THE DAMNED ENGINEERS

by JANICE HOLT GILES

The Enduring Hills
Miss Willie
Tara's Healing
40 Acres and No Mule
The Kentuckians
Hill Man
The Plum Thicket
Hannah Fowler
The Believers
The Land Beyond the Mountains
Johnny Osage
Savanna
Voyage to Santa Fe
A Little Better than Plumb (with Henry Giles)
Run Me a River
The G. I. Journal of Sergeant Giles (editor)
The Great Adventure
Shady Grove
Six-Horse Hitch
Wellspring
Around Our House (with Henry Giles)
The Kinta Years
Act of Contrition

THE DAMNED ENGINEERS

JANICE HOLT GILES

Commonwealth Book Company
ST. MARTIN, OHIO
2019

Copyright © 1970 by Janice Holt Giles
Copyright © 2019 by Commonwealth Book Company, Inc.
All rights reserved
Printed in the United States of America

ISBN: 978-1-948986-09-0

FRONT COVER PHOTOGRAPH: Railroad viaduct destroyed by the 291st Engineers on December 22, 1944.

To
Colonel David E. Pergrin
and the men he commanded,
the 291st Engineer Combat Battalion

JANICE HOLT GILES, 1950

JANICE HOLT GILES (1905–1979) was born in Arkansas and raised there and in Oklahoma. In 1941 she accepted a position at Presbyterian Theological Seminary in Frankfort, Kentucky. On a bus trip to Arkansas in 1943 she happened to sit next to a soldier returning to Camp Swift, Texas, from a furlough at his home in Adair County, Kentucky. After 48 hours on the bus together, Henry Giles and Janice Holt would not see each other again until 1945. But when Henry shipped out to Boston and then to England to participate in the Normandy invasion, he and Janice began a correspondence that would last through the war, and resulted in their marriage in 1945. In 1949 Janice published her first novel, *The Enduring Hills*. Over the next three decades she produced over twenty novels, mostly set in Kentucky and the frontier west, and was one of the most beloved authors of the mid-twentieth century.

Henry's wartime letters to Janice numbered over six hundred and, along with a detailed journal he kept, formed the basis of a project dear to Janice, her edited publication of *The G. I. Journal of Sergeant Giles*. Henry was a sergeant in the 291st Engineer Combat Battalion, a small unit that played a pivotal role in stemming the German counter-offensive in the Battle of the Bulge in 1944. Following extensive research and countless interviews, and expanding on her work with *G. I. Journal*, Janice published in 1970 the critically well-received history of the 291st Engineers in World War II, *The Damned Engineers*. It is no mere accounting of events, causes, and results, but rather it conveys the real experiences of ordinary men who, when placed in extraordinary circumstances, displayed the courage and fortitude to get the job done. And, as Janice wrote, the 291st Engineers not only got the job done, but they "gave a damned good account of themselves."

Introduction

by Martin Blumenson

THE GENESIS of this book arises out of those misty and far-off days of World War II, now more than a quarter of a century away, when Henry Giles entered the Army and was assigned to the 291st Engineer Combat Battalion. His letters to his wife during training and during the subsequent campaigns in Europe formed the basis of an exciting book that transcended the individual experiences of Sergeant Giles; it captured the essence of and illuminated the sense of the daily lives of all the American soldiers who suffered boredom as well as fear, anguish as well as danger, loneliness, hardship, and fatigue, and who had the stamina, courage, and stability to overcome hazards and difficulties they could hardly have imagined.

While editing *The G.I. Journal of Sergeant Giles*, which was focused firmly on her man, Mrs. Janice Holt Giles came to appreciate and understand that her husband's personal life in the Army was more than the sum of his own thoughts, observations, and feelings. His existence — that is, his well-being, comfort, outlook, activities — all this was inextricably tied to his unit.

A conglomerate mass of Americans gathered from all walks of life who had been shaped into a cohesive organization for the purpose of performing certain military tasks, the unit was no ephemeral entity, not simply the place where members lived and worked, ate and slept; the unit was the soldier's family. His buddies were his brothers. All the others he knew by sight or recognized as belonging were like cousins.

All shared a common experience that resembled that of the other units, depending on what they did and where they were; but all the members of the unit family shared a unique experience of their own. They had their own particular joys, their own peculiar customs, their own special gripes, likes, problems, and brand of humor. And they mourned deeply those they lost despite the surface indifference and callousness they assumed for self-protection.

The unit was the family, and it was part of a larger clan, the Army itself, which appeared wise and stupid in turn, which was vast and uncomprehending while at the same time omniscient and sometimes even kind.

This is what Janice Holt Giles set out to explore and explain. She built on her husband's continuing attachment to his unit, which had been formally dissolved immediately after the war, and to his friends, who, although scattered throughout the country, wrote to each other and occasionally gathered together, they thought to recall the days of their youth but in reality to perpetuate the mystique of the unit, which still bound and held them all.

What better way, she thought, to make this all clear than to show what happened to the soldiers of her husband's unit during their most harrowing test? What better way to demonstrate the strength of those family bonds than to see how the men reacted when all seemed lost, when they were menaced by overwhelming force that promised only death and destruction? What, she asked herself, became of feelings of unity when they were under extreme stress and strain, under the duress of a world suddenly turned upside down? Could the family cohesion withstand an enormous crisis?

The best example of this sort of situation was quickly apparent.

Introduction

The 291st Engineers had been in the Battle of the Bulge. They had stood in the way of the German onslaught. They had taken a mighty blow. And like many other units, they reeled, staggered, and, although frightened, fought back.

The German counteroffensive, launched in the Ardennes on December 16, 1944, caught the Allies by surprise. Yet it was, in retrospect, in line with traditional German military thought. German military doctrine had, for many years, stressed the decisive act. The conduct of war was essentially a matter of finding the opportunity to launch the bold stroke that would overwhelm and smash the enemy and gain victory quickly.

The Schlieffen Plan, executed in 1914 upon the outbreak of World War I, sought to conquer France at once. That was the German method. That it failed, that the swift wheeling movement through Belgium and northern France ultimately bogged down and degenerated into trench warfare, was no fault of the strategic concept. The static warfare that ensued, the awful battles of attrition as at Passchendaele and Verdun, this was not in the German manner. And as soon as the Germans could do something else, they set off the gigantic and daring counteroffensive put into motion by Ludendorff in the spring of 1918. That Ludendorff failed to win the war was no fault of his idea, which was conceived within the framework of proper German doctrine.

So too in World War II. The Germans overwhelmed Poland in 1939, then crushed France in 1940, and tried the same blitzkrieg pattern against Russia in 1941.

Three years later, when the Western Allies invaded Normandy in June 1944, the Germans reacted by making an immediate search for the place to explode their decisive counterthrust. The best way to drive what Hitler called the Anglo-Saxons back into the sea, they discovered, was to attack at Bayeux. But they were unable to mass their troops and deliver the mighty blow for a variety of reasons.

Not until the first week of August did Hitler see another opportunity for a decisive operation. Hoping still to defeat the Allies, now strongly lodged on the Continent, by means of a single blow, he ordered what the Germans call the Avranches counterattack and the Allies regard as the Mortain counterattack. His field commanders had little confidence in Hitler's grandiose vision. They believed it to be unrealistic if not sheer madness. A lack of understanding between Hitler and his field commanders was, in large part, responsible for the defeat of the operation. But there were other reasons why the blow was blunted.

Persisting in his quest for the massive all-out attack that would end the war in his favor, Hitler finally found what he was looking for in the Ardennes counteroffensive of December. Although his field commanders thought him unrealistic if not completely mad, Hitler gained overwhelming surprise over the Allies and came very close, for a short while at least, to achieving his purpose.

Like Ludendorff's offensive in 1918, which frightened the Allies but which in the end signified that Germany had lost the war, Hitler's Ardennes counteroffensive shook and shocked the Allied camp and in the end revealed the bankruptcy of the German military position.

What stopped the German steamroller in the opening weeks of World War I, what halted Ludendorff's offensive in the closing months of that struggle, what blunted the German thrust through Mortain toward Avranches in August 1944, what destroyed the validity of Hitler's Ardennes counteroffensive was, above all, the tenacious courage of small groups of Allied soldiers who refused to admit defeat. They offered resistance where and as they could. And in the final analysis, they broke the force of the blow and won.

In Belgium, in December 1944, the 291st Engineer Combat Battalion was one of many such groups. Outflanked and overrun, they nevertheless fought. Despite high odds against them, they

Introduction *xiii*

reacted out of cold anger with the skill that has always marked the best efforts of well-trained and proficient soldiers struggling to overcome the fear and adversity created by the unexpected and the unknown.

The military expert moves symbols across a map, applies the vague and abstract principles of war to real situations, shifts forces to attain local superiority in numbers — in short, uses all the means at hand to defeat the enemy. But the theories spun by the military thinkers and the plans formulated by the strategists and tacticians, even the technical concepts of battlefield leaders, are at the mercy of the actions of men under fire. They resolve the issues.

The battle is, indeed, the payoff, and wars are won or lost in the outcome of combat between men fighting as individuals and as members of small groups.

The field of battle during the actual contest cannot be plotted and organized in formal fashion. The fog of warfare, which hangs over battlefields in times of combat, obscures what is supposed to be an orderly ebb and flow of units, one against the other. What happens in reality is a widespread individual and small-unit reaction which is anything but orderly. Momentary panic, intuitive flight, irrational acts of bravery occur. And then the habit of obeying orders reasserts itself and takes over. Somehow a pattern emerges — a pattern in which a helter-skelter chaos jells into a comprehensible outcome, which gives a significant result, a result measured by the temporary disruption of an enemy timetable, by a cut in the enemy's communications, by the work of a roadblock holding up a scheduled enemy movement, by a volley of fire that forces an enemy group to take cover and lose time.

Fighting is not only shooting. It is a multitude of actions, like delivering a message through an area infested by the enemy, bringing ammunition forward along a road under enemy artillery fire, manning a roadblock, blowing a bridge, serving hot food, taking care of the wounded and injured. When actions such as these are performed in the most miserable conditions of weather and despite the attempts of the enemy to discourage and prevent them, when they are performed willingly as a matter of course, as a matter of simple duty, as an inevitable result of upbringing in the unit family, they are normal — and heroic.

Bernie Koenig holding a bazooka without ammunition and sitting on a hilltop without complaint in freezing temperatures for twenty-eight hours because someone had to be lookout.

Vince Consiglio, a motor mechanic trapped in a house with thirty-two other men under attack from German tanks and infantry, going a little out of his head for a few hours, observing for tank destroyer guns, firing his rifle, manning a machine gun, helping the wounded, and finally, when just twelve men were left alive, going for help through a hail of bullets and shells.

Sergeant Jean Miller calmly waiting to destroy a bridge at the last and most effective moment even though the Germans might discover and kill him.

Jeff Elliott and Red Richardson volunteering to take bazookas forward through enemy-held territory to Malmédy, which might be in enemy hands — and making it after a terrifying jeep ride through the night.

Bernie Goldstein guarding a road all alone with his rifle out in front of his unit and challenging a column of German tanks to halt.

Johnny Rondenell stringing a necklace of mines across a road even with a German half-track practically on top of him.

Paul Kamen, dentist, coming forward to Malmédy because the battalion medical officer, the physician, was away on other business and because Kamen could administer drugs and bandage wounds and even perform simple surgery; Kamen making it to Malmédy even though his truck was riddled with bullets when he arrived; Kamen doing so because he was needed.

And more than anyone else who personified the virtues of the

Introduction

291st Engineers, the quiet, unruffled man who was hard but fair, who, knowing the individual strengths and weaknesses of his men, tried to make them look good, who gave them pride and dignity in their work and understanding of their role in the larger scheme of things, and who made them feel that their unit-family was the finest in the world — David Pergrin, their battalion commander.

It is not easy to catch the pervading spirit of a thousand soldiers who are manhandling heavy equipment, building bridges, sawing logs, picking up mail, keeping records, and waiting — although they don't know it — for the fury of the Ardennes counteroffensive, which will shatter the order of their routine into a million fragments, each a sharp particle that prods men into unanticipated patterns of behavior.

But Janice Holt Giles has done so. Her descriptions of the 291st unit-family, of the Malmédy massacre and its effect on the Americans, of the German attack shifting into high gear, and, above all, of what happens to men in battle are among the best I have ever read.

The 291st Engineer Combat Battalion was one of many units — infantry, artillery, armor, signal, quartermaster, medical, and the rest — which found themselves swept up into the maelstrom of the German Ardennes counteroffensive. By virtue of their steadfastness and fortitude, they destroyed the German hope of victory.

The Damned Engineers shows how they did it and why.

Contents

PART I
The Allied Side, 1

PART II
The German Side, 95

PART III
Confrontation on the Amblève, 153

EPILOGUE, 371

APPENDIXES, 379
BIBLIOGRAPHICAL NOTES AND ACKNOWLEDGMENTS, 383
BIBLIOGRAPHY, 386
INDEX, 393

Illustrations

following page 138

Col. David E. Pergrin, Commander, 291st Engineer Combat Battalion

Officers of 291st Engineer Combat Battalion in June 1944

Company B men and their wood-burning machine

Company C sawmill at Trois Ponts

Lt. Ralph W. McCarthy, Capt. Frank W. Rhea, Lt. W. L. Colbeck

Company B sawmill at Stavelot

Col. David E. Pergrin, 1/Sgt. William H. Smith

Mined trees on Highway N–32, near Malmédy

Oberst (Waffen-SS) Jochen Peiper at Kaiserbaracke crossroads, December 17, 1944

Oberst (Waffen-SS) Jochen Peiper and one of his officers walking along road

Pvt. Bernard Koenig and T/5 Burnie Hebert

Sgt. R. C. Billington

German tank destroyer which collapsed the Petit Spai bridge

Company A building a timber trestle bridge in Luxembourg

Company B men at work in sawmill in Stavelot

Company B maintaining Highway N-28 between Eupen and Malmédy

Gas dump north of Stavelot on old Francorchamps road

following page 266

Tiger Royal tank near Petit Spai. Capt. James H. Gamble and Lt. Arch L. Taylor

T/5 Vincent Consiglio

First Lieutenant Albert W. Walters

Warche River bridge after being blown

Company B emplacement near big viaduct. Radio Operator Frederick Bryans and Sgt. Munoz

Big railroad viaduct blown on December 22, 1944

Bomb damage in Malmédy, December 24, 1944

291st Engineers fighting fires the same day

Wreckage caused by bombing in Malmédy

291st Engineers in rescue work

Christmas Eve in command post at Malmédy

Men of Company C sweeping snow from bodies of victims of Malmédy massacre

Bodies of victims uncovered and tagged with numbered markers

Last bridge in Belgium, over the Our River, built February 3–5, 1945

Battalion staff near Rheinbach, Germany, March 1945, after award of Presidential Unit Citation

Illustrations

MAPS

1. The Western Front — December 15, 1944   25
2. Route of Company A from Werbomont to Amblève, December 16   40–41
3. 291st Engineers' defense positions in Malmédy, December 17–18   89
4. Route Plans of *I SS Panzer Corps*   116
5. Crossroads at Baugnez, near Malmédy, and Massacre Field   165
6. Company C roadblock at Stavelot, December 17   215
7. Battle of Stavelot, December 18   228
8. Battle of Trois Ponts, December 18–22   249
9. Habiemont bridge blown, December 18   259
10. Skorzeny's predawn attack on Malmédy, December 21   308
11. Meuse Barrier Line positions of 291st Engineers, December 19, 1944 to January 4, 1945   325

PART I
The Allied Side

I

IN DECEMBER of 1944 the men of the 291st Engineers were having a good war and they knew it. They were in houses, there were girls, there were good pass towns, there were bars, and they were not building Baileys. Bars, girls and passes were important to individuals according to their needs or capacities. Important to the entire 291st were houses and relief from bridge building.

Since the first week in November they had been in small Belgian towns and they had had four walls around them and a roof over their heads. Unbelievable comfort after the months of foxholes and pup tents. And with the houses had come a new assignment. They were pulled off bridge building and put to sawmilling. With a few rotations out for road maintenance and patrolling they were working shifts on a routine as regular as if they had been civilians. Even those who drew the timber details, sawing down the trees and hauling logs to the sawmills, were grateful not to be heaving Bailey panels into place.

Sir Donald Bailey may have invented the greatest sectional steel bridge ever known to man and it may have been a boon to military science, but to the engineers who had to lift the sections, push them out over some icy river, bolt and weld them together, they were pure hell. A Bailey was never built without its quota of injuries, running from wrenched kidneys to crushed feet, skinned hands and even, occasionally, temporary blindness from using a blowtorch without safety goggles. To this day when the men of the 291st speak of a Bailey bridge they swear.

But in December of 1944 Baileys were at least temporarily behind them. Their assignment now was what they called a good deal and they agreed that this was the way to fight a war. They highly approved of all this comfort and luxury and devoutly hoped it would last until the end of the war, which anybody could tell was almost in sight. The Krauts were on their last legs. It was obvious. One more big offensive and they would give up. If they were lucky, the 291st just might see the end of the war right here in these fine and fancy houses of theirs.

True, they were all split up. Companies were spotted here and there and platoons and squads were distributed around over a fifty-mile radius. But as long as the basic unit, the platoon and its squads, was relatively intact the men did not feel dislocated. The company was the integral unit, but within it the squad was the family and the platoon was its home. Besides, all of eastern Belgium was not much bigger than some counties back home and the distances seemed short and the roads were pretty good. They were making out fine.

And if there was one thing the 291st was by December of 1944 it was experienced in the arts and skills of making out. From the beginning they had been making out, for they had no past and no future beyond the end of the war. They were an expediency of the war, created solely for the purpose of war, and when the war was over they would cease to exist as an outfit just as swiftly as they had become an outfit.

As a battalion they had no long proud, glorious military tradition to live up to. They wore no division patch on their shoulders, no Big Red One, no Bloody Bucket, no Lightning Streak. They were combat engineers, working under First Army. They were troubleshooters, going where First Army assigned them, doing whatever First Army sent them to do. Their only shoulder patch was First Army's big "A."

The Allied Side

But they were proud and they were perfectly willing to write their own history and make their own traditions, and they had their own ways of doing both, some of which are unprintable and unmentionable.

They had been activated as the 2nd Battalion of the 82nd Engineer Combat Regiment in January of 1943 at Camp Swift, Texas. This was a big, new raw camp near Austin. A cadre of NCOs formed the core of the outfit. They were mostly Regular Army, old-line NCOs and pretty hardbitten. For some of them this was the third or fourth time they had helped shape up an outfit.

The men began arriving at Camp Swift early in February. They were largely from New York, Pennsylvania and New Jersey. There was one fairly sizable contingent from Louisiana and there were lonely little sprinklings from Virginia, Kentucky, Oklahoma and various other states. In the main, however, they were upstate New York and Pennsylvania.

They were mostly very young, draftees just reaching draft age. If they were older, they had been exempted until now because of some slight physical defect which in 1943 no longer counted, or because of being married.

They were a mixed broth stirred up from Hell's Kitchen, the hills of New York and Pennsylvania, the bayous of Louisiana, the mountains of Virginia and Kentucky, college campuses, farms, cities, nonessential industries. They had unpronounceable names like Oswiecimski, Pasciucco, Nowaskowski, Olsewski, Spadiccini, L'Hommedieu, Courvillion, Chetneki, mixed in with the more familiar names of Smith, Miller, White, Walker, Martin, Jones and so on.

But whatever the name, whatever the background, whatever the size, the condition when they arrived at Camp Swift was the same for them all — rookie, first class.

Basic training began immediately and it was the same Basic every rookie in the United States Army got. Drill, calisthenics, rifle cleaning, drill, marches, inspections, drill, calisthenics, machine gun classes, drill, field marches, inspections, drill and drill and drill, until the men developed an abiding conviction that a platoon sergeant was a monster who took special delight in killing them by slow degrees.

On March 28 they got their new designation. They became the 291st Engineer Combat Battalion, assigned along with their sister battalion, the 82nd, to the 1115th Engineer Combat Group, VIII Corps, Third U. S. Army.

New officers now began arriving. In April came young Captain David E. Pergrin to be Assistant Engineer, and throughout the rest of the training period various young first and second lieutenants kept streaming in. The old-line NCOs watched them come and watched them shape up, and sized them up with wise, experienced, unblinded eyes. Men who had already cadred three or four new engineer outfits, they had seen every kind of officer and they could rarely be fooled. Evidently they liked what they saw coming into the 291st, for they stayed with it.

Using the pipelines they knew so well how to use, these men had moved in almost a solid body whenever they chose, from California to Missouri to Wisconsin to Texas. Customarily when they finished taking a new bunch of recruits through Basic they moved on, and although a new camp went up in Colorado and they could have once more cadred out together, very few of them did. Of course they may have been tired. Three or four Basics in a year and a half is a lot of Basic. Or maybe they just did not like Colorado. For whatever reason they found a home in the 291st and thus the battalion always had the balance wheel of an unusually high percentage of old-line NCOs.

Basic training continued and at its end the men held the traditional beer bust to celebrate their graduation from rookie to soldier. They were considerably thinner, many shades browner and several inches taller. This was not unique to the 291st. Basic was the same everywhere and rugged. What *was* unique was

The Allied Side

that it had taken sixteen weeks, instead of thirteen, to shove these men of the 291st through. They were a steamy, raffish bunch to handle and they did not become soldiers easily.

And now they had their engineer Unit Training — map reading, bridge building, road building and maintenance. They went to Louisiana on maneuvers and if they learned more about heat, mud, swamps, mosquitoes, hogs and watermelons than they did about engineering it was not the fault of the Third U.S. Army. The idea evidently was maneuvers under the most trying conditions. The men got a different idea. They were convinced they were headed straight for the jungles of the Pacific.

They had landing practice on the Gulf Coast finally and then headed back to Austin. They passed all their endurance tests and Unit Training tests, and now training time was running out. In September 1943 the 291st was tapped to sail for England to take part in the Bolero construction program. For this they got a new commander. Lieutenant Colonel John R. Hayes was transferred to the Engineer School at Fort Belvoir, Va., and David E. Pergrin, who had made major in July, took over the command of the battalion.

At this time Major David E. Pergrin was twenty-six years old, younger than many of the old-line NCOs in the outfit and senior to most of his company and platoon commanders by not more than a year or two. He came from Elizabeth, Pennsylvania, and was a graduate of Penn State College with a degree in civil engineering. He had been called up from ROTC in June of 1940, shortly after graduating. He had served on the staff at Fort Belvoir until April of 1943 when he had been sent to the 291st.

Pergrin was a broad-shouldered, well-built, sinewy man standing about five foot eleven. He had dark hair and eyes and he wore glasses. He had an infectious crooked grin and by any standards would have been called a handsome, clean-cut young man. He was serious for one so young and he was aggressive, with a lot of drive. He had a strong determination that the 291st should live up to its capabilities. He welcomed responsibility and he had an inbuilt capacity for carrying it. He was efficient and if he had any inner uncertainties they did not show. He was calm, had a good basic grounding for engineering and although he was not West Point he was not afraid of this new assignment. He and the 291st would get the job done.

The outfit sailed from Boston on the *Santa Elena* (South American Line) on October 7 and landed in Liverpool on October 19. For eight months, then, they built hardstands and barracks in southern England for the big build-up of American troops needed for the invasion.

In England the 291st became part of the 1111th Engineer Combat Group, commanded by Colonel H. W. Anderson. Anderson was a veteran of World War I when he had been an engineer battalion commander. The other battalions in the 1111th Group were the 51st and the 296th.

In England, also, Pergrin worked toward shaping up his outfit for war. He shifted officers and men about, transferred out troublemakers, shored up weak spots and acquired extra strength. By the time of the invasion he had the 291st pretty well set up. He had the usual complement of Liaison, Administration, Intelligence, Operations, Supply, Communications, Medic and Motor sections. He was up to combat strength, around 619 officers and men for the full battalion. He had fifteen officers with him at Battalion Headquarters.

The average age of these men at Battalion was twenty-five, the oldest being thirty, the youngest twenty-two. All the officers had graduated from OCS at the engineering school at Fort Belvoir. Besides Pergrin, however, only Captain Edward R. Lampp, the Operations Officer, had had civil engineering in college. The Liaison Officer, Captain Lloyd B. Sheetz, had had three years of metallurgical engineering and various others had had some schooling in different phases of engineering.

"The problem," Pergrin said, "was always a balance between

The Allied Side

Battalion and the line companies. You had to put your engineers in the line companies, but you had to have men at Battalion who understood the problems and also had some engineering skill. It never really equaled out. You just had to spread out what you had and do the best you could with it." He *did* put his engineers with the line companies.

He left the NCOs who had cadred the 291st spread out in the companies and platoons pretty much as he had inherited them, which was wise. However intelligent and able the officers were they were essentially civilians and only temporarily military men. Many of the old-line NCOs were making the army a career and they were a good counterbalance, knowledgeable as they were, experienced and usually pretty unflusterable. They knew how to keep a company or platoon sharp and effective, at the same time meshing the gears and keeping it livable.

Came June 6 and the invasion and the 291st, now with First U.S. Army, landed at Omaha Beach on June 24 before the beachheads were expanded. Their landing was the last unhurried moment they were to know for a long, long time. They plunged immediately into hard, backbreaking, unromantic, unglamorous work at a killing pace, under unrelenting pressure. They were under artillery fire within hours of their landing and almost the first thing they learned how to do was to dig a good safe foxhole.

Until the breakout in late July they continued to repair roads, build bypasses, install bridges and culverts, clean up debris and open bombed-out roads, under the German guns. At Carentan they kept the main supply line up the Cherbourg Peninsula open, ducking the artillery fire on the Tucker Bridge as they daily, and sometimes hourly, repaired the direct hits on it. Many of their first wounded were at that bridge.

They were quickly blooded but miraculously they had nobody killed. The most serious casualty was that of Pfc. Francis Buffone who lost both legs in a land mine explosion. He was the only mine casualty the battalion ever suffered.

After the breakout they went into St. Lô and started clearing a road for the huge army of vehicles to follow. They went into Mortain while it was still hot and smoking and did the same. In the swift advance across France, moving almost faster than their equipment and supplies could keep up, they mended roads and built bridges. Bridges and bridges and bridges, Baileys, timber trestles and culverts. One-night stands, two nights, they were lucky if they stayed longer than that in one place. But they made out.

They made out in Paris on a grand scale, then they swung over into Luxembourg and Belgium. They were slowly becoming experts in the business of making out. They looked like Bill Mauldin's cartoons but they were becoming very ingenious at taking care of themselves. Like every other outfit they learned to raid, swipe and steal equipment and gear. They recovered abandoned vehicles and repaired them, made them run again and worked them into their own equipment. An officer found an English trailer and appropriated it for his traveling home. The Communications Section found that a German truck made a very useful extra vehicle for them. And T/4 Jeff Elliott, who was wild about anything with a motor, tried to hang on to a Mark IV tank. Much abandoned German gear and equipment found its way into the 291st.

The early summer in France was wet and chilly and the men quickly learned that dry footgear made the difference between good feet and bad feet and many of them carried an extra pair of socks in their hip pockets. The ground was often muddy and pup tents or foxholes were cold at night, so they picked up blankets thrown away by the infantry, tarps and slickers that had been discarded and fattened their bedrolls. One sergeant had a sleeping bag that was the envy of all his frieinds. He had eight blankets in it.

The men snitched or bought or swapped for all the extra food they could find and ingratiated themselves with the villagers to

The Allied Side

get invited into their homes for hot meals. And so excellent were their instincts for finding wine and beer and cider, to say nothing of the ingredients of a lethal moonshine made from grain alcohol and fruit juices, that few of the drinking men in the outfit, who made up easily 90 percent, were ever totally without.

As they moved into southern Belgium and Luxembourg and the cold rains of autumn came on, they began to wonder if they were going to spend the winter in tents. But when the swift advance across France into Belgium and to the German border ground slowly to a halt in late September and early October, First Army looked ahead to the discomfort of the winter months for front-line troops and to the need for bridge timbers for the Rhine crossings the next spring and assigned its First Army engineer battalions to a winterization program.

The 291st was collected up around the 1st of October from their last bridge-building jobs near Longuyon and Salmchâteau and transported north to the forests near Hockai, southeast of Liège. Here they bivouacked, until assigned, in pup tents in the middle of a dense, drippingly dank pine forest. There was nothing much to do but watch the buzz bombs headed for Liège go over, duck when one cut out, stand guard and write letters home. It was a time to try their souls because they were uncomfortable and bored and the new assignment did not come until the 1st of November. Then they were ordered into towns and houses, sawmilling and the winterization program. Well, God bless the winterization program and long may it last!

The 1111th Engineer Combat Group had moved the 291st to Hockai in the knowledge this assignment was coming. With three battalions under his command and a quota of board feet of timber to be cut and sawed, as well as bridges and roads to be built and maintained, Colonel Anderson had assigned his 51st Engineers to the primary task of sawmilling and sent them southwest to Marche. In that vicinity they operated thirty-eight sawmills. Anderson had assigned his 296th Engineers primarily to road building and maintenance in the forward zones of First Army's V Corps, and sent them northeast to Sourbrodt.

He had kept his 291st Engineers as his security battalion, near himself, and they were given a hodgepodge of jobs, sawmilling, road maintenance and watchdog for Group.

First U. S. Army, Lieutenant General Courtney H. Hodges commanding, was headquartered at Spa with various rear supporting elements at Chaudfontaine a little farther north. Anderson put his Group headquarters some thirteen miles almost due south of Spa at the charming little village of Trois Ponts. With Trois Ponts as the center he then strung the 291st out on either side of him, on an angling northeast-southwest line twenty-five miles long. From Trois Ponts the front at Losheimergraben on the German border was some twenty miles almost due east.

Colonel Pergrin set up the 291st battalion headquarters at Haute Bodeux, less than three miles west of Trois Ponts. He was so near Group that actually Anderson had a working battalion command post right under his hand.

Pergrin sent his Company A to the point on the line farthest west, Werbomont. Werbomont was approximately eleven miles west of Trois Ponts. He sent Company C to La Gleize, a lovely little mountain village about four miles north of Trois Ponts. He sent Company B to the point on the line farthest northeast, Malmédy. Malmédy was about eleven miles from Trois Ponts. The 291st was thus stretched out along a natural defense line in front of First Army at Spa, with their own Group command post almost exactly in their middle. And they had drawn a beautiful segment of Liège Province as their assignment.

Jubilantly the men spread out into the villages assigned to them and into the houses requisitioned for them. At Werbomont, Company A set up, with the command post in a schoolhouse and the officers and men living in houses nearby.

At La Gleize, Company C set up in an historic old château

which they proudly spoke of as their "castle." And Company B went to Malmédy with whoops of joy. It was the largest town in the area and it was well known to have the best bars in the area. Company B's commander, Captain John T. Conlin, rubbed his hands together with glee. "Good deal," he chuckled, "good deal."

But these were only the company headquarters. The work took the platoons on detached service over a much wider area. Platoons were operating sawmills in Sourbrodt, Montenau, Born and Vielsalm, in addition to two sawmills in Trois Ponts and one each in Malmédy and Stavelot. The outfit was operating eight sawmills in all.

The men moved where they were ordered and daily their trucks, jeeps, bulldozers, dump trucks, air compressors and other vehicles crisscrossed the network of roads, firebreaks and forest trails. From Sourbrodt to Malmédy and Stavelot and La Gleize. From Montenau and Born to Trois Ponts and Werbomont. From Werbomont to Trois Ponts and Malmédy, to Grand-Halleux and Montenau and Born. From Malmédy to Butgenbach and Elsenborn and Büllingen. This entire area became their home and they soon knew its road system as well as if it had been a county back home.

By November 8 the 291st had settled in and was in business. Individually the men were in business at the Saturday night dances, on passes to Spa, Verviers and Eupen, as well as Liège and Brussels. They had nightly movies in the company headquarters towns, they had mineral baths in Spa, they had hot meals and they met the girls. It was much better than they were used to, and much better than they could have hoped for. They set about making the most of it.

To their east lay the front, at a distance varying from twenty to thirty-five miles depending on the curves and bulges of the line itself. In their sector it lay principally along the international boundary between Belgium and Germany, with one fist-like bulge over into Germany along the Schnee Eifel.

Visualize a 600-mile line, a long snaking line with its head in Holland and its tail near the Swiss border. This was the entire Allied front. Farthest north, in Holland, was the British area, where Field Marshal Sir Bernard L. Montgomery's 21 Army Group directed the First Canadian Army, the Second British Army, and, temporarily on loan, the Ninth U.S. Army. In the center was Lieutenant General Omar N. Bradley's 12th Army Group with Hodges' First U.S. Army and Patton's Third U.S. Army. Farthest south was Devers' 6th Army Group, composed of Lieutenant General Alexander M. Patch's Seventh U.S. Army and a French Army.

Hodges' First U.S. Army was therefore holding the center of the Allied front. It was composed of three corps. Farthest north was Major General J. Lawton Collins' VII Corps, which touched the Ninth U.S. Army on the left. Farthest south was Major General Troy Middleton's VIII Corps, which touched the Third U.S. Army on the right. In the middle was Major General Leonard T. Gerow's V Corps.

The 291st lay behind V Corps and the 1111th Engineer Group was supporting all V Corps operations.

Thus we find the 291st behind the center of the entire Allied line in the 12th Army Group, behind the center of the 12th Army Group in the First U.S. Army, and behind the center of First Army in the V Corps. They were also centered in a hilly, wooded area known as the Ardennes, and they were almost due west of the only natural gateway through a range of rough hills. The gateway was the Losheim Gap.

But nothing much had been happening along the front in their sector for several weeks. It was a quiet front just now. On both sides it was as if Germans and Americans alike were just resting awhile, licking their wounds after the bloody battles around Aachen and in the Hürtgen Forest, just lying still and breathing

The Allied Side

deep. In a segment around eighty-five miles long on the V and VIII Corps' front about the only activity was the daily patrols and a little artillery fire. It was mostly a rest front, where troops could relax and recuperate, running as it did through the Ardennes from Monschau to Echternach. That was what the whole winterization program was about. The troops along this eighty-five-mile front would sit still most of the winter, waiting for the spring offensives. First Army meant to make them as comfortable as possible.

That this line was very thinly held, as Eisenhower beefed up both ends for winter offensives, the 291st was unaware. Nor did it occur to them that their own long, angling twenty-five-mile line was squarely astride a natural defensive position, defined much of the way by the Amblève River. They knew the river was there, for heaven's sake. They crossed it constantly and they had built those timber trestles across it at Trois Ponts, and at one of its tributaries at Malmédy and another of its tributaries near Werbomont. But it was just another river and this whole country was a jigsaw puzzle of little streams and rivers that had to have bridges. That the Amblève would have enormous importance very shortly was unimaginable even to First Army, much less the 291st Engineers.

Nor did any of the men think much about the immense concentration of First Army supplies north of the Amblève. They knew the installations were there. They wove their way back and forth between them constantly — mountainous depots, supply dumps and service installations, of ordnance, medical supplies, food, clothing, gasoline and lubricants. They knew these things were densely packed all around Spa and that Liège was the biggest supply depot on the continent. They knew that was why the buzz bombs streamed overhead toward Liège so constantly. Without knowing there were over 2,000,000 maps in it, they knew First Army's main map depot was in Stavelot. Without knowing there were 2,500,000 gallons of gasoline in them, they knew there were long gas dumps alongside the roads near Spa. They knew these things without thinking that actually the whole vital pulsing heart of First U.S. Army was centered above the Amblève, behind their 291st towns and houses, nor what the implications could mean for them.

For it never occurred to them, either, that while they thought of themselves as a service unit, in the First Army's Table of Organization and Equipment they were a combat unit. Few of them remembered, probably, that in their own combat engineer's manual it said, in not very fine print, that in critical situations they should serve as infantry. They had had a lot of experience as engineers, but the combat part had never been tested and it had never occurred to them it would be. But there they were, strung out for twenty-five miles along a line and in a position which nobody ever thought would be, even in the most fantastic eventuality, a strategic position.

It was a time of rosy euphoria for all the Allied armies. The end of the war was in sight, the Germans were about to collapse and soon they would all be going home. Blithely unaware, comfortable, fairly happy, the men of the 291st went about their work, gave thanks for this assignment and figured they had it made to the end of the war.

This, then, is where they were and what they were doing on December 14, 1944. The 291st had come a long way from Camp Swift, Texas, and they had a little history behind them. Because engineers do not normally have much of a turnover in replacements, they had become, by squads and platoons and companies, tightly welded and close-knit. To the men in the line companies Battalion was a little vague, but it was there, it was their head. So were the other line companies there, not too familiarly known but a part of the outfit. To every man, actually, the 291st was his own squad, his own platoon, his own company. These men, with whom he slept and ate and joked, with whom he worked, were his brothers, were his family, were his home and his world.

The Allied Side

They knew each other better than they would ever again know another human being, even their wives — down to the most irritating little personal habits, up to the noblest qualities of selflessness.

There were among them gentle men and men as hard as nails. There were thinkers and men who rarely thought beyond the next meal. There were men who looked with wondering eyes, even in war, on the historic beauty all around them, and men who never saw it at all. There were men whom the total unprivacy daily abraded, and men who never noticed it. There were men who missed their freedom of action and felt roped and hogtied by army rules and regulations, and men who sank down into them and felt freed by their lack of responsibility. There were men who did more than their share of the work, and men who could avoid it most of the time. There were men capable of almost any crime, and men capable of mercy toward them. There were eightballs, oddballs and screwballs. There were strong men, weak men, rough men, soft men. The army put them all in uniform and made soldiers of them but it could not change the private nature of a single one of them.

But in the composite they were swaggering, wild, high-spirited, wanton, cheerful, flexible, careless, casual, and comically, ridiculously, eternally wisecracking. If the British cultivated the casual manner, the understatement, as an armor against fear and tears, the American GI cultivated the wisecrack. And typically GI the men of the 291st met their problems with a wisecrack.

They were open and friendly and pretty naïve, big, handsome, healthy men, a good-natured crew. They were rowdy and rambunctious and people feared for their daughters — with good reason — but they were also gay, generous, quick with their sympathy and their help. They chewed gum incessantly, were irreverent about Belgian traditions and customs and property, unimpressed and more than a little arrogant in their Americanism. They said O.K. — O.K. to everything and it became part of the vocabulary of Europe. They spoiled the children of Belgium just as they had spoiled the children of England and France, just as they would spoil the enemy's children when they got to Germany. A kid was a kid no matter what language he spoke and when he tucked a small soft hand into their big hard ones and begged for chewing gum and chocolate he usually got it. Big, soft-hearted, unsophisticated patsies — for a pretty girl, for a little kid, for a helpless old man or woman.

What it all boiled down to was that they were typical GIs, indistinguishable from a million other GIs and, as yet, undistinguished. If Colonel Pergin occasionally wanted to crack a few of their heads together, when the chips were down they got moving swiftly, and if not exactly soldierly, always effectively. They were the 291st, a Class A outfit of engineers, physically hard, able, highly trained, ingenious, disciplined in their own way, and immensely efficient in a careless, messy, casual fashion. And to hear them tell it they were "the best goddamned engineer outfit in the whole European theater."

They would have a chance to test it shortly.

But for the time being they were working, it was all very pleasant and they hoped they were settled for the winter. By December 14 Colonel Pergrin knew that one company would soon be moving out.

2

THE ALLIED ARMIES had swept swiftly and victoriously across France and Belgium and Holland through the summer and early autumn. But in September they ground slowly to a halt. From late September through October Eisenhower had been occupied with stabilizing the long line, in reorganizing the combat units and in making preparations for further offensive actions.

Thousands of tons of supplies were moved from the ports and beaches into the rear areas, railroads were slowly repaired and put into operation, hundreds of bridges were built and the road systems were improved. Casualties among the combat units were slowly replaced.

Then in the middle of November Eisenhower ordered the British 21 Army Group and Bradley's 12th U.S. Army Group to close to the Rhine before winter locked them into a static position. They made a valiant effort, but the November offensive rolled right into some of the heaviest fighting the Allied armies had ever known. It rolled, to put it bluntly, right into a hornet's nest. The British did not even clear the Meuse until December 4. Ninth U.S. Army could not close to the Roer River which was a natural barrier between them and the Rhine. It took Patton's Third Army two weeks to capture Metz at an enormous cost in casualties, and First Army's right flank fought through the deadly Hürtgen Forest, a dense, tangled wooded area which had to be penetrated before the Roer River could be reached on their front.

This was the bloodiest and costliest sector of the entire front. Parts of three whole divisions were cut to pieces and commanders were bitter as they saw their divisions take three, four and even seven thousand casualties. Two divisions, the 28th Infantry and the 4th Infantry, were so badly mutilated that they had to be withdrawn and were sent to the quiet front in Luxembourg to rest and reorganize. They had suffered such heavy losses they were simply no longer fighting units until their casualties could be replaced.

General Bradley and his commanders had expected strong resistance. They were coming up against the German West Wall. But they had not expected anything as fanatical, as do-or-die, as they ran into. After two weeks of bitter fighting the Ninth and the First U.S. armies had advanced only ten miles and were along the Roer River for a distance of about twenty miles.

But now a new problem arose. On the headwaters of the Roer the Germans had built a series of dams which could release floodwaters to inundate the entire Roer valley. Not much thought seems to have been given to these dams in the overall planning. It was apparently expected they would be captured in the forward push. But the German resistance had been too stubborn, and the dams had not been captured. Now it seems to have occurred to the strategists that the dams provided the enemy with a strong military weapon. All they had to do was open the gates and all U.S. troops in the Roer valley would either be isolated or flooded out. So first priority was now given to destroying these dams.

The job was given to the Air Command to blow up the two big key dams, the Urft and the Schwammenauel. But they were huge earthen affairs and could not be knocked out, even by direct hits. The bombing of the dams got to be a not very funny joke as the bombers daily reported no success. The air attacks

The Allied Side

were finally called off and the job of capturing the dams was given again to First Army.

Hastily General Hodges organized an attack, this time from farther south in a flanking movement. Bluntly and impatiently he gave the job of taking the dams to his V Corps, under Major General Gerow.

General Gerow's V Corps consisted of four infantry divisions and parts of two armored divisions and one cavalry group. He had three infantry divisions in the line, the 8th on the extreme left, touching VII Corps to the north. Next came the 78th Infantry, a new division. At Monschau the 99th Infantry took over in November, also a fairly new division in the line. Gerow's 2nd Infantry was in reserve, resting in Middleton's Corps down along the quiet front.

The 99th Infantry line was about fifteen miles long, running from Monschau to the northern edge of the Losheim Gap. It was the division the 291st knew best. Its headquarters were at Butgenbach, a mere thirteen miles east of Malmédy, and its positions were largely in front of the 291st positions.

The Losheim Gap was the historic natural gap in the range of hills called the Schnee Eifel through which the German divisions had poured in 1914, and again in 1940. But right there the 99th Division's responsibility ended. Not only did the division's responsibility end there, but the Gap marked the seam between Gerow's V Corps and Major General Troy Middleton's VIII Corps, and a unit boundary is always a vulnerable point on a front.

The Gap itself was Middleton's responsibility. Across its nine-mile width, however, was spread a very meager defense, a light task force of only around 450 men, the 18th Cavalry Reconnaissance Squadron of the 14th Cavalry Group, with one company of three-inch towed tank destroyers attached. There was no real line, as such, across the Gap. The men were spread out in outposts in several villages, from Kobscheid to Lanzerath.

The last 99th Division outpost was on a ridge just north of, and overlooking, the hamlet of Lanzerath. Here an Intelligence and Reconnaissance platoon of the 99th occupied well dug-in positions with excellent fields of fire. Across town from them, about two miles distant, a small party of Company A, 820th Tank Destroyer Battalion, was positioned. There was telephone communication between the two units, but it was rarely used because the two little units were not only answerable to different divisions, they belonged to different Corps. In the event, this was to have tragic consequences.

South of the Gap, the VIII Corps positions began, at this time, with Gerow's 2nd Infantry Division resting in Middleton's line. Below this division came the 28th Infantry Division, mutilated so badly in the Hürtgen Forest. Below the 28th lay one combat command of the 9th Armored Division, also new in the line, and farthest south came the 4th Infantry, another badly mauled division.

When Gerow received orders to take the Urft-Roer dams he decided to pull his 2nd Infantry back home and give them the job. The hole they left in Middleton's line was then plugged with the 106th Infantry Division, the newest and greenest division on the continent. They had just arrived from the States. This transfer was effected and the 106th closed in their new positions on December 11. They inherited the 2nd Infantry's dugouts, outposts and defense plans.

It is well to take a good look at this long eighty-five-mile line. The 99th Infantry was new and had been in the line only about three weeks. The Losheim Gap was very vulnerable and was weakly defended with 450 men. The 106th Infantry had been in the line only a few days and did not even have all its equipment yet. Below them were two badly hurt infantry divisions, the 28th and 4th, and one armored combat command very new in the line. It looks like madness, but Bradley and Eisenhower both have said it was a calculated risk to stretch this segment of the front so

The Allied Side

paper thin. Montgomery was preparing to take the offensive and he had been given much U.S. strength. Patton's Third Army was preparing to take the offensive and Patton had been beefed up. The line could not be strong everywhere, so the strength was diverted to both ends. Nobody knew, of course, that this thinning in the middle was playing right into German plans.

Gerow worked out his attack to capture the big dams. The 2nd Infantry would carry the assault, moving through the 99th's positions south of Monschau and supported by them. But when 2nd Infantry got through the forests and came out into the open country it would need tank support. Gerow could not spare his own armored units, so to give the 2nd Infantry the tank support it would need, Hodges reached down into VIII Corps and plucked one of 9th Armored's combat commands. This was CCB, commanded by Brigadier General William M. Hoge.

Now it also became obvious to everybody that once CCB and its tanks got into good tank country they would run into dense minefields. The Germans would never leave good tank country unmined. So CCB had to have some engineer support.

Well, First Army was using the 1111th Engineer Group in support of any and all V Corps operations. So First Army Engineer, Colonel W. H. Carter, tapped 1111th Group to furnish one company of engineers to detect and clear minefields for CCB of 9th Armored.

Colonel Anderson, of Group, looked at the disposition of his battalions and tapped the 291st to furnish this company. Colonel Pergrin called in his mine detectors and had them put in good repair and started pondering which of his companies to give the job to.

Gerow's 2nd Infantry, Major General Walter Robertson commanding, jumped off their attack on December 13. General Hoge marched his Combat Command B north from their VIII Corps positions on this same day. His assembly point was Faymonville, a village about ten miles north of St. Vith. He closed at Faymonville late in the afternoon of December 14. He reported to V Corps headquarters at Eupen, then went over to Monschau to watch the progress of the attack. His tanks would not be engaged until 2nd Infantry got out of the woods.

Anderson, of 1111th Engineer Group, had a liaison officer at V Corps headquarters, so he was apprised when CCB closed in Faymonville, and he now ordered Colonel Pergrin to move his 291st company into that vicinity immediately.

On December 15, therefore, Pergrin sat in his quarters in Haute Bodeux and looked at his map once more.

His Company C was up at La Gleize, with two platoons running the two sawmills in Trois Ponts, and its detached 3rd platoon was operating a sawmill in Sourbrodt, northeast of Malmédy.

His Company B was intact in Malmédy, operating a mill in Malmédy and one in Stavelot.

But his Company A was widely scattered, and furthermore it was scattered in the right place. Its 3rd platoon was running sawmills in Montenau and Born, just a few miles south of Faymonville. Its 1st platoon was south of Trois Ponts at Grand-Halleux, operating a sawmill in Vielsalm. Its 2nd platoon was in Werbomont with Company headquarters. Company A could move its headquarters, say, to Born, where its 3rd platoon was already working, pick up its 1st platoon from Grand-Halleux, and be in position to support CCB, 9th Armored, with no waste of movement. So, Company A it would be. His decision made, Pergrin went to Werbomont for a conference with Company A's commanding officer.

Company A's command post was set up in a schoolhouse about three quarters of a mile north of a crossroads of main north-south and east-west highways, with the officers and men living in houses nearby. The only line platoon Captain Gamble had with him in Werbomont, 2nd platoon, lived in a house angled across the street from the schoolhouse. It was a semide-

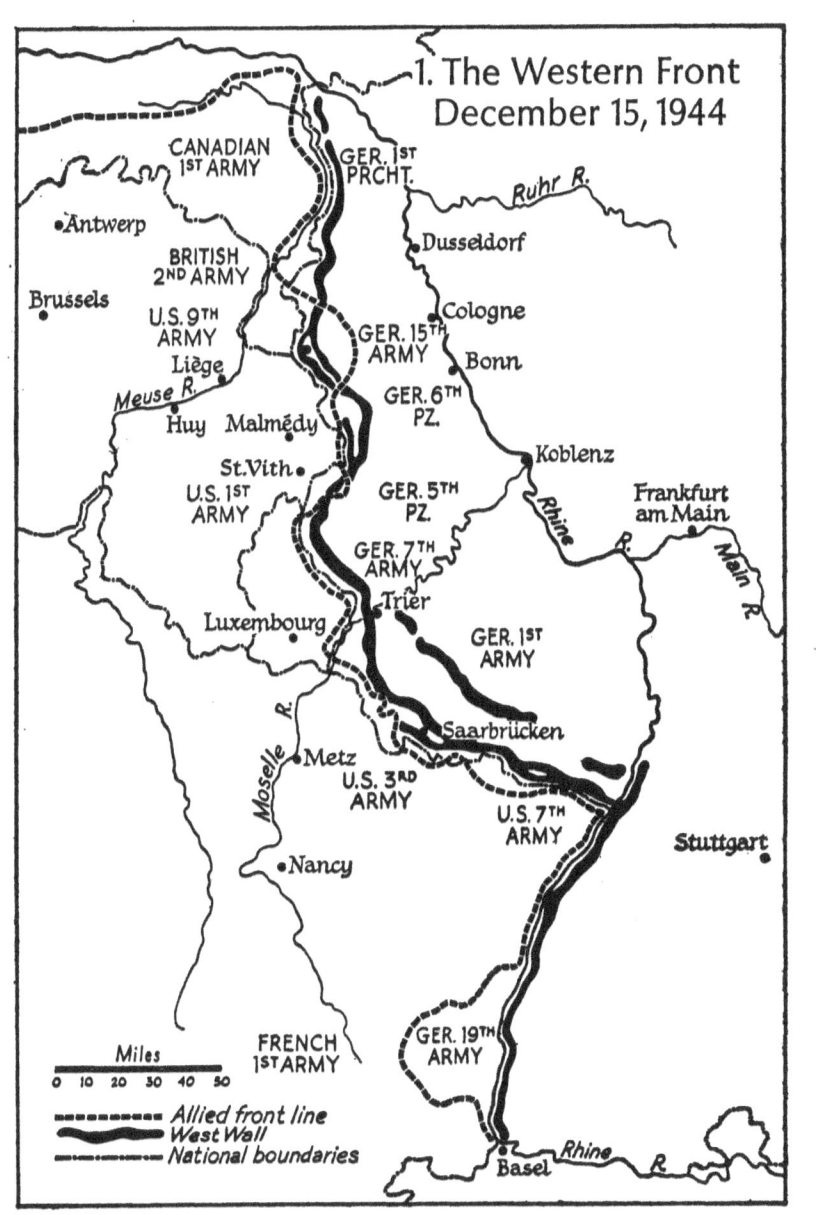

tached house, one half unoccupied at the time, cared for by the family in the other half.

Second platoon, who lived there some six weeks, came to know their landlady very well, and the 3rd squad leader, Sergeant Robert C. Billington, who had a little college French, occasionally played cards with her and her brother. Billington was always losing his buttons. His Belgian landlady taught him to sew them on strongly.

Nearly every night the men of Company A drifted down to a tavern at the crossroads. In the bar there they could get beer, but the principal attraction was the pretty blond seventeen-year-old daughter of the proprietor with whom they laughed and flirted. After England, all barmaids were Peggy to the 291st, so the place became known as Peggy's tavern.

When Pergrin sat down at a table in Company A's command post and laid out his map to outline the move the company would make, the man who faced him across the table, who would make the move and take the new assignment, was carried on official military records as Captain James H. Gamble. But only in the army was he James. His middle name was Harry and that was what he had always been called.

Perhaps more than any other officer in the battalion he looked the part. He was fair in coloring, of middle height, slim and flat, with strong blue eyes and good clear skin. He had a very erect military bearing. He had a fine mind (his I.Q. was near genius), was high-spirited and proud. He was twenty-three years old.

The two officers knew each other well. They had been at Fort Belvoir together and they had come into the 291st within a month of each other and had been together all the way. As Gamble looked at Pergrin he knew, from experience, that his commander was a driver, with great ambitions for his battalion, and with an unalterable sense of duty and a stern insistence on soldierliness and efficiency.

When Pergrin visited Company A, Gamble was frequently a

little desperate in his efforts to shield his rambunctious outfit from the commanding officer's eagle eye. Company A had a pretty rampaging record. In an effort to stimulate efficiency Pergrin had set up a Battalion Meritorious Service Award. Company A rarely won it. They failed to see much to recommend it as compared to big, swinging drunk weekends which might or might not result in a considerable number of AWOLs.

And while they were dependable and got moving swiftly and effectively when there was a job to do, Company A did, without a doubt, build the messiest bridges in the battalion. They got the job done with good, strong bridges built in record time. They just did not see any reason for tidying them up. The company's first sergeant, William H. Smith, always said finally, "Hell, that'll hold 'em up," and when 1/Sergeant Smith said a bridge would hold 'em up, it would, and that was good enough for Company A. There were better things to do than tailoring up bridges.

So, frequently when his commanding officer came visiting Gamble was on the defensive, inclined to ask himself immediately, Lord, what have we done now! He went to bat for his outfit without fail, but he nearly always had something to go to bat for. Even as he swore, "No, sir, there's no whisky in the camp," he had to pray that that corporal sharpening tools over in the edge of the area would not try to get up off his log and walk away.

For his part, when Pergrin conferred with Gamble he saw deeper than the clean-cut military man. Gamble came from a small Blue Ridge mountain town in Virginia. Beneath his correctness was a country kid who could pick a five-string banjo, still loved country music and had a natural ebullience which occasionally boiled over into mischief.

Now the two officers who knew each other so well, deeper than military etiquette allowed them to show, faced each other and Pergrin told Gamble to close up shop at Werbomont and to move, at the earliest hour possible the next morning, here — and his finger pointed to Born. He gave no reason for the move. When Company A was actually assigned to CCB would be time enough to give Gamble further orders. For now, it was just move. And when Gamble got set up in Born he was to bring his 1st platoon over from Grand-Halleux. With the 3rd platoon already at Born and Montenau, Company A would then be intact. Pergrin then left.

Gamble was perturbed about this order to move. It was not only unexpected, it reversed the expected which had settled Company A in a winter routine. It was a move much nearer the front, and it was dangerously near the limits of radio communications to Pergrin at Battalion.

Separated though the line companies were at present, they were linked to Battalion by radio. As an engineer outfit, the 291st did not possess powerful radio sets such as the infantry and artillery had. Each company had a Signal Corps Radio Model 284. This set was capable of transmitting and receiving on an assigned frequency with a capability of thirty miles continuous wave (Morse code) and up to ten miles by voice.

These rated distances were not entirely trustworthy because of various factors, such as changing atmospheric conditions, contour of terrain, actual locations of sets working with each other, radio traffic by other and sometimes more powerful sets nearby, and there was, of course, always the possibility of enemy interference. Because the line companies were so widely separated now, Morse code was used exclusively with them. Each company had three radio operators who worked a twenty-four-hour day. All messages had to be encoded and decoded.

The 291st Communications Section, of which T/Sergeant John L. Scanlan was chief, had only one overhead telephone which went to Group Headquarters in Trois Ponts, and to the Battalion Motor Pool at that same place.

Group had radio, of course, but it also had telephone commu-

The Allied Side

nications with First Army in Spa, and First Army had telephone communications all over eastern Belgium, including the town of Malmédy. So, through Group and First Army, Battalion had telephone to Company B in Malmédy. It was awkward and it was cumbersome and it took a lot of time through various switchboards, but in an emergency it was useful. But there were no telephone communications to A and C companies. The 291st was not equipped to lay and maintain such long overhead lines. Besides, radio communications were entirely satisfactory.

In addition to the SCR 284, each of the companies in the 291st had about six walkie-talkie battery-operated radio sets. They were strictly voice radios, Model SCR 300, capable of transmitting and receiving from three to five miles. A few men in every platoon of each company had been trained to operate this radio fairly well.

The three line companies also had a few field telephones, a small amount of wire, some wire climbers and other equipment. This was purely for their own internal use. The three line companies used jeeps to make a daily pickup of written orders from Colonel Pergrin, and the mail. Battalion used a three-quarter-ton weapons carrier truck to pick up written orders from Group, and the mail from the nearest Army Post Office section.

The importance of communications cannot be stressed too much. Communications meant more than a channel through which an outfit's affairs were conducted. Communications meant eyes and ears, direction and orderliness, and security. No commanding officer felt so lonely and so isolated as when he was out of radio contact — out of touch. In touch — they were immensely necessary words, immensely reassuring and comforting. When the German offensive began on December 16, the factor contributing most largely to the utter chaos and bewilderment and confusion was the loss of communications, among all outfits, along the entire front. The men in the communications sections played an unromantic, largely not understood, but tremendously important role. When they could not function, the whole army was blind and deaf.

Gamble, therefore, did not like having his radio link stretched so far. He called in the two officers with him at Werbomont, Lieutenant Alvin Edelstein, leader of 2nd platoon, and the Administrative Officer, Lieutenant Frank R. Hayes, and his 1/Sergeant, William H. Smith, and informed them of the order to move. They discussed every possible reason for it among themselves but could not fathom its purpose. They all agreed, however, that something out of the ordinary was in store for them, something probably disagreeable and possibly damned dangerous.

Then Lieutenant Hayes, who loved maps and had hoped to be assigned to the topographical engineers, got out his maps and set about plotting the route for the move.

The news was filtered down to the squad leaders and trucks and jeeps went fanning out to alert and bring in any men on special details.

That night Sergeant Billington, 3rd squad leader, 2nd platoon, played one last game of cards with his landlord. The men went for one last time to Peggy's tavern to drink a final beer and flirt one last time with the pretty blond daughter of the proprietor.

They were unhappy about this move, too. They were comfortable where they were, they liked the people of Werbomont, it was close to Spa and passes were easy to get, and they had thought they were settled for the winter. The way it filtered down to them, now they were going to some little town over in Germany. To this day many men of Company A believe that when they made this move they went into Germany.

They certainly did move into a Germanic area of Belgium. It has to be understood that First Army troops were densely packed into a bulge in the eastern tip of Belgium which had been part of Germany until 1919. The old German-Belgian border

The Allied Side

had run north and south from the Dutch border just east of Aachen, east of Eupen and Malmédy, on southward to the Luxembourg line. Eupen, Malmédy, Sourbrodt, Butgenbach, Büllingen, St. Vith, Montenau, Born — all these towns had been in Germany. For 105 years, since 1815, the entire tip in which most of the American military units were now deployed had been German. Generations of the inhabitants had thus been German citizens, German in all their habits of life, their language, their attitudes and their loyalties. Only one sixth of the population of some 60,000 people were Walloons and French-speaking. Five-sixths were German.

But this area, which was composed of the districts of Eupen and Malmédy, was highly developed by Germany during this period and efficient and extensive railway and road systems were built. At the end of World War I the Allies contended that these districts had been made a base for German militarism and that in order for the Low Countries to be safe the Eupen-Malmédy districts must become Belgian. No plebiscite was held. The Treaty of Versailles arbitrarily pinched off these two districts from Germany and gave them to Belgium. The new boundary line was therefore considerably farther east than the old one and all the towns lying east of the Eupen-Malmédy line, which had been German for so long, suddenly became Belgian. People do not so easily transfer their loyalties. A simple parallel would be if the State of Maine were suddenly pinched off the United States and given to Canada. At least as long as the old U.S. citizens lived, there would be divided feelings and loyalties. Those people born before 1919 had been German. In that year, by edict of the Treaty of Versailles, they became Belgian. In 1940 they became German again by reattachment through Hitler's victorious invasion. In September of 1944 they were Belgian again. By the end of December 1944 they would be German once more, and by the end of January 1945 would again be Belgian.

The 291st positions lay directly athwart the old boundary line. The men stationed in Werbomont, in La Gleize and in Trois Ponts were in towns which had always been Belgian. Those stationed at Malmédy, at Sourbrodt, at Montenau and Born, were in towns with a long German history. In these towns were people fiercely loyal to Belgium, of course. But there were people equally loyal, and equally fierce about it, to the old German ties. And it should be further understood that Hitler made a political distinction between the two sections of Belgium. His troops *occupied* Belgium proper. But in the Eupen-Malmédy districts Hitler felt he was simply taking back land and people rightfully German. The occupation in those districts was therefore a reannexation, as in the Rhineland.

It was early recognized by the U.S. authorities that Eupen and Malmédy were hotbeds of unrest with their large German populations. And to add to the problem these towns, as well as neighboring villages, held many refugees from the combat zones near the front. One of the first things the First U.S. Army had done upon settling into its headquarters at Spa had been to make a systematic comb-out of the Germanic towns to the east — Losheim, Krinkelt, Rocherath, Waimes, Sourbrodt, Büllingen, Honsfeld, Manderfeld, Butgenbach and others. Many of the people were removed simply for their own safety — especially in the belt around Honsfeld-Büllingen-Butgenbach where antiaircraft batteries were set up to shoot down the buzz bombs. But others were shifted and interned because they were known to be active Fifth Columnists.* They would be dangerous to have wandering freely about among American troops and installations. They could spy too easily and all too easily pass on vital information.

Into Malmédy, Eupen, Stavelot, Grand-Halleux, Ligneuville and other villages, there then flowed the families and friends of people interned nearby, all disgruntled by the evacuation and internment, many of them actively hostile to the Belgian and U.S.

---

* Pogue, Forrest C., *The Supreme Command* (Washington: Office of the Chief of Military History, Department of the Army, 1954).

The Allied Side

authorities. They were ready fuel for the flames of insurgency and they formed a vast recruitment for a large and effective Fifth Column.

When the men of the 291st settled into their Belgian towns, those of them stationed in Malmédy and east of Malmédy slowly began to feel as if they were in Germany rather than Belgium. They bumped into the German language constantly, many of the people had German names, street signs and town businesses were most often in German, and the attitude of the people was certainly strange.

Fresh from France where they had been joyously hailed as liberators, covered with kisses and every man made to feel a hero, they noticed they were welcomed with less than total joy in these towns. In fact, there was a distinct air of sullenness, of wary watchfulness that bordered sometimes on plain unfriendliness.

Malmédy, for instance, might be beautiful and picturesque and historic, but it was also pervaded with a murky restraint. Many of the people did business with the Americans and were friendly. But some of the citizens not only paid the soldiers scant attention but acted as if they were invaders and the town would have been better off without them. Malmédy, in fact, had a vaguely fated feeling about it, a volcanic feeling as if something seethed under its skin, ready to boil over and destroy.

When the men of Company B got to know the people of Malmédy well enough to go into a few homes, they were bewildered to see large photographs of sons, brothers, husbands, hanging on the walls and standing on the tables. Not that one did not expect to see photographs of men in uniform in honored positions in Belgian homes in 1944. But it *was* confusing to see that the men in these photographs did not, in the main, wear Belgian uniforms. They wore the field gray uniform of the German Army. It was, to say the least, uncomfortable to visit in such homes.

And the cemeteries in these towns had many graves marked

with crosses on which hung a German helmet, or which centered on them the German Iron Cross.*

The men of the 291st in the old German area were indulgent. They thought perhaps the people had lived so long near the German border they had intermarried and had mixed loyalties. Because there were also many loyal Belgian patriots in most of the towns, they cultivated them and continued their careless, easygoing friendliness.

But Company A in Werbomont had had no experience with mixed loyalties and with only the vaguest knowledge of the new boundary line between Belgium and Germany, and none whatever of the old, they did know that Born, where they were going to move, was damned well German. The people were German, they spoke German, the street signs and business signs were in German, so the town was obviously in Germany!

Unhappy about the move as they were, orders were orders, and the men griped and complained but in the end shrugged it off with a joke. "Oh, well, the old 291st — always in the right place at the wrong time for trouble." And they bedded down ready to roll when roused the next morning.

Remember that Gamble only had one line platoon with him in Werbomont. His 3rd platoon was already in Montenau and Born where he was going to move next day. As has been said, 3rd platoon was running two sawmills, one at Montenau, the other at Born. But Lieutenant Archibald L. Taylor, leader of the platoon, had his command post at Montenau. He had two squads working there, only one squad at Born.

Taylor was a tall, thin, slow-talking North Carolinian. His brother officers said he talked so slow it took him a full minute to answer yes or no to a question. He was a quiet, resourceful southern gentleman, of sound judgment and excellent qualities of leadership.

* Various Company B men to author, particularly T/Sergeant John T. Scanlan and Private Bernard Koenig.

The Allied Side

Taylor had enlisted in the army in 1939, with three years of college behind him. He had therefore been Regular Army before going to OCS. "I sometimes wished," he said, "I hadn't made officer at all. It was mighty lonesome, especially when we were on detached service." But his background as an old-line NCO made him a very good officer. He understood the free and easy companionship of his men, how they thought and what could be expected of them. If he missed it for himself, it still stood him in good stead and he had a good solid platoon.

Taylor, on detached service, had no radio to Company or Battalion. He depended entirely on jeep messengers and the mail deliveries for news and orders. The night of December 15 he had no idea the rest of Company A was preparing to catch up with him. He and his men turned in after a routine day. Nothing much ever happened in Montenau or Born. The men went to Malmédy or St. Vith for a little fun and companionship.

Gamble's other line platoon was at Grand-Halleux, five miles south of Trois Ponts. First platoon's leader was Lieutenant Albert W. Walters. He only had two squads of his platoon with him. His 1st squad was Gamble's security squad at Werbomont.

Walters was twenty-three years old, a pretty rugged individual whose native environment was the coast country near Seattle. He had a thatch of straw-colored hair and was good-looking in a rough-crafted sort of way. More importantly, he had a good head on his shoulders, had his feet firmly planted on the ground and carried his load without fuss or much bother from above or below. He was aggressive and had initiative.

At Grand-Halleux, Bucky Walters was also ignorant of Company A's proposed move, but when he turned in the night of December 15 he was troubled, for various reasons. First, he had watched the 106th Infantry Division move through Vielsalm on their way to the front. They were the first of the eighteen-year-old draftees and they looked like babies in their young green innocence. They had also had a rugged trip across France in open trucks in rain and cold. They were exhausted, sick and miserable. The outfit did not have all its equipment nor even all its men. Walters noticed, especially, that they did not yet have their division engineers. "My God," he said to his platoon sergeant, "if that's what is going up to the front we may as well get ready for trouble!"

Also Walters' timber squad had been cutting in the area east of Grand-Halleux for about five weeks and he was beginning to need a new stand of timber. He went across the Salm River that day, December 15, to look over the timber stands on the west side. Several civilians and American soldiers over there had a strange tale to tell. A small plane had circled the area just at twilight for two days now. It appeared to be dropping small parachutes.

When Walters returned to his CP in Grand-Halleux he issued orders that everybody, without fail, was to go under arms at all times from now on, and if there was anything unusual or out of the ordinary it was to be reported to him immediately.

He felt in his bones that trouble was brewing, though he could not put his finger on it. However, the mail had been brought down to 1st platoon that day, December 15, and a few more Christmas packages from home had arrived for the men. They were saving them to have a Christmas party for the children of the parish. Big plans were being made for much food, much fun, much singing and a big, fine Christmas tree for the children.

Up at La Gleize the night of December 15 everything was routine with Company C.

At Sourbrodt, C Company's detached 3rd platoon also had had a routine day. Nothing much ever happened in Sourbrodt. The men went to Malmédy for the movies and bars.

At Malmédy on the night of December 15, the men of Company B who had passes used them as tickets at a restaurant where GI food was cooked by civilian cooks. Not only was the food good, it was served by pretty young Belgian waitresses.

Afterward, those who wanted to went to the nightly movie. Others went visiting in Malmédy homes. The lucky ones, with dates, found various secluded trysting places. When they went to bed they slept the sleep of the tired, the virtuous and the just, unapprehensive.

3

THE NIGHT of December 15 was a short night for Company A in Werbomont.

The men were roused around 3:00 A.M. to get ready to roll. The vehicles growled into place in a long line and the equipment was slowly loaded on. The kitchen and the radio were the last two setups to be taken down. The men had to be served breakfast and Corporal Dennington, head of Company A's radio section, wanted to stay in the Net until the last minute. The pre-dawn hours were cold and dark and a fine drizzling rain was falling.

Around 6:45 Company A was ready to leave. Corporal Dennington had tapped out QLV, meaning "I am reporting out of the Net," and had received in return Battalion's QMX, meaning "Report back in as soon as possible." The antenna had then been taken down.

Sergeant Scanlan, Battalion's Communications Chief, had been informed that Company A would be moving to Born today. He had located the place on his map and mentally reviewed the communications picture. The trip was about thirty-five road miles, but he expected it might be night before the boys reported back into the Net. Scanlan did not like having any company out of his Communications Net but the 291st was not equipped for mobile operations, so the best he could do was acknowledge Dennington's message and begin to worry, for he is a conscientious man and he *will* worry until Company A is back in the Net and he can feel he has all his chickens under his wing again.

Like Captain Gamble, what perturbs him most is that this move takes Company A dangerously near the maximum radio range and they may even prove to be beyond communications with Battalion. He can only wait until they are set up again and see, but it will be on his mind the entire day.

It was nearing 7:00 A.M. when Company A started rolling. Winter comes early and miserably in the Ardennes. The region lies where two weather systems meet, the weather moving east from the British Isles and the weather moving west from Russia, and both systems affect the climate and make it difficult to forecast. Through November and early December there are many overcast days and much rainfall. There are freezes and light snows which will deepen as winter slowly locks in, and there are gusty, harsh winds sweeping over the ridges and plateaus. Thick, peasoupy fogs rise from the rivers about daylight and sometimes last until noon before burning off. One old-line sergeant grumbled at breakfast one morning that the fog was so thick you couldn't see ten men behind you in the chow line. "It's like living inside a cow," he opined.

The cold is raw and damp and penetrating and days are short and dark and gloomy. Snows of ten or twelve inches can fall overnight and snow lasts a long time in the Ardennes — but the deep snows do not occur until late in December and through January.

It was a typical December day as Company A started up its vehicles and began to move out of Werbomont, darkly overcast, foggy, murky, with a cold light rain falling. There had been snows earlier but only old patches were left on the ground on December 16. Daylight came around 7:50. The sun rose at 8:29. It would set at 4:35. This was army time, which during the winter was the same for both the Allies and the Germans. In mid-

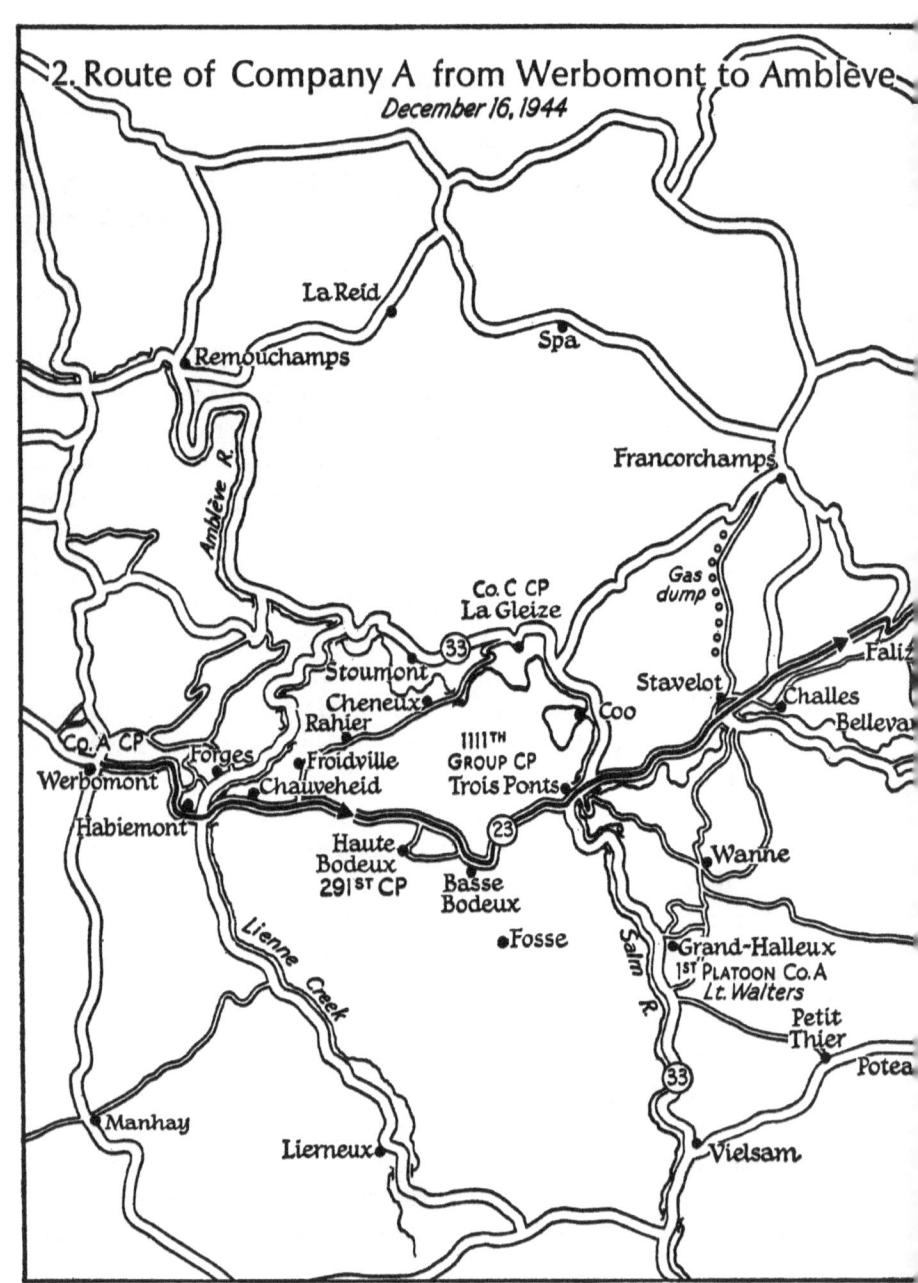

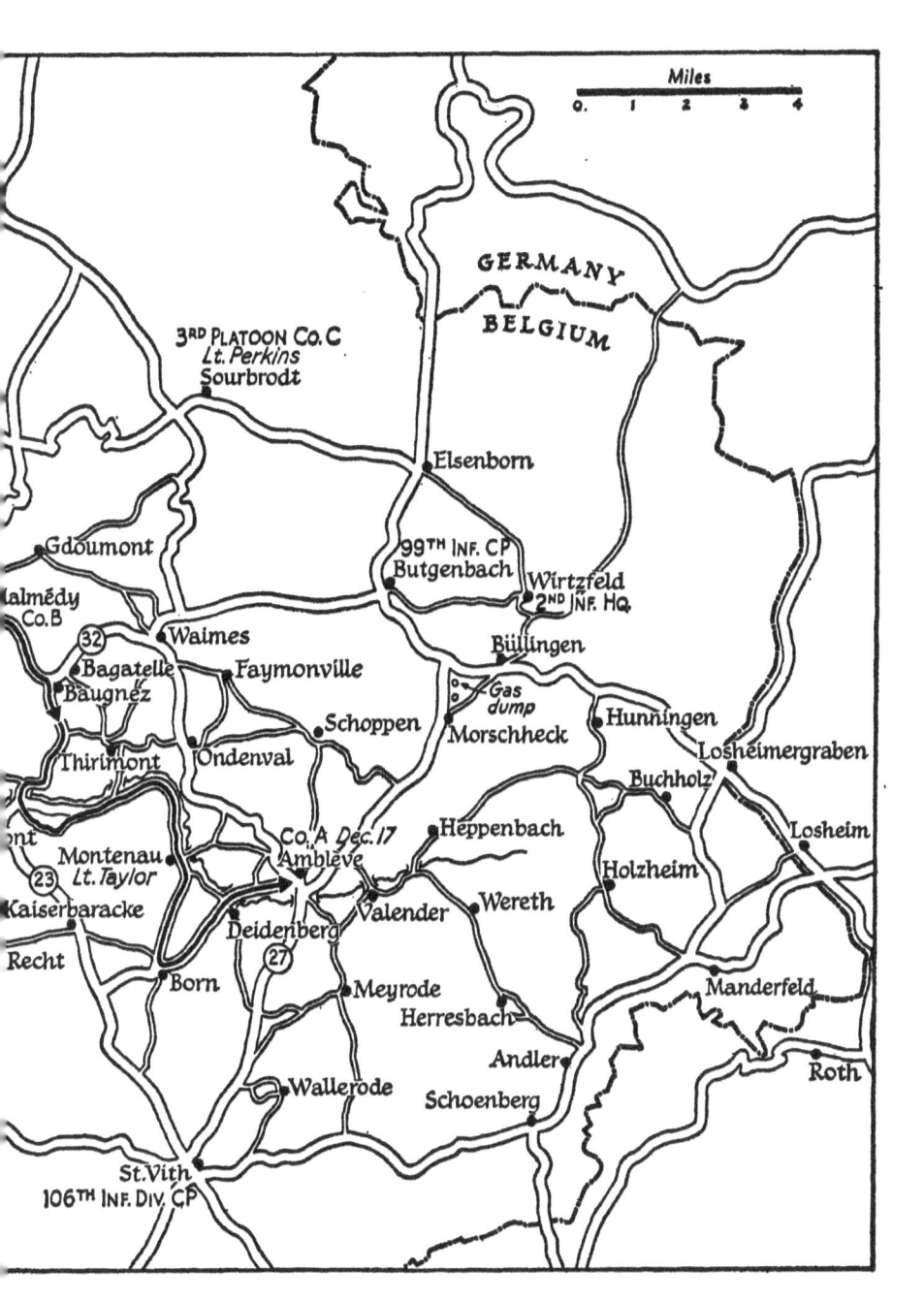

December the daylight hours were very brief and the twilights were short, adding only thirty-eight minutes to the hours of light, morning and evening.

Led by Captain Gamble's command car, the convoy moved out. Because they had to get gas for their vehicles and that had to be done at the depots in Malmédy, Lieutenant Hayes had routed them through Trois Ponts and Stavelot to Malmédy, thence southeast to Born.

Follow carefully this route Company A now takes, for this will soon be the battlefield and the geography is extremely important. Notice every stream, every bridge, every hill, every bend and turn, the road intersections, the railroads and viaducts, even the houses. Notice especially the four towns, Werbomont, Trois Ponts, Stavelot and Malmédy, for in these four towns the confrontation will occur and they and the 291st will all play a vital role. By one of those strange coincidences which war is so full of, Company A will touch all of these vital points of the battle of the Amblève as it moves on December 16.

With no foreknowledge the men are only cold, sleepy and disgruntled over having to move at all as the small convoy rumbles out just before daylight, about 7:00 A.M.

Werbomont lies on a slight plateau at the junction of two main highways, N-15 running north and south between Liège and Houffalize, and N-23 running east and west. Beyond Werbomont N-23 angles northwest and leads to Huy, where it crosses the Meuse River. Company A, however, turns east and heads for Trois Ponts, some eleven miles away.

About two miles out of Werbomont the road becomes very crooked, winding and turning as it begins a long descent into the valley of Lienne Creek. Partway down this long hill, but off to the left, lies the village of Habiemont. It is reached by a byroad.

The Lienne valley is rather broad with fairly unobstructed views across it. At the bottom of the hill, as one approaches

The Allied Side

Lienne Creek, the highway is bisected by the road coming up from Lierneux to the south, which goes on northward to Targnon and Stoumont. There are a few farmhouses nearby and near the bridge, on the left, sits a single building, a café.

The bridge across the creek is a wooden trestle bridge which Company C of the 291st built earlier in the fall to replace the one destroyed by the Germans as they retreated. This bridge, known to the men as the Habiemont bridge because of its proximity to the hamlet of that name, is to become vitally important and to attain a place in history.

Having crossed the bridge, Company A follows the highway, N–23, in a sharp bend which then curves right and climbs around a rocky hill mass. The road then straightens out. There are several byroads and driveways which lead to small settlements and private estates.

One byroad, a secondary road, comes in from the north. It originates in La Gleize, crosses the north-flowing Amblève River at Cheneux, and meanders down through the villages of Rahier and Froidville before debouching into Route N–23. This road will be of great significance shortly.

Now Company A has a more or less straight route to Basse Bodeux and on to Trois Ponts. Basse Bodeux is the twin village of Haute Bodeux where Battalion is stationed. It is on the highway, however, where Haute Bodeux is behind and in a pocket of hills off the road. It is perhaps a mile and a half from Basse Bodeux to Trois Ponts.

Trois Ponts, whose name of course means Three Bridges, is a pretty little village built in a valley overlooked by four hills, where three rivers come together. From the south the Salm River flows directly northward through the town, most of which is built on the west bank, but part of which extends across the river onto a narrow strip along the east bank, along the foot of a high, abrupt and cliffy hill mass.

Just north of the village the Amblève River comes in from the east and joins the Salm. There are two bridges across the Salm and one across the Amblève, which gives the village its name. Strangely, as the river flows on northward to the Meuse it loses the name Salm and takes the name Amblève.

As Company A proceeds through the town they pass a hotel on their left. This is the main headquarters for Colonel Anderson and the 1111th Group. Behind the hotel, and at the foot of a hill on the bank of a little creek, is one of the sawmills operated by Company C. The mill is running busily, as usual, this morning, for it runs twenty-four hours a day, seven days a week.

Immediately beyond Group Headquarters, Company A crosses the Salm River, in the heart of town, and at the end of one short block the highway makes a sharp left turn. To their right as they make this turn lie the tracks of a main railroad line which runs from Luxembourg to Liège. The railroad hugs the river because this strip of land on the east bank is so narrow. The beetling cliffs of the hill mass almost overhang it. The railroad station is a little south of the bend in the highway, and the other Company C sawmill, the Robert Crismer mill, is opposite the station. The high hill mass rises behind all this section of Trois Ponts very sharply and steeply. On this hill mass, about three and a half miles away, is the village of Wanne. A secondary road leads from Wanne down this steep hill and enters Trois Ponts on this narrow east bank. Wanne and this road will have serious consequences later.

A very short distance after they make their left turn, perhaps a hundred yards or so, the highway crosses the Amblève River, which here runs westward but only a stone's throw away joins the Salm and flows north. The bridge here is another wooden trestle, built by Company B earlier in the fall.

After crossing the Amblève, Company A passes a row of some six or eight buildings, some of them family homes, some business buildings, all on their left. Between two of them, Battalion's

The Allied Side

motor pool is located in a garage. All the men of the battalion have come to know the people living in these houses as they have come and gone from the motor pool.

For a short distance Company A is not only traveling on N-23, but is using N-33, a major north-south highway which runs from Aywaille to Vielsalm. But they leave it just beyond the row of houses and turn sharp right back onto N-23. They pass under a railroad viaduct and head for Stavelot. N-33, which goes on north, also passes under a railroad viaduct. There are thus two viaducts at right angles to each other. In the forested, hilly Ardennes, Belgian highways either cross over or under the railroads. There are few level grade crossings. This makes innumerable bridges — all vulnerable to enemy attack, but also naturally good defense points. The viaduct on N-23 is to have special significance.

About 500 yards from this viaduct, a dirt road enters the highway from the right. The road has crossed the Amblève River on a very light flimsy bridge. It is the Petit Spai bridge, and the Petit Spai road has wound down off the heights from the village of Wanne. This bridge will be of utmost importance very soon.

It is about four miles to Stavelot and the road is dotted by homes all the way. As Company A nears Stavelot, on their left is a small hotel. Lieutenant W. L. Colbeck, whose platoon operates the B Company sawmill in Stavelot, lived in this little hotel for a while. He knows the family well.

Beyond the hotel but across the highway from it lies the sawmill which Colbeck's platoon operates. Beside it is the rather imposing residence of a man named Legaye. Lieutenant Colbeck has come to know this family well, also. Before long this home will be the scene of grim tragedy.

As Company A rolls by the sawmill they can see a small house trailer in the mill yard. This is where Lieutenant Colbeck, his driver and two cooks are now living.

They come into the heart of Stavelot and pass the MP at the

intersection of the main streets. To their right at this point, some three blocks south, flows the Amblève River. It is crossed there by a very old, very heavy stone-arched bridge. The main part of Stavelot lies on the north bank of this river, but an extension lies across the river in the valley and flows part of the way up a high hill mass. A secondary road winds up the hill to this height of land. This bridge and this road will have strategic importance within thirty-six hours.

To their left at the intersection in Stavelot, the old road to Francorchamps crosses a branch railroad track then climbs and winds up a hill. The town of Stavelot thus lies astride the Amblève River, in its valley, with hills on either side. Perhaps a mile northward, up the Francorchamps road, is the big gas dump with over a million gallons of gasoline and related products stacked along the road in five-gallon cans. It is guarded by a unit of the Belgian Army.

Company A moves straight on through Stavelot. As they clear Stavelot, fog and drizzle from the pine trees which line the road drip gloomily. It is somehow a sad and dismal scene. Few of the men liked these ranks of pine trees which were everywhere, all over the country. They made it all look like one big cemetery and the trees seeped constantly as if forever weeping.

Just this side of Malmédy they reach an intersection where the road from Spa comes down, and they make another very sharp horseshoe turn right. Briefly they are almost doubled back on themselves. They cross the branch railroad on a highway overpass, double sharply to the left, completing a big S-bend, then cross the Warche River, a tributary of the Amblève, on a wooden bridge Company B had built in place of the old stone-arched bridge the Germans blew in their retreat.

Now they straighten out for the approach to Malmédy, passing a big paper mill on their left. Across the street from it is a single residence, the only building on that side of the road. All the rest is an open field. After passing these two buildings, the

The Allied Side

paper mill and the residence, it is around a quarter of a mile to a long and very high viaduct on which the railroad track again crosses the highway. This viaduct is so high that the rails are some sixty feet above the highway. The paper mill, the single residence, the big viaduct will all feature shortly in important events.

Now they swing right and are in Malmédy. It was one of the most beautiful and picturesque little towns in the Ardennes. It was also one of the largest with its population of around 5000. It lay in folded hills southeast of Spa, the hills running up north into the wild and rugged forests of the Hertogenwald. Like most Belgian towns it is built around *places*, or squares, with a complexity of mazelike streets running into the business concentration on the principal square.

The Warche River, which rises away to the northeast of the city, winds around it on its western limits, then meanders off southward and empties into the Amblève. The railroad, which comes up from Stavelot, curves around the southern edge of the town, then winds off eastward to the German border. This railroad meanders under and over the roads, entering the city from the west and south, and continues eastward, crossing N–32 in a system of overpasses and underpasses. This railroad played a surprisingly important part in all aspects of the Battle of the Bulge on the northern shoulder.

Malmédy was a very important town to First Army. Its facilities and its strategic location behind the front at the intersection of all major roads, east and west and north and south, made it an obvious installation point. It became a service and supply center and it was also used as a rest area for front-line troops. It was jam-packed with ordnance and quartermaster supply units, there were several big gas depots, there was a replacement depot, the 44th Field Evacuation Hospital was located there and a detachment of the 518th Military Police was stationed in the town. It was busy, overcrowded with people, hustling and lively.

Captain John T. Conlin, commander of B Company, had found a big two-and-a-half-story white stucco house in the southeastern part of town for his headquarters. The house had belonged to a man named von Renz. The street on which the house faced was actually a section of the main Eupen–St. Vith highway, as well as N–32 which ran east to Butgenbach and the German frontier. All through traffic, therefore, passed Conlin's CP.

All the Company B platoons were living in Malmédy. First platoon was quartered in a small hotel in the downtown area. They were operating the sawmill in Stavelot but they drove back and forth daily. Second platoon was cutting timber and hauling logs to the two sawmills, but they, too, drove back and forth to the woods daily. It is not known where they lived, but S/Sergeant Walter J. Smith, their platoon sergeant, has said it was "some big barn of a place." Third platoon lived in the von Renz house in which the command post was also located.

Company A reached Malmédy at midmorning and to their amazement they found the whole town milling and boiling with excitement and apprehensive civilians and soldiers. They saw damaged buildings, shattered trees and they recognized squads of Company B men at work cleaning up a lot of debris in the streets. The town looked as if a big windstorm had hit it.

Around 5:30 that morning, about the time Company A was loading up to leave Werbomont, there were suddenly violent explosions in Malmédy, explosions which shattered windowpanes and shook the earth, which sent up immense clouds of black smoke from which rained the debris of brick, stones, mortar and splintered wood.

The men of the third platoon, Company B, were jolted out of their beds in the flowery-papered rooms of the von Renz house by the roar and rumble and reverberations of the huge explosions. Hitler's secret weapon, they told each other, awed and scared by the deep intensity of the explosions. They piled out and

The Allied Side

dressed, tensely wondering what next. Buzz bombs they were used to, but buzz bombs were not causing these thundering explosions. What kind of scary, eerie thing was it? Where had it come from? Would there be more?

The first explosions had sounded deep and intense but rather far away to 1st platoon in their quarters downtown. But the final one hit right next door and was like the thunder of doomsday. A deafening crash, a jolting of the whole building, then breaking glass and falling plaster. The men of 1st platoon threw themselves to the floor and arms over their head waited for the next one, and the end of time. It did not come. That was all. Finally they picked themselves up and looked around, weak in the knees, examined themselves and found a few cuts and scratches, then began chattering. "What in the hell *was* that?" Like 3rd platoon, they thought it was a new, weird weapon. Whatever it was, it was enough to curl your hair.

Conlin drove quickly into town to see what had happened and to make certain his men were safe. He made his way through the debris on the streets, the bricks and stones of fallen walls, the shattered glass from windows, the limbs and branches of splintered trees.

He found all his men safe. Except for some scratches and bruises nobody in Company B was injured. The Military Government was already on top of the situation and Conlin was asked to put his engineers to work with their bulldozers and trucks cleaning up the debris.

When Conlin returned to his CP he knew what had happened. In all, four mammoth 310-mm. shells had fallen in the town, fired by the big German railroad guns far behind the German lines. But the men, generally, did not find out until much later. They continued to speculate and wonder among themselves. Some changes were made in the daily routine. Instead of going to work in the sawmills, certain squads were detailed to clean up the debris in the streets.

Private Bernard Koenig was in one of these clean-up squads. Three American medics from other units in the town had been killed and Koenig's squad drew the detail of cleaning up the area where they had been hit. It made him thoughtful. Malmédy was some thirty miles behind the front and yet here they were washing up the blood of three American medics just killed. Not yet knowing the details of the shelling, the men were filled with an uneasy sense of foreboding. They still believed the explosions, so far behind the front, had been caused by some new, weird secret weapon, and the strange and mysterious were always the scariest things to face. What must they look for? What safeguards should they take? Would another rain of the things begin again any minute? And what on earth did it all mean?

As the hours passed and no more shells fell, the men of Company B began to feel a little more relaxed. Company A arrived at midmorning and were in turn made somewhat apprehensive by what they learned from the work details. Nobody could make heads or tails of the event.

Gamble sent his vehicles to a gas depot and he visited with Conlin at the command post. "What the hell's going on here?" Gamble wanted to know.

Conlin lifted his big shoulders. "All hell busted loose about seven o'clock this morning," he said. "We got four big blockbusters in a row. No warning at all. Just peace and quiet and then suddenly, varoooooom, here they come!"

"But why? Why Malmédy? My God, this is thirty miles behind the front!"

Conlin had no answer either.

He was a dark, solid man, a graduate of the University of Wisconsin with a degree in political science. If Colonel Pergrin had had a favorite among his officers it would have had to be Conlin. He called him a "wild fighting Irishman." Conlin's energy, his fighting spirit, his driving determination that B Company should be the best outfit in the battalion, made him a man after Pergrin's

The Allied Side

heart. Pergrin had that same determination for the battalion.

Physically strong and compulsively active, it may be that Conlin would have been more at home as a tank commander under, say, General Patton. The prosaic work of engineers was probably a constant frustration to him. But his drive made Company B a very able, sharp company. Not that they lacked any of Company A's rowdiness. They had about the same amount of that wild rampaging spirit. But Conlin was more of a rough rider than Gamble, cracking down harder and tougher more often. Unable to get into combat, he used his company combatively, in fierce competition with the other companies.

He had telephoned the colonel, he told Gamble now, and Pergrin had told him to carry on, he would be over later. Both officers were perturbed but they were more puzzled than anxious. The Allied front was of course invincible. There was no real cause for concern. The fact that there were four shells and no more probably meant it was just some freak firing.

Gamble also discussed this move he was making with Conlin. Conlin had heard nothing about it. The colonel had told him, on the telephone, that Company A was moving to Born and he was going down there later, but he had not said why A Company was moving — and B Company certainly had received no orders. It was something which apparently involved only Company A. Gamble could only wait and see.

With his vehicles as full of gas as the rationing allowed, Gamble left Malmédy around 11:00. From the command post the convoy went southeast on the highway which, for a short distance, was both N-32 and N-23. About two and a half miles out of Malmédy they came to a little crossroads hamlet named Baugnez, although none of the U.S. troops in the area called it that or perhaps even knew its Belgian name. They called it Five Points, because five roads came together at this point.

There was a café at the intersection and two or three farm homes nearby and that was all, except for some open fields and woods. There was nothing about it to indicate it was destined shortly to become the most famous single location, outside of Bastogne, in the entire Battle of the Bulge.

At this place Gamble stayed with N-23, the road which went south to St. Vith, while N-32 led on eastward to Butgenbach and the German border. Three miles south of Five Points he came to the beautiful village of Ligneuville, one of the loveliest resort towns in the Ardennes. The royalty of Europe had always enjoyed the village and stayed in the charming Hôtel du Moulin. Gamble may or may not have known that the village was now the headquarters of the 49th Antiaircraft Artillery Brigade and that its commander, Brigadier General Edward J. Timberlake, now lived in the Hôtel du Moulin.

At Ligneuville Gamble swung over by a secondary road to Montenau to alert Lieutenant Arch Taylor that he was moving into the area. It may be that Taylor warned him that he would find Born pretty full and that he might have difficulty setting up there. Taylor might have suggested Deidenberg or Amblève, both on a dogleg between Montenau and Born.

At any rate, Gamble did find Born full to the bursting point, with 106th Infantry troops. There was not one single building or home available for Company A. The 106th had just moved into the line, remember, on December 11. The division CP was at St. Vith. Major General Alan W. Jones had put his reserve, the 2nd Battalion of the 423rd Regiment, in Born.

Gamble huddled with his officers and they decided to backtrack to Deidenberg and over to Amblève. They were checked suspiciously by the 106th security points and they began to feel pretty much out of pocket.

They reached Amblève about 3:00 P.M. It took a while to find places to stay, the day was dark and overcast, a light rain was still drizzling down, and with the sun setting at 4:35 there was very little daylight left by the time they got squared away. Gamble took over a schoolhouse for his CP, and houses nearby

The Allied Side

in a sort of court, or square, were found for the men. By sheer coincidence Gamble has picked a town which within twenty-four hours will be of significance to a German colonel.

The cold gray stone houses of the village looked unfriendly and the men noticed that the signs on the cafés and business buildings were all in German. The people of the village watched them unload in a silence as chill and gray as the stone houses. There was no smiling warmth for them here as there had been in Werbomont. "What a dump!" Gamble said to his administrative officer, Hayes.

He was feeling more and more uneasy. There had been something very jittery about the 106th's security checks. They had been insistent on the full procedure of identification and had even then eyed the little convoy suspiciously. Gamble was anxious to get the radio set up so he could report in, but the radiomen were having trouble putting the antenna up. He was out on a limb over here, practically on the German border, and he wanted a link to Battalion as soon as possible. Rumors that the Germans had broken through the front were also beginning to sift in.

The men were busy getting set up, but from Gamble right down to Pfc. Louis T. Dymond who pulled guard at the CP that night there was an apprehensive feeling — nothing you could put your finger on, but something was haywire. They did not like this town and they devoutly hoped they would not have to stay long in it.

As dark came on, Company A's own security was posted and road patrols were assigned.

Two men, off duty, went to a tavern for a beer that night. They were Pfc. George Courvillion and Corporal Vincent Fresina, long-time friends from the same general neck of the woods in Louisiana. Courvillion was Louisiana French and spoke and understood French. He overheard a civilian tell the bartender that soon their friends, the Germans, would be returning, and he saw the two men exchange guarded but pleased and understanding looks.

Courvillion and Fresina reported what they had heard to 1/Sergeant Smith, but Smith, like any other good 1/Sergeant intent on keeping his outfit unflustered, dismissed it profanely. He told the two men to get the crap out of their ears and hit the sack.

Thus Company A finished their move, in Amblève, and bedded down.

Over at Grand-Halleux, Bucky Walters and his 1st platoon had carried their guns all day, but it had passed in a routine way. Walters had driven up to Trois Ponts that morning to ask about the military situation and to report the small plane and the parachute drops. He was told everything was normal. Walters disagreed. Something was out of kilter, but he had only some vague rumors to go on.

Back at Battalion the day had not gone by the books at all. When Conlin telephoned Colonel Pergrin and told him Malmédy had taken four direct hits from big 310-mm. shells, that there were some killed and wounded people and much debris, Pergrin had listened, asked a few questions, then said he would come over later. Conlin already had things under control.

No more than Conlin could Pergrin account for the shells, but knowing as he did of the 2nd Infantry attack toward the Urft-Roer dams he privately thought the enemy might be counterattacking against 2nd Infantry. In fact, a counterattack could be expected. Pergrin was therefore not unduly perturbed. The shelling was not conducive to peace of mind, but every counterattack the Germans had thrown at the front had been swiftly checked, so it could be assumed if this was another one it would be quickly choked off. It was the only reasoning that made any sense. Otherwise it was simply a freak. Maybe the Germans

The Allied Side

were just sighting in their big guns and had fired at random. Pergrin's mind was pretty full just now of Company A's forthcoming activities in support of CCB, 9th Armored, and what it entailed.

He went to Malmédy that afternoon, talked with Conlin, checked around the town and surveyed the damage. He spent several hours there and it was almost dark when he left to go on to Born and check up on Company A. Nothing new had been learned and there had been no more shells.

At Haute Bodeux, as the day progressed Sergeant Scanlan had grown increasingly uneasy about his communications with Company A. When they had not reported in by dark he decided to go to Born himself. If they were in trouble with the set perhaps he could help. He got permission to go, picked up Corporal Bevis to drive him, and the two men loaded the three-quarter-ton truck with the mail for Company A. It was heavy with Christmas packages, which would be very welcome to the boys. They left Haute Bodeux around 8:00 P.M.

They had to hunt for Company A, since they were not in Born, so it was between 9:30 and 10:00 P.M. when they reached Amblève. If he asked, Scanlan must have learned that Colonel Pergrin had been there and had just left. He dropped off the mail and looked up the radio boys. They told him they had had a rough trip and had had a lot of trouble getting set up, primarily getting the antenna on the roof, but they were just ready to go. Corporal Al Schommer was at the set. He tuned in and tapped out his call letters.

Back at Battalion, Corporal Thurston, on duty that night, picked him up immediately and sent back to Schommer, who had no difficulty receiving him. Scanlan smiled and relaxed, his biggest fear relieved. Company A was in business again, back in the Net, not out in the void alone where he couldn't reach them.

Scanlan and Bevis left Amblève then and got back to Haute Bodeux around midnight. Scanlan did not know whether

Colonel Pergrin had returned yet or not. He was thinking of going to bed but wondering a little if there was much use in it. Having picked up the rumors swirling around Company A he had a premonitory feeling that the times were out of joint and he was not going to get much sleep anyway.

Pergrin had got back. He had reached Amblève about 7:30, also having had to hunt for Company A, shortly before Scanlan left Haute Bodeux. He heard Gamble's report of the trip down, checked the details of the setup and approved it, and listened to Gamble's report of the rumors Company A was catching.

Pergrin was a quiet controlled man, his nerves and emotions well leashed. He did not get fussed easily. By his manner he was a calming influence on his men. It was Gamble's duty, however, to report these rumors to his superior officer. Pergrin, believing this was simply a counterattack against the 2nd Infantry Division, made few comments. It had nothing to do with his orders. His orders had been to move a company to support CCB, 9th Armored. He had done so. There had been no change in his orders. So, when he left Amblève his orders to Gamble remained unchanged. Get Bucky Walters moved over from Grand-Halleux the next day, carry on and wait for further orders. He got back to his own headquarters a little before midnight.

Around 1:00 A.M. Corporal Rufus Oliver, on switchboard duty at Battalion that night, made his hourly test call of all local and long distance telephone lines. He could not get Group at Trois Ponts. He reported this to Scanlan at once. It was unusual enough to make everybody sit up straight. Scanlan himself then tested the lines. Local lines in Haute Bodeux were O.K. But the line to Trois Ponts was out.

Scanlan reported to the Duty Officer who promptly reported to Pergrin, who had not yet gone to bed.

Immediate preparations were made to send out a repair team with wire climbers and wire test equipment. In the meantime, the radio operator on duty, Thurston, followed emergency pro-

The Allied Side

cedure and switched over to the frequency of Group Radio Net. As with Battalion, which was always on continuous watch with its companies, Group was always on continuous watch with the battalions.

Group advised they were taking care of the break, but they put Battalion on continuous watch with them until the line was repaired. Everybody tensed up. The telephone break was so unusual that the feeling was general that it was sabotage. Scanlan definitely was not going to bed now.

At Amblève, Corporal Schommer received Battalion's alert signal to stay on continuous watch. About half an hour later he heard his call letters again and took down a message, or tried to. When he tried to decode the message, however, it made no sense at all. It was a bunch of garbage, a mess of nonsense words. He had to do something with it, however, so he finally put it down precisely as it decoded. He then wakened 1/Sergeant Smith, who read the nonsense message, blistered Schommer's ears for waking him with a message nobody could make heads or tails of, and went back to sleep. Neither he nor Schommer had any way of knowing that communications in the area were in an immense snarl, that the Germans were jamming and sending on all frequencies to increase the general confusion behind the American lines.

On guard at the schoolhouse CP that night, Pfc. Louis T. Dymond heard a lot of traffic most of the night. He wondered about it, but he had no way of knowing that a massive retreat of rolling vehicles was occurring. None of it was passing his post, which was in a sheltered court, so he simply heard it and wondered. In the earliest hours of his watch, some of the vehicles might have been those of 2nd Battalion, 423rd Regiment, 106th Infantry Division, moving up to a badly fractured front. General Alan W. Jones had called up his only reserve to help protect St. Vith, some five miles south of Company A at Amblève.

In Trois Ponts, at 1:30 A.M. while the repair team was still trying to find the break in the telephone line to the 291st headquarters in Haute Bodeux, Colonel Anderson of Group received a message from Headquarters, Army Security Command at Spa. The 1111th Group was in the Net of Army Security and the 291st was actually Group's security battalion at the time. The call was an alert notifying all Subarea Security Commanders of the possibility of a large-scale enemy attack, accompanied by paratroopers, and orders were to disseminate the information through the proper channels and take the proper precautionary measures.

Manifestly Army Security Command did not go into details as to how they had received their information. But First Army Intelligence had been warned by an agent behind the German lines that a brigade of paratroopers numbering between 1000 and 1200 men were assembled at Paderborn aerodrome, preparatory to taking off in some 120 JU-52 planes. The exact drop point was not known, but it was believed to be in the vicinity of Aachen.

As a result of the alert, rigid security measures went into immediate effect. Colonel Pergrin was notified by special messenger. Special patrols were ordered by Colonel Anderson, and additional security guards were posted at road crossings, bridges and other strategic points.

The alert filtered from unit to unit and within two or three hours the first ripple of fear of paratroopers behind every bush, at every crossroads, in every patch of woods along the roads, sped up the Amblève line. They could be anywhere, these paratroopers, in the house next door, behind that familiar building, around that bend in the road, unseen, lurking, positioning themselves for sabotage or attack.

News spreads in many unofficial ways. There is always the heavy travel on all the roads. Men stopped by guards at checkpoints were told some paratroopers had been dropped. There are many pipelines between units. The news travels up and

The Allied Side

down them. The civilians pick up whispers and begin passing them on. By morning the news and rumors were general.

Not long after Pergrin was notified of the Security alert, Group reported they had found and repaired the break in the telephone line. It was not a reassuring report. The line had been cut. By whom? The men had no idea. Privately Pergrin thought of paratroopers.

Nobody in the U.S. Army knew that on this night six or eight American jeeps, occupied usually by four soldiers in American uniforms, were crisscrossing the whole rear area along the Amblève. The jeeps bore the correct identification numbers for the sector. The men in them spoke English, or at least one man in each jeep spoke English fluently and without accent. They carried the correct identification cards, wore dog tags and knew the passwords. They drove freely about observing and talking and listening, collecting valuable information concerning American positions, movements, reserves and supply depots. They checked bridges, river crossings, road intersections, traffic intersections. At night they quietly cut telephone lines, changed road signs, made sudden appearances in towns and spread rumors.

Among the telephone lines cut by one of the jeep teams that night was the line between Trois Ponts and Haute Bodeux. It amounted to little more than harassment, for it was easily mended. But it caused a wave of fear, it added to the ripples already beginning. And like Scanlan, Pergrin did not go to bed that night, either.

At 3:00 A.M. German planes appeared over some woods about ten miles north of Malmédy. Incendiary bombs suddenly turned the woods and the villages in the area bright with their red light. In the flare of the flaming incendiaries there was shortly a mushrooming of white umbrellas, swinging, balancing, swaying. Like beautiful white blossoms the parachutes hung in the red sky and descended gracefully and quietly to the earth near a crossroad called Mon Rigi.

That night two American divisions up north were beginning to move south. From Holland, 7th Armored Division was ordered to St. Vith to help the beleaguered 106th Infantry. From behind Aachen, the 26th Regiment of 1st Infantry Division was ordered to Elsenborn, to bolster up the equally beleaguered 99th Infantry Division. Both columns of march saw and heard the planes and were lightly bombed on their roads. They wondered why so many flares and incendiaries were being used.

Over at Sourbrodt where Company C's detached 3rd platoon was stationed, running one of the 291st's sawmills, men on guard duty that night also saw the flares and heard the planes. And they, too, wondered about the unusual night display.

At Spa, General Courtney Hodges in the Hôtel Britannique did not see them. He knew his V Corps had been in trouble all day, and he knew that his VIII Corps, around St. Vith, was taking a knock, and he had taken the precautions of starting reinforcements to both Gerow and Middleton. But when General Gerow had asked permission that day to call off 2nd Infantry's attack toward the Urft-Roer dams, Hodges had refused. He simply did not yet have enough information to know or even begin to guess the extent of what was happening all along the entire front of his First Army. It was entirely too inconceivable.

4

AT TROIS PONTS, the morning of December 17, there was an air of alertness at Group Headquarters but it was controlled and contained within the Staff. And near Group headquarters a security detail which had been sent down from Company A at Werbomont several days earlier changed shifts routinely. The detail was in charge of S/Sergeant Paul Hinkel. Hinkel was actually from H/S (headquarters) Company, but he had formerly been a platoon sergeant in Company A. Wounded near the Tucker Bridge at Carentan back in July, he was out of the battalion until October and lost his job as a result. Since he was still a staff sergeant, however, a place was made for him with S–2, Intelligence and Reconnaissance, at Battalion. He and his detail were due to be relieved in regular rotation next day, but on December 17 Hinkel and his men were still on duty and everything was routine.

Elsewhere in Trois Ponts that morning routine was also followed. Company C's men on the day shift at the sawmills arrived on time and took over and the mills hummed busily. Up at La Gleize, no rumors of any kind had yet been heard by Company C. It was another gloomy routine day, and cold.

At Battalion, in Haute Bodeux, as the long night came to an end, Corporal Thurston in Communications, almost ready to go off duty, did a quick check on other radio frequencies and reported that everything was unusually quiet. Normally radio traffic was extremely heavy at all times. Thurston laughed and said, "If this keeps up, the 291st will practically have the airwaves to themselves."

Scanlan laughed, too, but he did not feel very good about it. There was too much a feeling of ghosts walking or witches brewing trouble, a heavy sense of the air itself being troubled, as if something was threatening this secure ring of air which their sets and their keys held around Battalion and its units like a sheltering cloak. No, Scanlan did not like this quietness in the air at all.

Up at Sourbrodt, north of Malmédy, the day began normally for Company C's detached 3rd platoon, but it very shortly broke into pieces. The village was full of rumors — about a breakthrough on the front, about a paratrooper drop in the woods nearby. And there was beginning to be an extremely heavy increase in the flow of vehicles passing through. All, interestingly, headed north — away from the front.

Company C's 3rd platoon was commanded by Lieutenant John T. Perkins, who came from Louisville, Kentucky. He was an exceptionally capable officer. He was also a very quiet man who had no chatter in him. At staff conferences he rarely spoke up unless asked a direct question. He then replied accurately, succinctly and sensibly. His men swore by him. "It was a pleasure to serve under him," they said.

He had the able assistance of a very good platoon sergeant, Ed Keoghan. Keoghan had one squad cutting and hauling timber to the sawmill and another squad was running the mill. His third squad was not with the unit in Sourbrodt. It was on road patrol out of La Gleize.

Lieutenant Perkins was troubled by what he was hearing and seeing and as soon as his men were all at work, therefore, he decided to drive down to Battalion, at Haute Bodeux, report what he was seeing and hearing and see if anybody down there knew what was going on.

Shortly after Perkins left an infantry officer came to the sawmill and asked Sergeant Keoghan if he could spare some men for special duty. "The Krauts dropped a big bunch of paratroopers in the woods last night," he said, "and we've got to try to round 'em up."

Keoghan chose three or four men and, leaving the mill in charge of one of his squad sergeants, led the detail himself. For several hours he and his men barged around through the woods. None of them saw any paratroopers.

The paratroopers were there, but not where they could easily be found. At noon of this day they were in the deep middle of the forest setting up their base camp. They had not yet begun to fan out into the countryside.

But if Keoghan did not see any paratroopers, he did see much else that troubled him. On every road going north he saw long lines of hurrying vehicles, big cranes, prime movers, dump trucks, trucks of every kind, weapons carriers, jeeps, command cars, antiaircraft guns and tank destroyers, every kind of equipment on wheels the army possessed, barreling north as fast as they could go. More and more it looked to him as if there was some truth in the rumors of an enemy breakthrough. Why else was the whole First U.S. Army on the move?

For at the same time he was seeing all this movement northward, he was seeing tanks and infantry going south, or trying to, on the same crowded roads. It was eye-opening. Never before had he seen anything like the desperation and the hurry and the snarl and the mess. It was also frightening.

About noon he arrived at a crossroads, probably Mon Rigi. The MPs there were trying to straighten out a massive traffic snarl and they were very upset and angry. "We had some boys going down where that breakthrough's at," they told Keoghan, "and some damned jokers changed the road signs. They sent the whole outfit on west, down the wrong road! When we got on the trail of it there was two of 'em still standing out here in the road turning 'em wrong. Hell, those boys have got to go all the way around by Malmédy now to get to Waimes where they were supposed to go."

This was probably the 16th Infantry Regiment, 1st Infantry Division, moving on orders from near Aachen to Waimes. Both Colonel Pergrin and his liaison officer, Captain Lloyd B. Sheetz, saw the 16th Infantry pass around the north edge of Malmédy on December 17 and remember that they took the secondary road through Chodes and Gdoumont to reach Waimes, instead of the main highway, N–32 — for fear of running head-on into the enemy.

Keoghan asked who had changed the road signs. "Krauts," he was told. "Some of them paratroopers, likely. In American uniforms, too. They had a jeep and when we got here they jumped in and made off so fast one of 'em was still standing on the front bumper hanging onto the wire clippers. They hauled out of here going fifty miles an hour!"

Keoghan laughed. The Germans had a nasty way of stretching piano wire across a road and a man driving an open jeep very fast could be decapitated when he hit it. After a few sad experiences, most jeeps were fitted with an upright bar filed very sharp on its leading edge to clip such wires.

But this news gave Keoghan pause to think. Krauts wearing American uniforms? Roaming around behind the lines changing road signs, spying, lurking, perhaps sabotaging? He wondered if perhaps he and his men might not have met and even talked to some of them and, ironically, asked about paratroopers. He decided he had better get back to the sawmill. The boys there would be ignorant of this information and they might innocently get themselves into a lot of trouble.

When he got back to Sourbrodt it was around 1:00 P.M. He found Lieutenant Perkins there, back from Haute Bodeux, with

The Allied Side

orders for 3rd platoon to get back to La Gleize immediately.

When Perkins had arrived at Battalion he had been told there *was* a breakthrough on 99th Infantry Division's front and Colonel Pergrin had just left for Malmédy with orders to defend, and he should get 3rd platoon out of Sourbrodt and back to La Gleize at once. Perkins lost no time. He got to Sourbrodt shortly before Keoghan did and they began to load up the outfit.

It was around 2:00 P.M. by the time they got started, with three trucks. Within thirty minutes they were enmeshed in so much traffic that they got separated. Perkins, in his jeep, and one truck managed to stay together. Keoghan, in the platoon truck, managed to hang on to the other squad truck, but the two sections were hopelessly lost from each other. So it was each section for itself, but they all knew they were headed for La Gleize. The job was to keep maneuvering in that direction as best they could. Perkins made it by the morning of the next day. Keoghan never did get to La Gleize at all.

At Malmédy the morning of December 17, Company B's platoons turned out to go about their regular and routine work. First platoon loaded into their trucks and made the short drive to Stavelot for their day in the sawmill there. Recall that their leader, Lieutenant Wade L. Colbeck, was living in Stavelot in a house trailer parked in the mill yard.

The mill was owned by a civilian of Stavelot. It was quite modern, with all-electric saws and equipment. The owner had his office in a brick building near the mill, in which he also lived in an apartment run by his seventeen-year-old daughter. It is not necessary to say that the daughter was the apple of the entire platoon's eye.

Second platoon, which was cutting timber and hauling logs for the mills in both Malmédy and Stavelot, went to work in the woods as usual. Their leader was Lieutenant John C. Kirkpatrick. He was a new officer in the battalion and on December 17 he was still something of an unknown quantity to the men because he had taken them over only a week or two earlier. The platoon had had a high turnover of platoon leaders, for one reason or another, but it had functioned ably largely because of a fine platoon sergeant, S/Sergeant Walter J. Smith.

When 2nd platoon had left for work, Lieutenant Kirkpatrick apparently went to La Gleize, whether on a social visit or on military business is not known. But all the officers in the battalion liked to visit in La Gleize because Company C's command post was in the beautiful old Château Froidcour.

Company B's 3rd platoon went about its chores routinely, also. For several weeks a road crew from B Company had been working on the roads east of Malmédy, toward Waimes and Butgenbach. On this morning, December 17, the road crew turned out to report for work on the primary road, N–32, in the vicinity of Waimes. The work came under the general supervision of 3rd platoon's leader, Lieutenant Frank W. Rhea.

The men left in their truck shortly after 7:00 A.M. They were shivery in the raw, damp misty cold of the murky morning, and shivery also from the rumors that had drifted in of a German parachute drop. These were added to the rumors that the enemy had launched an offensive and broken through the front. As they wheeled out onto N–32 toward their work point they began to meet a solid stream of westbound traffic. They blinked and wondered, what the hell?

The vehicles they were meeting were mostly those of service and supply units, the usual rear echelon units that must always build up thickly behind any front to keep it alive. This road, N–32, was the main artery, east and west, from the front back to the immense service and supply depots beyond the Amblève, and there was always a lot of traffic over it, but nothing like what they were meeting this morning. Also among the service and supply vehicles, disturbingly, were some artillery units, some antiaircraft batteries, armored vehicles, jeeps and trucks of all kinds. Something was going on up front. That was for sure.

But the sergeant in charge of the work detail kept the driver pushing on. The line of vehicles was a steady stream but it was not yet a traffic jam. It was moving and it was going one way. At their work point the men unloaded and got out their shovels. They were filling potholes with rock gravel. Dump trucks full of the gravel would shortly be arriving.

Lieutenant Rhea's 1st squad was on road patrol at this time with the limits of Ligneuville and Stavelot. The men making their first trip out to Ligneuville that morning could not get there. Their road, too, was jammed with traffic, a solid stream of it. They decided finally to turn around and go back to the CP. Something was happening and Captain Conlin ought to know about it.

From a height of land south of Malmédy the men on road patrol could look down on the town in its nest of folded hills. Private Bernie Koenig said it was a dreamy, unreal scene. Malmédy looked exactly like a giant anthill somebody had stirred with a stick. Out all the radial spokes of the highways were long lines of streaming black ants — the heaviest vehicular traffic the men had ever seen. The ants were streaming into the anthill from the east and the south, and out of it to the west and north. It was strange and foreboding, after the shelling of the day before, after the paratroop alert of the morning. Malmédy was suddenly becoming a weird, eerie place, as if it were marked or doomed, as if it had somehow been pinpointed for trouble.

Around 7:30 A.M. Lieutenant Frank Rhea climbed into his jeep and started out to see how the road work on N–32 was going.

Rhea was the only West Point man in the entire 291st Battalion. He was also one of the youngest of the officers, barely twenty-one. He was from Waldo, Arkansas, and he had graduated from West Point in June of 1943. He had reported to the 291st just three days before it left Camp Swift for Port of Embarkation. He spent the three days qualifying to go with the battalion.

He was a big husky youngster with shoulders like a football player and a plain simplicity of manner and quick easy sense of humor which endeared him to his men and made for a good camaraderie with them. A good athlete, he was always ready to wrestle or box with them after hours. T/5 Vincent Consiglio, a motor mechanic, remembers many wrestling matches he had with the lieutenant. Rhea was the champion checker player of the outfit and jokingly maintained that he had won his appointment to West Point by beating his senator in a game of checkers. He was as jaunty and rowdy as any other twenty-one-year-old. But just the same he was a competent engineer, he had a good sensible head on his shoulders, he had initiative and he was perfectly willing to take responsibility and entirely capable of carrying it. His brother officers called him Big Junior, because he was Frank W. Rhea, Jr.

As he wheeled out on N-32 this morning of December 17, he was soon engulfed in the heavy westbound traffic on the road. "What the hell's the matter with everybody this morning?" he grumbled to his driver. "Where's everybody going all at once?"

By the time he arrived at the work point he had seen enough and pondered it long enough to determine to go on to Butgenbach and see if he could find out what was going on. He stopped at the work point long enough to tell the sergeant what he intended to do and to keep the men working.

He did not quite get to Butgenbach. Just west of that village, where 99th Infantry's headquarters were located, there was a road intersection. An MP was frantically trying to control the bumper-to-bumper traffic. Rhea parked his jeep and watched for a few moments. Now he could plainly hear the sound of small-arms fire in the distance ahead of him. And he was fascinated by a flight of American planes which were obviously dive-bombing something over beyond the hills and out of sight. They swooped in, bombed and strafed, then swooped up and circled about.

Rhea went over to talk to the MP on duty at the intersection. By now it was around 8:15. "What's going on here?" he asked.

"The Krauts have broken through the 99th's lines," the MP told him. "They're attacking just over that hill. All hell busted loose over there about daylight this morning."

Rhea wasted no more time. He got back to the work point and ordered the men back to Malmédy, then he headed for home himself. Around 9:00 or 9:15 he was reporting to Captain Conlin in the CP. Conlin took the ball quickly. Pergrin had to be notified, and if Pergrin ordered defensive measures they would need all the guns and ammunition, mines and demolitions they had in Malmédy. Also all the men. Conlin ordered Rhea to get going on these things, while he called the Colonel.

Shortly afterward Conlin got through by telephone to Colonel Pergrin. He reported what Lieutenant Rhea had seen and heard, then he added eagerly, "Colonel, this may be our chance to get a crack at the Krauts ourselves."

Listening, Pergrin grinned. It was a typical Conlin comment, he thought, exactly what this wild Irishman who commanded B Company would say. But Pergrin did not commit himself except to say, "Maybe. You can begin defensive preparations. I'll be over shortly."

This was good enough for Conlin. He wanted all his men in Malmédy so he sent runners to bring Lieutenant Colbeck and his 1st platoon up from Stavelot, and to bring 2nd platoon in from the woods. And he and Lieutenant Rhea began to map out some roadblock positions.

At Haute Bodeux, Pergrin called in his Operations Officer, Captain Edward R. Lampp, and his Liaison Officer, Captain Lloyd B. Sheetz, gave them Conlin's information and told them to make preparations to go to Malmédy with him. Before Pergrin could leave, however, he had a telephone call from Colonel Anderson at Group, in Trois Ponts.

At 10:05, Colonel Anderson had had a telephone call from Major Richard Carville, his Liaison Officer at V Corps forward CP at Elsenborn. Carville said that enemy tanks had penetrated the 99th Division positions, and early that morning, before daylight, they had got into the vicinity of Butgenbach and 99th's headquarters had moved out. He said the tanks had been repelled. He added that the tanks had got around the CP of the 629th Engineer Light Equipment Company. This was a company of the 1111th Group which was operating rock quarries and furnishing gravel for its road building and maintenance operations. Their headquarters were near Butgenbach.

Anderson told Major Carville to send the 629th, with its big and expensive equipment, over to Malmédy. He then told Carville to keep in touch. Anderson could not know it but this was to be his last contact with Carville for several weeks.

Anderson immediately called Pergrin, about 10:15, and told him of the breakthrough and directed him to go to Malmédy and ascertain the situation there, told him the 629th would be coming there, directed him to take command of all the 1111th units in Malmédy. In addition to the 291st's Company B, this would be the 629th and the 962nd Engineer Maintenance Company, already stationed in Malmédy. Pergrin was also ordered to take defensive measures.

It is to be remembered that in no sense was this breakthrough yet considered a serious threat or a real crisis. Actually not enough was yet known about it. And everybody in the American Army was suffused with confidence. Everybody was girded about with an abiding faith in the invincibility of the Allied armies. This was regarded as something troublesome and that was about all. There had been a breakthrough of some kind. It was being a nuisance and at least temporarily the lines in front of

Büllingen and Butgenbach had given way. But nobody really believed the enemy could make a deep penetration. It was not yet recognized as an all-out offensive. It was probably a counterattack, more or less expected in response to the 2nd Division's offensive toward the Roer dams. Reinforcements would be thrown in quickly and it would shortly be checked. Note that Pergrin was not ordered to hold Malmédy at all costs. It was not expected that Malmédy would have to be held. Under the circumstances it was sensible to see what the situation was and to take precautionary measures. Nor would Pergrin be the only officer in Malmédy. Malmédy was full of troops. So Pergrin was not ordered to take command of *Malmédy*. He was ordered to take command of all 1111th Engineer units there and to take defensive measures.

In the light of Colonel Anderson's orders, however, Pergrin did take two more men with him to Malmédy besides Captain Lampp and Captain Sheetz. They were the assistant Operations Officer, Lieutenant Thomas F. Stack, and the assistant Intelligence and Reconnaissance Officer, Lieutenant Leroy H. Joehnck.

The party left immediately, Lieutenant Stack riding with Pergrin in his command car, the others following in jeeps. It is between twelve and thirteen miles from Haute Bodeux to Malmédy, but it took almost forty-five minutes to drive it that morning. The difficulty began at Trois Ponts when they started meeting part of 7th Armored Division.

The evening before General Eisenhower had been sufficiently uneasy about the varying reports beginning to reach his headquarters concerning the breakthrough that he had advised General Omar Bradley to loan First Army a couple of armored divisions. Bradley had therefore directed Patton to release the 10th Armored Division to go north from the Saar sector to Bastogne, and he had directed General William Simpson of the Ninth U.S. Army to send the 7th Armored Division south from Heerlen, Holland, to help out the 106th Infantry Division around St. Vith.

On the evening of December 16 these two points seemed to be in the greatest need of help.

First Army had then worked out the route marches for 7th Armored and assigned them two roads. The first, or west route, went through Verviers, down to Stavelot, to Trois Ponts, and south on N-33 from there to the assembly area at Vielsalm. CCB was assigned this road, and as he went to Malmédy Colonel Pergrin was meeting the vehicles of this column.

The other road, or the east route, assigned to 7th Armored, went from Aachen through Eupen, down to Malmédy and on to Ligneuville and Recht to Vielsalm. Combat Command R was given this road and as Pergrin drove into Malmédy its lead elements were passing through that town.

Pergrin got to Malmédy around 11:00 A.M. Conlin quickly went over the situation with him. There were no firm facts and there was no new knowledge. The extent of the breakthrough or its strength was not known. Conlin then told Pergrin the steps he had already taken and the defensive measures he had in mind. He had sent a runner over and brought Lieutenant Colbeck and his platoon back to Malmédy. Colbeck was already home and he and Rhea were rounding up men, equipment, trucks and were already beginning to set up roadblocks in the east end of town. He had sent a runner into the woods and recalled 2nd platoon. These men should be coming in any time. He had also sent a reconnaissance patrol out eastward and if anything unusual was seen, the men would alert the command post immediately.

Fine. This was all good and Pergrin had seen for himself as he came in that Rhea was installing machine guns on the squad trucks and loading them with mines, demolitions and bazookas preparatory to setting up roadblocks.

But having met one of 7th Armored's columns going through Trois Ponts, and having seen another passing through Malmédy, both headed for the relief of the 106th Infantry at St. Vith, Per-

The Allied Side

grin was now deeply uneasy about Company A in Amblève. Here in Malmédy they were some thirteen miles west of Butgenbach where the breakthrough appeared to have occurred, but Amblève lay only seven miles south of Butgenbach. And the men at Amblève were only a few miles north of St. Vith. If the 106th was having trouble at St. Vith, and the 99th was having trouble at Butgenbach, Company A was right in the middle, in a position to get squeezed and might soon be, if they were not already, in the middle of a hornet's nest.

Priority, therefore, went to Company A and before he began to map out any further defenses of Malmédy Pergrin sent a radio message. From Malmédy he had no direct communications with Company A. He had to go through Battalion. He sent a message to Battalion, therefore, to radio Company A to come home. And for urgency he ordered it sent in the clear. This was no time to be messing around with the slow process of encoding and decoding. The message, as best he could remember it later, said: ENEMY DANGER IMMINENT. RETURN FORMER POSITION. The former position, of course, was Werbomont.

By the time Company A received that message they did not have to be told enemy danger was imminent. They were having some direct experience of it.

5

In Amblève the morning of December 17, Corporal Al Schommer was still on radio duty. Daylight came at 7:50, but it was such a dark and murky day that it was between 8:30 and 9:00 before there was any appreciable difference in the light. Schommer got up from his seat, stretched and yawned and went over to the window to draw back the blackout curtains. He stood at the window, amazed at the enormous amount of activity that was going on outside. Trucks, guns, jeeps, armored cars, big equipment trucks, vehicles of every sort and kind were jamming the streets, all flowing westward. It looked to him like a massive retreat flowing all about Company A in this forbidding village.

Suddenly he noticed a flight of planes up northeast of Amblève, swooping and diving and climbing. He wondered what they could be bombing up that way. Then he saw one of the planes burst into flames and begin a slow over-and-over fall to the earth. He saw the black blossoms of flak bloom all about the squadron of planes. Another plane was hit then and exploded in a great orange burst. Flak? Enemy flak this far behind the lines? The skies should be safe for U.S. planes up there. But they were being shot at and hit.

Schommer went into action. He went looking for 1/Sergeant Smith. The first sergeant watched the planes a moment, then said, "Something's going on up there. I'd better find out what it is."

The Allied Side

Sergeant Smith got a weapons carrier, a submachine gun, and headed northeast. It was about 9:30 when he left. Around 10:30 he came barreling home with startling news. "Captain, there's a whole column of German tanks up there, headed in this direction. If we don't get out of here fast, we're not going to get out at all!"

It was fantastic and unbelievable. German tanks so far behind the lines? The whole area up there, Butgenbach, Elsenborn, Büllingen, Honsfeld, was a complex of U.S. installations, divisional headquarters, rest areas. And all of it was very rear area. It did not seem possible there could be an enemy penetration up there. But 1/Sergeant Smith was not an easily flustered man or one given to hallucinations. If he said he saw German tanks not far north of Amblève, headed toward Amblève, he saw them and that was that.

Gamble had no orders to displace, but under the circumstances he would assume that responsibility himself. He went into action at once. He was very low on gas. Rationing was so rigid that his vehicles had been allowed not much more gasoline the day before than they needed to get him to Amblève. Their tanks were almost dry now, and there was no time to go to Malmédy for more. But he had some equipment vehicles he could do without. He therefore ordered Smith to put the men to work siphoning the gas from their tanks into the platoon and squad trucks. He also told Smith they would take only what they most needed — rifles, machine guns, bazookas, all their ammunition, and the radio and kitchen setups. Everything else would be left.

Fortunately Gamble had not yet ordered Lieutenant Walters and his platoon to move from Grand-Halleux to Amblève. He now sent a runner directing Walters to displace and join the main unit in Werbomont.

Then Gamble himself drove over to Montenau to alert Lieutenant Taylor and his platoon. It was around 11:30 A.M. when he reached Montenau. Taylor was in the woods with a crew but his platoon sergeant, Malvin Champion, was at the CP. Gamble told him to get Taylor and alert the platoon immediately. He went back to Amblève at once.

When he got there, about noon, he was greeted with the news that there had been a radio message from Colonel Pergrin ordering them to return to their former position. Gamble, Lieutenant Hayes and 1/Sergeant Smith grinned at each other. They had got the jump on the colonel by a full hour and were far readier to leave than the colonel could have expected. Lieutenant Hayes had even already plotted their route back, through Poteau, Vielsalm, Grand-Halleux and Trois Ponts.

About this time the truck of another engineer outfit came racing into the area. A handful of men were in it. They were babbling with terror. They were men of the 168th Engineers, they said, and they had been on a water point detail near St. Vith. There they were, they said, going about their regular morning work. Nobody had warned them. And all at once the Krauts were right on top of them — and the whole outfit was overrun. They were the only ones left. The others had all been killed or captured. Only because they had been nearer a truck had they managed to escape. The truck had been shot at and one or two of the men had been slightly wounded. "Can we stay with you, Captain? Can we go with you?" they pled.

Gamble said sure they could. "We'll be leaving soon. You can tag on."

An artillery outfit had gone through Amblève about half an hour earlier. Suddenly half a dozen men from the outfit came tearing back into the area. They had run smack into German tanks. "They got the whole outfit," one of the men said, "and damn near got me. Which way's the rear?"

T/4 Jeff Elliott pointed it out to him and the man took off.

Others stuck around, however, and pled with Gamble to be allowed to go with him. "Sure," he said, "we'll take everybody we can."

The Allied Side

But the radiomen were having almost as much trouble taking their antenna down as they had had putting it up the evening before. And now, at about 12:00 noon they began to get some artillery fire. As the shells started crunching into their area, 1/Sergeant Smith, in exasperation, climbed up on the roof to help take the antenna down, cussing the radiomen, cussing the Germans, cussing the antenna.

Even while ducking shells this delighted the radiomen. Sergeant Smith had an unalterable conviction that radio operators were the prime goldbricks of the outfit and he had long threatened to get them on some real work details. It gave the radiomen exquisite pleasure to see First Sarge up on that roof ducking artillery fire trying to get their antenna down for them. Shells bursting all around evidently inspired 1/Sergeant Smith to noble exertions, for the antenna soon came down.

As the shells began to explode in the courtyard, T/4 Jeff Elliott, who drove Lieutenant Hayes' jeep and who was sitting in it at the time hiding from the work of loading up, flew into the CP. He grabbed up a pair of binoculars on the table and looked out the window toward Meyrode and St. Vith. He could see a lot of black smoke and much activity on the road. Then, at a crossroad only one mile south of Amblève, he counted three German tanks and saw three or four German armored cars and a bunch of infantrymen.

Elliott's stomach plunged clear down to his boots and he yelled for the captain and handed him the binoculars. Gamble took a look and yelled for 1/Sergeant Smith, who had just succeeded in getting the antenna down and loaded. Smith yelled, "My God, we got Krauts north of us, we got 'em east of us and now we got 'em south of us. We're practically surrounded! Let's get the hell out of here!"

Elliott, who had just unloaded the officers' liquor ration a short time before and set it on the table, reached for the bottles to load them again into Lieutenant Hayes' jeep. Hayes shouted at him to forget 'em. Leave the damned stuff. Liquor was expendable.

It wasn't to Elliott. He mourned over having to leave the beautiful stuff for the Germans. But he left it.

At 12:20 they wheeled out of Amblève. As they left, Gamble stopped at an intersection and offered to take all the MPs there. The MP on duty shook his head. They had to stick around, he said.

Thirty minutes later the Germans overran Amblève. The fate of the MPs is not known.

Only one road out of Amblève was open. It led west to Deidenberg. Gamble took it, then he turned left to Born and on to Recht. He went on through Recht to Poteau and there he ran flat into the biggest logjam of traffic this road system had ever seen. Seventh Armored Division was trying to go east from its assembly area at Vielsalm to St. Vith. Everything else, wild, panic-stricken, crazy, was trying to go west to safety. There were trucks of every kind and size, artillery, jeeps, officers in command cars, and they were all trying to get away as fast as they could go — west. It was a terrible sight — the American Army running away. It was not a retreat. It was a total rout, out of control, ugly, everybody in the whole mess trying to get somewhere else, somewhere that was safe.

Some of these people *were* running, just as hard as they could run, scared out of their wits. It did not matter what direction or road they took so long as it got them away from the Germans. In most cases, however, they were small units who had lost communication with their main unit. Some of the units had orders to move back, as did Gamble and Company A. They knew where they were supposed to go. But they, too, added to the whole big clotted logjam.

Gamble pulled up to study the situation. While he was halted Lieutenant Taylor and 3rd platoon caught up with him. Taylor had quite a tale to tell.

When his platoon sergeant had found him in the woods and given him Gamble's message, Taylor had brought his work crew in and then he told Sergeant Champion, "If we're going to move we've got to have some gas. You better send the platoon truck to Malmédy and get some."

Two men were dispatched in the truck. They went due north to intersect a secondary road near Thirimont which went west to Ligneuville. It was perhaps one mile from Montenau to the intersection. It was about 12:00 noon or shortly after when they left.

Between thirty and forty minutes later they were back in Montenau on foot, dirty, disheveled and scared half to death. They were almost incoherent. "They shot us up, Lieutenant! They shot the truck up! A Kraut tank shot us up!" Taylor managed to calm the two men and get their story.

They had reached the intersection and were just turning west when all at once they were under fire from a German tank coming southeast on the intersecting road. It was impossible! German tanks did not suddenly appear on a friendly, peaceful road miles behind the front! It was like something out of a nightmare.

But it was possible all right. The tank saw them and opened fire on them with its machine gun. The truck was hit and went out of control. The driver hung on and steered it into the ditch where it turned over on its side. The two men in the cab were thus protected from the machine-gun fire. Stunned by the suddenness and the whole wild implausibility of the event the two men nevertheless had the wit to huddle down in the cab and lie still. Mercifully the tank did not stop. It rolled on by, followed by several others, who fired their machine guns into the overturned truck.

Then there was a lull and the two men were inspired to frenzied activity. They crawled out of the truck and fled along the ditch to a culvert. Beyond the culvert lay the railroad tracks on a high embankment. They crawled through the culvert, sprinted for the tracks, leaped them in one bound and slithered down the other side into the lee of the embankment. They lost no time hotfooting it home, then.

Taylor was slow-talking but he could make a fast decision. He had to get 3rd platoon out of here if German tanks were wandering around on the loose. He left Champion to load up the equipment and he drove down to Born and picked up his men there. He badly needed gas, however, so he decided to make another try to get into Malmédy. A little road went through the woods and hit the main Malmédy–St. Vith highway about two miles west. He would take that road and see if he could make it.

As he came out on the main highway, however, he met a jeep carrying an officer, a major. The major stopped him. "Where you going?"

"Well, sir," Taylor said, "I'm going to Malmédy. I've got to get some gas."

"Well, I'll tell you, son," the major said, "unless you've got something to fight armor with you'd better not go into Malmédy because there's plenty of it there right now."

So. O.K. You did the best you could with what you had. Taylor turned around and retraced his steps. He would run his vehicles as long as he could — he would pick up gas if he could, wherever he could find it. But he was going to get 3rd platoon out of there. He would head for Trois Ponts, and maybe he had enough gas to get that far.

He went back through Montenau and made the dogleg east through Deidenberg. He did not go to Amblève. He figured Gamble would already have left. He cleared Deidenberg around 2:00 P.M. and went on south to Born. His heading from there would be Recht and Poteau, and from there he meant to go to Vielsalm and up to Trois Ponts.

Not five minutes after Taylor cleared Deidenberg, German troops poured into the village and a brisk firefight began between them and the Americans in the village. Totally unaware of the presence of the enemy Taylor's vehicles moved steadily onward and he and his men did not even hear the firing behind them. But for a long time the people in Montenau believed that the tall, thin, nice American engineer officer and his men were wiped out in Deidenberg.

As Taylor and his men went through Born they saw vehicles of the 14th Cavalry Group in the town. Taylor's men who had been stationed in Born for five weeks remarked on them. "That's a new outfit here. Never saw them here before."

No, they had not been in Born before. They were men of the 18th Cavalry Squadron who had been positioned in the villages in the Losheim Gap. The day before they had occupied the villages of Kobscheid, Roth, Auw, Krewinkel, Berterath, Merlscheid and had tied in to the 99th Division's position at Lanzerath. By noon they had been overrun by elements of three German divisions in their advance. They had slowly drifted back, from one defense line to another, until around noon on this day all that was left of the 18th squadron had come to rest in Born.

Lieutenant Taylor and his men moved on through Born and took the heading for Recht and Poteau. When he caught up with Captain Gamble at Poteau, Taylor walked up to the head of the column to let Gamble know he had joined the party. There was a conference between the officers. Nobody knew much about the logging trails and firebreaks through the woods, but it was obvious they were not going any further if they got mixed up in this mess on the primary road. They decided to take a chance on the woods.

The word went back down the line, "Hang on!" Within fifteen minutes after they turned onto the forest trail every man in the outfit was lost. They had no idea where they were or where the captain thought he might be going. He was giving them a very rough ride, and they only hoped he knew what he was doing. If he didn't, they might all wind up in a POW camp in Germany.

That Sunday morning started normally up at Grand-Halleux with Lieutenant Walters' 1st platoon. Walters was using his 3rd squad, under Sergeant Williams, to cut timber in the woods east of the village. He was using his 2nd squad, Sergeant Abe Caplan, in the sawmill in Vielsalm. Recall that his 1st squad was Captain Gamble's security squad and was traveling with Gamble.

Sergeant Williams took his men into the woods punctually as usual. But he brought them in around noon. They had seen some German armored vehicles about a mile east of them, he said, headed north toward Stavelot on a byroad. Williams was of the opinion it was a German recon or armored patrol unit. The Germans had not seen Williams and his men. But under orders to report anything unusual to Lieutenant Walters, Williams had decided German armored vehicles in this area were plenty unusual. It was good enough to stop work and bring his men in.

Walters got on the ball quickly. He sent a messenger immediately to notify Sergeant Caplan and his squad at Vielsalm. Then he put Sergeant Williams and half of his squad to work felling trees and setting up a roadblock on the road which led east. The men cut down several big trees across the road, then positioned themselves with their rifles and a .30-caliber machine gun behind them.

With the other half of Williams' squad Walters began preparations to evacuate the area.

Shortly, Sergeant Caplan returned with his squad. He had not yet reached Vielsalm, because of the heavy traffic on the road, when he met several trucks of an engineer bridging company. He stopped them to ask what was going on. The driver of the lead truck told him about the breakthrough and said if St. Vith was not already in German hands it soon would be. The driver said they were lost from their main unit and were trying to find it. Caplan, who outranked the driver by perhaps one stripe, attached the trucks and said, "Follow me." They were glad to.

When Caplan arrived back at Grand-Halleux Walters briefed him on the situation and set his squad to helping load up the equipment.

About 3:30 P.M. the messenger Gamble had sent arrived, telling Walters to move out. Walters was almost ready to go by then and by 4:00 P.M. he led his men north toward Trois Ponts. It was about five miles by the primary road, N-33, but that road was clogged with 7th Armored vehicles. It was about ten miles around up the heights and through the village of Wanne, but that road was also clogged with retreating vehicles. Walters therefore began zigzagging about on his own logging trails cut by his own men in their five weeks in the woods. It was to take him twelve hours to get to Trois Ponts.

6

AFTER COLONEL PERGRIN radioed Company A to come home he could turn his mind to the defense of Malmédy.*

The enemy, his intentions, his strength, his direction unknown, was east of Malmédy. If he came any further, if he was not stopped at Butgenbach, he would of course approach from that direction, so obviously the first and deepest defense should be made in the eastern end of the town. It was difficult because the eastern section of Malmédy was a whole complex of avenues and streets and branching roads. But Conlin had already made a start.

Two major roads entered from the east. The first and most important was the primary road, N-32, which came in through Five Points and ran past the command post. Conlin was taking care of this road with a roadblock about halfway out to Five Points, backed up by two more roadblocks at street intersections inside the town limits.

---

* The story of the defense of Malmédy was given to the author in personal interviews and/or written accounts by: Col. David E. Pergrin, Lt. (now Colonel) Frank W. Rhea, Lt. W. L. Colbeck, Capt. Lloyd B. Sheetz, Lt. Thomas F. Stack, Sgt. (later Lieutenant) Ralph W. McCarty, Pvt. Bernard Koenig, S/Sgt. Walter J. Smith, Cpl. Edmond Byrne, S/Sgt. Albert D. Melton, Squad Sgt. Sheldon T. Smith, T/5 Vincent Consiglio, all of whom were present from December 17 to December 27, 1944. Roadblock positions were painstakingly worked out with Col. Pergrin, Lt. Rhea, Lt. Colbeck, S/Sgt. Melton, Cpl. Edmond Byrne, Sgt. Ralph W. McCarty, Lt. T. F. Stack and Pvt. Bernard Koenig.

The Allied Side

The other important road from the east was a secondary road which branched off N-32 at Waimes and entered Malmédy farther north through the villages of Gdoumont and Chodes. Conlin was putting a roadblock halfway to Chodes, and backing it up with another roadblock at a street intersection within the town limits.

Because of the paratrooper alert that morning he already had a roadblock north of the town on the road which led to Eupen.

Pergrin absorbed this information and approved. This all seemed wise and good to him, to block the eastern approaches immediately as heavily as possible. But he considered the whole situation, the entire perimeter, especially the southern edge of town. His finger traced the railroad which came up from Stavelot. It bent eastward just south of town, crossed the main Stavelot highway, N-23, on the big viaduct, then ran in a curving line on a high embankment along the whole southern fringe of the town to the railroad station, not far from the command post.

Three secondary roads came winding up from the south, intersecting the railroad. The railroad crossed the Route de Falize on an overpass. It crossed the next southern road, the Route de St. Vith,* on an overpass. But just south of the command post, and near the railroad station, the embankment leveled down and the third southern road, a farm road, crossed on a level grade crossing. All these four railroad crossings were vulnerable because of the roads, but they were also excellent defense points. However, Pergrin thought, if Malmédy got hit and it was necessary to defend the entire extensive perimeter, there were enough troops in Malmédy, there would be no difficulty manning it.

He also pinpointed a back road which wound off up toward Spa. That road should have a guard on it. In the event of the impossible it would make a good escape hatch. In all Pergrin pinpointed eleven positions which would constitute a good pe-

* Bernard Koenig recalled the names of these roads because the sawmill was located nearby.

rimeter defense of Malmédy. In addition, at the last moment, he thoughtfully marked the old stone bridge which crossed the Amblève River in Stavelot. It could be a vulnerable point in the defense of Malmédy should the enemy get across and cut the road system.

By this time it was nearing 11:30. Pergrin gave the marked overlay to Captain Edward Lampp, his Operations Officer, and directed him to return to Trois Ponts with it and go over it with Colonel Anderson. He said he would report to Anderson personally but Anderson would need to see the map. Then from Trois Ponts, Lampp was to go on to Haute Bodeux. Pergrin was temporarily without an executive officer, so he deputized Lampp to act in that capacity and Lampp was to take over at Battalion in Pergrin's absence. Lampp left Malmédy immediately.

When Lampp had left, Colonel Pergrin telephoned Colonel Anderson and reported. There was nothing new to add to the general picture. He gave Anderson his defensive setup, told him he had ordered Company A to come home, and told him he was sending Lampp back to take charge at Battalion.

Anderson acknowledged and said he would be in Trois Ponts with his finger on the overall situation. He then said he was going to close down communications with Pergrin. He did not think it a good idea to be on the air with him with the enemy so near. He said he would keep in touch through Lampp. His final orders to Pergrin were to carry on. What this closing down of communications with Group meant of course was that Pergrin was now on his own. Henceforth most of his orders would come through First Army directly. Note also that Pergrin is still not ordered to "hold at all costs." Presumably he is left to use his own discretion at Malmédy.

Since about 10:00 that morning Lieutenant Frank Rhea, who had discovered the breakthrough at Butgenbach and brought news of it, had been busier than a cranberry merchant. He and Captain Conlin had made a preliminary survey of the equipment

The Allied Side

available for the defense. Company B had its quota of TNT and mines. His men had their rifles and the normal quota of ammunition. Conlin had six or eight bazookas, perhaps six .50-caliber machine guns, four of them mounted on the platoon trucks, and he had about a dozen .30-caliber machine guns. Conlin may have had a little more than his quota, for he was an aggressive leader and the leader of any unit liked to have something extra squirreled away. But it was not much more than the usual engineer company would have.

Conlin had then turned over to Rhea most of the responsibility for gathering up the men of Company B and setting up the roadblocks. When Rhea pulled his men out of the sawmill and told them they were going to man roadblocks and maybe fight the Germans, they did not know whether it was a big joke or not. Somebody stuck a sign on the sawmill door, "Out to lunch." It turned out to be a long lunch hour. Company B never returned to that sawmill.

For a while the only officer helping Rhea was Lieutenant Phillip Lassen, B Company's Administrative Officer, but around 10:30 Lieutenant Wade L. Colbeck and his 1st platoon arrived from Stavelot.

Colbeck was a little shorter than average height, a modest and very earnest young man, but as spunky as a raccoon. With his round, fresh-looking face he looked like a kid, but he was a driver and Conlin thought highly of him as a platoon leader. He was from Michigan and he was twenty-three years old.

Conlin's runner had caught Colbeck at the sawmill and said there was a "small breakthrough" somewhere east of Malmédy and the captain wanted him to bring his men in. Colbeck had closed down the mill and left immediately. He left all his personal gear in the trailer and also left his kitchen setup.

Rhea was delighted to see him. He turned over to Colbeck the job of setting up three of the roadblocks and told him where to position them.

Colbeck took his 1st squad out to set up the roadblock of first importance, the one about halfway to Five Points. He found an ideal place for it, actually about two thirds of the way to Five Points. From the command post the highway angled southeast along the railroad for a short distance, then the railroad crossed it on a overpass. Just beyond the railroad overpass the highway made a sharp right bend and then ran beside a hotel. A little farther on a small stream bordered the road. On the other side was a steep drop of between fifteen or twenty feet. No vehicle could possibly get past a roadblock at that point, with the stream on one side and a drop on the other.

The road was mined along the shoulders and a daisy chain which could be pulled aside for friendly traffic was laid across it. A bazooka team was placed about thirty yards behind the mines, and the platoon truck with its .50-caliber machine gun was parked off the road and about thirty yards behind the bazooka team. Later machine guns would be dug in, but for the present the truck had to serve. All the trees on both sides of the road were wired with quarter-pound blocks of TNT. The squad leader, Sergeant Charles Dishaw, was put in charge of the roadblock. This roadblock was in position by noon.

Behind it, all along the street, the trees were also wired with TNT and Lieutenant Phillip Lassen put a squad of H/S platoon men with a .30-caliber machine gun to guard. T/5 Vincent Consiglio, bulldozer operator Red Ball Renson and other mechanics and specialists manned this roadblock.

Colbeck put another of his squads at another back-up roadblock just north of the command post where four main streets made a junction. The trees were mined here, also, and a .30-caliber machine gun was set up.

Finally, Colbeck took his last squad out the Gdoumont road. A little southwest of Chodes the road made a great looping bend and was joined by a minor road coming in from the south. Colbeck positioned his men just at the loop in order to guard both

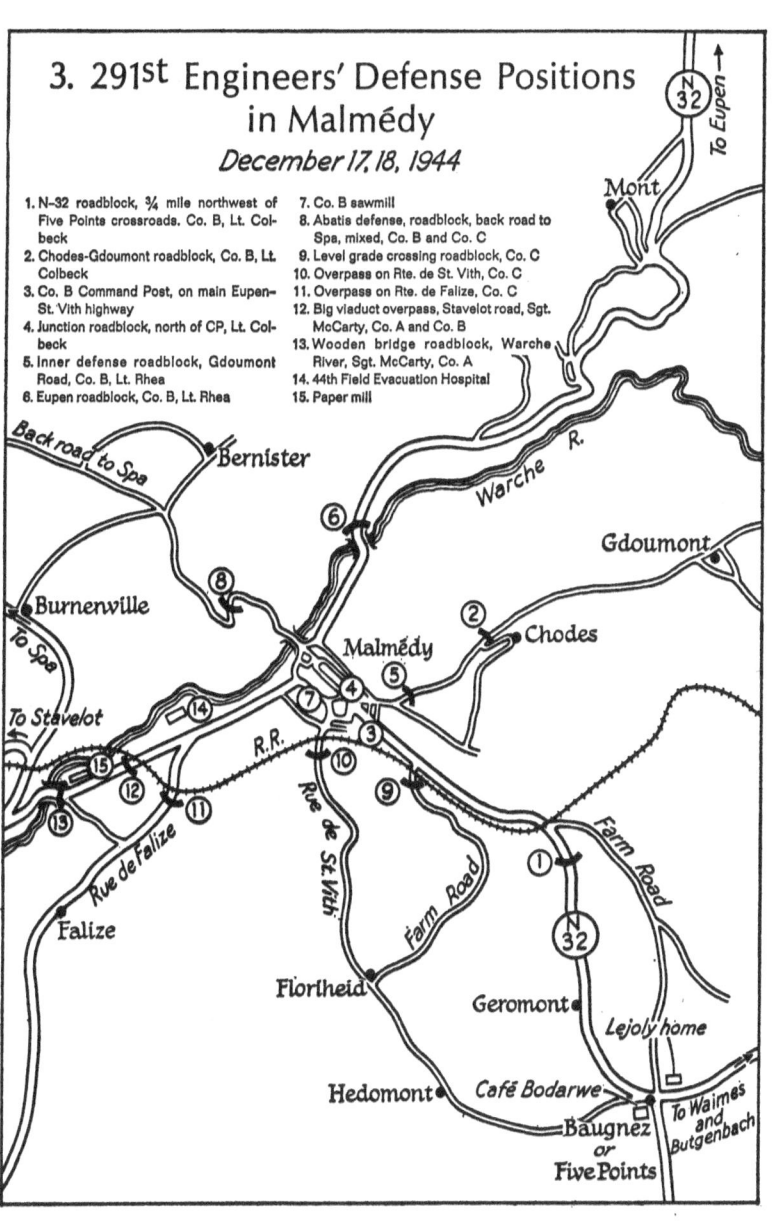

roads. He put mines, a bazooka and another .30-caliber machine gun here.

A good many of Lieutenant Rhea's men were on the security checkpoints which had been set up earlier in the morning because of the paratrooper alert. One of his squads, for instance, was guarding the entrance to Malmédy from the north on the Eupen road. His 1st squad was on road patrol, and when it came in because of the heavy traffic, the men found him installing .30-caliber machine guns on the various squad trucks. Rhea promptly latched on to the men and gave them a job, sending them, with their squad leader, Sergeant Munoz, to an inner defense where the Gdoumont road came into town. For this roadblock he had two bazookas and the TNT in the demolition chest of their squad truck, but no mines. The men mounted a .30-caliber machine gun on their truck and began to inch their way through the milling traffic in the town toward their position.

And now B Company's 2nd platoon came in from the woods. Rhea spread these men around, sent some of them to the railroad overpass behind Lieutenant Colbeck's advance roadblock, and sent others to cut down trees and set up an abatis defense on the back road to Spa.

The immense snarl of military traffic and civilians swirling about was maddening and frustrating to the small units of Company B who were trying to get into the positions assigned to them. Bernard Koenig was in the unit which set up the block where the Gdoumont road entered town. He recalls that his squad leader, Sergeant Munoz, wondered how in the hell a defense could be set up when the street was packed and jammed with people and vehicles. All he could do was go as far out the street as he could, park the truck with its machine gun to one side and put TNT on the trees. He had no mines. He had two bazookas but when he looked for ammunition for them there was none.

Koenig was handed one of the bazookas. Such was the frame of mind of the men at this point that it didn't strike Koenig as

The Allied Side

strange at all that he should be given a bazooka without ammunition and told to climb up onto the hill on the north side of the street and take up a lookout position there. With a useless bazooka, which he unquestioningly took, and his M–1 rifle, he climbed his hill. The other men stayed with the truck and began wiring trees. One man was put on the machine gun in the truck.

The officers, trying to get men into positions, trying to funnel more men and equipment to them after they got into position, were constantly fighting the streaming traffic in the town, cursing it and worming through it.

Pergrin set up his command post on the second floor of Conlin's headquarters. Shortly after he finished reporting to Colonel Anderson, the commander of the 629th Engineer Light Equipment Company reached Malmédy and came to the command post. Questioned by Pergrin, he had very little information beyond what had happened to his own outfit. Shortly before daybreak that morning three or four enemy tanks had suddenly come prowling up the road toward his CP near Butgenbach. A tank destroyer outfit had fired on them, however, and they had pulled back. But what everybody wanted to know was how the *hell* had enemy tanks gotten so far behind the front line!

Pergrin had actually not learned much more than he already knew, and he thought surely the situation must be in hand over around Butgenbach and Büllingen by now. He radioed Battalion that the 629th had reached Malmédy and asked them to pass the information along to Colonel Anderson.

As Pergrin was talking to the officer of the 629th, around 11:45, a little convoy of some 140 men in twenty-eight or thirty vehicles led by a jeep was entering Malmédy on the other side of town, from the Eupen road on the north. The small outfit bore left on the route which bypassed the business section of town. Because of the snarling mess of traffic in the town it moved very slowly. It was about 12:15 before it was halted by the guards in front of Pergrin's command post. Pergrin was notified and went out to see who they were. They were three serials of Battery B, the 285th Field Artillery Observation Battalion.

Riding in the jeep which led the convoy were two officers, Lieutenant Virgil T. Lary, commander of the lead serial, and a captain in charge of keeping the battery in its route slot with CCR of 7th Armored. The outfit was identified and told Pergrin their route directions. Then the captain wanted to know if a combat command of 7th Armored had passed through.

It had, Pergrin told them. In fact, it had just cleared Malmédy.

Fine. This was precisely what the captain wanted to know.

The 285th Field Artillery Observation Battalion was stationed near 7th Armored Division, at Heerlen, Holland. Battery B had been assigned to accompany the division south and they had been given a route interval between the combat command which had just passed through Malmédy and the 7th Armored Artillery which was following on their heels.

In fact, even as Pergrin stood talking to the two officers in the jeep the lead company of the 440th Armored Artillery Battalion was entering Malmédy from the north.

But Colonel Pergrin was answering the questions of the captain with Battery B. He warned the officer of the breakthrough and told him German tanks had been seen near Butgenbach. He suggested it might be wise to change the battery's route and go by way of Stavelot. The officer pondered a moment and decided to risk the assigned route. It was a very tight fit they had and if he got out of his slot he might never get back in.

The little column moved on out, headed for Five Points, then Ligneuville and Recht and southward. Tacked on to its tail was an ambulance. It belonged to the 26th Regiment of 1st Infantry Division and had just been repaired and repainted in Verviers. When the 26th was ordered south toward Butgenbach at midnight the night before, two medical corpsmen were sent to Verviers to get the ambulance and bring it to the new regimental

The Allied Side

headquarters. The driver had fallen into line behind Battery B at the Mon Rigi crossroads. He planned, however, to leave the convoy at Five Points and go out N-32 toward Waimes and Butgenbach.

At 12:30 or thereabouts, after Battery B had passed on out the highway, the two men who had been sent on reconnaissance out N-32 burst into the CP, wide-eyed, out of breath, shaky with what they had seen and inclined to babble with excitement. "There's a big Kraut column coming! Colonel, they've got tanks and half-tracks and armored cars, everything, and there's a hell of a lot of 'em! It looks like the whole German army!"

Pergrin pinned them down. "Where? Where did you see them? Where were you? Where are they coming from?"

They told an unbelievable story. They had been patrolling, prowling cautiously eastward. Believing that an armored column would be most likely to travel on the main highway, they had avoided N-32, beyond Five Points, and had nosed down a little secondary road which led to Thirimont and which the 291st kept in more or less repair as an additional access road. Suddenly, just about noon or a little before, they had seen the hair-raising sight of a long enemy armored column moving west out of Thirimont. Nerves prickling and urging them to get out of there fast, they had stayed long enough to count sixty-eight armored vehicles, thirty of them tanks. That was not the total or the end of the column, but it was plenty. They turned their jeep and raced, accelerator undoubtedly floorboarded, to report as fast as possible.

Well, this was the moment of truth. The absolutely impossible had happened. The breakthrough had not been contained at Butgenbach. And the enemy, in great strength, was now knocking on Pergrin's front door. A column that big and strong? My God, they would run right over him, with his little squads here and his little squads there and his mined trees and his half a dozen bazookas and his eight or ten machine guns and his daisy chains.

This, and there was no denying it, might just be the end of Company B, 291st Engineers.

But what on earth were they doing coming around that little secondary road when N-32 was wide open? Even in the middle of consternation and shock Pergrin's analytical mind puzzled over it. Why were they coming from that direction? How many of these German penetrations were there, and where were they going? Was this the same bunch that had broken through at Butgenbach?

The sergeant and the private who had constituted the reconnaissance detail had barely finished their report when, around 12:45, a sound was heard which made everybody stop still and listen. There was no mistaking the sound — it was the crump of a shell, then there was another and another, then the crackle of machine guns, then more shells, goose-stepping up the road into the edge of town, nearer and nearer, then crumping and exploding so close that the windows of the CP rattled and in the soles of their feet the officers felt the tremble of the floor. It sent a shudder rippling up the spine.

In the quietness of the command post Pergrin spoke. "That little FOB outfit has run smack into that Kraut column."

PART II
The German Side

7

THE GERMAN OFFENSIVE was entirely Hitler's own idea and it was under his personal direction from start to finish.

It began to take faint shape as early as July 31 when the Allied armies broke out of Normandy and began their great triumphant sweep across France. At a Staff conference that day, though he rambled and ranted as usual, he did say again and again that the final decision must come in the west and that if necessary the other fronts must suffer in order that a concentrated effort be made there.

He furthermore stated, at this same conference and with bitterness, that he himself would assume the responsibility for planning and commanding such an effort. He was still recovering from injuries received in the July 20 bombing attempt on his life, still much shaken by the evidences of treason. Henceforth, he seemed to be saying, he would trust nobody but those sacred few to whom he was talking, Colonel General Alfred Jodl, Field Marshal Wilhelm Keitel and one or two others. And it must be kept so secret that not even the Commander-in-Chief West should be told. Only the Führer and this small operational staff should know.

He had time to brood in the next week or two as he continued to nurse his injuries and he seems to have reached a realistic conclusion. With Allied armies now sweeping across the continent itself he had a bad war with two fronts, the Russians on one side, the British and Americans on the other. The only chance he had, his only hope, was to do something, somewhere, somehow, to break up the Allied coalition. If he could do that he could have himself a new war. He could free himself of his threat in the west and could then turn all his strength to defeating the Russians in the east.

The diaries of the War Conferences during this period indicate over and over how his mind was trending. Frederick the Great, of course, was his shining inspiration. He had won his war by a breakup in the coalition against him. And in 1940 Hitler himself had broken up the British-French coalition and knocked France out of the war. If he could sweep the British off the continent again, cause disruption and dissention between them and the United States, there was a good chance this Western coalition could be knocked into a cocked hat and he would have the new war he needed. Probably he never seriously considered any method or place other than those he had used in 1940 — a great offensive through the Ardennes.

In the next two weeks, apparently, his plan was worked out, for he announced on August 19 that he was going to take the offensive at the beginning of November when the Allied air forces would not be able to fly because of bad weather, and he ordered large allotments of men and matériel for shipment to the Western front.

On that same day, August 19, at 7:20 P.M. the 10th Polish Mounted Rifle Regiment, of General Montgomery's forces, touched the 90th Infantry Division, of the U.S. 12th Army Group, at Chambois to close the Falaise Gap.

In the days which followed this debacle for German troops Hitler went steadily ahead with his plans for a great offensive. He established the *Sixth Panzer Army** and he ordered the prepa-

---

* All German units are italicized for the purpose of distinguishing them from American units.

The German Side

ration of the road and railway systems for the heavy traffic they would have to bear.

In the first week in September, as General J. Lawton Collins' VII Corps, First U.S. Army, entered Belgium, Hitler recalled Field Marshal Gerd von Rundstedt from retirement to take over as Commander-in-Chief West, and Field Marshal Walther Model, an ardent Nazi, was given command of *Army Group B*, which would make the great assault.

Rundstedt, however, was not taken into the planning. His prestigious name was needed to inspire the German troops and to lull the Allies. Rundstedt was a brilliant commander, for whom the Allied generals had great respect, but it was well known that he went by the book. Rundstedt would throw no surprises on his front. Hitler was planning the greatest surprise of the war and he had no intention of allowing Rundstedt to direct it, but with Rundstedt facing them, Allied commanders would feel certain they knew what he would do — conserve his forces and defend brilliantly as long as he could. It was the only sensible thing to do and Rundstedt was above all a practical, sensible, logical commander.

Early in September Field Marshal Model was told that the retreating German armies *must* hold forward of the Siegfried line, the West Wall. The area behind was needed for the regrouping and reorganizing of the troops for the offensive.

On September 2, Hitler ordered the creation of an "operational reserve" of 25 new divisions. The task of manning these divisions was entrusted to the faithful Goebbels who was ordered to "comb out" industry, the Navy and the Luftwaffe, the overage and the under-age for men. Artillery units in the Balkans were withdrawn for use in the offensive and some of the troops employed in Finland were made available.

On September 4, the British 11th Armoured Division entered Antwerp, and on September 11, First U.S. Army units set foot on German soil in the vicinity of Aachen. On the same day Patton's right flank touched the French II Corps, under General Patch's Seventh U.S. Army at Sombernon, and a front was now established reaching from Switzerland to the Baltic.

The second week in September Hitler had encouraging reports from the Western front that the German troops were getting a toehold along the line and that the enemy's action was rapidly slowing down. Hitler was not surprised. He had predicted that they would outrun their supply line. Hitler now ordered his German line to stand to the last man, to give up not one inch of ground. This order and the fanatical holding which resulted were what the Allied armies ran into in their November offensive toward the Rhine, especially at Aachen and the Hürtgen Forest.

In spite of his "operational reserve" Hitler had to depend primarily on units already in the Western line and now all SS panzer divisions were ordered out of the line to be refitted and reformed and given to the *Sixth Panzer Army*. They were to be the backbone of the offensive.

On September 16 Hitler announced to his Staff that the offensive would be launched through the Ardennes and that its objective would be Antwerp. Studying the daily reports, studying the war maps, he had hit upon the perfect place to cause the utmost confusion and dissension among the Allies — the seam between the British and the U.S. troops. He must have exulted when his Intelligence reports also told him that this Ardennes segment of the front was also the most thinly held of the entire line. It played perfectly into his hands. It must have tickled his sense of history, also, to use once more this historic gateway through which German troops had poured in 1914 and again in 1940. It would be a gesture like a small boy cocking his nose at his enemy.

Antwerp had to be his strategic goal, although his military commanders would never quite understand why. To them it seemed totally unrealistic. But the penetration *had* to reach to

The German Side

the sea. Hitler wanted another Dunkerque. He wanted to roll the British back and get them entirely out of the war. There would be such rage and dissension and confusion then among the Allies that he could handle the Americans, alone.

On September 25, Jodl was ordered to begin the detailed and comprehensive plan for the attack. As outlined the plans were:

1. The attack should be launched sometime between 20 and 30 November when flying weather would be bad.
2. It should be made through the Ardennes in the Monschau-Echternach sector.
3. The initial objective would be the seizure of bridgeheads over the Meuse River between Liège and Namur.
4. Thereafter Antwerp would be the objective.
5. A battle to annihilate the British and Canadians would ultimately be fought north of the line Antwerp-Liège-Bastogne.
6. A minimum of thirty divisions would be available, ten of which would be armored.
7. Support would be given by an unprecedented concentration of artillery and rocket projector units.
8. Operational control would be vested in four armies — two panzer armies in the center and two infantry armies to cover the flanks.
9. The Luftwaffe would be prepared to support the operation.
10. All planning would aim at securing tactical surprise, and speed.
11. Secrecy would be maintained at all costs and only a very few individuals would be privy to the plan until the last moment.

The only changes ever made in this plan were the delay in opening the offensive from late November to December 16, and the decision to keep an infantry army holding in the north against the British until the Allies had fully reacted to the attack.

On September 25, the same day Jodl was ordered to prepare the battle plans, the 291st Engineers were building bridges in southern Belgium and in Luxembourg. Company A finished a bridge at Steinfort, Luxembourg, on the 24th and moved to Ettelbruck where Company C joined them and they put a bridge across the Alzette River. At the same time Company B was building bridges at Longuyon and Bereldange. The first week in October all the companies joined Battalion at Bastogne for their next assignments.

The first week in October the Germans began strengthening the Rhine bridges which would shortly have such heavy traffic over them. Bridge piers and pillars were reinforced. Railway lines were laid across highway bridges and rail ferries were set up. Supply dumps and depots were established and a complete overhaul of the German State Railways began. Emergency schedules and controls were established.

On October 8, the 291st Battalion and Companies B and C moved to Hockai and bridges were built at Trois Ponts, Malmédy and Habiemont. Company A went to build a bridge at Salmchâteau.

The morning of October 21 Hitler signed the "unalterable" plan and letters of instruction went to Rundstedt, Commander-in-Chief West, and to Model, commander of *Army Group B*. This was Rundstedt's first knowledge of the plans for the offensive. At this time Hitler also gave the offensive a sly name, "Watch on the Rhine." It was a name that could be leaked to the enemy and lend further credence to the belief that there were no plans for any offensive.

On October 21 the 291st were living in tents in the Hockai forest waiting for their assignment to the winterization program.

In the afternoon of that same day a handsome young giant who stood six feet four without his boots was brought by order to Hitler's headquarters. He was Lieutenant Colonel Otto Skorzeny, considered by Allied Intelligence to be the supreme commando of the German forces and their most dangerous agent. He had rescued Mussolini from the capitulating Italians in 1943, and only recently he had made a foray into Hungary and kidnapped the regent's son and seized the seat of the Hungarian government.

The German Side

Skorzeny was Austrian and came from a long line of soldiers who had served the Hapsburgs. He had had a Spartan upbringing and his face bore the honorable dueling scar of the saber. But he was also Viennese and had their nonchalant grace and charm and wit and easy humor.

Now Hitler told Skorzeny he was going to give him the most important job of his life.* He wanted Skorzeny to raise an armored brigade in the image of the Americans, wearing their uniforms, driving their vehicles, speaking their language. Such a body of troops could mingle with the Americans, take part in the chaotic rout and retreat which would occur when the offensive began, seize and hold the Meuse bridgeheads for the advancing panzer divisions. Also small commando units in jeeps and Recon cars could scout at random behind the lines and gather important information, commit some sabotage and add further to the demoralization of the U.S. troops.

The plan was given the name Operation Greif, after a mythical bird something like a hawk or condor. For the Allies it came to have one meaning only, grief. It caused plenty of it.

English-speaking volunteers were requested and began arriving at Skorzeny's headquarters. His Special Services troops had been the envy of adventurous young men in all branches of the German armed services ever since they were organized in 1943. There was no lack of volunteers, but Skorzeny quickly learned that practically all of them had considerably shaded the basic requirement — the ability to speak English. Skorzeny therefore went to the High Command and convinced them that in the brief time allowed him he could never create a full brigade of English-speaking troops. He demanded a different composition for the brigade — and he got what he demanded, two tank battalions, a paratroop battalion, and signalmen. To these he added two battalions of his own troops. He thus came up with a bri-

* All details of plans and operations of Skorzeny's brigade, Ethint 12, Oberst (W–SS) Otto Skorzeny, "Ardennes Offensive, an Interview with Obst. Skorzeny" (Aug. 12, 1945). Also Skorzeny's own book, *Skorzeny's Special Missions* (London: Robert Hale Limited, 1957).

gade of experienced, very tough men who constituted a real striking force. This was Skorzeny's *150th Panzer Brigade*.

He put the volunteers into a special commando company, which would meet the second half of Hitler's orders — disguised scouts and jeep teams to infiltrate behind the American lines, gather information, commit sabotage and create confusion. This special company was the only one that was perfectly Americanized, with American uniforms, jeeps, scout cars, trucks, and at least one man in each vehicle who spoke English fluently.

Collecting the U.S. equipment was a headache for Skorzeny. He wanted twenty Sherman tanks. He has said he got two. For the rest he had to make do with German Panthers plated over to look like Shermans. But it was expected that all he needed would be captured as the offensive gained momentum.

Skorzeny wanted many jeeps. He says he got thirty. He knew there were numerous jeeps in the German units on the Western front, but nobody who had one wanted to part with it. Officers therefore hid them from Skorzeny's searching eyes. Again it was expected that many would be captured. He painted German Fords khaki and added some Czech and French cars to make up the number he needed.

Nearly 3000 men cannot be brought together for special training, put under rigid security and told nothing of the purpose without many rumors starting. The objective finally hit on as being the most reasonable was based largely on Skorzeny's own record of kidnap. It was believed that this time he was going to kidnap Eisenhower. Skorzeny allowed the rumor to gain ground because it served well enough as a cover story.

Now, "Watch on the Rhine" moved forward rapidly, all through November, but even so Hitler's first date in late November could not be met. The opening day of the offensive had to be postponed until the next siege of unfavorable weather, December 16.

On December 4 another special mission was organized. Baron

The German Side

Friedrich A. von der Heydte, a brilliant paratroop commander, was ordered to take charge of a regiment of parachutists to be dropped behind the lines the night of December 15, a few hours before the offensive opened.*

Von der Heydte had helped plan and put into operation the drop in Crete in 1941 which had been so successful. At the time he received Hitler's order for the offensive he was in command of the paratrooper school in Bergen Op Zoom, in Holland.

He was told his brigade would consist of around 1200 men drawn from various parachute regiments. He would have preferred his own men, whom he had been training in Holland, but he was told it would jeopardize secrecy to move an entire regiment. He was allowed, however, to choose his own company and platoon leaders.

He met his brigade for the first time in Dalhem, some eight miles east of the front at Losheimergraben, on December 11 and he organized them into four companies of light infantry, one company of heavy weapons, a signal platoon and a supply platoon. The parachutes and other equipment arrived on December 13 and a very short training period was begun. All of the men had jumped before but none of them very much and none of them very recently.

On December 14 von der Heydte was called to the headquarters of Field Marshal Walther Model, who was to direct the whole offensive, where he was given the full details of the offensive for the first time. His mission, he was told, would be to open the way for the *Sixth Panzer Army* and to block all northern roads so the U.S. could not reinforce their First Army from the north.

Following his conference with Model, von der Heydte had a conference with the commander of *Sixth Panzer Army*, General

---

* Details concerning entire operations of the von der Heydte kampfgruppe from MS. B-823, Oberstleutnant Friedrich August Baron von der Heydte, "Kampfgruppe von der Heydte."

Sepp Dietrich, and his chief of staff, General Fritz Kraemer. Kraemer gave him written orders:

> On the first day of the attack the Sixth SS Panzer Army will take possession of Liège or the bridges across the Meuse River south of the city. At early dawn on the first day of the attack, Kampfgruppe von der Heydte will drop into the Baraque Michel mountain area, eleven kilometers north of Malmédy, and secure the multiple road junction at Baraque Michel for use by the armored point of the Sixth Panzer Army, probably elements of the 12th SS Panzer Division. If for technical reasons this mission is impracticable on the morning of the first day of the attack, Kampfgruppe von der Heydte will drop early on the following morning into the Amblève River or Amay area to secure the bridges there for the advance of the Sixth SS Panzer Army's armored points.

Dietrich was drunk and he was brusque with von der Heydte. Von der Heydte persevered, however, and succeeded in having some kind of boundary established between his area and that of Skorzeny, and he was able to get the services of an observer from the *12th SS Panzer Division* equipped with a radio.

Fearing the radio might be damaged in the drop, von der Heydte asked for carrier pigeons. Dietrich snorted at the idea. "I don't run a zoo," he said. "Besides, you won't need carrier pigeons. I will meet you north of Malmédy within twenty-four hours." Von der Heydte had to be satisfied.

Following this conference he went to learn the flight plans. He was told they would be:

1. The transport planes would fly from Paderborn toward the front on a route lit by searchlights. Near the front the planes would illuminate their own positions with flares and form in columns for the drop. The searchlights and flares were necessary to keep the young green pilots from plowing into each other.
2. A JU-88 would precede the squadron by a quarter of an hour to prepare for the drop by releasing four small groups of incen-

The German Side

diary bombs in the form of a cross from one to two kilometers in diameter. The paratroopers would jump within the limits of the cross.
3. For half an hour to two hours after the drop the planes would continue to circle over the area dropping flares and incendiaries so that the paratroopers could see to rendezvous.
4. In between times they would circle ten to fifteen miles farther away and drop dummy paratroopers in widely scattered areas, around Elsenborn, up behind Ninth U.S. Army, near Spa and Stavelot.

The drop was set for 3:00 A.M. on December 16, the flight to leave from two aerodromes, Paderborn and Lippspringe, at midnight. Trucks were to transport the troops to the aerodromes on the evening of the 15th after sundown. In the event, the flight had to be postponed until the following night for the simplest of reasons. The trucks did not have enough gas to haul the paratroopers to the aerodromes!

On December 11 the build-up of men and matériel for the German offensive was almost complete. A miracle of scraping the barrel for men and supplies had been accomplished, to say nothing of moving them into position. Early that morning Hitler moved into his new headquarters near Ziegenberg in order to keep close personal control of the whole offensive.

On December 11, Colonel Pergrin was notified that he would be expected to furnish one company from his 291st Engineers to support CCB of 9th Armored Division in the offensive toward the Urft-Roer dams.

On the evening of December 12 Hitler called a meeting of the division commanders. The Army and Corps commanders who would lead the assault had been brought into the planning in October and November, but for the first time the men who would actually direct the tactical operations were now brought into the picture, only hours before the offensive actually opened.

For an hour the generals listened to a political and historical harangue and probably listened inattentively because a harangue from Hitler was customary.

Hitler then launched into the general overall plan of the offensive. It is necessary now to look at the map of the front line. The German offensive would pierce through the center of the line along an eighty-five mile segment from Monschau on the north to Echternach, Luxembourg, on the south. The entire segment was defended by First U.S. Army, and very weakly. Only the 99th Infantry Division of its V Corps lay within the segment, but all of its VIII Corps fell within it. Therefore, the segment the Germans meant to attack was defended by four infantry divisions, one task force of 14th Cavalry Group consisting of 450 men, and one combat command of an armored division. Against these thin-stretched units the Germans had massed three full armies.

Hitler had given his *Sixth Panzer Army* the most important role and placed it on the north, facing the U.S. 99th Infantry Division along its entire line from Monschau to the Losheim Gap, and most of the 14th Cavalry Group in the Gap itself.

The *Sixth Panzer*'s role was to sweep through the 99th Infantry, race for the Meuse, then bend northwest and penetrate to Antwerp. While its armor raced forward its infantry divisions were to form a wall from Monschau westward to Liège. This was known as the northern shoulder and the wall would seal off the possibility of any reinforcements from the U.S. and British units in the north.*

The *Sixth Panzer Army* was politically colored, all its armored divisions being Waffen-SS. Hitler did this purposely and intentionally gave it the most important role to play. He was still sore and tender and angry about the attempt on his life and the evidences of treason in the Wehrmacht. He meant to deny them

---

* Details of plans and operations, MS, A-924, Brigadeführer der Waffen-SS. Fritz Kraemer, "Operations of the Sixth Panzer Army" 1944-45 (National Archives, Washington, D.C.).

The German Side

any part of the glory in this offensive. But there was a more practical reason. This army, made up largely of dedicated Nazis, sworn to obedience, could be counted on to make a hard try for Antwerp. Hitler knew his Wehrmacht commanders were skeptical of this goal and he was afraid they would settle for the "small solution" pinching off only those enemy troops east of the Meuse. Hitler had to have the "big solution." He had to have a new war. Thus he gave the most important role to his loyal, obedient SS officers. On paper this army was not referred to as the *Sixth SS Panzer Army*, but Hitler occasionally slipped and called it that, and as we have seen Colonel von der Heydte's written orders called it that.

Hitler gave the command of this army to his old and valued Nazi friend, Sepp Dietrich. Dietrich was a rough, brawling, burly man. Like Hitler he had fought in World War I and he had reached the rank of sergeant in a tank unit. Forever after he thought of himself as an expert in tanks.

He was a jovial, hearty man, loving food and perhaps overly loving drink, and with his rough manners was about as different from the Wehrmacht officers as a pig from a thoroughbred horse.

He had been a faithful follower of the Führer's from the earliest days. He was quickly converted to Hitler's cause and he faithfully followed him all the long climb up the ladder and he had never failed to serve him well and loyally.

For all these reasons, Hitler rewarded his loyal old comrade with the command of this important army and tried to play safe against any hesitation on the part of the Wehrmacht officers. He hedged his bet on Dietrich a little, however, by putting a brilliant Wehrmacht strategist with him as chief of staff, General Fritz Kraemer.

Although the goal was Antwerp, and understood, to achieve it Kraemer had prepared an excellent encirclement of Liège. Kraemer's plan swung one wing north of Liège and sent another to cross the Meuse south of Liège. Having thus enclosed not only Liège and its vast tons of supplies but all the densely packed First Army installations in the vicinity of Spa, the penetration could then proceed farther west along the Albert Canal.

The *Sixth Panzer Army* was given the elite of the SS armored troops and a strength that was formidable. It consisted of four armored divisions, two for the spearheads and two for the second wave of assault, and five infantry divisions. It also had the most and the best of the matériel.

South of the *Sixth Panzer Army* came the *Fifth Panzer Army*, The line dividing them was loosely St. Vith, Vielsalm, Werbomont and Huy, as it bent west and northwest. The *Fifth Panzer Army* was commanded by Baron Hasso von Manteuffel, a descendant of a family of famous Prussian generals. Manteuffel was given two objectives. He was to encircle the Schnee Eifel and pinch off two regiments of the new green 106th Infantry Division and capture St. Vith, the most vital rail and road center in the sector. The rest of his army was to thrust across Luxembourg, race for the Meuse and cross between Namur and Dinant, then swing north to protect the flank of the *Sixth Panzer Army*.

Below Manteuffel's *Fifth Panzer Army* came the southernmost German troops, the *Seventh Army*. It was an infantry army and its role was to seize the Vianden-Echternach area, then push west to protect the entire southern flank against any possible reinforcement from Patton's Third U.S. Army. It was commanded by General Erich Brandenberger.

Hitler may have been sick, his left leg and arm may have been trembling, but he could still light a fire, in himself and in those he addressed. And as he briefed his division commanders that night of December 12, he lit one. The generals were thunderstruck and awed by the daring of the plan, and almost immediately they were seized with great hope and excitement. It was wonderful to have a bold plan again, to turn around from the defensive and sweep once more with victorious German armies against the

The German Side

enemy. After the event many would say they never believed it would work, but they did not act that way that night. They were fired with enthusiasm and they fired their corps and regimental commanders with the same zeal and enthusiasm in turn.

Hitler concluded the briefing with an order which would be implemented only too well by some elements of his troops. "This battle will decide whether Germany is to live or die. Your soldiers must fight hard and ruthlessly. There must be no pity. The battle must be fought with brutality and all resistance must be broken in a wave of terror. The enemy must be beaten — now or never! Thus will live our Germany! Forward to and over the Meuse!"

Prisoners of war and helpless Belgian civilians would be engulfed in the "wave of terror" thus enjoined.

Directives were issued to all the German armies concerning the conduct of the troops in the occupied enemy territories: "The principle is to follow the behavior of the local populace." And Gauleiters were brought to move with the troops and take over control of the occupied territories — Seyss-Inquart for Holland, Grohe for Belgium and Simon for Luxembourg.

On the 14th and 15th of December, Colonel Pergrin was detailing his Company A to move to Born, and he was having his mine detectors put in good repair for their use in support of 9th Armored's CCB.

Even with all the secrecy imposed by Hitler from the beginning, it is impossible not to ask how three full armies and all the men, all the weapons, all the equipment, the machines and vehicles, all the mountains of supplies, could be assembled and moved without some knowledge of it by the Allies.

It could be done several ways and Hitler used them all. First, the basic premise was met. Nobody was suspicious and Hitler took good care to arouse no suspicions. Both the British and American Intelligence were lulled into a state of overconfidence by the swift, almost easy advances made so far. It was assumed that this advance would be resumed as soon as the supply situation could be untangled and when the Roer dams were taken. It was believed Hitler was on his last legs. He had been fighting for five years. He was down to the bottom of the barrel in both men and matériel. The war was as good as won. In September men began counting on it being over by Christmas. Even Eisenhower made a bet at that time with Field Marshal Montgomery that it would be over by December 31. An offensive? It was out of the question. It was never even considered.

Of course the Germans were given credit for knowing a major offensive of our own would be mounted toward the Rhine sometime soon. After all, Rundstedt was no fool. And he would react with vigor. So, when aerial photographs showed increased rail traffic and movements of troops and tanks and guns, Intelligence promptly interpreted these as being moved to use in a defense against the Allied offensive.

For the same reason, Hitler could boldly assemble the entire *Sixth Panzer Army* in front of Cologne and let it sit there. Intelligence did precisely what Hitler wanted them to do. They decided this army was there to blunt the Allied offensive. And "Watch on the Rhine" was going to be, of course, Hitler's last-ditch stand in front of the Rhine.

Both the 99th Infantry Division and the 106th reported hearing much movement behind the German lines the nights of December 14 and 15, but no account was taken of the reports. In fact, the 106th officer reporting was told pretty testily not to be so jittery. "They're probably playing records to make it sound like movements," he was told. Both divisions were new in the line and, humble in their inexperience, did not press their uneasiness.

A few prisoners taken in the last days before the offensive spoke of it. But prisoners rarely knew plans on a very high level and besides prisoners always insisted Germany was going to do

The German Side

something big very shortly — usually with Hitler's much vaunted secret weapons.

On December 15 a woman told some officers of the 28th Infantry Division in Luxembourg that she had been visiting behind the German lines and she saw a great assemblage of tanks and troops there. Intelligence officers of the 28th were impressed enough to send her to VIII Corps, where she told her story again, and she was then sent to First Army. But by now it was too late.

The truth is that Allied Intelligence was simply asleep at the switch. Blinded by their own overconfidence they fell for every ruse Hitler used, beginning with his own reputation. Hitler was dismissed as a fanatical maniac. He was fanatical in the sense that he believed invincible will could make a dream come true, but he was not a maniac. And the man who conquered one European country after another in 1939 and 1940 was no military fool. He had read a considerable amount of military history and a lot of what was called his "intuition" was something pulled out of the enormous storage and retrieval system of his photographic and retentive memory. Of the plans for this offensive, Rundstedt himself said, "The operational idea as such can almost be called a stroke of genius." * Because the man was conscienceless, shrewd and cunning, he was all the more dangerous.

He used Rundstedt to lull the Allied command. He cunningly used the very name of the offensive to misdirect Allied attention. And better than anybody, having used it consistently, he knew how well total surprise worked, in the paralysis of communications, in terror and chaos. He mixed a clever bag of tricks and Allied Intelligence fell for them all. They failed and failed miserably at their job, and it was an immensely costly failure.

* Cole, Hugh M., *The Ardennes: Battle of the Bulge* (Washington, D.C.: Department of the Army, 1965), p. 20.

8

And so the morning of December 16 came. Company A of the 291st Engineers moved in convoy out of Werbomont, through Trois Ponts and Stavelot, to Malmédy, where four 240-mm. shells fell. They went on through Ligneuville to Amblève, which lay some seven miles southwest of Büllingen, some five miles north of St. Vith, and around ten miles behind the front in the Losheim Gap.

Shortly after Company A was roused up to have breakfast and begin loading their trucks the German guns all along the Ardennes front opened in their thundering, rolling barrage. Cannons, mortars, rockets and 88s shrieked and screamed and blazed and rumbled down the eighty-five-mile segment of line. It was one of the most intense bombardments American GIs had ever seen or heard. At every point along the front it lasted an hour and in some areas it went on for two or three hours.

When the bombardment ceased finally, communications all along the front were in a snarled mess and precisely the chaos and confusion Hitler had wanted was achieved. Platoons could not contact companies, companies could not contact battalions and battalions were in very limited contact with divisions. The surprise was total, and it would be days before the American corps and army commanders could piece together anything like an accurate picture of what was happening.

The German Side

When the bombardment stopped, at different times in different places, there was a benumbed and unbelievable silence, then out of the silence fog-wrapped figures loomed like ghosts walking. Slow, steady, implacable, ten or a dozen abreast the German infantry came on, gray ghosts walking in dim gray light until, nearing an outpost or dugout or foxhole, they broke into a run and launched themselves, screaming "Heil Hitler!" at the stupefied GIs. It was like something out of *Frankenstein*, and it was a moment to try any man's nerve.

There were no tanks in this predawn hour, only the knots of gray men here and there, but coming in a relentless and growing stream. The German plan was for the infantry, down the entire front, to lead and make an opening for the tanks which would follow.

Caught off guard, lulled in security, dazed by the heavy artillery concentration, scared by the whole eerie, unbelievable thing, men did still rally and fight, in little units here and little units there. Not knowing the full strength of the offensive, small groups were caught up in fierce, swirling action, not understanding but instinctively reacting. Most of them believed they were in some kind of local attack limited to their own positions. With communications so snarled it was impossible to know much more.

They rallied and hung on, with sometimes deadly results to the advancing enemy. From Monschau to Losheimergraben, the full length of the 99th Infantry line, Dietrich's infantrymen of the *Sixth Panzer Army* ran into the stiffest opposition of the day. Around Monschau and Höfen the *Hitzfeld LXVII Corps* attack was stopped dead in its tracks and never did really get going again. And below there the Germans ran head on into the stubborn resistance of both 2nd Infantry, which was attacking toward the Roer dams through the 99th's lines, and the 99th Infantry. German Intelligence had failed there. They knew about the attack toward the dams, but they believed it to be a

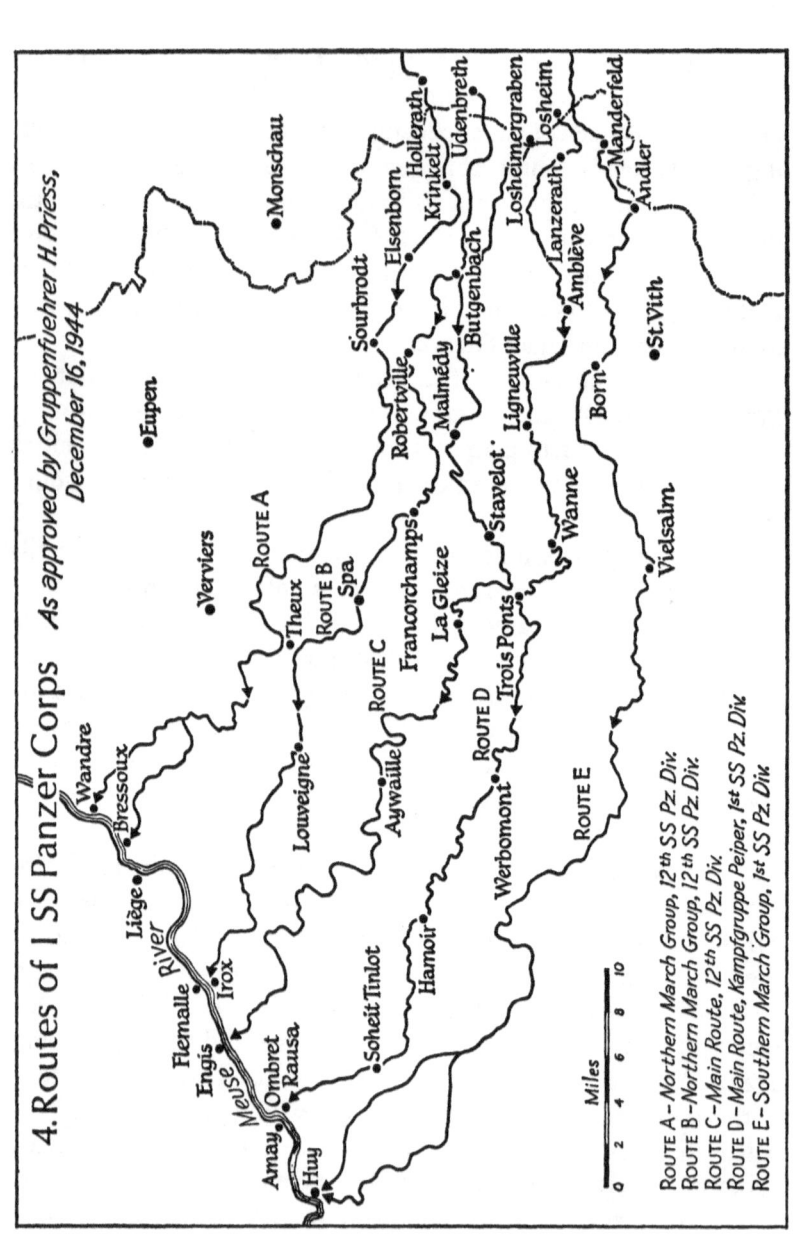

99th Infantry Division attack. They had 2nd Infantry positioned on their maps well behind the lines, in reserve.

Around 11:00 A.M., as Company A left Malmédy to proceed to their new position, General Gerow at his V Corps headquarters in Eupen had enough information to know that his right flank was in trouble, precisely where it joined Middleton's VIII Corps in the Losheim Gap. One hour later, at noon, the Gap was overrun and the men of 14th Cavalry Group were being forced back as *Sixth Panzer Army*'s southernmost infantry division, *3rd Parachute Division,* poured through the nine-mile gateway.

It was the only appreciable penetration made that day by *Sixth Panzer Army*.

If Hitler had rested his highest hopes on the *Sixth Panzer Army*, Dietrich pinned his on his crack *I SS Panzer Corps*. It had been beefed up until it was the strongest corps in the entire offensive. It was commanded by SS General Hermann Priess and all its armored troops were SS. There were four armored divisions but two, the *2nd* and *9th*, would remain in reserve to be committed in the second wave. In the top sector of the *1 SS Panzer Corps* sector, the leading armored division was the *12th SS Panzer Division (Hitler Jugend)*. In the bottom sector it was the elite *1st SS Panzer Division (Liebstandarte Adolf Hitler),** commanded by SS General Wilhelm Mohnke.

The sector assigned to *I SS Panzer Corps* was narrow, lying roughly from just north of Hollerath along a northwest angle to cross the Meuse just above Liège, to the seam with *Fifth Panzer Army* in the south, which followed, roughly the St. Vith–Vielsalm–Menil highway.

Five roads within this sector were assigned to the advance, the

---

* MS. A–877, General der Waffen–SS H. Priess, "Commitment of the I SS Panzer Corps During the Ardennes Offensive" (Dec. 16, 1944–Jan. 25, 1945), National Archives.

three most northern roads to the *12th SS Panzer Division* (*Hitler Jugend*) and the central and southern roads to the *1st SS Panzer Division* (*Liebstandarte*).

The top road, Route A, debouched across the border between Hollerath and Udenbreth, swung northwest through Sourbrodt, angled up through Sart, Pepinster (on the fringe of Verviers), on to Nessonvaux, then up to cross the Meuse at Bressoux and Wandre.

Route B, just below Route A, crossed the border south of Udenbreth, swung northwest before reaching Losheimergraben, went through Robertville, Beverce, Francorchamps, Spa, Theux and on to cross the Meuse in the suburb of Seraing and at Irox.

Both Routes A and B were to be used by the *12th SS Panzer Division*'s armored infantry and reconnaissance battalion.

Route C, which would be used by the armored column of *12th SS Panzer Division*, moved from Losheimergraben up through Büllingen, on to Malmédy, thence to Stavelot, touched Trois Ponts but turned north to La Gleize, followed the bends and turns of the Amblève River through Remouchamps and Aywaille and crossed the Meuse at Engis.

Route D, assigned to the armored column of *1st SS Panzer Division*, the *Liebstandarte Adolf Hitler*, debouched from Losheim, went through Lanzerath to Honsfeld. Thence it moved on to Heppenbach, to Amblève and up to Ligneuville. At Ligneuville it was to take to very bad secondary roads across country to Wanne. It was to cross the Salm by the lower bridge south of Trois Ponts and pick up Highway N–23 which it would then follow to a crossing of the Meuse at Huy and at Ombret Rausa.

Route E, which crossed the front near Manderfeld, ran through Andler, up to Wallerode, through Born, Recht and Poteau to Vielsalm. Thence it ran through Lierneux, Menil, then swung up through Modave and Barse for a Meuse crossing at Huy. Route E was assigned to the southern march group of

The German Side

1st SS Panzer Division, a reinforced armored infantry regiment and the division's reconnaissance battalion.* (See map for routes of proposed commitment of *I SS Panzer Corps*.)

These were the routes mapped out by the Corps' staff. However, they were not obligatory. Priess himself has said, "The Corps — and under Corps command, the divisions — had freedom of movement within this area. Thus march routes did not have to be rigidly adhered to. Each division had express permission to deviate from prescribed march routes whenever the situation demanded."

In the event, one column, the armored column of *1st SS Panzer Division*, would deviate considerably from its prescribed route.

The *I SS Panzer Corps* was loaned three infantry divisions to make the breakthrough for their two spearhead tank divisions. From north to south they were the *277th Volksgrenadiers*, the *12th Volksgrenadiers* and the *3rd Parachute Division*.

The *277th Volksgrenadiers* were to break through for the *12th SS Panzer Division*, on a broad front generally north of Udenbreth leading through Krinkelt-Rocherath to Butgenbach and westward along the highway N-32, which was the road assigned to *12th SS Panzer Division*'s armored column.

The *1st SS Panzer Division* (*Liebstandarte Adolf Hitler*) was given a sector lying between the highway N-32 and the Andler–St. Vith–Poteau highway N-26 on the south. The *12th Volksgrenadiers* and the *3rd Parachute Division* were to open the *Liebstandarte*'s sector for them.

Because this study is largely concerned with the *Liebstandarte Division* something must be known about it. It is helpful in trying to understand its savagery to know something of its background. In the beginning, the SS (Schutzstaffel) was organized

---

* All details concerning the commitment of *I SS Panzer Corps*, and the map of proposed routes, are taken from MS. A–877, General der Waffen–SS H. Priess, "Commitment of the I SS Panzer Corps During the Ardennes Offensive" (Dec. 16, 1944–Jan. 25, 1945).

by Hitler as a small elite unit of some 280 men, sworn to absolute obedience and loyalty to him personally. They were his bodyguard. Himmler then took this small nucleus and enlarged it into the great, effective organization of Black Shirts which became so widely known as the SS. It was composed of various military and civilian branches with varying duties and characteristics. But the Waffen-SS was strictly military.

The *Liebstandarte Division* had its proud origins in the elite and original bodyguard unit, but its crack armored regiment, *1st SS Panzer Regiment*, was also a Death's Head unit. The Death's Head units had begun as concentration camp guards. In 1940, however, the youngest and best of these young men had been winnowed out and formed into military units. *First SS Panzer Regiment* was therefore not only *Liebstandarte* but *Totenkopf* — and their insignia was the Death's Head.

The *Liebstandarte* had taken part in the fighting in Normandy and in the retreat across France. Two months before the offensive, however, they were pulled out of the line and sent to the Minden area of Westphalia to regroup and reorganize. They were brought up to full T/O strength of around 22,000 men, given about 200 new tanks and much other new equipment, and they were strengthened with corps artillery and antiaircraft guns.

About three weeks before the offensive was to begin the division was moved into *Sixth Panzer Army* reserve at Blisheim, about 12 kilometers east of Düren. By this time the division consisted of *1st SS Panzer Regiment*, two armored infantry regiments, the *1st* and *2nd SS Panzer Grenadier* regiments, an armored reconnaissance battalion double the size and strength of the usual reconnaissance battalion, an antiaircraft regiment with 88-mm. guns, an engineer battalion, and one battalion of corps artillery consisting of 150-mm. and 210-mm. howitzers.*

* The basic documents for the commitment of the *Liebstandarte Division* and for the route, movements, plans and battles of *Kampfgruppe Peiper* are MSS. C-004 "Kampfgruppe Peiper" — Ethint 10, 1 SS PZ Regt. 11-24 December, 1944, and Ethint 11, 1 SS PZ Regt. 16-19 December, 1944.

The German Side

On December 13 the *Liebstandarte* was given a detailed march order by *I SS Panzer Corps*. No mention was made of an impending offensive. The order contained nothing except the route of march and the new assembly area, which was Marmegen-Blankenheimerdorf-Schmidtheim. Advance elements of the division were already in Dahlem.

Special precautions were taken to conceal the movement. The troops were not told the purpose of the movement. A complete blackout and radio silence were observed. No signs marked the route except plain yellow arrows without division designation. The division moved out at 7:00 P.M. on December 13, in a dense fog which still prevailed when they scattered into the woods of their new assembly area at 10:00 A.M. the following day.

Before noon on this same day, December 14, General Mohnke called a meeting of his commanders at his headquarters in Tondorf. Present were Lieutenant Colonel Jochen Peiper, Colonel Hanssen, commander of *1st SS Panzer Grenadier Regiment*, Colonel Sandig, commander of *2nd SS Panzer Grenadier Regiment*, Major Gustave Knittel, commander of the reconnaissance section, and Skorzeny and several of his officers.

At this meeting General Mohnke, the *Liebstandarte*'s commander, announced the entire plan for the offensive and read the detailed Corps order which assigned various routes and fixed the morning of December 16 as D-Day.

Each commanding officer at the conference — that is, Major Knittel, Colonels Hanssen and Sandig, and Peiper — was given a marked map showing the routes of advance. The commanders were given to understand that the *Liebstandarte* had been given the most important role in the whole offensive, and within the *Liebstandarte* the most important role, the key spearhead thrust, was to be given to a very strong armored combat group. At this meeting Jochen Peiper learned, officially, that he was to command this kampfgruppe.

Peiper has said that five days earlier he had deduced there was to be an offensive and he was to have a key role when General

Kraemer, chief of staff of *Sixth Panzer Army*, had asked him what he thought of an offensive through the Eifel and how long did he think it would take an armored regiment to travel 80 kilometers. Not wishing to guess, Peiper had taken a Panther tank and driven it 80 kilometers and learned that alone, on a fairly good road, he could drive 80 kilometers in one night.

Peiper was given the composition and strength of his command. Based on the *1st SS Panzer Regiment*, it was enlarged and reinforced to the size of a full combat group. He had all of the division's tanks — two companies of Mark IVs and two companies of Mark Vs (Panthers), or around 100. In addition he was given the use, when needed, of one battalion (around 42 tanks) of Tiger Royals loaned by *I SS Panzer Corps*.

For infantry he was given the *3rd Battalion* of the *2nd SS Panzer Grenadier Regiment*, which was fully motorized and armored and had the self-propelled assault guns which the German infantry leaned on so heavily and which were the envy of every American infantry commander. This unit was commanded by Major Josef Diefenthal. The rest of this regiment would follow Peiper's kampfgruppe.

Peiper had two companies of combat engineers (*Pioneers*), and he had his share of divisional and corps artillery and antiaircraft guns, plus the usual Service/Supply and Headquarters units. In addition, Peiper has said that each combat team in the division had a group of the special Skorzeny units, and that each unit consisted of around 500 men, 20 Sherman tanks (or Panthers plated over to look like Shermans), some German tanks, about thirty 2½-ton trucks, and from 30 to 50 jeeps.

Peiper has said that he was not given any tactical control of the Skorzeny units attached to his kampfgruppe and under interrogation after the war, when asked what he thought of the value of these units during the offensive, he said they might just as well have stayed home because they were never near the head of the column where they had planned to be.

It was at this conference that Peiper was told not to bother

The German Side

about his flanks but to drive rapidly to the Meuse River, making full use of the element of surprise. He was told that his kampfgruppe was expected to make the first Meuse crossing.

Peiper objected immediately to the roads on his route. They were very poor, occasionally being mere dirt tracks. He said the roads were unfit for tanks, were suitable only for bicycles. No discussion was allowed. He was told the Führer himself had chosen the route. It was supposed to have one virtue. There were not many bridges along it. Since Peiper was not alloted any heavy bridging equipment this was expected to be helpful to him. He was expected to take such bridges as he needed through the swiftness of his attack and the element of surprise.

At the conference it was also announced that two trainloads of gasoline needed by the division had not arrived, therefore orders were issued to all units to supply themselves with captured gasoline. Division Intelligence had a situation map purporting to show American supply installations. The complex of gas dumps around Spa was indicated, and the gas dump at Büllingen was shown. It is interesting that the big gas dump south of Francorchamps was not known to the Germans.

Peiper has said there were no other shortages. There was enough ammunition to last four or five days, by which time it was expected supplies would have caught up with the advance elements.

The *Liebstandarte*'s forces were to be committed on two routes. Peiper's kampfgruppe was to lead on the northern route in the division's sector.

The other infantry regiment, *1st SS Panzer Grenadiers*, and Major Gustave Knittel's reconnaissance battalion were to take the southern route. Peiper has said that all the *Liebstandarte*'s units were committed with the intention of reinforcing his spearhead eventually. This southern march group had no tanks but was to be assisted, if necessary, by Tiger Royals from *I SS Panzer Corps*.

Concluding the division conference, General Mohnke read

aloud most of Hitler's December 12 speech to the division commanders. It will be recalled that this was the speech which ordered the offensive to be waged ruthlessly and in a wave of terror.

Following the division conference, Peiper returned to his own command post in a forester's hut near Blankenheim and called a conference of the commanders of the units assigned to him. He organized his column into two battalions, with his two companies of Mark IVs in the 1st Battalion and his Panthers in the 2nd Battalion, the half-tracks and armored infantry intermingled and meshed in. These were his combat elements, to be followed by his engineers and artillery, the battalion of Mark VIs (Tiger Royals) following at the very tail. The route intervals were organized so that the entire column was about 25 kilometers long.

After organizing his kampfgruppe into its march column Peiper drove over for a conference with General Gerhard Engel, commander of *12th Volksgrenadiers*, the infantry unit which was to make the breakthrough for him. Engel told Peiper that he expected to make his initial penetration by 7:00 A.M. on the 16th. Peiper then asked him to clear the main road of mines in the Losheim area.

On the 15th there was a conference at *I SS Panzer Corps* headquarters consisting of the division commanders, the commanders of all combat teams and eight or nine of Skorzeny's officers. At the conclusion of this conference Peiper conferred with the Skorzeny men and the details of the advance were discussed. It was understood that Skorzeny's unit assigned to Peiper would move with his column, overtake the tanks as rapidly as possible, then infiltrate behind the American lines to cause confusion by dropping off fake MPs to misdirect traffic, by seizing centers of communications, command posts and the like. They were also to seize and hold Peiper's bridgehead on the Meuse, either at Huy or Ombret Rausa.

Peiper has said that the special precautions taken by Skor-

The German Side

zeny's men, who of course were in American uniforms and in American vehicles, to protect them from being fired on by German troops were quite simple. All tanks would keep their guns at nine o'clock throughout the journey, with no shooting at first. If they met German troops later the soldiers were to take off their American helmets. And all vehicles bore small yellow triangles in the rear.

On the morning of December 16, Dietrich opened the artillery barrage in the *Sixth Panzer Army* sector early, around 4:00 A.M. By 5:00 A.M. the *12th Volksgrenadiers* moved into their infantry attack in the vicinity of Losheim. Peiper was present in General Engel's command post to observe the infantry attack, so that he could estimate precisely when to launch his own push. It turned out that the infantry could not make their promised penetration by 7:00 A.M. nor even by noon. It was 2:00 P.M. before Peiper left Engel's CP to begin bringing his own column forward.

Meanwhile, the entire *1st SS Panzer Division* had been slowly inching forward on one road, from Schmidtheim to Dahlem, to Kronenberg and Scheid. At Hallschlag the southern march group branched off onto the road to Ormont. By this time Corps had ordered the division artillery to move up, and since the division artillery was horse-drawn, the road became hopelessly clogged.

There was a further holdup in the advance at a highway bridge which crossed over the railroad tracks between Scheid and the international boundary line. The Germans had destroyed the bridge themselves during their retreat and it had never been rebuilt. Not a wheeled vehicle could move until the bridge was repaired. The engineers were there but a truck containing some vital equipment was lost somewhere back down the line. The road became an immense logjam of vehicles, everything from tanks to the horse-drawn artillery, packed wheel to wheel and as immovable as if fixed in concrete.

When Peiper returned from General Engel's command post around 2:30 P.M., he was so angered by the imbecility of the whole mess that he ordered his own column, led now by himself, to move on by ruthlessly shouldering anything and everything that got in its way off the road. Horses, guns, trucks, all were shoved mercilessly into the ditches. But Peiper was moving.

When he got up to the railroad cutting, he examined it, found a place where it was slightly shallower than on the road, and led his column down the steep bank, across the tracks, and up the far side. By a little after dark he was leading his column up the international highway toward Losheim.

He reached Losheim around 7:30 P.M. Here he received a radio message from Division. General Priess, commander of *I SS Panzer Corps*, has said that when the *12th SS Panzer Division* failed to open their attack that day, and it was learned that the *9th Parachute Regiment* of the *3rd Parachute Division* had taken Lanzerath, Peiper was unleashed and ordered to take over the attack from Lanzerath. This was precisely what Peiper wanted to hear. Now he could *go!*

Colonel Otto Skorzeny had also had a frustrating day, his *150th Panzer Brigade* units meshed into *1st SS Panzer Division*. As the hours frittered away he saw the chances of success in their mission being drained off. As his units were caught in the immense logjam of snarled traffic, Skorzeny tried to get up forward to see what was causing the long delay. He had to walk most of six miles because of the indescribable mess of vehicles on the road. In a copse of woods near Losheim he found his Headquarters Company, the one perfectly Americanized company of his brigade. Skorzeny has said that he now decided, with the success of his most important mission fading, to send out jeep teams from this company. Some nine of these teams were sent on December 16, to infiltrate behind the American lines and begin to create chaos and confusion. Varyingly the teams were successful or not.

The German Side

One jeep team, led by the former commander of a frigate in the German merchant marine, was cruising around Malmédy about the same time Colonel Pergrin reached that place on December 17, and boasted that he had had a drink with a U.S. soldier in a café in the town. The captain reported back that Malmédy was occupied only by service units and that these service units were rapidly leaving town.

As we know another jeep team changed the road signs at the Mon Rigi crossroads the morning of December 17 and sent the 16th Regiment, 1st Infantry Division, around by Malmédy and delayed their arrival at Waimes.

But the most successful team was the one that was captured near Eupen on December 17. Three men of the team were captured and they talked before being shot as spies. They admitted they were members of a special force and that there were many of them, German soldiers in American uniforms, knowing the passwords, roving around at will behind the lines in American vehicles, charged with wrecking communications, sabotaging supply dumps, misdirecting traffic and generally creating havoc.

One of the prisoners really started the ball rolling for the amazing psychological success of the whole operation. He said Operation Greif had another primary objective besides sabotage, that the most important mission was the abduction, by Skorzeny himself, of General Eisenhower.

With Skorzeny's reputation, it was believable. Thus Operation Greif became Operation Grief as a period of suspicion, panic, confusion and much tightened security began. With typical GI ingenuity some way-out passwords were created and nobody escaped suspicion, from General Omar Bradley and Field Marshal Montgomery to any T/5 driving a truck. Unless a man could correctly identify "dem Bums," give the name of President Roosevelt's dog, tell who Betty Grable's husband was, he was suspect and likely to be hauled off for questioning.

General Eisenhower was a victim of the story, too. Such a

strict cordon of security was thrown around him that he was literally held a prisoner in his own headquarters for the best part of a week.

But all of this was still ahead as Skorzeny ordered his jeep teams to begin working their way behind the American lines, while the rest of his brigade frittered the hours away on December 16.

At Losheim, following the radio message from Division, Peiper headed toward Lanzerath.

Peiper was around thirty years old at this time. He was a slight man with slick straight dark hair. His face was lean, with strong jaws, a high-bridged nose with flared nostrils, and he had steady, well-set dark eyes. He had fine white teeth and a wide, engaging smile. He was highly intelligent, personally charming, literate and capable of courtesy and good manners. He was a brilliant tank tactician and he was also an ardent Nazi. He afforded himself the luxury of excellent cigars.

After the end of the war, Major Ken Hechler of the U.S. Military History Section interrogated Peiper. He found him arrogant, extremely proud of his regiment and of his division, and quick to make derogatory remarks concerning other units. Major Hechler also learned, by accident, that Peiper spoke English fluently. He heatedly interrupted the interpreter from time to time to correct his German translation. Peiper supplied the impeccable English.

Peiper understood the whole Nietzschean philosophy which underlay Nazism and was passionately dedicated to its dream. He had a full grasp of the dream — one Europe, under Germany. How ideal it would be if all of Europe were German. What a great culture that would create and what fine supermen, what a splendid race could be bred! He believed in the "higher" type of man who would be bold and vigorous, cruel if necessary, and powerful — a man of the ruler caste, a superman, capable of being Nietzsche's "lord of the earth." That the dream would wipe out whole races of people was unimportant. They had the

The German Side

slave mentality and needed to be exterminated anyway. Pity for them, and mercy, was a weakness. The correct words were invincible will, power, daring, ruthlessness. And all the bloody means were fully justified by the beautiful Nazi dream. One Europe — under Germany.

Peiper had been Himmler's adjutant, perfectly willing to see six million Jews exterminated. He acquiesced in and apparently was perfectly willing to implement all the inhumanity of the concentration camps. It was not pretty but it was necessary.

As the commander of a tank battalion on the Russian front he had served daringly and with enough savagery that a legend had grown up around him. His outfit in Russia had become known as the Blowtorch Battalion because allegedly it burned two villages and totally wiped out all the inhabitants. He was a commander after Hitler's heart. He let nothing stand in his way. Hitler had been excited by Peiper's exploits and had praised him and furthered the Peiper legend throughout all Germany until the man was a full hero. Peiper wore the Death's Head insignia on his military cap with pride.

This was the man who was given the most important role in the entire offensive — to spearhead the advance of the *Liebstandarte Division* — Hitler's own division. The job and the man fitted together like ham and eggs.

As Peiper swung his column onto the road to Lanzerath he shortly found it to be a death trap of mines. The column was rolling along, using headlights for speed, which in themselves drew antitank fire, when the second or third tank behind the lead suddenly hit a mine and burst into flames. Then a following half-track hit a mine and exploded. The one behind it hit another mine and lost its tracks. Peiper halted. He asked one of his officers where the mine detectors were. Back with the engineers, he was told. But Peiper could not wait for them to come up. He gave the order to proceed and clear the road by rolling over the mines.

It was an order fraught with terror for his men. Ten vehicles could safely pass a buried mine, the eleventh might veer perhaps only a few inches and blow up. By the time the column had passed through the mined area Peiper had lost five tanks and five half-tracks.

The task force reached Lanzerath about 11:00 P.M. It was a hamlet of twenty-three houses, a church and a grubby little hotel, surrounded on all sides by woods, the forest of Büllingen.* Peiper rolled up in front of the small hotel and strode in looking for the commanding officer of the paratroop regiment supposed to be waiting for him here. He found him. The commander of the *9th Parachute Regiment* was a Luftwaffe colonel, a staff officer with no ground experience. He had his headquarters in the dingy café of the little hotel. Both German and American soldiers were sprawled about, many of them asleep. Fourteen of the American prisoners were from the 99th Division's I & R platoon. This platoon, it will be recalled, was half of the link between General Gerow's V Corps and General Middleton's VIII Corps, at the seam near Lanzerath between the two. The other half was a section of guns from Company A, 820th Tank Destroyer Battalion, attached to the 14th Cavalry Group.

Early in the fighting that day the detachment from the 820th had pulled out, but the men of the 99th's I & R platoon had fought all day from their well dug-in positions and had held off attack after attack of the *1st Battalion, 9th Parachute Regiment*.

---

* A vivid description of this entire episode is given in John S. D. Eisenhower, *The Bitter Woods* (New York: G. P. Putnam's Sons, 1969), pp. 217–220.

On February 3, 1945, after the Germans had been pushed back beyond their original line, Company A, 291st Engineers, arrived in Lanzerath to take up quarters. The author's husband, Henry E. Giles, was the weapons sergeant of 2nd platoon, Company A. He remembers Lanzerath well, because he had a narrow personal escape from death by artillery fire the night of February 3. Second platoon stayed in the large cellar of a big building in the hamlet. It may have been this grubby hotel in which Peiper's famous confrontation with the 9th Parachute Regiment commander took place. Sergeant Giles described the village as dank, dismal and dreary, in the midst of big pine woods which all the men of the 291st had come to loathe. He put it succinctly, "It was god-awful." Company A stayed in the village until February 8, when they crossed the bridge they had built themselves into Germany.

The German Side

Not until they were out of ammunition did their leader disperse them, every man for himself. He and his runner, both wounded, stayed together and were captured along with the other men of one squad. He was Lieutenant Lyle C. Bouck.

Peiper was already in a foul mood, from the long day's frittering away of time, from the need to sacrifice his men and vehicles on the mined road, and now he saw nothing here but a bunch of men sprawled out asleep. Cursing, he asked the officer what was going on. The colonel actually ranked Peiper but he was Luftwaffe while Peiper was SS and a Hitler favorite. He could be arrogant with officers higher than colonels if he chose. The colonel told him the woods were heavily fortified and that scattered fire from prepared pillboxes along the road was holding up his advance. He told Peiper it was impossible to advance without heavy artillery.

Pressing the colonel, Peiper learned that he had not personally made a reconnaissance, nor had his battalion commander, nor had the captain who reported the American strength. The word of a handful of men had been accepted. Peiper grew furious. Icily and contemptuously he cussed out the paratroopers and ordered the colonel to give him one of his battalions. He would lead his own breakthrough. He barked out an order which sent a probing force of tanks and infantrymen toward Buchholz. These troops overwhelmed the 99th Infantry's forces at Buchholz — two platoons of Company K, 3rd Battalion, 394th Regiment — without difficulty, between midnight and 1:00 A.M.

In the café, Peiper pinned a map to the wall with bayonets and studied it. His route lay through Buchholz to Honsfeld.

He held a conference with his officers at 1:00 A.M. (December 17) and organized his attack as follows: Two Panther tanks to lead the column as the point, followed by a series of armored half-tracks and a mixture of Panthers and Mark IVs. The battalion of paratroopers would march alongside for flank protection, with one company riding the decks of the tanks. The balance of the regiment would hang on to his tail and reach their destination along the northern shoulder. So. The hot words ceased and Peiper set about deploying his troops. His attack order was for 4:00 A.M.

At the same time Peiper was in Lanzerath, von der Heydte's brigade of paratroopers finally took off from the Paderborn and Lippspringe aerodromes. That afternoon of December 16, following the cancellation of the drop the night before, von der Heydte was telephoned by General Sepp Dietrich and told that the offensive was not going well and that the Americans were trying to reinforce the northern shoulder. The drop would therefore be made that night, in the zone of the original directive, the Baraque Michel crossroads north of Malmédy. Von der Heydte was told that if he could not wholly stop the concentration of American troops, his mission would be to hinder them as much as possible.

On this night the trucks found enough gas and the brigade was shortly in the air. There was a very strong head wind and the flight was rough. There was also a considerable concentration of antiaircraft fire when they flew over the front. Von der Heydte saw several of the planes go plummeting down.

At the jump zone, von der Heydte, who had to jump with a broken arm still in a splint, watched the parachutes descending and realized there were far too few of them. Not more than one fourth of his men were dropping. Where were the other planes? What had happened to his men? It would be a long time before he would learn the answer. Roughly some 300 men out of 1200 rendezvoused with him in the drop area and von der Heydte felt that his mission had ended in total failure.

Peiper's column left Lanzerath and rolled through Buchholz between 4:30 and 5:00 A.M. They found the village empty.

The German Side

Only one man of Company K had escaped being engulfed earlier. The radio operator had hidden in a cellar. Now, as Peiper's column rolled through the radio operator observed, counted the tanks and half-tracks, estimated the infantry and reported it all to 99th Infantry Division headquarters at Butgenbach. It was a report of incalculable value.

As Peiper moved out of Buchholz onto the Honsfeld road, he found it full of retreating American vehicles. Fine. He simply held up his column until there was a gap, then he slid his leading tanks into the gap and he calmly advanced merged into the American vehicles. He denies that a man with a flashlight walked ahead of his point guiding the column. He has said that the paratroopers walking beside each tank used white handkerchiefs to guide the tanks.

The column entered Honsfeld between 6:00 and 7:00 A.M. The big Panthers prowled up the streets, the paratroopers jumped off their decks and ran quickly into the buildings, rounding up GIs right and left. And it was swiftly done. Caught by surprise, there was little resistance.

Among the units overrun was the 14th Cavalry Group's Troop A, 32nd Squadron, which had moved into Honsfeld only the night before. Lieutenant Bob Reppa had set up his command post in a house in the edge of the town. This was the first house entered as Peiper himself rolled up in his own command tank, a Tiger Royal. When Reppa and his men were flushed out, Peiper took it over for his own use as he sent out probing units, waited for reports, waited for the town to be subdued and made further plans.

Honsfeld was a rest area for the 394th Regiment of the 99th Infantry Division and was well behind the lines. Nobody at all was expecting the enemy. There was only a very thin provisional defense. In the darkness, in the immense and shocking surprise, the Germans had it all their own way. Americans fled, some escaped, some were captured, and many were killed. Peiper has said they took much booty here — fifty reconnaissance vehicles, including half-tracks, about eighty 2½-ton trucks and fifteen or sixteen antitank guns.

Peiper was running low on gasoline. He has said they used up as much gasoline in twenty-five kilometers as they would normally have used in fifty on account of the mountainous terrain of the Eifel. Knowing as he did that there was a big fuel depot at Büllingen, he determined to refuel there. He flung one company of paratrooper-infantry forward immediately, with two platoons of Mark IV tanks, to overrun Büllingen.

He sent a reconnaissance probe toward Heppenbach and learned that the road in that direction was impassable for his tanks. It had frozen and thawed, frozen and thawed until it was mushy with mud.* The last thing Peiper wanted was to get mired down. He was now ready to make his dash westward. He has said he could tell from the noise off to his right that the *12th SS Panzer Division* was not making very good progress. He therefore determined to make use of their road briefly and to go to Büllingen.

But it is also likely that here in Honsfeld Peiper learned for the first time that the 49th AAA Brigade had its headquarters in Ligneuville. Honsfeld lay in "buzz bomb alley," the belt in which the 49th had positioned its antiaircraft guns to shoot down the buzz bombs. A number of prisoners were taken at Honsfeld. Peiper has said he learned of the 49th's headquarters through an officer taken prisoner. It was probably here in Honsfeld.

At any rate, this was a big and important headquarters numbering over 400 men. Peiper has said he was eager to capture it. His route from Honsfeld to Amblève and Ligneuville by way of Heppenbach was closed to him, but if he proceeded to Büllingen, he could not only refuel but he could pick up the main

---

* MS. A-877, Gruppenfuehrer Hermann Priess, "The Commitment of *1 SS Panzer* Corps During the Ardennes Offensive, December-January, 1944–45" (March 1946), p. 29.

primary road from Büllingen to St. Vith, take Amblève as he was supposed to do, then swing on up to Ligneuville.

At this time it is also likely that he decided to divide his column and send one arm around north of Ligneuville, while he came up from the south, thus completing a double envelopment of the 49th AAA Brigade.

At about dawn a squadron of American planes summoned by 99th Infantry to come to the assistance of their beleaguered units at Losheimergraben circled over Honsfeld, observed the battle going on there and lent a hand diving, bombing, strafing, wheeling and harassing. Peiper's antiaircraft guns formed up and opened fire on them and several planes were shot down.

These were the planes Lieutenant Frank Rhea, of Company B, 291st, saw from the intersection near Butgenbach, as they circled and dived, swooped and strafed and bombed. They were also the planes Corporal Al Schommer, Company A's radio operator, saw from the window of their command post in Amblève and which caused him, when he saw them being shot down, to alert 1/Sergeant William H. Smith. This early on the morning of December 17, therefore, Peiper's movements are beginning to affect the moves and actions of the 291st.

Peiper did not linger long in Honsfeld. He released the *9th Parachute Regiment* here and left the mopping up of the town to them. He kept command of only one battalion which, for the most part, would ride his tanks all the way with him.

In Honsfeld, however, Peiper's outfit set a pattern they were to follow from now on in disposing of their prisoners. Nineteen American soldiers who had surrendered and been disarmed were shot down in cold blood. Hitler's order that the offensive must be waged ruthlessly and without pity suited the Death's Head kampfgruppe perfectly.

And so Peiper now headed for Büllingen some three kilometers northwest. He has said that about one kilometer out of Honsfeld they ran into small-arms fire from some American unit which delayed them about half an hour. This, he said, gave his rear vehicles time to catch up.

About one o'clock that morning of December 17, the 254th Engineer Combat Battalion had been attached to the 99th Infantry Division and ordered to Büllingen to prepare positions covering the entrance to the village from the east and the south. Twice in the predawn hours they had beaten back attacks by the infantry paratroopers of *9th Parachute Regiment* sent ahead by Peiper.

When Peiper's advance tanks hove into view at Büllingen, shortly after 7:00 A.M. (almost an hour before daylight), the engineers fell back into the shelter of buildings in the west end of the village and did what they could to hold off the tanks. Around this same time the 99th's headquarters nearby in Butgenbach moved out, the word having reached them that enemy tanks were in Büllingen.

Around 8:00 A.M. the engineers were ordered to fall back to higher ground, about 1000 yards back on the road which led to Butgenbach. Only two companies were intact enough to follow orders. They retreated to the position directed and were joined by a hurriedly assembled group of cooks, clerks, drivers and mechanics from 99th Division's headquarters, some antiaircraft artillery units in the vicinity and four guns from the 612th Tank Destroyer Battalion. Here these units joined forces and dug in.

This defense line was somewhere in the neighborhood of the 629th Engineer Light Equipment Company's headquarters. A platoon of Mark IV tanks, which had helped overrun Büllingen, probed up this road and these were the tanks which the surprised engineers saw prowling about their command post just before daylight. They were fired on by the guns of the 612th Tank Destroyer Battalion and several tanks were disabled. The rest of the Mark IVs retreated.

The German Side

As Peiper's main column moved up toward Büllingen from Honsfeld, about 8:30 A.M. his tankers saw a small airfield, off to the left of the road, near the village of Morschheck. This field was used by liaison and observation planes. Planes were on the field, but taken by surprise few of them could get off the ground. Peiper has said a defense was attempted, with machine guns, but the field was soon overrun. He has said that 12 planes were destroyed. A unit of the battalion of armored infantry with Peiper was sent to finish off the American contingent and take the booty. Much of it consisted of clothing, very welcome to the Germans, and many of them blossomed out in flight suits, jackets, gloves and scarves belonging to American airmen. One piece of clothing taken as booty may have gone to Major Josef Diefenthal himself. He was later seen wearing a light tan leather jacket which much resembled the pale beige jackets American pilots wore. It stood out in great contrast to the black leather jackets worn by the other German officers.

Peiper was in command of Büllingen and his vehicles had begun refueling before 9:00 A.M. The prisoners taken were forced to do the refueling. Peiper has said he captured 200,000 liters (50,000 gallons) of gasoline at Büllingen and used 50 prisoners to fill all of his tanks. He has said that about 9:30 A.M. the American artillery up around Butgenbach laid a heavy barrage on the town causing some casualties among his troops. This artillery fire came from the guns of the 26th Infantry Regiment now reaching Butgenbach. Peiper believed that civilians at Büllingen observed for the artillery because of its accuracy.

The advance elements of Peiper's kampfgruppe began to wheel out of Büllingen between 9:30 and 10:00 A.M. They took the main Büllingen–St. Vith road, which led down through Amblève. The little defense line dug in on the road between Büllingen and Butgenbach were much astonished to see the German column moving off toward the southwest. They had expected an all-out attack on their own position. They attributed the German movement to the intervention of some friendly fighter-bombers who suddenly appeared and began to strafe and bomb the German column. They were a squadron of the 366th Fighter Group, one of two which had been called into the area earlier by the 99th Infantry Division. The squadron claimed a kill of some 30 tanks and armored vehicles but it is doubtful if this is true. Peiper scattered his vehicles into the nearby woods. He has said he lost one Tiger Royal tank. He was able to move on quickly with little loss of time when some ME-109s dropped out of the sky and sent the U.S. squadron away.

Behind Peiper, at Büllingen, the usefulness of the prisoners was now over and a few were loaded into vehicles to be taken along and questioned. The rest, fifty men who had surrendered and were disarmed, were shot. One civilian was also killed.

Now, remember that this same morning, around 8:30 or a little later, Corporal Al Schommer, the radio operator on duty with Company A, 291st Engineers, in Amblève, went to the window, pulled back the blackout curtain and saw American planes being hit by enemy flak in the Honsfeld-Büllingen area. That he alerted 1/Sergeant William H. Smith, who decided a reconnaissance should be made and made it personally. Which road Sergeant Smith took toward Büllingen is not precisely known, but it will be remembered that when he returned to Amblève, in haste and what for Smith was great excitement, around 10:30, he reported having seen a German armored column headed straight for Amblève.

At the time Smith saw the column, Peiper's kampfgruppe was probably just heading down the Büllingen–St. Vith road. We know that Captain Gamble began preparations immediately to leave Amblève.

About three miles out of Büllingen a road to Heppenbach branched off the Büllingen–St. Vith highway. Here Peiper divided his column. He led one contingent down this road through Heppenbach to Amblève, along his assigned route. He

Colonel David E. Pergrin, Commander, 291st Engineer Combat Battalion

291st Engineer Combat Battalion Officers, photographed in England, June 1944

1st row, l. to r.: Capt. William L. McKinsey, Warrant Officer Robert D. Bryant, Warrant Officer John K. Brenna, Warrant Officer Coye R. Self, Capt. Walter A. Kaplita, Lt. Martin D. Tintari, Capt. James H. Gamble, Capt. John T. Conlin

2nd row: Capt. Max Schmidt, Lt. Thomas F. Stack, Lt. Leroy H. Joehnck, Lt. Albert W. Walters, Lt. Frank R. Hayes, Lt. Alvin Edelstein, unidentified, Lt. Frank W. Rhea

3rd row: Capt. Edward R. Lampp, Lt. Thurston K. Lowrie, Capt. James K. Walton, Capt. Lloyd B. Sheetz, Lt. Donald J. Gerrity, Lt. Archibald L. Taylor, Lt. Warren R. Rombaugh, Capt. Lawrence R. Moyer, Lt. Wade L. Colbeck, Lt. Donald T. Davis, Lt. John T. Perkins

Right above: Company B men and their wood-burning washing machine

Right below: Company C sawmill at Trois Ponts

Lt. Ralph W. McCarty, Capt. Frank W. Rhea, Lt. W. L. Colbeck, all of Company B

Company B sawmill at Stavelot

Col. David E. Pergrin, 1/Sgt. William H. Smith, Company A. The man on the right is not identified

Mined trees on Highway N-32, Malmédy, just below the command post

Left: Oberst (Waffen-SS) Jochen Peiper at Kaiserbaracke crossroads, December 17, 1944. With Peiper is the driver of his command car and a Nazi lieutenant. Captured German photograph. *Above:* Peiper, on right, and one of his SS officers walking along the road at Kaiserbaracke crossroads, the same day. Note that Peiper still has the cigar that was clenched in his teeth
U.S. Army Photographs

EDITOR'S NOTE FOR THE 2019 EDITION: Subsequent research with additional photographs has established that the attribution in these photographs from the U. S. Army Photographs is not correct. The soldiers in these photographs were part of Peiper's rear guard. See Donald M. Goldstein, *Nuts! The Battle of the Bulge: The Story and Photographs* (Washington: Brassey's, 1994) pp. 65-68.

Pvt. Bernard Koenig and T/5 Burnie Hebert in Malmédy. A few days later Hebert's leg was shot off by an 88-mm. shell

Sgt. R. C. Billington

German tank destroyer which collapsed the Petit Spai bridge on December 21, 1944. Company A treadway bridge beyond, Company A men on bank

Company A building a timber trestle bridge in Luxembourg

Company B men at work in sawmill in Stavelot

Company B maintaining Highway N-28 between Eupen and Malmédy

Gas dump north of Stavelot on old Francorchamps road

The German Side

sent another section of his kampfgruppe along secondary roads through Moderscheid, Schoppen, Ondenval, Thirimont, to enter Ligneuville from the north.

Since most of the tanks known later to have been at Baugnez, near Malmédy, were Mark IVs with a sprinkling of Panthers mixed in, it appears that Peiper took with him most of his Panthers and sent his Mark IVs around north of Ligneuville under the command of Major Poetschke, the commander of *1st SS Panzer Regiment*. Along with Poetschke he also sent Major Josef Diefenthal and his *3rd Battalion* of the *2nd SS Panzer Grenadier Regiment* (armored infantry) and their half-tracks and self-propelled assault guns. The number of armored vehicles seen by witnesses at Baugnez, and counted by some of them, would indicate that only about half of Peiper's tanks went by that route.

Peiper and his section moved through Heppenbach and were approaching Amblève around 12:00 noon. We know that Company A of the 291st Engineers began to receive artillery fire in their area at that hour. Since no other enemy unit with tanks or artillery was in the vicinity, this shelling had to come from Peiper's tanks. Elements of *3rd Parachute Division* were moving up the alley between Lanzerath and Amblève but at this time they were just overwhelming Holzheim. The southern march group of *1st SS Panzer Division*, the *1st SS Panzer Grenadier Regiment* and the reconnaissance battalion had been much delayed because of mines in the vicinity of Manderfeld and were at this time held up by heavy traffic on the roads near Andler. This group would not reach the Wallerode-Born-Recht area until after midnight, when they would run into elements of the 7th Armored Division near Recht and be stopped cold in their advance.

We know that when Amblève started getting shells, T/4 Jeff Elliott fled into the command post and grabbed a pair of binoculars and peered toward Meyrode where he saw "three tanks, several armored cars and a bunch of infantry." These were a probing unit moving ahead of Peiper's column, the infantrymen being 3rd *Parachute* troops riding the decks of the tanks.

We know that Captain Gamble led Company A out of Amblève at about 12:20 P.M. on December 17, under artillery fire, and that within twenty to thirty minutes Amblève was overrun by Peiper's troops.

It will be remembered that Lieutenant Arch Taylor and his 3rd platoon of Company A moved through Deidenberg on their road to Born, Kaiserbaracke, Recht and Poteau around 1:30 P.M. And that the people of Deidenberg and Montenau believed he and his men had been wiped out by the German troops who entered the village from Amblève so close on his heels that they were entering as the last of his vehicles was leaving. These, too, were Peiper's men.

This was how close Company A came to being swallowed up, at Amblève and at Deidenberg, by Peiper's column. By a hair they got away.

Between 2:00 and 2:30, Peiper's elements were moving toward Born. And it is necessary now to reconstruct the movements of the 14th Cavalry Group for, not knowing of Peiper's diversion southward through Amblève, Deidenberg and Born, historians have always been mystified by the movements of this unit on this particular afternoon. No German units were known to be anywhere in the vicinity, and yet the elements of 14th Cavalry Group mysteriously retreated from their excellent positions in Born and Wallerode about 3:00 on this afternoon.

The 14th Cavalry Group had been attached to the 106th Infantry Division on December 11 when the 106th moved into the line. Colonel Mark Devine was the commander of the 14th and it consisted of two squadrons, the 18th and the 32nd Cavalry Reconnaissance Squadrons, and one company of the 820th Tank Destroyer Battalion was attached.

Since October 19, the 18th Cavalry Squadron had been occupying positions on a line Lanzerath-Krewinkel-Roth-Kobscheid across the Losheim Gap north of the Schnee Eifel. In small

The German Side

units, platoon size or less, the 18th Squadron occupied Kobscheid, Roth, Weckerath and Krewinkel. Sections of Company A, 820 TD Battalion, occupied three villages on the left, Berterath, Merlscheid and Lanzerath, where they tied into the 99th Infantry Division with a patrol to the 99th's I & R platoon across the town.

This squadron had been attached to 2nd Infantry Division since October 19, and these positions occupied. When the 2nd was pulled out of the Schnee Eifel positions to make the attack toward the Urft-Roer dams, it was replaced by the 106th Infantry Division. And now Colonel Devine's entire 14th Cavalry Group was attached to the 106th.

Major General Walter M. Robertson, commander of the 2nd Infantry, had always been uneasy about that thin spread of cavalrymen across the Losheim Gap. In the first place, motorized cavalry was not meant to be put in set positions. The purpose of motorized cavalry was reconnaissance and mobility. The only guns they had were the machine guns mounted on their vehicles. In static positions, as they were now being used, all that could be expected of them was delaying action. They were not equipped to do anything more. General Robertson had therefore kept his reserve battalion directly behind the cavalry positions and he had worked out a defense plan which called for them to withdraw from their outpost villages to Manderfeld to form a defense line, at which time his infantry would take over with a counterattack.

Colonel Devine left his 18th Squadron and its attached tank destroyer company where they had been since October, in their outpost villages. His 32nd Squadron was in Vielsalm being refitted.

Neither General Alan W. Jones, commander of the 106th, with his headquarters in St. Vith, nor Colonel Devine, with his command post in Manderfeld, had had very much time to weigh their situations or to establish their relationship with each other before things got cracking on their front, hot and heavy.

Devine and his staff studied the defense plan they had inherited from 2nd Infantry and worked it out more fully, detailing specific roads to be used in a withdrawal and defense lines on which to fall back. Devine made several attempts to reach an understanding with General Jones concerning this defense plan, but there is no evidence that 2nd Infantry's defense plan was accepted by General Jones and his staff. Devine finished his more detailed plan by the night of December 15, but there was no time to circulate it.

When the offensive opened at daybreak on December 16, Devine's little units got hit with elements of three German divisions, from two different German armies. On his right, in Roth and Kobscheid, his men were swallowed up very early by elements of Manteuffel's *Fifth Panzer Army*, his *18th Volksgrenadiers* attacking around the north end of the Schnee Eifel.

At Krewinkel his Troop C held out valiantly until ordered to withdraw against the *1st Panzer Grenadier Regiment*, which was spearheading the southern march group of the *Liebstandarte Division* of *Sixth Panzer Army*.

On his center and left, the sections of tank destroyers, Company A, 820th TD Battalion, were overrun by *3rd Parachute Division, Sixth Panzer Army*. The section stationed at Lanzerath, which formed the tie with 99th Infantry Division on the left, pulled out very early, without authorization. Thus not only was Devine's contact with the 99th lost, the 106th Division's contact was lost and the door through the middle, along this vulnerable seam, was wide open.

By 9:30 the morning of December 16, Colonel Devine realized he was in deep trouble and his executive officer telephoned General Jones for permission to move his 32nd Squadron up from Vielsalm. Unaware as yet of the enormous strength of the offensive, Jones gave permission only to alert the squadron, not to move it. Devine persisted and thirty minutes later he did receive permission to move the 32nd up. It arrived at his headquarters in Manderfeld around 11:00 A.M. Devine spread the men along a ridge line behind Manderfeld in accordance with

The German Side

his defense plan and sent one troop to Andler to guard the Our River bridge there. Troop A was sent to Holzheim to guard the Group's rear and left. This was all well planned and well executed.

Then Colonel Devine telephoned General Jones for the second phase of the defense plan, which called for a counterattack northward from the infantry. Right there the plan broke down. Apparently not alarmed at all by what was happening in the 14th Cavalry Group sector, but very much perturbed over what might be happening to his two regiments in the Schnee Eifel, Jones replied that no infantry counterattack could be made at this time. Not realizing the absolute impossibility of it, Devine closed the conversation by saying he hoped to organize a counterattack himself to restore his line.

But shortly Devine realized that his units in their outpost villages were being swallowed up and he ordered them, at 12:00 noon, to withdraw to Manderfeld. Only his Troop C could comply. They moved over from Krewinkel, Afst and Weckerath and reached Manderfeld by 12:40. As they left Krewinkel they saw German troops entering. This was the *1st SS Panzer Grenadier Regiment* who poured on through Wischeid toward Andler.

By early afternoon they were streaming past Manderfeld to the south and *3rd Parachute Division* men were pouring past to the north. In spite of this, Devine organized a counterattack with Troop C and some assault guns and at 2:00 P.M. Major J. L. Mayes led this unit in an effort to retake Lanzerath and reestablish contact with the 99th Infantry. Near Lanzerath it was beset on three sides by *3rd Parachute* troops with self-propelled guns and had to fall back.

At 4:00 P.M. therefore, Devine asked permission to withdraw from Manderfeld to a line Andler-Holzheim and received permission. By 5:00 P.M. the withdrawal was completed. Manderfeld was set afire in the attempt to destroy the Group's records.

The dispositions of Devine's units, then, were: Troops E and

C of the 18th were sent to Holzheim, where Troop A of the 32nd was already stationed. But at 6:30 the 18th's units pulled out, presumably on their own commander's orders, and joined him and the remainder of the 18th at Wereth, near Amblève. Troop A, Lieutenant Bob Reppa commanding, of the 32nd then moved over to Honsfeld and was swallowed up before daylight next morning by Peiper's column. Troop B of the 32nd, which had been posted at Andler to guard the Our River bridge, remained at Andler. Troops E and C of the 32nd and the squadron headquarters went to Heeresbach. Colonel Devine set up his command post at Meyrode, and then he went to St. Vith to confer with General Jones and receive further orders. He saw him briefly, Jones made no comment on the various movements of the Group and told him simply to wait there at headquarters. Devine waited.

At 9:30 P.M. there was a telephone call from 99th Infantry headquarters and Colonel Devine was asked to speak to them with regard to re-establishing contact with them. He agreed to make the attempt from Wereth.

Colonel Devine waited all night to see General Jones and get some kind of orders, some kind of agreement or understanding from him, some kind of support. At no time during the 16th or the night of the 16th did Devine receive any orders from his commanding officer.

Jones, of course, was deeply perturbed about his two regiments in the Schnee Eifel. From all accounts, he was a man who gave the appearance of calm, quiet efficiency, but it must be remembered that he was inexperienced and untried in combat command. He seems to have reacted sluggishly all day of the 16th, perhaps out of fear that this was purely a local attack and he did not want to push the panic button on it. When the first reports began to come into his VIII Corps headquarters at Bastogne, General Middleton had telephoned General Jones, telling him he could have General William Hoge's Combat Command B, 9th

The German Side

Armored, which was at Faymonville. Jones made no move to shift this strong unit of tanks to his own front, leaving them instead "attached in place" at Faymonville until the night of the 16th. Then, aware that his regiments in the Schnee Eifel were in serious trouble, he ordered Hoge south.

On this night of the 16th, General Jones was trying to get some kind of understanding with his own commander, General Middleton, about withdrawing these two regiments from their exposed positions. There seems to have been total misunderstanding between them. Perhaps a bad telephone connection can be blamed for the confusion, or perhaps it was simply army verbalese which did not make things clear. At any rate, General Middleton believed that Jones had understood he was to withdraw the regiments, and General Jones understood that he was *not* to withdraw them. The result was that between eight and nine thousand men remained in their positions on the Schnee Eifel and were slowly encircled by one German division, the *18th Volksgrenadiers*, which split into two sections to achieve the encirclement.

General Jones' fears for these regiments were increased by the fact that his own son, Lieutenant Alan W. Jones, Jr., was serving with one of them. Added to the tensions of the commander, therefore, were the personal and emotional involvement of the parent. It was a bad situation, and Jones seems to have almost totally ignored any danger to his position from the north and what was happening in the 14th Cavalry sector, and had his mind concentrated wholly on relieving his regiments. He seems to have become monolithic in this concentration and apparently was incapable of an appreciation of his total situation. He collapsed with a heart attack several days later and one wonders if he was not already a very sick man.

At any rate, Devine sat all night, never did get any further word with General Jones and returned to his command post around 8:00 the morning of December 17.

Although he did not know it, his Troop A, 32nd Squadron, had been scooped up by Peiper in Honsfeld, before daybreak, and his Troop B, same squadron, at Andler had been hit at dawn by Tiger Royal tanks of the *506th Panzer Battalion*, sent by *Sixth Panzer Army* to reinforce the *Liebstandarte*'s southern march group. After this brush, Troop B moved from Andler to Schönberg, nearer St. Vith, and Andler and its Our River bridge fell into enemy hands.

Shortly after Devine reached his command post in Meyrode, he had a report from the commander of the 18th Squadron, at Wereth, that his scouts had just seen German troops *north* of Wereth. This was about 10:30 A.M. These were probably *3rd Parachute* units, the *5th* and *8th* regiments, moving northward to take up their positions along the highway N-32 on the northern shoulder. At any rate, this meant that Devine's Holzheim-Andler line was cut and no longer tenable. Devine did not even try to get permission to withdraw now. On his own, therefore, he ordered a withdrawal to new positions. Those elements remaining of his 32nd Squadron he moved to Wallerode, about a mile and a quarter northeast of St. Vith, and the remnants of his 18th Squadron, some sixty-odd men, he moved to Born. The units took up their new positions by noon. Recall they were in position and were seen by Lieutenant Arch Taylor's men as they passed through Born between 1:30 and 2:00 P.M.

Devine then telephoned General Jones, from Born, and told him the positions he now occupied. He believed they would be final and he could now counterattack and try to restore contact with the 99th Infantry Division. He was told to stay where he was, and that a liaison officer was being sent.

But even as Devine was telephoning, Peiper's troops were moving into Amblève, only two and a half miles northeast of him in Born, and between 1:30 and 2:30 P.M. these troops were on the edge of Born itself.

Colonel Devine hurriedly ordered his units to back up to

The German Side

Recht. He had nothing in Born with which to fight tanks and armored infantry. He ordered the men of 18th Squadron to take a position in Recht itself, and he ordered the 32nd elements to take a back-up position astride the Recht-Poteau road on the Recht River. But these units could not reach Recht now — not from Born. Peiper's men were moving into Born.

Recall that there was an immense logjam of traffic in and around St. Vith. Devine's units had to sideslip down into this traffic because the only route open to them was through St. Vith. Devine's units inevitably got mixed up in all the traffic. Three recon teams of the 18th eventually reached Recht, but all the other units went on to Poteau and some of them passed on through Poteau. Devine set up his command post in Poteau, also.

Then he set out, around 5:00 P.M., with some of his staff officers for St. Vith to report once more. It was impossible for him to get to St. Vith on the road which led directly from Poteau. This road was clogged with 7th Armored vehicles moving over from Vielsalm to St. Vith, via Poteau. Devine therefore went by Recht and from there to a crossroads called Kaiserbaracke, where he would hit the main Malmédy–St. Vith highway and swing right.

At Kaiserbaracke, however, he ran smack into Peiper's column, still moving northward on this highway toward Ligneuville. Devine was fired on, of course, and his command car was wrecked. He and two of his officers escaped on foot. They made their way to St. Vith and at General Jones' headquarters Devine was heard with skepticism. It was now shortly after dark. Understandably Devine was excited, having just been shot at by German tanks and set afoot. To Jones and Brigadier General Bruce Clarke, commander of CCB, 7th Armored Division, who was with Jones at the time, he sounded hysterical. "We've got to run," he is reported to have said, "I was practically chased into this building by a Tiger tank . . ." *

---
* Eisenhower, John S. D., op cit., p. 229.

The two generals listened, but did not believe. There was *no* enemy north of St. Vith. The enemy was still east of St. Vith. And this colonel was simply hysterical. According to their position maps and their information there was no enemy north of St. Vith and there most certainly was no enemy armored column on the main Malmédy–St. Vith highway! Obviously the pressures on Colonel Devine had simply been too much for him. He was distraught and hysterical, was seeing ghosts and having hallucinations. There were no German tanks north of St. Vith. The two generals knew it. General Clarke reportedly said to Jones, "I suggest we send Colonel Devine back to Bastogne. Maybe he could give General Middleton a first-hand account of the conditions up here." *

Thus Colonel Devine, whose small outfit had been hit hardest of any outfit along the front, by elements of three German divisions, who had seen his command almost disappear from existence (their casualty loss was 48 percent), who had tried repeatedly to get orders, had tried to follow a defense plan, but who could not somehow ever penetrate General Jones' fixed gaze on his own regiments, was relieved of his command.

He returned to his own command post at Poteau, arriving there, according to the 14th Cavalry Group After Action Report, at 11:30 P.M. still on foot. His Executive Officer, Lieutenant Colonel Augustine Duggan, who had been with him in the skirmish at Kaiserbaracke, had not yet made his way back to the CP. Therefore, relieved of his command, Colonel Devine called in the commander of the 18th Squadron, Lieutenant Colonel Damon, and gave command of the remnants of the Group over to him. Colonel Devine then retired. At 2:00 in the morning, he was evacuated to Bastogne, through medical channels, as a nonbattle casualty.

Command of the 14th Cavalry Group, or what was left of it, changed hands several times but eventually 32nd Squadron was

* Ibid.

The German Side

absorbed into 18th Squadron and Lieutenant Colonel Damon was put in command of all.

But Colonel Devine was not hysterical and he had not been seeing ghosts. He had not had hallucinations. He had not disobeyed orders to stay in Born without good reason. Had he remained in Born, Peiper's men would have squashed him like a bug under their feet. But because Peiper's column turned north on the Malmédy–St. Vith highway, went to Ligneuville and Pont and did not ever appear on the St. Vith scene, their presence in that vicinity has not been known until now.

We have two photographs of Peiper himself taken at the Kaiserbaracke crossroads. Both are dated December 17, 1944, and both are captured German photographs. Both photographs are taken so as to show prominently the road signs at the crossroads. The photograph of Peiper studying his map and the road sign looks posed as if it were a deliberate intention to show his superiors the extent of his breakthrough. The officer leaning against the side of the command car is an SS lieutenant, probably Lieutenant Krenser, commander of the *2nd SS Panzer Company* of Panther tanks. Note that Peiper has a cigar clenched in his teeth.

In the second photograph, Peiper and the same lieutenant are walking north past the road signs, the command car having evidently pulled ahead, the cigar still in Peiper's mouth. A halftrack is halted precisely at the crossroads behind them. Obviously the column did not come from Born on the secondary road which enters at Kaiserbaracke, but came by another secondary road which entered perhaps three quarters of a mile farther south. Again the road signs are prominent. And only at Kaiserbaracke do the precise distances on the road signs — Malmédy 13 kilometers — St. Vith 8 kilometers — apply.

Historians have generally supposed that Peiper and his entire kampfgruppe followed the northern route around by Schoppen and Baugnez to Ligneuville. But at any point on this route Peiper would have been much further from St. Vith than eight kilometers. At Moderscheid he would have been 14 kilometers from St. Vith and 16.5 kilometers from Malmédy. At Schoppen he would have been 14.5 kilometers from Malmédy and 12.5 kilometers from St. Vith. At Thirimont he would have been 7 kilometers from Malmédy and around 15 kilometers from St. Vith. The location of these photographs, therefore, is definitely Kaiserbaracke. Furthermore, Kaiserbaracke was on Peiper's officially assigned route.*

It gives one chills to note how narrowly Combat Command R of the 7th Armored Division escaped colliding with Peiper's kampfgruppe that day, not once but twice. First, as they moved south through Malmédy and the Five Points crossroads they barely missed a collision with the northern wing of Peiper's column. Then as they proceeded down the Malmédy–St. Vith highway toward Vielsalm they barely cleared the Kaiserbaracke crossroads before Peiper appeared there.

Not until the driver of 7th Armored Division's chief of staff stumbled into CCR headquarters in Recht around 8:45 that night and reported that the officer, Colonel Church M. Matthews, had been killed near Pont in a collision with an armored column was it accepted by 7th Armored and General Jones that the enemy had indeed penetrated to their north.

*

* The first identification of Peiper as the officer in Photograph No. 1 which this author saw was made by Brigadier General S. L. A. Marshall in the *Reader's Digest Illustrated History of World War II*, published in 1969. It is on page 396. Following this, the identification of him in Photograph No. 2 is elementary. In fact, T/Sergeant John L. Scanlan identified Peiper in this photograph after its appearance in John Eisenhower's book, *The Bitter Woods*, also published in 1969.

The author obtained these photographs from the U.S. Army Photographic Section and they were examined for her by the U.S. Army Corps of Engineers Map and Photographic Department, Louisville, Ky. Under magnification and filter there is no doubt of the identification. Under magnification, also the small sign between the two highway signs reads, "253 Ord. MM." This is a U.S. military unit finder sign. The "Z" sign at the top of the road sign is a sector direction sign.

The German Side

At any rate, the northern elements of Peiper's column, which amounted to about his *1st Battalion*, mostly Mark IV tanks with two or three Panthers in the lead, elements of armored infantry with their half-tracks and self-propelled guns, and at least one company of engineers, had moved along on the northern route. At Moderscheid they had a small brush with a handful of Americans, and proceeded to Schoppen, Ondenval and on to Thirimont.

At Thirimont the road led straight ahead by another dirt track to Ligneuville. However, this was a soft dirt road. The 291st Engineers had kept a short byroad which swung north to the crossroads of Bagatelle in fairly good condition with grading and some rock on it. The column decided to swing north on this road, hit the hard-surface highway, N-32, turn left a short distance to the Baugnez crossroads, then head south again on the main Malmédy-St. Vith highway, N-23.

We know that it was along here, in the outskirts of Thirimont, that Lieutenant Taylor's platoon truck, going to Malmédy for gas around noon, was destroyed by the lead tanks of Peiper's column. And that it was as Peiper's column moved through Thirimont that Company B's reconnaissance patrol spied them and counted 68 tanks and half-tracks in the column before racing back to report to Colonel Pergrin in Malmédy.

As the column swung northward from Thirimont, only a rolling field about a mile wide at its base and narrowing to a third of a mile near Bagatelle lay between them and the main road, N-23. It was two miles from Thirimont to Bagatelle.

As the advance rolled along that short distance from Thirimont to Bagatelle, about halfway up they topped a rise of land and had a panoramic view spread before them. And across the rolling field, which was on their left, they saw a small convoy of American vehicles going south on the road they themselves were headed for. The lead tanks in the German column opened fire with their big 75-mm. guns.

*

In Malmédy the guns were heard in Colonel Pergrin's command post and after listening a few moments Colonel Pergrin said, "That little FOB outfit has run smack into that German column."

And Battery B, 285th Field Artillery Observation Battalion, led by Lieutenant Virgil T. Lary in his jeep, had indeed run smack into that German column.

PART III
Confrontation on the Amblève

9

WHEN THE TRUCKS carrying the 140 men of Battery B, 285th Field Artillery Observation Battalion, rolled away from Colonel Pergrin's command post in Malmédy around 12:30 P.M. on Sunday, December 17, 1944, they were under the shadow of dark wings. Some of the men in the trucks had about thirty minutes to live. Most of them had less than two hours.

The little convoy moved slowly out the street. Less than a mile from Pergrin's CP they went under the railroad overpass, bent sharply right and very shortly passed Lieutenant Colbeck's B Company roadblock. A little beyond the roadblock they slowly ground up a long steep hill, then descended to the crossroads the GIs in Malmédy called Five Points.

Exactly at the crossroads, to their left, was the farm and home of Henri Lejoly. Lejoly was entirely German in all of his feelings and loyalties and he had never made any secret of it.*

Diagonally across from Lejoly's house, but below the crossroads, was the café home of Madame Adèle Bodarwé.† Madame Bodarwé's sympathies are not precisely known. Her son, Louis, was serving in the German army at that time. He lives today at

---

* Toland, John, *Battle: The Story of the Bulge* (New York: Random House, 1959), pp. 60 ff. Also Mulligan, Hugh, AP News story, December 14, 1969, "The Bulge: Memories of '44's Blackest Day."

† Identification and positions marked on his own old Army map, GSGS 4141 of Malmédy and its environs, by Lieutenant W. L. Colbeck for the author.

the crossroads and he maintains that his mother was a loyal Belgian.

Two MPs from the 518th Military Police detachment in Malmédy had been on duty at Five Points that day. The military police headquarters in Malmédy had been alerted that elements of 7th Armored Division had been routed down this road. The first segment would be Combat Command R. The second segment would be the division's artillery. Slotted between them in a very tight fit was Battery B, being sent with the artillery to observe.

The two MPs had smoothly handled Combat Command R, but shortly after noon the last vehicles of this segment cleared the intersection. It is not known whether the MPs knew that Battery B was spotted between the two big segments. They did know that the next big segment would be the artillery and that it would probably be an hour before they came along. If they knew that Battery B was assigned between the two segments they evidently decided one MP could handle it, for when the last vehicle of CCR cleared the intersection the two men decided that this was a good time for one of them to go into Malmédy and eat his lunch. One did. The MP who remained on duty was Pfc. Homer Ford.

The lead vehicle of Battery B's first serial arrived at the intersection around 12:45 P.M. It was the jeep in which the 7th Armored captain and Lieutenant Virgil Lary rode. It was waved on to its proper road by Pfc. Ford.

A bulldozer was dawdling down the road some distance ahead of them as Lary's driver turned the jeep southward on N-23. It would have been a piece of luck too good to be true if this had been a 291st dozer, especially if it had been the 291st famous operator, Red Ball Renson. Every man in the 291st knew a good story about Renson, who undoubtedly was the sloppiest GI in the entire United States Army. The stories ranged from their crossing to England when Renson got tired of climbing five

Confrontation on the Amblève

decks with full field pack and all gear every time there was a submarine alert and just dumped everything he owned overboard, to inspections when Renson had to be put as far back as possible to escape attention, to a fantastic fifty-mile nonstop drive he made across France one time. Nobody ever made a soldier out of Renson. He remained an individual to the bitter end. But this was not a 291st bulldozer and Red Ball Renson was at that very time manning a machine gun on Lieutenant Phillip Lassen's roadblock of mechanics and drivers on the street below the command post.

As the little convoy made its turn on to N-23, Pfc. Homer Ford kept the vehicles moving smoothly. The last vehicle, the ambulance belonging to 26th Infantry Regiment, halted a moment and asked for directions to Waimes. Ford gave them and thumbed the driver and his companion due east.

This finished Ford's duties for the moment. He thought he might as well go into Madame Bodarwé's café and take shelter out of the cold until the next segment of 7th Armored arrived. Madame Bodarwé already had one visitor. At some time during the passage of all the vehicles Henri Lejoly had walked across the road from his home to the Bodarwé café. Undoubtedly the two discussed the meaning of this big movement of American armored vehicles, and it is at least within the realm of possibility that Lejoly had some word of the German advance. Recollect that the Skorzeny jeep team commanded by the merchant marine captain had cruised at will around Malmédy on this morning. He certainly had some contacts, for somebody willingly told him about the 291st roadblocks, describing them as manned by six or eight men, consisting mostly of trees mined with TNT, a few land mines and several machine guns. But it can never be known precisely how much Lejoly knew, nor what he and Madame Bodarwé discussed together as they watched the movement of American vehicles.

The MP turned to walk the short distance to the café. Ford

had taken perhaps half a dozen steps when suddenly there came the boom and crump of a cannon, followed immediately by more heavy gun explosions. He swung swiftly around and to his horror saw that Battery B, some three hundred yards down the road now, was being shelled. He saw a German armored column, across the open field, coming north on a secondary road. Almost paralyzed by astonishment and consternation he saw German infantry dismount from the decks of the tanks and pour across the field, their machine pistols and rifles crackling. He saw the bulldozer take off as if it had suddenly sprouted wings.

In front of his unbelieving eyes Ford also watched the disintegration of the small convoy as trucks slewed across the road, piled into each other, slid askew into the ditches on both sides of the road. He watched men pile out of the trucks, taking what shelter they could find. He stood stock-still watching this, in a paralysis of amazement and disbelief. What in the *hell* were German tanks doing this far behind the lines!

Then Ford saw several men of the Battery running up the road toward him and he came to life. He beckoned them furiously, waving them on to hurry, hurry, and he led them around behind Madame Bodarwé's café.

When Madame Bodarwé and Henri Lejoly heard the firing they had come out of the café and were at this time standing on the edge of road watching.*

As Ford and the three or four men of Battery B with him hid behind the café, Ford watched, anxiously and observantly, as the skirmish continued. He saw the tanks rumble past the crossroads and make room for themselves by shoving the Battery's vehicles off the road, raking them with machine-gun fire until many burst into flames. He saw the men of Battery B, like insects in the ditch, occasionally become frantic enough to try to escape,

* Eisenhower, John S. D., *The Bitter Woods* (New York: G. P. Putnam's Sons, 1969), pp. 237, 260.

Confrontation on the Amblève

mowed down as they tried to flee in the woods. More German infantry poured across the field and down the road joining the skirmish. Other armored vehicles of the column passed the café and completed the encirclement of the little convoy.

Then a half-track rolled up, an officer in a light tan leather jacket got out and the firing died off. He seemed to be giving orders. There were a few more pops of rifle fire, a few more bursts from the machine guns, then Ford saw the men of the Battery start climbing out of the ditch beside the road with their hands up. The little outfit was surrendering. Ford watched as they threw down their rifles, watched as the Germans collected the guns. He watched as the Germans searched the prisoners for additional weapons, saw them poking and prodding, rifling through the men's pockets, shoving and pushing them onto the shoulder of the road. The Germans were in great good humor, laughing loudly among themselves.

Ford noticed that they were especially happy with the gloves they took from the prisoners, drawing them on their hands with pleasure, showing them to each other. He thought it strange that these Germans, who had the best guns ever made and the best tanks ever made, should have no gloves. And he watched as the Germans lit up and puffed with enjoyment on the American cigarettes taken from the prisoners.

Then the officer in the light tan leather jacket walked up the road, got into a half-track, and shortly the German armored column began to move again, headed south down N–23. The officer in the light tan leather jacket was, of course, Major Diefenthal.

A command car had now driven up with another officer in it and he took over as the column got moving. The Germans have said he was Major Poetschke, the commander of the tank battalion.[*] Whether it was Poetschke or not, he made a useful scape-

---

[*] Gallagher, Richard T., *The Malmédy Massacre* (New York: Paperback Library, 1964), pp. 103, 116.

goat in the Malmédy Trial later, because he was killed in the spring of 1945 on the Austrian front and he could not deny giving the gruesome order later.

Ford now saw that the line of prisoners was moving up the road toward the intersection, and all at once he did not feel very safe behind Madame Bodarwé's café. He looked about for a better hiding place. There was an outbuilding not far away. He told the handful of men with him they had better get inside that barn, out of sight. The Germans would find them where they were.

It was only a short distance to the outbuilding but it was across an open stretch of ground. Ford led the way and the men followed, sprinting across the open stretch. They hid inside but they could still see what was occuring down on the road.

The Germans brought the line of prisoners on up to an open field just below the café and crossroads. Here they herded them into the field and made them line up, shoulder to shoulder, very closely, in rows. There were eight rows. The men appeared to be taking their capture quietly. There was no confusion, no trouble of any kind. They stood quietly in the field, hands in the air. Ford could see why. There were many Germans, all of them with guns. There was only a handful of Americans, all without guns. It would have been suicide to make trouble.

Suddenly, as Ford watched the prisoners so intently, eight or ten Germans swept around the café and converged on the barn. He swore and told the men to be quiet. "Maybe they won't find us."

But the Germans surrounded the building and shouted for them to come out, threatening to burn the building if they did not. Ford said to the other men, "Well, I guess they saw us run in here."

Perhaps. Or perhaps Henri Lejoly had given them away. At any rate, it was their turn now. They came out, hands up, and threw their weapons down. They were all searched immedi-

Confrontation on the Amblève

ately. Ford wore an excellent pair of gloves which were taken, and his pockets were rifled of all his possessions, wallet, loose coins, wristwatch, cigarettes and cigarette lighter. The other men were also thoroughly searched.

They were then prodded into the field along with the other prisoners. It was a dark, gloomy, overcast day, the cold was raw and penetrating, and the men in the field were cold and shivery. The field was brown with dead grass and weeds and it was slushy and boggy underfoot. Old patches of snow lay banked here and there. As the men huddled closely in their rows they noticed that other prisoners were being herded in with them, men whom Battery B did not know. They spoke briefly with them and learned that they had all been captured earlier in the day. There were around twenty of them, among them five MPs, overrun in their positions as the German column advanced, a mess sergeant who happened to bump into the column near Schoppen, a staff sergeant and a handful of engineers who had been taken at Büllingen.

Among the last prisoners herded in with them were the two medical corpsmen who had been in the ambulance belonging to the 26th Infantry Regiment, Samuel Dobyns and Roy Anderson. They had bumped smack into the German column between Five Points and the next little crossroads, Bagatelle, only a third of a mile away. They had been run into the ditch and captured, and now they, too, were brought into the field to join the rows of prisoners. Their ambulance had been burned.

The captured men knew who their captors were. One of the tankers had laughed at them and said, in good English, *"First SS Panzer Division* welcomes you to Belgium, gentlemen." And they were all a little uneasy because these were SS troops. Also the tankers had worn the Death's Head insignia on their caps.

The men stood in the field waiting, wondering what the long delay was about. Most of them believed they were being kept waiting in this field until trucks could be brought to transport them to some POW camp. "What a hell of a way to spend Christmas," one of them said.

They watched, uneasily, as a German officer stopped one of the passing self-propelled weapons with an 88 mounted on it, and the half-track maneuvered around trying to bring the big gun to bear on them. The gun would not depress far enough. The officer waved it on, but it got stuck in the soft mud of the road shoulder and caused a minor traffic jam as the following vehicles had to veer around it. Horns beeped and men yelled lusty oaths at the unfortunate driver. Angrily the officer stopped the next two tanks arriving and they maneuvered into a position which allowed them to cover the field from either end. They then brought their machine guns to bear on the prisoners. There followed, then, another delay.

When the firing broke out, Lieutenant Virgil T. Lary, in the lead vehicle, looked wildly around, trying to take in what was happening.* The first shell had blown the left wheels off one of the lead trucks. Another shell exploded on the road in front of Lary's jeep. Then another shell fell and another, then machine-gun fire began to crackle, and shortly rifle fire was punching at them, all coming through the screen of trees on their left.

As Lary glanced back he saw that his column was powerless to move, the vehicles plunging into the wildest kind of chaos. It only took seconds for Lary to absorb this, then he and the captain riding with him hit the ditch. They ducked down to escape

* Knowing Lieutenant Lary was a native of Kentucky, the author began trying to locate him in February of 1965. She was successful in finding him in April of the same year. From his home in Fort Lauderdale, Florida, Lieutenant Lary wrote the author several times concerning the massacre and referred her to the best account of it from his point of view, an article written by him and published in the *Field Artillery Journal* in February 1946. At the time the article was written, Lieutenant Lary was a civilian again and a student at the University of Kentucky. The events were still vivid in his mind and he was even then preparing to go to Dachau to testify in the trial, Malmédy: Case-64. Subsequently obtaining the article and reproducing it for her files, the author found it as detailed and articulate as Lieutenant Lary had said.

Confrontation on the Amblève

the fire, got their breath and talked briefly, trying to decide what they could do. Was there any defense they could make?

How? With what? Rifles? Against tanks and cannons? Some of Lary's men were valiantly potshotting away with their rifles from the ditch but they were hopelessly outnumbered and hopelessly outclassed as to weapons. They would all be killed, every one of them, if they tried to resist. What was an officer supposed to do in such a situation? Sacrifice his men in a hopeless gallant stand? Or give up, surrender? Either alternative was sickening. Lary and the captain talked it over and decided they would surrender. There was no way out of the trap, there was no defense to be made except literally a last-ditch stand.

So. O.K. Lary crawled down the ditch to tell his men and to pass the word along to stop the firing. They were going to surrender. As he reached the first of the men he heard a tank coming down the road from the crossroads. He felt a sudden spurt of hope. He knew the 440th Field Artillery Battalion was not far behind him, assigned to this same route. Maybe they had arrived! Maybe this was one of their big tanks with its 105-mm. howitzer. Maybe Battery B would be saved even at this late hour and would not have to surrender.

Lary raised his head above the ditch to look and looked right down the muzzle of the big cannon of a Tiger Royal tank. A half-track was behind the tank and an officer in it suddenly stood up, raised his pistol and fired at Lary. Lary ducked behind the wheel of a vehicle and rolled back down in the ditch.

He felt hopeless now. They were entirely boxed in. He ripped the officer's insignia off his uniform and smeared mud on his helmet in the hope he might pass for an enlisted man. He passed the word down that they were all to throw down their weapons, put up their hands and crawl out of the ditch. Now! Lary himself led the surrender.

So Battery B surrendered — or what there was of it in the ditch. There were around 140 men in the little outfit at the time of the ambush. Some had been killed in the trucks. Some had been killed as they leaped to safety in the ditch. Some had been killed in the ditch. Some had been killed as they fled into the woods. Some had escaped. How many actually surrendered has never been known, but it was around 120, as best official figures could show later. They crawled out of the ditch, hands up. The captain, assigned fatefully to Battery B only to ride with them and keep them with 7th Armored, and who had made the fateful decision to keep to the assigned route, was not among them. He had been killed in the ditch.

As the MP had seen, there was a brief period of milling about as the prisoners were searched, and the Germans were in a jovial, laughing mood. This had gone their way easily, as smoothly as cutting butter with a hot knife. Then an officer, presumably Major Poetschke, arrived and brusquely ordered the armored column to get moving quickly, quickly. He had a rendezvous at Ligneuville to keep.

The prisoners were now lined up along the shoulder of the road and prodded and shoved northward toward the crossroads. Lary warned the men to obey all orders. Under the Rules of Land War they would be safe.

One man who had been in the ditch with them had not surrendered, however. He found a little stream nearby with about a foot of water in it. T/5 Warren Schmidt splashed into the stream and simply lay down in the water. It was icy cold and it took his breath away, but he forced himself to submerge all but his nose and he dragged mud and weeds over himself and tried to look very dead.

The prisoners were lined up in the field in a small space perhaps fifty feet square. The effort was made to use the big gun of a half-track to guard them, and failed, and then the officer in charge stopped two tanks. He wanted some heavy weapons to guard the Americans, he explained.

The tank commanders were not anxious to obey, but did. The

Confrontation on the Amblève

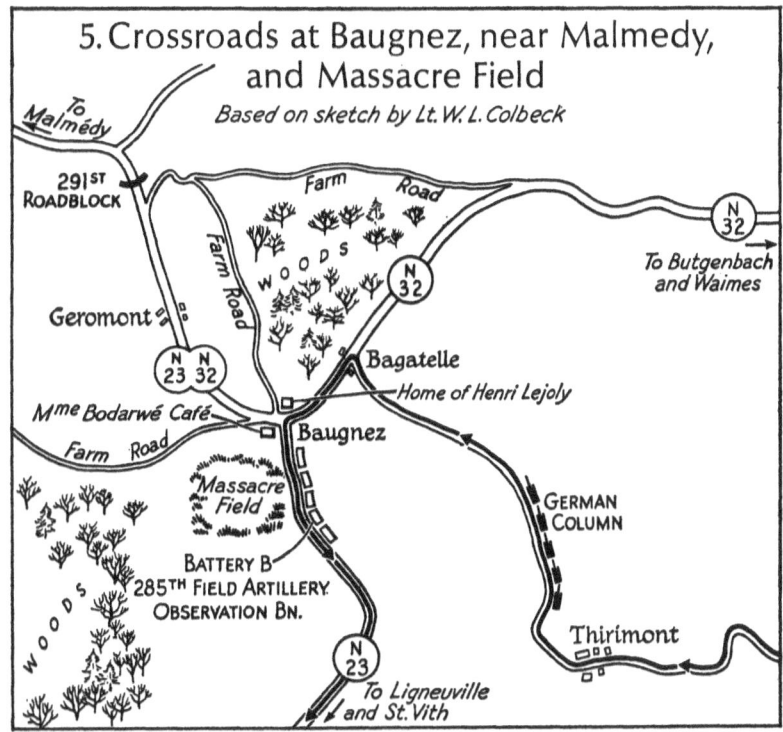

first tank flagged down was Tank No. 731. This meant 7th Company, third platoon, tank no. 1. The commander was M/Sergeant Hans Siptrott. The tank was a Mark IV. The driver was Corporal Gerhard Schaeffer. The rest of the crew consisted of a Corporal Wetengel, gunner, Private George Fleps, assistant gunner, and Private Arnhold, radioman. Fleps stood in the tank turret with his pistol in his hand, guarding the prisoners.

The other tank was No. 732. It was a Mark IV also. The commander was Sergeant Clotten, whose driver was Corporal Koewitz. Another member of this crew was a Private Vogt.*

There was now a long lull in affairs. The prisoners stood in the field and waited. They were cold and they were apprehen-

* Deposition of George Fleps, War Crimes Branch Report, USFET, 1946.

sive, but they were behaving correctly. As has been said, they believed the long wait was for transportation to come up and take them to some POW camp.

Actually the wait was for rear elements of the column to come up.

The first rear unit to come up was a company of combat engineers, the *3rd SS Pioneer Company*. Major Poetschke conferred with their commander, then left.

Shortly after he left, one of the *Pioneer* officers approached the first tank, No. 731. "The prisoners are to be killed," he said to Siptrott, the commander, "and it must go quickly. Everybody is needed up ahead and there is no time to waste."

Siptrott said, "I don't have much ammunition."

The officer told him to do as he was ordered. Siptrott turned to Private George Fleps, who had his pistol out already, and told him to start shooting. Fleps raised his pistol and selected a target in the first row, took deliberate aim and pulled the trigger. The pistol shot sounded like a short, explosive pop. The bullet slammed into the driver of Lieutenant Lary's jeep, who was standing immediately beside Lary. To Lary it looked as if Fleps had aimed directly at him. The man fell, toppling backwards, so that he knocked down several men behind him.

Inevitably there was a reaction among the prisoners. The men started yelling, and at least two men standing in the front row swiveled about and began bulldogging their way through the group to the rear. One of them was Private James P. Massara of Battery B, and the other was the medical corpsman, Samuel Dobyns. Lary called out, fearing the men would break and run and call down further fire, "Stand fast! Stand fast!"

Fleps' pistol popped again and a medical officer, standing next to Sergeant Kenneth Ahrens, in the front row went down. Immediately after this shot was fired, within seconds, the machine guns of both tanks opened fire. The prisoners screamed and yelled, many of them instinctively throwing themselves on the

Confrontation on the Amblève

ground, others milling about. Methodically the guns raked across the group, left to right and back again, over and over, and again, mowing the men down like ranks of tenpins, until the whole group, except one man, were sprawled on the ground. Fleps has said that one man remained standing, by some miracle, and that he raised his pistol again and shot him. Then his tank, No. 731, started moving. The driver jerked the tank unevenly as he moved off and Fleps was thrown against the edge of the turret, hurting his hip. He swore and rubbed his leg.

The machine gun in Tank No. 732 continued to spray the fallen figures. Screams, cries, shrieks and groans filled the air at first. But slowly, gradually, as the machine gun played back and forth over the fallen figures, all sounds ceased. It had taken perhaps five minutes. The time was now about ten minutes after two. Tank No. 732 moved on down the road.

Up the road from the slaughter pen which the field had now become, Henri Lejoly had witnessed the entire scene.

The prisoners fell singly and they also fell in piles and heaps, and miraculously when the machine guns ceased their chatter not all of them were dead. One who still lived, though he was badly wounded in the back, was Sergeant Ahrens. In the front row, Ahrens had been hit immediately, as he whirled about and flung himself onto the ground.

Another who still lived was Lieutenant Lary. Lary had thrown himself to the ground when the machine guns opened fire and he was not hit until on one of the later bursts a bullet went through his foot, and another bullet hit in the fleshy part of the calf of the same leg. Both Lary and Ahrens had the wit to lie absolutely still and draw no further fire to themselves.

The MP, Pfc. Homer Ford, was not dead. He had thrown himself to the ground and had been hit in the arm. He, too, lay perfectly still and played dead.

Others still living were Private James P. Massara and William Reem who were not even wounded. Like a football tackle Massara had butted his way to the rear when Fleps fired the first time. There he had flung himself down and was shortly protected by the bodies in front of him. Still others living were T/5 Theodore Paluch, Kenneth Kingston and Carl R. Daub, a man named Smith and one named Profanchik. The medical corpsman named Samuel Dobyns had four wounds in four different places, but he was alive. Four different times as the machine guns traversed left to right a bullet had plowed into him. His companion, Roy Anderson, was also living.

There were others, more than one could have believed, who had lived through the brutal execution. Some lived through the first stage only to be killed a short time later. For as the column continued to roll by on the road, machine guns on the vehicles raked the bodies, and any man with a pistol or rifle who felt like it took a potshot at the figures lying in the field.

But now began the worst of the horror. Soldiers of the *Pioneer* unit came into the field and walked around among the piles and heaps of massacred men. If there was a sign of life the men were shot in the head, or had their heads bashed in with rifle or pistol butts. When a head was bashed in with a gun butt there was a sickening thump of crushing bones.

Private Jacob Weiss, of a communications platoon, arrived during this mop-up. He stopped his half-track and saw most of it. He took no part in it but he watched as the *Pioneers* went among the men looking for a live one. He saw one *Pioneer* testing for death by kicking men in the testicles. A live one invariably reacted. He was then shot.

As Weiss watched he saw another *Pioneer* find a live one. He jerked the wounded man to his feet and stripped him of his field jacket, then his shoes and pants. Then Weiss heard the *Pioneer* say, "You can go back to sleep now," and he put a bullet in the man's head.

Another member of the mop-up party Weiss watched was Private Gustav Sprenger, who was eighteen years old at the time.

Sprenger found five Americans piled together, too badly wounded and in too much pain to lie perfectly still. As Weiss watched, Sprenger put one bullet into each man. When he finished, he turned back to the first man and shot them all again. Six times he did this. When he finally stopped he had fired thirty-two bullets into the five men. His pistol barrel was too hot to touch. He was aglow with killing! Excited and laughing.*

To Sergeant Ken Ahrens, who made himself lie still where he had fallen, all the Germans seemed to be laughing. They were having a very good time with their killing. Only a few bodies away from him Ahrens watched as one of the Battery B medics, unable to bear the sounds of pain from a man beside him, raised up one knee and took his first-aid kit from his pocket and plugged the man's bullet hole with a wad of bandaging. In spite of the machine gunning, the medic evidently believed the Red Cross on his helmet would be honored. Ahrens watched as one of the *Pioneers* walked over and stood beside the medic, waited for him to finish the bandaging, then shot the bandaged man and the medic. He was joined by another *Pioneer* and the two men turned about, laughing together.

The two walked toward Ahrens and he thought his time had come. He breathed as faintly as he could. "Dead," they said, and walked on. Ahrens guessed that the wound in his back had soaked his uniform with so much blood it was easy to believe he was dead.

One of the German soldiers approached Lieutenant Lary and stood beside him while he loaded his pistol. His heavy boots were right beside Lary's head. Then a bullet went through the head of the man next to Lary, and Lary lay tense and waited, expecting to be next. "Tot," the German said, "dead," and moved on.

Lary was apparently the only officer to escape death. Private

* Deposition of Jacob Weiss, War Crimes Branch Report, USFET, 1946.

Massara watched four of the *Pioneers*, led by one of their officers, carefully search out the American officers and make certain they were dead by putting additional shots into them. Lary escaped because he had removed his insignia and smeared mud on his helmet.

Eventually it all stopped. Either the Germans were sated with killing or they were satisfied all the Americans were dead. And now the long column passing on the road had all gone by. No more vehicles were passing to take potshots at the men in the field. Lary was not absolutely certain but he later told Colonel Pergrin that he had counted around fifty tanks and about the same number of half-tracks that passed, after the massacre.

The men in the field still living lay still for perhaps twenty or thirty minutes after the long column stopped rolling by, but they were whispering to each other. "Anybody else alive?"

"Me."

"And me."

"Here."

"And here."

How many men were still living and spoke up is not precisely known. But when they began to talk about making a dash for it, some fifteen or twenty thought they were not too badly wounded to try. And they wanted to do it right now.

Lary urged the group to wait until dark. A unit of Germans was still about the crossroads. They knew it. They could occasionally hear them talking. "We'll have a lot better chance to make it after dark," Lary insisted.

But the men also had good reasons for not waiting. "More Krauts may come along and finish us off."

That was a cogent argument, even to Lary.

It was finally Private James P. Massara, one of those not wounded at all, who stood up and said, "Let's go!" and led the men in the sprint. In a more or less solid pack they ran northward, up the field, toward Malmédy.

Confrontation on the Amblève

After one dumbfounded moment the Germans left to guard the crossroads recovered and turned their machine gun on the fleeing men. Lieutenant Lary, who had decided to make the dash when the men did, saw one of the men drop. The others kept going.

Massara and a man running neck and neck with him reached the woods safely and hid.

William Reem, Smith, Profanchik and one other man also made the woods safely and hid.

Pfc. Homer Ford and three men with him fled straight up the field, reached the woods and were safe.

Sergeant Ken Ahrens and the men with him reached the safety of the woods and hid.

But about twelve men swerved toward Madame Bodarwé's café when the machine gun opened fire on them, Lieutenant Lary among them, and T/5 Theodore Paluch. Lary yelled at the men not to go inside, to follow him. Paluch and three men did follow Lary around behind the café. Six or seven of the men, however, could not resist ducking into the café. Lary ran around behind it, saw a small shed and dived into it. It held a pile of straw and other debris in one corner and he hid in it, pulling the straw over him. Paluch and the men with him evidently did not see where Lary had gone, for they remained behind the café.

The Germans guarding the crossroads had seen the men run into the café, of course, and shortly they turned their attention from the fleeing men to those who had gone into the café. They dismounted their machine gun and approached. When they could not flush the Americans out with threats, they set fire to the café, and they did a thorough job. Before long the men were smoked out and as they tried to crawl out the windows and doors, the Germans turned the machine gun on them and mowed them down. Behind the building Paluch and the men with him had played dead once more, in case the Germans came prowling. But they did not, and when the building began to burn the men crawled off, partially hidden by clouds of smoke, and made it safely to the woods.

From his hiding place in the shed, Lieutenant Lary heard the screams of his men as they were burned out and shot down.

Madame Adèle Bodarwé had a mysterious fate. She simply disappeared. She was never seen again after this dreadful afternoon.*

---

* Eisenhower, op. cit., p. 237. Also Mulligan, op. cit.

The story of the massacre is reconstructed largely from the stories of the survivors rescued by men of the 291st Engineers. Colonel Pergrin interrogated every one of the seventeen survivors assisted by Company B, took down their names, rank and serial numbers and their stories. He recounted many of them to the author. The Inspector General's Department, First U.S. Army, took sworn statements. Many of these sworn statements were released to publicize the event through the U.S. Army newspapers, *Stars & Stripes* and *Yank*. The author has a file of both newspapers from July 1944 to the end of the war in 1945. Also the issues of *Yank* were compiled into a book in 1969. Both American and German depositions taken at the Malmédy Trial are contained in the files of USFET, War Crimes Branch Report, 1946.

10

Up at the 291st's B Company roadblock, a short three quarters of a mile northwest of the Five Points crossroads, the men on the roadblock heard the opening guns of the skirmish down at the crossroads and the crackle of small-arms fire. Since Battery B had just passed their position a short time earlier, they knew it had run into something pretty big down there. Only tanks or artillery would have cannon. They tensed and waited, ready with their bazooka, their .50-caliber machine gun, their daisy chain of road mines, but especially with their mined trees, to do all they could to stop whatever it was, if it came their way. One squad of engineers, in charge of Sergeant Charles Dishaw.

The firing was still going on at the crossroads when they saw an armored car coming up the road. It approached fast, without any hesitation, as if expecting no opposition. It got some and it was probably Sergeant Dishaw himself on the .50-caliber machine gun who opened fire on it. The car swerved almost off the road and screeched to a sudden stop and the men on the roadblock thought it had been hit. Then it squirmed frantically around and took off back down the road like a scared jackrabbit, machine gun bullets chasing it up the hill and out of sight. The men expected tanks next and watched the crown of the hill intently for the first hull to heave into sight. Nothing came and the firing at the crossroads died away and there was only a profound, strangely disquieting stillness. Remember that this roadblock was less than a mile from the crossroads. What had happened down there? And what was going to happen next?

As the shells fell in the southeastern section of Malmédy they touched off the panic that had been building up all morning as long, bumper-to-bumper lines of retreating vehicles poured through the town. They came from the south and from the east and as they ground into clotted halts in the streets and on the squares inevitably they passed on the frightening word: "The Krauts have broken through!" Some, coming from the Butgenbach-Büllingen area knew there was a battle raging there and brought firsthand evidence of it.

Add to that the rumors of paratroopers dropped in the vicinity, the posting of extra security guards, the movements of various American service units out of the town, and the situation was dynamite waiting only for the match. The shelling of the town was the match.

Civilians who had been apprehensive all morning now panicked and added to the great confusion. On foot, carrying their possessions, on bicycles, pushing handcarts and wheelbarrows loaded with their belongings, they contributed to the massive traffic jam, pathetic though their situation was.

All of the military units in the town which had not already left were suddenly seized with urgency and their vehicles added to the moiling, snarled mess. Shortly the entire town was infected with madness, utter chaos and confusion. The 44th Field Evacuation Hospital decided it was time to go and loaded up the convalescent soldiers and nursing staff, abandoning most of their stores and equipment. Quartermaster and ordnance units, supply units, heavy equipment units, all merged into the mass of movement. Everywhere, all over the town, everybody was in a frantic hurry, panic-stricken and terrified, wanting only one thing — to get out, and get out swiftly. Colonel David E. Pergrin, Lieutenant Frank Rhea, Lieutenant W. L. Colbeck, in fact all the 291st men who were in Malmédy remember this mass panic and chaos. It was an unforgettable memory. Colonel Pergrin said: "The fastest way to get around in Malmédy that day was on foot. It was almost impossible to drive in certain areas. It was the worst traffic mess I ever saw and it greatly hampered our efforts to set up our defenses."

About 1:15, or shortly thereafter, the guards in front of Pergrin's command post halted another outfit. Pergrin went out to see who they were. The lead vehicle was a jeep carrying an officer, a major. He told Colonel Pergrin he was the commander of the lead company of the 440th Armored Field Artillery, 7th Armored Division. And he wanted to know what these signs saying the road was under enemy fire meant, and he wanted to know what this steady stream of U.S. soldiers and vehicles meant, and what the hell was all the mess around the town square!

Pergrin told him. He also told him that the enemy was just outside the town at Five Points, in great strength, and the major and his big guns had come just in time. Not so. The major said he and his guns were under orders to go to Vielsalm. He could not stop in Malmédy. Pergrin did his best to persuade him. "This is the front line now," he said. "You can't be needed anywhere else worse than right here!"

He told the officer precisely how weak he was against a column of enemy armor. "And everything else in town has left or is leaving. That's what all this traffic jam is about. Your artillery could save this place."

But the major shook his head. "Sorry. We're ordered to St. Vith. There's been a big breakthrough there, too." He told Pergrin his route had been through Malmédy, Ligneuville and Recht to Vielsalm. "You say there's German armor on that route?"

"And a hell of a lot of it," Pergrin said.

"Well, which is the best way for me to go now?"

Feeling more despair than he would have cared to admit at seeing this artillery pass on through when they were so desperately needed, Pergrin directed the officer to turn around and go west, proceed to Stavelot, to Trois Ponts, then turn south on N–33 to Vielsalm. He told him the streets to follow out of town.

Colonel Pergrin had one more hope of finding some reinforcements for his pitifully small defense units. All the service units that had been stationed in Malmédy had by now gone, or were going. But there was a replacement depot in the outskirts of town. Some 500 men were in that depot waiting for assignment. Making his slow way through the frantic and panicky mobs of people Pergrin drove to the replacement depot and spoke with the commanding officer. It seemed to him a reasonable request, that these unassigned men be used to defend the town in this crisis.

But the officer said, "Sorry. I have orders to move them to Liège. They're to be used in the defenses there. Most of them are already on the way."

So. Another unit was getting out. Everything was getting out — running away. Soon, Pergrin thought angrily as he fought his way back to the command post, there would be nobody left in Malmédy but Company B. He was right. One hour later there would be nothing left in Malmédy but Company B. Even the civil affairs unit had left.

Grimly he returned to the CP. It was now about 2:15. Captain Conlin was at the command post, Lieutenant Tom Stack was there, and several other officers. Pergrin reported that he had had no luck at the replacement depot. Somebody said, "Well, are we going to get out too, Colonel?"

Pergrin's head came up and he said firmly, "No. We are *not* going to get out. We are going to stick. We are going to stay here and make the best fight we can of it."

To this day Lieutenant Tom Stack remembers the shiver of pride he felt when the colonel said they were going to stick. Not that it didn't scare him. It did. He believed that probably the short sweet life of Thomas Finnbarr Stack would end right here in this dark Belgian town, but he was proud just the same, and he determined to do whatever was asked of him to whatever end it brought him.

Having made his commitment, Pergrin knew he had to have some help, and the only help he could call on were some more 291st men. Company A was out of pocket, but he still had Company C. So he wrote out a message for the radio operator for Battalion. Tell Captain Moyer, at La Gleize, to move to Malmédy with Company C as soon as possible. Also tell Captain Moyer to set up a roadblock at the bridge over the Amblève in Stavelot. One look at the map had told Pergrin how important this bridge had now become in the defense of Malmédy. If this German armored column should swing westward and get across the Amblève at that point, Malmédy could be cut off and isolated, to say nothing of the threat it would pose to First Army headquarters at Spa and all those supply installations north of the river.

Reinforcements ordered, Pergrin now said, "I'm going to make a reconnaissance out toward the crossroads and see what's going on out there." Since the first shells and outburst of firing there had been only the long, strange silence. It needed investigating.

Pergrin armed himself with a submachine gun, got Sergeant Bill Crickenberger to drive for him, took another enlisted man with him, and headed out. It was around 2:30 P.M. when he left the command post.

Shortly after 2:00 P.M. M/Sergeant Ralph W. McCarty, the construction chief of the 291st, came into Malmédy from Stavelot with three dump trucks of gravel. McCarty was a farmer from Kansas, a big, dark man, fundamentally earthy, strongly structured, sound and well adjusted. As construction chief it was his job to implement all the jobs laid out for the battalion. He was hauling crushed rock for the road-mending job near Waimes, on N–32, that morning.

McCarty was a good six hours late coming into Malmédy and he was pretty exasperated. He had been held up time after time by MPs at road intersections letting a lot of armor go through, and the roads were also cluttered with hundreds of other vehicles. McCarty wondered what the devil was making the whole First U.S. Army move from here to there on this particular Sunday. He was an aggressive, hard-pushing man and he had not taken kindly to the long delays.

He entered Malmédy, and headed for B Company's CP. To his surprise he ran into a roadblock at the street intersection just above the CP and Lieutenant Colbeck, who had set it up, was at the roadblock when McCarty was stopped for identification. McCarty wanted to know what was going on and Colbeck told him, and told him he had better report to the colonel for further orders.

As the two men stood talking together both heard a sudden burst of machine gun fire from the direction of Five Points. They stopped talking and listened. The machine gun firing did not last very long. There were several long sustained bursts, pauses, several more bursts, then it stopped. It was 2:15. Neither of the men knew they had just heard the massacre of around 140 men in the field below Madame Bodarwé's café.

McCarty and Colbeck listened, shook their heads, then McCarty led his trucks around to the command post. By the time he arrived, however, Colonel Pergrin had left on his reconnaissance. McCarty stuck around, picking up the dope on the situation from the men in the CP.

Colonel Pergrin and his reconnaissance party went through the roadblocks beyond the CP. At the last one, the outpost nearest the crossroads, they had to wait for the men to haul in their daisy chain. As he waited, Pergrin talked with Sergeant Dishaw, in command of the outpost, and Dishaw told him about the probe by the German armored car. Nothing else, he said, had come up the road. But, he added, there had been some machine gun firing down at the crossroads fifteen or twenty minutes earlier. If the colonel was going to make a reconnaissance he ought to be careful. The Krauts were still down there.

Pergrin drove on. Just beyond the roadblock the road began to climb. Pergrin wanted a high place from which to see over the intersection at Five Points. At the top of the hill, at the highest point, he ordered Crickenberger to stop. The men got out of the jeep and walked over into a cleared field which lay to their right. Pergrin hoped he could get a broad view to the south from there. However, at the southern end of the field a stand of woods obstructed the immediate view. Pergrin swept the area with his binoculars. In the distance there was nothing. No sign of the enemy.

He and his companions stood there looking and talking for a few minutes, when suddenly there was a lot of shouting and yelling, then there was a crackle of machine gun fire, then screams. The Krauts were still down there, all right, and something was going on.

Shortly after this disturbance four men came running and stumbling and screaming through the woods at the southern edge of the field, staggering toward Pergrin and his men, who ran to help them. They were the MP, Pfc. Homer Ford, and three companions, of whom one was a sergeant and one a corporal. All were wounded, and they were bloody, muddy, and as wet as drowned rats from lying in the slushy field. They were also almost incoherent, babbling and hysterical from their ordeal. Pergrin tried to calm them but they were too distraught. From their babbling stream of words, however, he could make out a few things. The Germans had killed everybody! Everybody! They had surrendered and then the Germans had lined them up and mowed them down with machine guns. Their whole outfit was gone . . . killed!

Pergrin and his men were horrified, but they hustled the survivors into the jeep and Crickenberger raced for Malmédy and the Company B aid station with them.

At about this same time Lieutenant Tom Stack and another officer were probing down the road in front of the roadblock when three men rose up out of the ditch alongside the road like muddy ghosts and frantically flagged them down. None of these men were wounded. Who they were is not precisely known but it seems likely they were William Reem and his companions. Stack raced them to the aid station, also.

When Pergrin got to the command post with the men he had rescued, everybody got to work immediately. Captain Conlin, Sergeant McCarty, the medics, everybody pitched in. They found dry clothing for them, heated food for them and their wounds were treated. As the men got warm and were fed they began to calm down and Pergrin could begin his interrogation. He needed to know three things immediately. They had surrendered? Yes. They were unarmed? Yes. They had made no attempt to escape? No. Not after they had surrendered. The MP and the sergeant got hold of themselves rather quickly and were able to tell a fairly coherent story, in its proper sequence. What they had seen, what had happened, what they had done. The stories of the other men, and those brought in by Lieutenant Stack, confirmed the horrible event in all its essential details.

There could be no doubt they told the truth. They had had no time to make up or even exaggerate their stories. They had been rescued within minutes of the final episode, when still terrified, still horrified by the ghastliness of what they had been through. They spilled it all out, just the way it happened, the truth of it, urgent, fresh, brutal and cruel, still making them shake.

The men also gave him more information concerning the full strength of the enemy column. For the first time Pergrin understood precisely how strong it was. "It took them an hour and a half to pass, Colonel," the men told him. "They must have seventy or eighty tanks and half-tracks, armored cars . . . everything."

Pergrin also learned the direction the column had taken. "They went south . . . down the St. Vith road," the men said. "They all turned south out there."

It was now around 3:50 P.M. Pergrin acted quickly. He wrote out a report for First Army containing the basic facts of the massacre, the approximate number of men involved, their unit and the present number of survivors rescued. He added the information concerning the strength of the enemy column and the direction it had taken. He added that he was remaining in Malmédy and gave his own strength. One wonders what the officers at First Army thought when they saw Pergrin's strength — seven officers and Company B — 152 men.

This message was first sent by radio. It was received, decoded and was being studied by First Army at 4:30 P.M. Later, when all the survivors rescued by the 291st had come in, Pergrin wrote a much fuller report which was taken to First Army headquarters by Captain Sheetz.

That evening Major General William B. Kean, chief of staff of First Army, wrote in his diary: "There is absolutely no question as to its proof — immediate publicity is being given to the story. General Quesada has told every one of his pilots about it during their briefing." *

By that time the Inspector General's Department had interviewed some of the survivors themselves, for Pergrin was ordered to send those able to travel to headquarters at Spa. There were five of them, the three unwounded, Pfc. Homer Ford and one other, and Lieutenant Tom Stack left for Spa with them shortly after dark that same day.

The decision to give wide publicity to the massacre was im-

* Eisenhower, John S. D., *The Bitter Woods* (New York: G. P. Putnam's Sons, 1969), p. 237.

plemented immediately. By midnight it had gone into almost every unit of First Army and by the next day very few GIs in the entire U.S. Army had not heard of the Malmédy Massacre.

It had the opposite effect from that which Hitler had expected when he ordered that this offensive be waged ruthlessly and without pity. This had worked in his onslaughts before, because the helpless civilians of overrun countries had to live with his hordes. It did not work with U.S. soldiers. Instead of dissolving the men of the U.S. Army into whimpering, cowering, panicky men, the massacre became the psychological turning point. It turned the vast conglomeration of careless, casual, nonchalant GIs into soldiers. It stiffened them, determined them, and its total effect was to weld them together again. After December 17 the U.S. Army had one more reason for defeating the enemy — to avenge the men of Malmédy.

After dispatching Lieutenant Stack and the first batch of survivors, Colonel Pergrin turned his thoughts to what more he could do in Malmédy. As thinly as Company B was already stretched, it had to be stretched a little thinner. A roadblock had to be set up at once at the big viaduct on the Stavelot road, and the structure had to be wired for demolition. Pergrin ordered Sergeant McCarty to take care of these things.

McCarty scrounged up a handful of men, three or four H/S platoon men, a machine gun and some mines, and around 5:00 P.M. he had a roadblock of sorts set up. Pergrin was running painfully short of all equipment and supplies by now. He therefore radioed Battalion to send him all the ammunition and explosives, mines and wiring, they could spare.

Pergrin then made another reconnaissance out toward the crossroads before full dark came on. Twilight was settling in with a deep sad cheerlessness as he drove out to the same high spot as before. A building at the crossroads was burning now, glowing redly against the sky. It was Madame Bodarwé's café. Reconnoitering carefully, on foot, Pergrin and Crickenberger probed clear down to the copse of woods at the southern end of the field this time. They could see the wreckage of the Battery B vehicles pushed off the road into the ditches, and Pergrin also saw a burned-out ambulance. This was the ambulance which had belonged to the 26th Infantry. The ditches of the road were a shambles of disabled, burned-out trucks and jeeps.

As Pergrin was finishing his reconnaissance, another party of survivors stumbled out of the woods where they had been hiding. They were T/5 Theodore Paluch of Battery B, a staff sergeant who had been shot in the throat and in the chest, and a medic who was wounded in the foot.

Pergrin brought them to the aid station in the command post. Sergeant McCarty, looking for some equipment, came in shortly afterward. He sat down beside the badly wounded staff sergeant and talked with him. The man had been captured at Büllingen and had been hauled around all day by the Germans, then herded into the field with the men of Battery B. McCarty tried to comfort him a little, then he had to leave.

Pergrin now realized he must have more medical help. There was no way of knowing how many more wounded would be brought in and the wounded already brought in had just about exhausted the medical supplies on hand and they had more than exhausted the medical knowledge of the B Company medics. So Pergrin radioed Battalion and ordered the 291st medical officer to come to Malmédy and bring with him more supplies and more medics.

Slowly other survivors made their way to the roadblocks and outposts to be brought in by the men of Company B. Pergrin talked with each of them, their wounds were dressed, they were given dry clothing and hot food and a place to sleep awhile.

About 4:30 that afternoon Private Bernard Koenig, who had been sent up on a hill with the useless bazooka, came down from his aerie to report. On that back road to Chodes and Gdoumont no enemy had been seen and there was little to report.

Lieutenant Rhea drove up shortly bringing some more mines and additional ammunition. He also brought the men some rations, and he directed them to move farther on out the road, to a deep bend, and set up a stronger roadblock. For the first time Sergeant Munoz and his men of Lieutenant Rhea's 1st squad learned how strong and ruthless the enemy was as he told them about the armored column that had hit in at Five Points, and about the massacre. Impressively he told them, "They've got eighty or ninety tanks, so stay on your toes. Keep alert!"

Rhea then left and the men moved on out the road and set up the new roadblock. Koenig says there was no panic about eighty or ninety tanks. In fact, most of the men admitted to a feeling of relief at knowing precisely what they were facing. There had lingered in their minds some haunting dread of something new and weird and strange and unreal. A tangible enemy, tanks and real men, they could face.

As the men stood talking together by the squad truck two GIs came staggering down out of the hills to the south. It was dusky dark. The GIs were in bad shape from shock and cold. They were almost incoherent and they muttered hoarsely as they told the same brutal story of the massacre down at Five Points. This was Private James P. Massara and his buddy who had escaped with him. They had been sheltering in the nearby woods until dark.

Sergeant Munoz sent them to the aid station. The men of his squad talked about it angrily together and they stiffened with a fierce impassioned determination. O.K. If this was the way the Krauts wanted it, it was the way they were going to get it. And they themselves would die to the last man before they would surrender.

Bernard Koenig then climbed back up on his hill, where he would spend a long lonesome night trying to keep from freezing to death.

Sometime after dark Sergeant Dishaw's men on the roadblock

nearest the crossroads rescued four more survivors. They came stumbling down the railroad track and blundered into the roadblock, stiff with cold, bloody, mumbling their story in half delirium.

A short while later T/5 Warren Schmidt, who had thrown himself into the icy water of the little stream and covered himself with mud and weeds, came looming out of the dark and almost scared the security man on point out beyond this same roadblock out of his wits. Schmidt still had frozen weeds hanging from him and he was encased in a muddy armor of frozen clothing. He looked like a man resurrected from the dead.

Down at the crossroads, now when it was dark, Lieutenant Lary crept out of the shed in which he had been hiding and limped down the country road that led west from Five Points. He hoped it would lead him to Malmédy where he knew there was a hospital. A hedge divided the field from the road and he stayed in the shelter of the hedge, hiding from any possible German patrols. As his wounds opened again they were very painful and he was shaking with the cold.

He finally decided the road was trending too far west to take him directly to Malmédy. He left the road, and guiding on the unusually heavy concentration of buzz bombs streaming overhead toward Liège he started working his way across the open fields and through the woods. He could finally walk no longer as the pain from his foot increased. He began crawling. It seemed miles and an endless time that he crawled, until finally he saw a dim light in a farmhouse. He could go no further. He had to take a chance on the occupants being friendly, which was not at all certain around Malmédy. He made his way to the door and knocked. It was opened and he was helped inside.

At 6:30 that evening Colonel Pergrin was ordered by First Army Engineer, Colonel W. H. Carter, to send the 629th Engineer Light Equipment Company and the 962nd Engineer Maintenance Company farther west. They were to report to Colonel Anderson at Trois Ponts for additional orders.

And now, except for some military police, Company B was entirely alone in the town, its sole defense. Seven officers, 152 men. They were spread out thinly in the roadblocks and outposts, knowing there was a powerful enemy somewhere out there in the black night. They had their trees wired with little quarter-pound blocks of TNT. They had daisy chains across some roads. They had a few machine guns and bazookas, and not enough ammunition for them. They had their rifles. But they stuck right there and they settled down to do what they could, if it happened, whenever it happened.

II

COLONEL PERGRIN'S MESSAGES to First Army at Spa and his own headquarters at Haute Bodeux started a trickle of men and supplies toward Malmédy.

First Army headquarters was electrified by his news that a strong enemy column was actually as far west as Malmédy. General Hodges had been proceeding on the theory that the attacks on St. Vith and Bastogne, in his VIII Corps sector, were the biggest threat to First Army. Gerow's V Corps, with 2nd Infantry and 99th Infantry Divisions, had not yet, he thought, been deeply penetrated. But he had rushed the 1st Infantry Division to bolster them.

General Bradley had also transferred the 30th Infantry Division from General Simpson's Ninth U.S. Army and at noon on this Sunday, December 17, Hodges had ordered it to begin to move southward from its position behind Aachen. Its destination was Eupen, V Corps headquarters, and it, too, was for General Gerow's use in bolstering his northern shoulder.

But here was a frightening penetration all at once. What concerned the higher commanders was that Malmédy was a strategic goal for the enemy. Its capture would open the roads to Eupen and Verviers to the north, and to Francorchamps and Spa and Liège, northeastward. Its capture would, in fact, lay bare the heart not only of First U.S. Army but of the entire northern

Allied effort. Liège was the biggest supply dump on the continent and was furnishing most of the supplies for the British as well as the U.S. armies. Malmédy must not be captured, therefore. It must be reinforced, and quickly.

The 30th Division had been resting near Aachen when the order arrived at noon to move to Eupen and the V Corps. It took the division only four and a half hours to get ready to take off, an incredibly short time. At 4:30 P.M., Major General Leland S. Hobbs, the division commander, reported he was moving out. That meant that he could not possibly get his men to Malmédy before morning.

The only thing First Army had to send to Malmédy immediately was some units of its own Palace Guard, its security troops. At 4:30 P.M., therefore, orders went out to the 99th Infantry Battalion (Separate), based at Tilff, a few miles northwest of Spa, and to the 526th Armored Infantry Battalion, a Twelfth Army Group unit based at Spa, and to one company of the 825th Tank Destroyer Battalion, also based in Spa. They were to proceed to Malmédy immediately.

The 99th Infantry Battalion (Separate) was a unit made up mostly of Norwegians who wished to continue fighting Hitler and were now attached to First U.S. Army. Their commander was Lieutenant Colonel H. D. Hansen, the Executive Officer was Major Bjornstad.

Colonel Hansen was given command of all three units which were formed into a Task Force, but to save time the orders were for each unit to proceed to Malmédy on its own and there to come under Colonel Hansen's command.

This provided two battalions of infantry, one of them armored infantry with their towed 57-mm. antitank guns, and one company of the big tank-destroyer guns. The 57-mm. antitank gun had already proved inadequate to fight tanks. It had to be towed, which made it poorly maneuverable, and it simply was not big enough or effective enough. But these units were all that

Confrontation on the Amblève

First Army could scratch up for the time being. In case of an attack on Malmédy they would have to hold at all costs, until some of 30th Infantry Division's units could get there.

Colonel Pergrin's radio message ordering Company C to Malmédy also electrified Battalion at Haute Bodeux, and Colonel Anderson of Group at Trois Ponts. For the message also contained as much information as he had when it was sent, around 2:30 P.M., concerning the strength of the enemy column. All he could tell them at that time was that the enemy had hit in at Five Points, and his strength was known to be at least sixty-eight tanks and half-tracks. Battalion was instructed to pass this information on to Colonel Anderson.

The entire headquarters force at Haute Bodeux was now gripped with the grim fear that Colonel Pergrin and Company B would be overrun and lost and they became intensely alert to Pergrin's needs in Malmédy. T/Sergeant John L. Scanlan, communications chief, personally got on top of communications. He worked in a nightmare of anxiety that he might lose his communications with Pergrin. Pergrin had three men in Malmédy on radio, and they would work their hearts out, but only Bill Crickenberger, whom Scanlan had loaned to Company B earlier, could really be rated expert. It was going to be very sticky and Scanlan wished he could get some more men into Malmédy. For the present, however, he could only field Pergrin's radio messages as rapidly as possible so there would be no delay in getting whatever he needed to him.

Pergrin's message ordering Company C to Malmédy was received and decoded by 3:00 P.M. The orders to Company C were relayed, received in La Gleize and decoded by 3:30 P.M. Captain Moyer called a conference of the officers with him in La Gleize to discuss the move and allot responsibilities.

In Haute Bodeux, Captain Edward R. Lampp, Acting Executive Officer and in command at Battalion, went personally to alert the Company C men working in the sawmills in Trois Ponts, and to confer with Colonel Anderson.

S/Sergeant Albert Melton, the platoon sergeant for C Company's 2nd platoon, recalls that it was around 3:30 P.M. when Captain Lampp came to his mill and told him to close it down and get the men ready to go to Malmédy with Captain Moyer when he came through Trois Ponts.

On receipt of Pergrin's radio message Colonel Anderson, however, decided the situation had now become so threatening that not only should Company C set up the roadblock Pergrin had ordered at Stavelot, but a roadblock must be set up at the Amblève bridge in Trois Ponts. So another radio message went to Moyer at La Gleize and he now had three responsibilities — move as many of his men as possible to Malmédy, set up a roadblock in Trois Ponts and another roadblock at the old stone bridge in Stavelot.

Captain Lawrence R. Moyer, commander of Company C, was twenty-four years old. He was a big, strong, sturdy man, mostly good-humored and entirely reliable in a slow-moving, patient sort of way. He had no engineering beyond OCS but he had been in construction work in private life and from practical experience was fully qualified.

In the conference he called that afternoon were four officers: Lieutenant Martin Tintari, Moyer's administrative officer; Lieutenant Donald T. Davis, 1st platoon leader; Lieutenant Warren Rombaugh, 2nd platoon leader; and Lieutenant John C. Kirkpatrick of Company B who had driven over from Malmédy that morning.

The staff conference was interrupted at 4:30 P.M. by the arrival of Squad Sergeant Sheldon T. Smith who had just returned from road patrol north of Waimes. He had witnessed the unbelievable traffic of the massive retreat and he had almost run into the German column at Five Points on his way home. Near Waimes an MP had warned him just in time and he had detoured

Confrontation on the Amblève

around through Malmédy by a secondary road. He had seen how empty and deserted Malmédy was by then.

Smith thought the officers were taking the order to move to Malmédy pretty casually. They kept talking about a "small breakthrough" over near Malmédy. Smith, therefore, stressed the seriousness of the situation to them. He was heard, thanked, and then told to get his squad ready to go back to Malmédy with Moyer.

Smith did precisely that. He got his men together, 1st squad of 3rd platoon, and told them to take all the extra clothing they had, in particular nobody was to leave his overcoat behind, and to take all the extra ammunition and food they could get their hands on. "This," he told them, "is going to be rough and you'd better be ready for it."

In the officers' conference the apportionment of responsibility was already laid out. It will be remembered that Moyer only had two line platoons available. His 3rd platoon, except for Smith's squad, was on detached duty in Sourbrodt. He was totally out of touch with them. Therefore Moyer decided he would take Lieutenant Davis and his 1st platoon, and as many other men as he could scratch up, to Malmédy with him. Rombaugh, 2nd platoon leader, was given the job of setting up the two roadblocks. Tintari, of course, would remain with the H/S personnel in La Gleize, in command of headquarters.

Lieutenant Kirkpatrick had to get back to Malmédy to rejoin his own platoon. It was decided he would go along with Rombaugh's men detailed to set up the roadblock in Stavelot. Rombaugh himself would go to the Amblève bridge at Trois Ponts.

The squads detailed to set up the roadblocks loaded up and set out shortly before 5:00 P.M. Moyer, however, was a deliberate man and he meant to take his kitchen setup with him. He therefore waited until the men had chow and were naturally all gathered together before alerting them to move. Lieutenant Davis' 1st platoon returned after chow to their quarters in the town, and loaded up. They were joined by Moyer's detachment and the entire group set out for Malmédy about 5:30 or 5:45 P.M.

They went to Trois Ponts and picked up the men at the sawmills, and with no difficulty except meeting the continuing heavy westbound traffic proceeded to Stavelot and on to Malmédy. Corporal Edmond Byrne, of 1st platoon, remembers that when they were stopped for identification by the MPs in Stavelot, the MPs shook their heads over their destination. They had been hearing all afternoon, from all the refugees from Malmédy, that Malmédy had been captured. Byrne remembers, also, that in the entire stretch of road from Trois Ponts to Malmédy they did not see another single vehicle of any kind going east. They met hundreds going west, but they themselves were the single detachment going east. It gave them a very strange and lonely feeling.

It was 7:30 P.M. when they arrived at the command post in Malmédy. When Captain Moyer walked in no man was ever more welcome. "Any trouble getting here?" Pergrin asked.

"No," Moyer told him, "except for a lot of traffic going west."

As Moyer reported, Pergrin learned the extent of the reinforcements he had brought with him. He had with him exactly one officer and forty-eight men, elements of three platoons but in total only a few more men than one full platoon. Men had had to be left in La Gleize and at Trois Ponts to guard equipment and quarters. Rombaugh had a detail on the Amblève bridge at Trois Ponts. One full squad had been detailed to the roadblock in Stavelot, and Moyer had only one squad of his 3rd platoon. He had done the best he could and the result was forty-eight men, himself and Lieutenant Donald T. Davis.

So. As to the guns and ammunition and supplies he could bring, they too had had to be divided up. There was not enough and Pergrin would still have to scrabble along. He hoped Battalion could send him enough for a little leeway.

He indicated to Moyer where he wanted his men sent, along

Confrontation on the Amblève

the railroad to plug the holes at the overpasses south of town. The details made up and fanned out. Lieutenant Davis put two of his 1st platoon squads just beyond the overpass on the Route de St. Vith, the secondary road which came up from the south, little more than a farm road but, with luck, passable for tanks. Sergeant Magliocco was in charge. The men placed mines on the road, positioned their .30-caliber machine guns on either side and put the truck with its .50-caliber gun behind the forward defense. They put two men on one-hour rotating duty out front as security.

S/Sergeant Albert Melton took parts of two squads of his 2nd platoon to the railroad overpass on the Route de Falize. He positioned his men in front of the railroad overpass, with a thirteen-mine pattern laid across the road. This was a fairly good secondary road which had been kept in repair by the 291st because it was constantly and daily used as a shortcut between Stavelot and Malmédy. The men called it the "mountain road" because of its winding, tortuous way. Behind his mines Sergeant Melton put a .30-caliber machine gun, on either side of the road. Behind the overpass he parked the platoon truck with its .50-caliber machine gun, which he took over personally. Then he settled down in the intense cold and the inky dark to watch and wait for the enemy.

Other Company C men were sent to the level grade crossing southeast of the command post and since every available man had to be used, this roadblock was in charge of the C Company mess sergeant, a man named Martin, and called, in the manner of all mess sergeants, "Mother" Martin.

With a mixture of B and C Company men at the abatis defense on the back road to Spa, Pergrin now had every road into Malmédy defended, to the thinly stretched extent of his men and equipment.

Squad Sergeant Sheldon T. Smith was sent, with his men, out N-32 beyond the roadblock near the crossroads and told to space the men in single positions along the side of the hill. It was so dark that, running without lights, the only way the truck driver, Bob Rolfes, could stay on the road was by guiding on the tops of the trees. It was a little less black above the treeline. Smith spaced his men out, about twenty feet apart. Then they, too, settled down to watch and wait.

All night these men of the 291st on roadblocks south and east of town were tense because they heard considerable enemy activity out in front of them — engines running, vehicles moving about and occasionally foot patrols coming so near voices could be heard. Always, however, the sounds receded without coming into direct contact with the outposts, save once. Around 8:00 P.M. an enemy half-track blundered up the road near the mess sergeant's roadblock. It was fired on, but was not destroyed. If it was hit, it was still able to get away.

For the most part it was simply a shudderingly cold, anxious and tense night of watching. In a very short time the men were fighting the cold, their feet paralyzed and with no feeling, their shoulders shaken from time to time by paroxysms of uncontrollable shivering.

In his lonesome vigil up on the hill above his squad's roadblock on the Gdoumont road, Private Bernard Koenig fought sleep desperately. He was afraid he would never wake up if he dozed off.

Around 8:00 that evening, Warrant Officer Coye R. Self reached Malmédy with the ammunition, mines and demolitions Colonel Pergrin had ordered from Battalion earlier.

The supplies were quickly funneled out to the men on the various roadblocks. Especially strengthened was the area west of Malmédy where Sergeant McCarty now had two roadblocks on the main Stavelot road. He had one at the wooden bridge over the Warche River, and another at the big railroad viaduct. Mines and demolitions were sent and McCarty and Lieutenant Rhea set to work to wire the two bridges.

Pergrin was still, however, very short of machine guns. His

officers kept asking for more and more machine guns for the roadblocks. He thought of Company A. They might be back home by now. He therefore radioed Battalion to send him the Company A machine guns and gunners. It was about 8:30 P.M. Battalion acknowledged and reported that Company A had not yet got in.

Between 8:30 and 9:00 P.M. Captain Paul Kamen, the battalion dental officer, arrived in Malmédy with more medics and medical supplies. Pergrin was amazed to see him. When he had radioed Battalion, he had ordered the medical officer over. Kamen explained that the medical officer, Captain Walter Kaplita, had not been in Haute Bodeux when Pergrin's radio message was received. Not wanting to delay, Kamen had reasoned that he knew more about administering drugs and deep dressings than the medics and that in a pinch he might even be able to perform simple surgery, so he had packed up and come ahead.

Artillery fire was now falling in Malmédy. "Any trouble getting here?" Pergrin asked.

"Well," Kamen said, "the truck got shot up pretty bad, but we got through. We came through a heavy bombardment on the road from Stavelot."

Pergrin went out to look at the panel truck Kamen had brought and could only shake his head. The body was literally riddled with holes. "How in the hell did you make it without somebody being killed?" he said.

Kamen did not know. He thought perhaps they had been driving too fast. Not a man had received so much as a scratch. Kamen plunged immediately into work dressing the wounds of survivors from the massacre who continued to be brought in. Although the flow of wounded survivors would cease, Kamen's work would not. For ten days he would be a very busy dental officer doing a medical officer's work.

It will be remembered that Company A was divided into two sections traveling toward Trois Ponts and home. Gamble had left from Amblève around noon, just minutes before the village was overrun by Peiper. Lieutenant Bucky Walters had left Grand-Halleux around 4:00 P.M.

As darkness came on, the two sections, traveling independently of each other, neither knowing where the other was, struggled on through the mazes of logging trails and firebreaks in the woods south of Trois Ponts. Progress was extremely slow after dark, not only because they were unsure of their way, but also because the roads were now iced over and, driving without lights, the vehicles were constantly slipping and sliding about. Yards were the measure of progress now rather than miles as they inched along.

It would have been hair-raising had they known that proceeding almost parallel with them, on a road almost as bad as theirs, and not more than three miles east of them, Peiper's long, strong, powerful armored column was now making its way to Stavelot.

At about the same time Peiper reached Stavelot, or a little later, Captain Gamble's little convoy — his H/S, 2nd and 3rd platoons — neared the end of its struggles. They had finally reached Wanne and now they came perilously down off the high ridge mass, by the steep winding road that debouched onto N–33 between Grand-Halleux and Trois Ponts. Not until then did the men in the trucks know where they were. Sergeant R. C. Billington said that it was so black and he was so lost he felt blind. When they came down off the Wanne hill onto the highway his sense of relief was mixed with surprise as he recognized the Salm valley and the Grand-Halleux road. As far as his sense of direction was concerned, they might as easily have come out at Stavelot or Malmédy. Whoever led them (some of the men think it was Captain Gamble, others remember it as Lieutenant Edelstein) had a sure instinct for direction. He hit the road he wanted right on the nose.

As they reached the road, however, they were stopped by a 7th Armored roadblock, two tanks, one on each side of the road. It took Gamble fifteen or twenty minutes to satisfy the officer

Confrontation on the Amblève

he was not straggling, that he was moving under orders, and that he had a first responsibility to his own unit. He was allowed to pass finally and the little convoy crossed the Salm on the lower bridge, reaching Trois Ponts about 8:30 P.M.

Here they stopped long enough at Group headquarters to pass on to Colonel Anderson their firsthand information and then they moved on to Haute Bodeux to report to Battalion. It was around 9:00 P.M. when they reached the battalion headquarters.

The men did not dismount from their trucks while Captain Gamble went inside to report, accompanied by 1/Sergeant Smith. In a few minutes Sergeant Smith came out and began to tick off the machine gunners. Colonel Pergrin, he said, wanted them in Malmédy. They were to load up and take their weapons and ammunition and leave immediately. A squad truck was hurriedly loaded and the detail was put in charge of Corporal Isaac O. McDonald of 2nd platoon.

Eight men in all were sent. The identities of seven are known. They were:

> Corporal Isaac O. McDonald, 2nd platoon, in charge
> Pfc. Louis Hernandez, 2nd platoon
> Pfc. Wiley Holbrook, 2nd platoon
> Pfc. Angelo Morello, 2nd platoon
> Pfc. Palmer, 3rd platoon
> Pfc. Diaz, 3rd platoon
> Private Joseph Spires, H/S platoon

When these men were detailed and had left, Gamble then led the rest of his men back to Werbomont. They arrived around 11:00 P.M. Sergeant Billington roused up his former landlord and obtained the 2nd platoon's old quarters for them. The others bedded down in the schoolhouse which once again became the Company CP. The radiomen set to work to put up their antenna and report back in the Net.

Captain Gamble had one big worry on his mind, however. Lieutenant Walters and his 1st platoon, by all odds, should have beaten him back to Haute Bodeux. Walters had been much nearer. But he had not yet arrived. Gamble could only suppose Walters was having problems on the road, as he had done. Gamble and his men had seen absolutely no sign of the enemy in the woods. There was no reason to suppose Walters had come to grief that way. But it was worrisome that he was still out of pocket. Well, Gamble had most of his boys back, the radio antenna was up shortly and they were back in the Net. It had been a long nightmare, but it was finally over. Or so he thought.

Shortly after Colonel Pergrin radioed for the Company A machine guns and gunners a runner arrived at his CP with the news that the road patrol on the back road to Spa had met the advance elements of the Norwegian Battalion who said they had been sent by First Army to reinforce Malmédy. A colonel was with them, the runner said. The colonel wanted to know how he should come into Malmédy.

This was the best news Pergrin had had all day. Finally a little help was arriving. "Tell him to stay on that back road," Pergrin told the runner. "Tell him the main road is under artillery fire. And bring the colonel to my CP."

At 10:00 P.M. Colonel H. D. Hansen and his Executive Officer, Major Bjornstad, arrived at Pergrin's command post. Not much time was wasted on formalities. Pergrin and Hansen were of the same rank, both lieutenant colonels. They shook hands and sat down to look at the map and study a reinforced defense line. Colonel Hansen had noticed the felled trees at the abatis roadblock on the back road. "How many men do you have here?" he asked.

"Approximately a hundred and eighty," Pergrin said.

Hansen stared at him, unbelievingly. "One hundred and eighty! And you stayed here? My God, man, why didn't you run like hell?"

Pergrin did not really know. It was a little bit of several

Confrontation on the Amblève

things, probably. Because everything else got out, he got stubborn and would not. And then that little Battery got it in the neck, and the SS troops had brutally murdered them, and something in him just dug in his toes and he would not join the pell-mell retreat going on all around him. There was undoubtedly much anger. But there was moreover that iron sense of duty he so constantly preached to the 291st. And there was the good engineer's knowledge that he might at least delay the enemy for a while with his mines and demolitions. And of course, and not least, there was just plain guts. What he could do, he would do, for as long as he could.

As the two lieutenant colonels studied the map in Pergrin's CP it was Hansen's opinion that a "damned good defense" had been mapped out. He was in advance of his own troops but when they arrived he would simply reinforce Pergrin's defense line. When the 526th Armored Infantry arrived, with the detachment of tank destroyers, they would put guns here and here and here — near the B Company roadblock on N-32, and south of Malmédy at the vital railroad crossings. They would fill in a perimeter line, then, with Hansen's infantry.

Pergrin was worried about the bridge at Stavelot and he told Hansen he had only one squad on the roadblock there. Well, Stavelot was much too important to be left with only a handful of engineers defending it and Hansen immediately realized it. He had no idea where the 526th Armored Infantry was at the moment, but he radioed First Army and asked that one company of the 526th and one platoon of the tank destroyer guns be diverted to reinforce the town and the bridge across the Amblève.

First Army immediately dispatched a runner to find the 526th.

A misunderstanding and some confusion had arisen as to how the units of Colonel Hansen's task force were to proceed to Malmédy. Orders had been for the Norwegians to proceed to Malmédy and reinforce the 291st Engineers. Orders to the 526th had been to proceed to Malmédy where they would be attached to the Norwegians. Orders to Company A of the 825th Tank Destroyer Battalion had been to march with the 526th and proceed to Malmédy, but upon arrival to report to Colonel Hansen and come directly under his command.

Colonel Hansen followed his orders and started his battalion moving directly to Malmédy, via Francorchamps. The 526th Armored Infantry assembled west of Spa at Remouchamps and by 7:00 P.M. were grouped and ready to leave. But somehow they believed they were to rendezvous with the Norwegians and they wasted two hours waiting for them. The company from the 825th had assembled at La Reid, between Spa and Remouchamps, where they waited, as ordered, for the 526th.

Someone with the 526th must have grown tired of waiting at Remouchamps eventually and sent to Spa to learn what had happened, for at 9:00 P.M. the 526th received orders to proceed to Malmédy on their own. The company from the 825th was moved from La Reid, joined the 526th, and the column moved southward via Stoumont, La Gleize and Trois Ponts. The roads were in very bad condition, iced over, and the convoy had much difficulty because of the blackout. Near Trois Ponts, one rifle squad, towing a 57-mm. antitank gun, was lost. The half-track slipped a tread and had to drop out of the column. This gun and its crew were to play a very important role later.

First Army's runner found the column around midnight. He carried written orders from the Provost Marshal directing the 526th to detach one company, plus one platoon of tank destroyer guns, to go to Stavelot and take over its defense. The 526th Executive Officer, Major Paul Solis, was given command of this small detachment. As the column went through Stavelot, Solis and his command dropped off. It was around 3:00 A.M.

The balance of the 526th, with the other three platoons of Company A, 825th Tank Destroyer Battalion, proceeded to Malmédy.

Meanwhile in Malmédy Pergrin and Hansen completed their

conference and Hansen left to set up his own command post. The 291st did not come under command of Colonel Hansen. The two officers were co-commanders in a defensive position.

Pergrin's officers had slowly become aware of the fact that a good many of their bazookas were useless to them because of the lack of ammunition. Since nobody knew precisely when the 526th and the 825th elements would arrive with some guns, and since bazookas were an excellent weapon against tanks, Pergrin sent one more radio message to Battalion. Send him Company A's bazookas, he said, and their bazooka ammunition. It was shortly before midnight now and this was the last radio message he was to send to Battalion. A short while later he lost his radio contact with Haute Bodeux. Enemy artillery was now shelling Malmédy and was making a mess of the air waves.

Around midnight the last of the survivors of the massacre the 291st would assist was brought into the aid station. He was Lieutenant Virgil T. Lary. He had fallen into the friendly hands of a farmer who was a Belgian patriot rather than a German sympathizer. He was given assistance and shelter. He wrote a note addressed to the hospital commandant in Malmédy and asked that an ambulance be sent for him. The farmer took it to Malmédy where he learned that the hospital was no longer there. He persisted in his search for help for Lary, however, until he located Company B's command post and aid station, where he delivered the note. Captain Kamen told him that he had no ambulance and the station was full of other wounded men who needed the attention of himself and his medics. Kamen sent sulfa and bandaging for Lary and the farmer promised to bring him in.

Returning to his farm, when Lary's wound was dressed the farmer found a stout stick and his daughter Marthe and her friend, Marthe Manx, assisted the wounded officer into the aid station. It was nearly midnight. Colonel Pergrin interrogated him shortly afterward. Lary was able to give the final confirmation, clearly, concisely and coherently of precisely how the massacre had occurred. Colonel Pergrin said, "Lary was in perfect control of himself, calm and collected. He related the entire sequence of events coherently and in good detail. There was no evidence of hysteria. Like a good officer, he made a good, clear report."

Between 3:30 that afternoon and midnight, seventeen survivors in all had made their way to places where men of the 291st could help them. It is known that 43 survivors of both the brief skirmish and the massacre lived and reached safety. There are 72 names on the monument erected by the Belgians in honor of the men massacred at the crossroads. The official records, however, list 86 names. A bleak testimony to the savagery of Peiper's troops.

About the time Lieutenant Lary was brought into the aid station Corporal Isaac O. McDonald and his detail of machine gunners and guns from Company A arrived in Malmédy. These men and most of their guns were all given to Sergeant McCarty for use on the Stavelot road. The roadblock at the big viaduct was strengthened, and a new one farther out the road was set up near the paper mill. Here the road crossed the little Warche River on a wooden trestle bridge which Company B had built in November, to replace one destroyed by the retreating Germans. The bridge was wired for demolition and a machine gun crew dug in with a .30-caliber gun on the far approach.

At Werbomont, Company A's radiomen had gotten their antenna up around 11:30. It seemed to Dennington, Schommer and Theodoseau that they had done nothing for two days but take down and put back up this blasted radio antenna. At midnight they received Battalion's message to send Colonel Pergrin

Confrontation on the Amblève

their bazookas and ammunition. The message indicated that Malmédy had been probed by German armor and was under heavy artillery fire.

The men had turned in and were sleeping. T/4 Jeff Elliott was asleep in the hall of the schoolhouse. He was roused by Corporal Dennington, the Company A chief operator, and told that Captain Gamble wanted to see him.

Elliott went sleepily into the orderly room where he found Gamble, Lieutenant Hayes, the administrative officer, for whom Elliott drove, and 1/Sergeant Smith and all three radio operators. All were discussing this order just received. Gamble explained the need for the bazookas. He did not order Elliott to take them over. He asked him if he would be willing to. Elliott said, sure, just give him time to get his stuff together.

Dennington went to find somebody to go with Elliott. The men of 3rd platoon were in an adjoining room in the schoolhouse. Dennington asked for a volunteer and Pfc. Red Richardson said he would be the man. Lieutenant Hayes unloaded his jeep while the two men got ready, and he and 1/Sergeant Smith helped load the bazookas and ammunition into the jeep.

When Elliott and Richardson were ready to go they reported to Gamble. "Battalion has just radioed that they have lost contact with Malmédy," Gamble said, "so you boys don't need to go if you don't want to. There's a big chance you will run into some real trouble. Malmédy may be in enemy hands."

Elliott said, "The colonel's not got any artillery, has he?"

"No."

"He needs the bazookas for tanks?"

"Yes."

"O.K. If he's still in Malmédy he's going to get the bazookas."

"Well," Gamble said, "if you run into any trouble don't try to be heroes. Abandon the jeep and get the hell out."

It was about 12:30 when Elliott and Richardson left the schoolhouse. It was black dark and in order to see better Elliott folded the windshield down. Richardson rode beside him, his rifle at the ready. Elliott had a Tommy gun which he placed across his knees. He was twenty years old and he was scared to death — so scared his teeth were chattering and he could not control them. It did not keep him from heading his jeep down N–23 toward Trois Ponts, eleven miles away.

He and Richardson went through Trois Ponts between 1:00 and 1:30 A.M. Their final checkpoint there was a roadblock at the railroad viaduct on the Stavelot road. The men had a daisy chain of mines across the road and a .50-caliber machine gun set up. When they learned Elliott and Richardson were going to Malmédy they tried to persuade them not to try it. "Malmédy has been captured," they said, "you'll never make it."

Stubbornly Elliott said, "We'll try it."

Richardson, sitting beside him, grinned. He was an iron-nerved man whom nothing ever seemed to faze. "Aw, what the hell," he said, "we just got one life to give for our country."

They drove on.

By this time there was a lull in the heavy traffic on the road. They met some but nothing like the solidly packed flow that had jammed the road earlier.

Just before they reached Stavelot, in its outer edge, the two men saw blue night lights approaching and Elliott pulled off the road and stopped. Richardson poked his rifle through the open windshield and Elliott picked up his Tommy gun. An American jeep approached and pulled up. There were four American soldiers in the jeep. Only one of them spoke. He asked if the road to Trois Ponts was still open. Elliott told him it was and the jeep moved on in the direction of Trois Ponts.

About that time the two men heard the clank of treads on a street above them and believing it to be an enemy tank, Elliott floorboarded the accelerator and took off through Stavelot like a scared jackrabbit.

Though they had no way of knowing it the jeep they had met

was probably a Skorzeny jeep and the officer who questioned them may have been the merchant marine officer who had cruised around Malmédy that morning. He had been at Peiper's command post just across the river earlier in the evening.* The tracked vehicle they heard belonged to the advance elements of the 526th Armored Infantry, now arriving at Stavelot.

Beyond Stavelot Elliott took the shortcut which wound around over the hills and came back into the main highway just below the wooden bridge over the Warche. As they got about halfway up this road, enemy artillery opened an intense barrage. Now their progress was a matter of ducking and dodging shells, and at least once, on a curve, a big bridging truck which came barreling down a long winding hill. Elliott hugged the side of the road, shut his eyes and prayed. The long truck whizzed by, its tail almost scraping the jeep.

The mountain road from Stavelot to Malmédy was such a harrowing experience, what with heavy artillery fire and bridging trucks zooming around curves at sixty miles per hour, that by the time the two men reached the command post Elliott was in a sweat and shaking all over. They went down the stairs to the basement, into which Colonel Pergrin had moved when the artillery fire began. Elliott drew himself up and saluted and said, "Well, Colonel, we brought the bazookas."

Pergrin blinked at him and Richardson. "How the hell did you get through? Are you hurt?"

"No, sir. They're plastering that road with artillery fire, but we made it," Elliott said.

Pergrin hauled out a bottle of whisky that had been liberated from stores abandoned by the 44th Field Hospital. He poured each man a good stiff drink. "Here," he said, "drink this. It'll ease those shakes."

He ordered the bazookas unloaded and then said, "Do you

* Eisenhower, John S. D., *The Bitter Woods* (New York: G. P. Putnam's Sons, 1969), p. 239.

want to try to get back to Company A, or would you rather stay here with us?"

Elliott and Richardson said they would prefer to go back.

"Well, you can't get back through Stavelot," Pergrin said.

"No, sir," Elliott said, "but I know all the roads around the back way. We'll make it all right."

Pergrin said O.K. and watched the two men leave. They looked like hell, he thought. Dirty, bearded, heavy-eyed, they looked like they had been hung over for two days. But they had brought the bazookas and he did not doubt they would make it fine back to Company A. They did, by going around by Spa and La Gleize.

Shortly after Elliott and Richardson left, the men of Colonel Hansen's Norwegian Battalion began to arrive, and between 3:00 and 4:00 A.M. the 526th Armored Infantry — minus one company directed to Stavelot — and the three platoons of Company A, 825th TD Battalion also arrived. Guides from Company C, 291st, led them to the roadblock positions along the railroad embankment and slowly, slowly the new units got into position.

The final reinforcements to arrive in Malmédy that night were a battery of 90-mm. antiaircraft guns under Lieutenant Robert Wilson of the 49th AAA Brigade, which had displaced from "buzz bomb alley" between Honsfeld and Butgenbach very hurriedly under Peiper's advance that morning. This battery was positioned on a hill overlooking both the Gdoumont road and N–32 east of town.

It was slow work moving the towed guns into position and yet the men worked feverishly against time. An attack was expected at dawn and when, around 5:30 A.M. the intensity of artillery fire suddenly increased, everybody in Malmédy believed it was the prelude to a general attack. The tempo became hectic. But both Colonel Pergrin and Colonel Hansen felt they had some chance, now. At least they could make a fight of it.

12

IN LA GLEIZE that afternoon Lieutenant Rombaugh detailed the 3rd squad of his 2nd platoon to set up the roadblock in Stavelot. The squad leader was Sergeant Charles Hensel. Hensel was a reliable man and Rombaugh did not hesitate to give him full charge. This squad was on the night shift at the sawmill and that was why they were in La Gleize instead of Trois Ponts.

Rombaugh called Hensel in and said, "You won't be going to the mill tonight."

Hensel said, "Good. The boys can do with a night off."

Rombaugh laughed and said, "You're not getting the night off. You're going to Stavelot and set up a roadblock."

Rombaugh then gave Hensel a brief outline of what was happening and impressed on Hensel the importance of the roadblock, and where it should be put, at the stone bridge.

Hensel alerted his men. The detail loaded up its squad truck with mines, wiring, demolitions, a .30-caliber machine gun, a bazooka and ammunition. Thirteen men, the entire squad except one who was in the hospital, made up the detail. The men were: Sergeant Charles Hensel, squad leader, Corporal Eugene Morris, assistant squad leader, Pfcs. John Leary, Francis Lynch, John McClements, Gadziola, Cole, Hahne, Sosa, Wettling, Bauers, Friedmann (driver of the truck) and Private Bernard Goldstein.

Rombaugh had told Hensel to move out as soon as possible.

The detail left La Gleize shortly before 5:00 P.M. It was just beginning to be dusky, twilightly dark.

They went south, toward Trois Ponts, and made good time until they reached the railroad viaducts in the edge of Trois Ponts where they had to turn onto the Stavelot road. Here they ran into a bottleneck of jammed vehicles and they were held up a considerable length of time. Finally there was a gap through which they could push their way and proceed.

Now it was full dark and at Stavelot they were surprised to find the town well lit as the long line of vehicles moved through the town with lights on. There was also an unusually heavy concentration of buzz bombs streaming overhead on a course toward Liège. It was around 6:30 as the squad approached the limits of Stavelot. In the heavy growl of the traffic with the great grinding engines of big trucks, bulldozers, prime movers, as well as all the other vehicles, they did not hear the guns of the German tanks arriving on the heights some two miles across the river.

But Peiper had now reached Stavelot.

Hensel and his men turned right at the main intersection in the heart of town and proceeded toward the stone bridge, from which they would ascend the long winding hill up to the heights. Hensel had a roadblock to set up and precise directions as to where to put it. Somewhere on that hill.

It will be recalled that when Peiper's northern wing left the Five Points crossroads they were in a great hurry to reach Ligneuville in order to surprise and capture General Timberlake and his 49th AAA Brigade headquarters and rendezvous with Peiper.

Until the early morning of December 16, life in Ligneuville had been a soldier's dream. The beautiful and exclusive resort town had three excellent hotels, the Hôtel du Moulin, in which the headquarters were, the Hôtel d'Amblève and the Hôtel des Ardennes. The hotels provided excellent quarters and the forests abounded in deer and wild boar, affording fine hunting.

The shelling of Malmédy on the morning of December 16 began to bring the dream to an end. All that day there was much speculation, many rumors and much apprehension.

After breakfast the morning of December 17 the rumors of a breakthrough were confirmed by the sounds of much firing over in the vicinity of Büllingen. Concerned over his batteries in buzz bomb alley, General Timberlake kept in radio contact with the 99th Infantry Division and finally received the message that a German armored column had indeed broken through at Büllingen and was probing toward Butgenbach. Timberlake issued orders to begin preparations to evacuate his headquarters.

Trucks were brought and loading of equipment began. Between 12:30 and 1:00 P.M. CCR of 7th Armored Division rolled through on their way to Vielsalm, and after a conference with the leading elements Timberlake issued orders at 1:00 that his units would move out of Ligneuville immediately after lunch. It was decided that a small command group of three officers and three enlisted men would be left to maintain communications with lower and higher units. Lunch was served and the tenseness of the atmosphere was somewhat relieved by the decision just made.*

Around 1:45 P.M. the bulldozer which had escaped from Five Points sounded an alert to all the headquarters units. It came barreling into town and pulled up in front of the Hôtel du Moulin long enough for the driver to shout at Captain Seymour Green, who had just finished his lunch and was standing outside, that a German armored column was coming, and that his bulldozer had been fired on. Then the driver tore off down the street and out of town.

Green was in charge of a section of the service train which belonged to CCB, 9th Armored Division. Recall that this Combat Command team had moved to Faymonville on December 14 to

* 49th AAA Brigade After Action Report and Unit History.

support the 2nd Infantry Division in their attack toward the Urft-Roer dams. Its service train had put up in Ligneuville. General Hoge had been ordered south the night before and was even now on the front near Winterspelt, on the other side of St. Vith. But elements of his service train were still in Ligneuville.

Green promptly got in his jeep and drove up the Malmédy road to investigate the bulldozer driver's report. He ran smack into the lead tanks of the German column and was captured.

The sounds of the firing up at the crossroads had been heard earlier by the men in the town. General Timberlake dispatched Major Kelakos to investigate the bulldozer's startling news and Kelakos returned within minutes with the astounding news that a German armored column was advancing down the road from the crossroads and was only minutes away from Ligneuville.

There was a frantic rush now to get moving. The route planned for the evacuation was over the winding, narrow road through the forests to Stavelot. Orders were to move by infiltration rather than in convoy — that is, each truck was on its own. General Timberlake's command car was the last vehicle to leave the town.

Timberlake's units made their way to Stavelot and on to Bomal, thence to Lambermont, near Verviers, where the evacuated AAA batteries from "buzz bomb alley" joined them and a defense line was set up.

Behind them in Ligneuville, as the lead tanks of the German column arrived they were advancing, as usual, with all guns firing. They met no opposition in the town itself and rolled up to the Hôtel du Moulin only ten or fifteen minutes after General Timberlake had left it.

Major Josef Diefenthal's men of the *3rd Battalion* mopped up in Ligneuville rapidly, bringing the prisoners they took into the hotel. Captain Seymour Green was among them. Later, eight were taken out and shot to death. Captain Green was not among those executed. He credited the hotel keeper, Peter Rupp, and his wife with saving the lives of the rest of the prisoners by serving the Germans their good wine until they were in such a state of high good humor they lost the wish to execute any more prisoners.

The tanks, meanwhile, had moved on through the town and in the southern edge of Ligneuville they met American tanks for the first time. These were with the supply trains of CCB, 9th Armored Division, and they were moving to join their unit near St. Vith. There was a brisk fire fight in which one of the German Panthers was destroyed and two armored cars. The supply train lost two Sherman tanks, one M-10 tank destroyer and several machine guns before they could break off and move southward to St. Vith.*

It was around 1:30 when the German column entered Ligneuville. The sharp skirmish with CCB's service trains, and the subduing of the town, disorganized the column. But it also had to wait here for its rendezvous with Peiper.

At some time during the period of reorganization and waiting, the commander of *1st SS Panzer Division*, General Wilhelm Mohnke, arrived at the Hôtel du Moulin and set up his headquarters in Timberlake's old offices. That evening Skorzeny arrived and set himself up in the chalet of Peter Rupp. †

While this fire fight and reorganization was going on in Ligneuville, Peiper himself was in the vicinity of Born, moving toward the Kaiserbaracke crossroads. The fact that CCB's service trains got away down this road to St. Vith without running into Peiper would indicate that he did not reach Kaiserbaracke until some time after 3:00 P.M.

It was only a little over three miles from there to Ligneuville, however, and rolling ahead of his column Peiper reached that point about 4:30. He learned that the double envelopment had not worked. The bird had flown.

Peiper also learned here that it would be impossible for him to

---
* Ethint 10, Oberst (W-SS) Jochen Peiper, I SS PZ Regt. (Dec. 15-26, 1944), p. 18.
† 49th AAA Brigade Unit History.

take the forest trails across country to Wanne. The Recon unit which Sergeant Williams of Lieutenant Walters' 1st platoon had seen in the forest as he and his men were cutting timber that morning was a reconnaissance patrol from Peiper's column.

Peiper would also have learned from Major Poetschke that there was no sign of any advance of the *12th SS Panzer Division* from Büllingen to Malmédy. Peiper would therefore know that it would be safe to advance from Ligneuville to Stavelot, usurp the *12th*'s road from there to Trois Ponts, where he would once again pick up his own road to Huy and Ombret Rausa. It is entirely possible that Peiper conferred with Mohnke at the Hôtel du Moulin and had permission to make this diversion.

Peiper's column was now in a terrible mess, strung out for miles, with long gaps between the units. Some were following his route down through Amblève and some were trying to follow Poetschke around through Schoppen and Thirimont. Peiper has said that few wheeled vehicles could use that road, however, because the tanks had turned it into a quagmire. They had all, therefore, trucks, artillery, flak wagons, to take the route through Amblève. The *2nd SS Panzer Grenadier Regiment*, at the tail of Peiper's kampfgruppe, also followed this route and got involved the next day in skirmishes with 7th Armored troops around Kaiserbaracke and Recht.

It was about 5:00 P.M. before the leading tank unit was ready to take the road toward Stavelot. It is not likely that Peiper himself accompanied the van of his column here. He had the rest of his column to pull together. It may even be true that Mohnke had ordered Poetschke on toward Stavelot before Peiper arrived.

Peiper's account of what occurred at Stavelot later in the evening is so jumbled and confused and disconnected that it lends credence to the belief he was not personally present but had the story secondhand from Major Poetschke.

The column now had a truly abominable road, little more than a forest trail through the dense woods, and General Timberlake's vehicles had not improved it any. Peiper's leading tank company turned it into a sliding, slithery soup for the vehicles following, and it was now dark. This section of his advance was a sheer nightmare for Peiper.

At any rate, his column plowed along its miserable road and reached the heights above Stavelot, but across the river from it, at about the same time Sergeant Charles Hensel and his squad of men were reaching the main town. From this good vantage point the Germans could see down into the town proper and what they could see didn't look too good. The town was full of great, crawling masses of vehicles moving with lights on. It gave the appearance of much strength being massed for defense. They halted, and halted for quite a while to ponder the situation, for if they had continued immediately, the lead tanks would have run into Hensel and his men at about the stone bridge.

But across the river in Stavelot, Hensel's squad reached the bridge. There was nobody at the bridge at all. It was entirely undefended. Corporal Eugene Morris has said that a "new officer in the battalion" was with them and that he directed the squad to cross the bridge, proceed up the hill and set up their roadblock somewhere near the top. He recalls that the officer told them they did not need to link their mines into a daisy chain, saying, "Anything that comes down that road will be enemy, so just lay your mines on the road." *

The truck moved across the bridge and proceeded a short distance to a point where the road curved left and began to make a steep, winding ascent up the hill. A line of houses was built on the left side of the road but the houses stopped where the bank on the outside fell away too sharply. After the houses ceased, it became a lonely road cut out of the hill, winding about. Toward

* All details of this entire event were given to the author in letters and many telephone conversations with four men who were involved: Sergeant Charles Hensel, leader of the squad; Corporal Eugene Morris, assistant leader; Pfc. John Leary, machine gunner; and Private Bernard Goldstein.

the top of the hill the road made a sharp right curve around a high rock cliff. Beyond this curve the ascent eased until the road flattened out at the top of the hill not far distant.

Hensel directed his truck driver to continue to the top of the hill. As they wound their way up he was looking for a good position for the roadblock. The truck could not have turned around on the narrow road, anyhow. At or near the top, with a broader road, and with Peiper and his tanks only a short distance farther on, they turned around and went back down the hill. When they rounded the sharp curve, with the high rock cliff left when the road was cut out of the hill, Hensel ordered the truck to stop. Here, he said, in this deep protected curve was the best place for the roadblock.

The rocky cliff made it a blind curve and the deep drop on the outside would prevent anything going around them. He set the men to work.

Pfc. John Leary and some other men tore down a wooden paling fence which had reflectors on it, which could have picked up headlights. Other men placed a thirteen-mine pattern across the road just below the curve in such a position that any vehicle rounding the curve could not see them until it was on top of them.

Hensel detailed Private Bernard Goldstein as the security man, on point, and Corporal Eugene Morris took him beyond the curve and positioned him behind a small white cement building. Neither man could know that at that very moment and not far away, the Germans were talking together about probing toward the Stavelot bridge.

When Morris returned from positioning Goldstein, Hensel put him and a man named Gadziola, with a bazooka, about 30 yards below the string of mines. Then below the bazooka team, about the same distance, he placed the .30-caliber machine gun with Pfc. John Leary and Pfc. Francis Lynch in charge.

By now it was nearing 7:30. Hensel had second thoughts

Confrontation on the Amblève 215

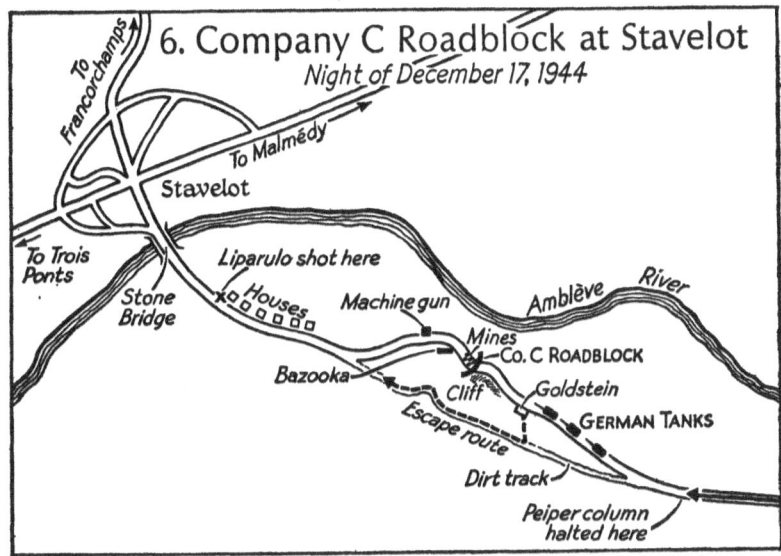

about leaving Private Goldstein on security alone. He decided to send another man to be with him. "Bauers," he called, "you'd better get up there with Goldstein."

Bauers was Goldstein's best friend in the squad. They had often pitched their pup tents together. Bauers said he did not know where Goldstein was positioned. "I'll take you," Hensel said.

In the meantime three tanks, with paratroop-infantry riding their decks, had started down the hill on the main road.

Behind his little cement building, entirely alone, with only his M-1 rifle, Goldstein kept watch. He has said it was pitch dark. Shortly he heard the tanks approaching, going very slow, almost creeping, as if they were feeling their way in the dark. They were going so slowly and so quietly that just beyond his position Goldstein could hear the men on the decks talking together. Goldstein understood German and spoke it a little. He heard the men and recognized their language.

At about the same time, Hensel and Charlie Bauers rounded the rock-faced curve and approached Goldstein's position. They both heard the tank motors at the same moment, when they were within perhaps thirty or forty feet of the building behind which Goldstein was posted. The tank engines were very low, barely turning, as if the tanks were either halted or barely moving, inching along. Hensel and Bauers stopped and within seconds, hardly believing their ears, they heard Goldstein challenge the tanks with a loud, commanding "Halt!" It was funny, it was wild, it was incomprehensible to them, but nonetheless, alone and with only an M–1 rifle, Goldstein had demanded that the tanks halt!

When Goldstein shouted the infantrymen on the decks scrambled to the ground and opened fire with their rifles. Hensel and Bauers took a potshot or two with their rifles, but then the machine guns on the tanks opened up and they beat a hasty retreat back around the rock cliff. Then one of the big guns, a 75-mm. gun, fired.

Goldstein has said that when this gun went off the shell went right over his head. He was blinded and deafened by the flame and thunder and the earth shook under his feet. He decided this was no place for a boy from Brooklyn and he took off up over the hill.

Below the curve, among the men of 3rd squad, there was a considerable amount of confusion now, with men running here and there. Morris and Gadziola fired the bazooka. Leary and Lynch did not fire the machine gun. There was nothing to fire at. The tanks did not come on around the curve. Up ahead of Leary and Lynch were only their own men, and a lot of noise and firing from around the bend. Some of the men came running back to them and said they were going to fall back to the bridge.

This did not happen immediately, however. The men on the roadblock were worried about Goldstein. He had not returned to them and they were afraid he had been wounded. They did

Confrontation on the Amblève

not want to leave him alone up on that hill. As the firing died down a little, Bauers pled to be allowed to try to get him. Hensel said O.K. Bauers crept around the cliff but was greeted with a fresh outburst of machine gun fire and had to withdraw in a hurry.

The men milled around awhile and waited about twenty minutes. Then they heard the tank motors rev up and tank treads clanking. Slowly the sounds receded. And now Gadziola wanted to try to reach Goldstein. Hensel again said O.K. Gadziola crept around the curve and immediately saw one tank still sitting there. The tank was slightly askew on the road, as if it had slid, or one of its treads had slipped. Gadziola did not tempt its machine gun fire. He returned and reported the tank's presence. Hensel now said they had to go back to the bridge. The truck was in position just below the mines, headed downhill. Everybody loaded on. They left the mines on the road but took the bazooka and machine gun and they coasted downhill, not starting the engine until they reached the bottom.

As they approached the bridge they met a jeep with an officer in it. His driver was Pfc. Lorenzo Liparulo of Company C. The identity of the officer is uncertain. Some of the men have said the officer was Lieutenant Rombaugh, but this seems to have been based on the fact that Liparulo was Rombaugh's regular driver rather than actual recognition of the officer. However, Rombaugh had fired Liparulo as his driver only a few days before, so he was not driving for Rombaugh at this time.

Others of the men have said the officer was "new in the battalion" and they did not know him. This could have been Lieutenant Kirkpatrick, who was the only new officer in the battalion, had just taken over command of 2nd platoon, Company B, in Malmédy, who was in La Gleize that day and who had either volunteered or been directed by Captain Moyer to see that the Stavelot roadblock was set up before he went on to Malmédy to rejoin his own platoon.

One thing is certain, the jeep was a Company C jeep and Pfc. Liparulo, whom all the men recognized as the driver, was carried on the roster of Hensel's own 3rd squad. Hensel himself has said he did not know the officer.

There was now at the bridge about a full platoon of men, around 40 or 50, and it was about 9:00 P.M. None of the men of 3rd squad knew the men at the bridge or had ever seen them before. Some of the men thought they were infantry, others who overheard Hensel and the officer talking thought they were an engineer outfit. For the bridge was now wired and ready to blow. Only engineers would have had the demolitions and wiring necessary. But while 3rd squad was up on the hill, the outfit had arrived and got the bridge ready to blow. The officer had evidently started up the hill to bring 3rd squad down before the bridge was blown.

As the squad truck and the jeep met at the south end of the bridge, the men in the truck overheard the officer say to Hensel, "Is this all of you? Have you got all your men down from the hill? The bridge is wired and we're getting ready to blow it."

When Hensel replied that he had had to leave one man up on the hill, the officer made no comment. Hensel proceeded across the bridge, the jeep turned around and followed, and another brief halt ensued.

Some of the men of 3rd squad have said the attempt to destroy the Stavelot bridge was made while they were still there and either the wiring or the explosives were defective, for it would not blow. Others do not recall it. Hensel has said that with the bridge now guarded by a full platoon he decided he should find Lieutenant Rombaugh and report to him. He therefore took his squad to Trois Ponts where he found Rombaugh and a detachment of Company C men at the Amblève bridge. Hensel's unit joined these men.

It seems likely that the officer was Lieutenant Kirkpatrick and that whether or not 3rd squad was still at the bridge when the

Confrontation on the Amblève

attempt to blow it was made, Kirkpatrick was and he reported the attempt to Colonel Pergrin when he went on to Malmédy, for Colonel Pergrin knew the bridge had been wired and an attempt to blow it had been made while he was still in Malmédy, before the battalion was reunited and the men of 3rd squad could have told him.

Who the unknown men were remains a mystery. A company of Engineers was in Stavelot. The 202nd Engineer Combat Battalion had been transferred a week earlier from Patton's Third Army to the First U.S. Army and temporarily assigned to the 1111th Engineer Group. Their Company C was due a rest and one of its officers chose Stavelot as the place for their rest. Company C had moved to Stavelot on December 13. Colonel Anderson, of Group, knew the 202nd had been assigned to him, but he did not know of the presence of its Company C in Stavelot.

All day of the 17th, the men of this Company C had heard disquieting rumors, seen the refugees from Malmédy, witnessed the vast movement of vehicles through the town. Finally Lieutenant Joe Chinlund, in command while Captain Peter Wolfe was recovering from an injury, called a conference at which it was decided that since Company C was in Stavelot of its own accord, had not been ordered there, it could leave of its own accord, and it should displace and try to find some heavy weapons outfit to which it could attach itself.

They went toward Trois Ponts and at that place ran into Colonel Anderson, who remembered that the 202nd had recently been assigned to him and ordered Company C back to Stavelot. His After Action Report does not indicate what orders he gave them beyond that, but apparently they were not ordered to beef up the 291st roadblock.

The 202nd's Company C returned to Stavelot and spent the night there. Sergeant Joe Josephs has said that nobody from this unit was anywhere near the bridge that night. He said that shortly after they got back from Trois Ponts somebody knocked at their quarters and asked directions to the bridge, saying they had orders to wire and destroy it if necessary. Sergeant Josephs said their own comment on this was short and sweet: "That's the army for you. With engineers already in Stavelot and demolitions running out their ears, they gotta send somebody else to do that job."

So a detail from the 202nd is ruled out as having wired the bridge.

There is a footnote to the attempt to blow the bridge. When the war ended the 202nd Engineer Combat Battalion was guarding prisoners of war at Le Havre. One day Sergeant Josephs and a companion were walking past the POW cage and a prisoner called out to them, in good English, "What outfit are you with?"

"202nd Engineers."

The prisoner laughed. "You were at Stavelot. I can tell you why that bridge wouldn't blow the night of December 17. We fixed it so it wouldn't."

Sergeant Josephs believed that the men who knocked at their quarters, and the men who were at the bridge when Sergeant Hensel came down from the hill, were Germans dressed as Americans.

However that may be, obviously the prisoner who spoke to Sergeant Josephs had been a member of a Skorzeny team and he and his team had sabotaged the effort to blow the bridge.

Colonel Pergrin was not only without an executive officer at this time, he was in Malmédy without any administrative staff, and keeping tidy records under the circumstances in Malmédy during this period was well-nigh impossible. It was ten days before the battalion was reunited, two weeks before an After Action Report could be filed, and the precise details of what happened at this roadblock on the hill across the river from Stavelot were never entirely clear until now. The official records of the 291st Engineers, therefore, have no details at all, except that the roadblock was established and that it was overrun. At the time

Confrontation on the Amblève

his After Action Report was filed, Colonel Pergrin believed that had occurred the following morning when Peiper attacked.

There has therefore been, through all these years, a deep mystery as to why Peiper halted at the top of this hill, coiled up and waited until the following morning to attack, when had he thrust forward boldly there was nothing for so venturesome a commander as Peiper standing in his way. Peiper himself has consistently maintained that his lead tanks that night were fired on by tank destroyers and sniped at by U.S. infantry. A bazooka rocket with its great blaze and explosion could easily have been mistaken for tank destroyer fire. And certainly some rifle shots were fired by the men of Hensel's squad.

Historians have not known what to make of Peiper's account.

Peiper's account, told to Major Kenneth W. Hechler on September 7, 1945, when he was a prisoner of war, says, "At 1600 on 17 Dec 44 we reached the area of Stavelot, which was heavily defended. We could observe heavy traffic moving from Malmédy towards Stavelot, and Stavelot itself seemed clogged up completely with several hundred trucks. That night we attempted to capture Stavelot, but the terrain presented great difficulties. The only approach was the main road, and the ground to the left of the road fell very sharply, and to the right of the road rose very sharply. There was a short curve just at the entrance to Stavelot where several Sherman tanks and antitank guns were zeroed in.

"Thereupon, we shelled Stavelot with heavy infantry howitzers and mortars, resulting in great confusion within the town and the destruction of several dumps.

"At the same time I ordered one of my Mark IV tank companies to try to find a way around Stavelot through Aisomont, Wanne and Trois Ponts. It proceeded along a small trail which was nearly impossible to negotiate. At 1800 a counterattack circled around a high hill 800 meters east of Stavelot and hit my column from the south.

"... the counterattack consisted entirely of infantry. After the counterattack was repulsed, I committed more armored infantry to attack Stavelot again. We approached the outskirts of the village but bogged down because of stubborn American resistance at the edge of Stavelot. We suffered fairly heavy losses, 25 to 30 casualties, from tank, antitank, mortar and rifle fire. Since I did not have sufficient infantry, I decided to wait for the arrival of more infantry."

The van of Peiper's column did not reach the top of the hill across the river from Stavelot at 4:00 P.M. as Peiper states. It was around 6:30 P.M. when the first tanks arrived. Stavelot was not heavily defended, but it is true much traffic was moving through it and it very likely gave that appearance.

If three tanks nosing down the hill road was an attempt to capture Stavelot, then an attempt was made. The description of the terrain is accurate.

Stavelot was not shelled that night. Malmédy was shelled, but not one shell fell in Stavelot.

The diversion of two, not one, Mark IV companies around by Wanne to Trois Ponts was made the following morning, December 18.

No counterattack of infantry around the "high hill 800 meters east of Stavelot" hitting Peiper's column from the south was made. Sergeant Hensel's squad of Company C, 291st Engineers, exchanged a few rifle shots with Peiper's men, fired their bazooka, disabled the lead tank and that was the "infantry counterattack."

No armored infantry was committed to attack Stavelot following this encounter.

Obviously Peiper confused the events of the attack the following morning with events of the night of December 17.

The truth, more probably, is that Peiper himself was not with the van of his column when it arrived on top the hill across the river from Stavelot. That Major Poetschke, commander of the tank battalion, cautiously sent three tanks probing down the hill and when they ran into the 291st's roadblock withdrew them and waited for Peiper to come up. Peiper accepted Poetschke's account that his tanks had been attacked by infantry, believed that American infantry was up on the hill with him, and in light of his badly disorganized column, strung out for twenty-five miles behind him, struggling desperately in the dark on a mushy, muddy road, decided to wait until his column closed up and make the attack at dawn the next morning. If Peiper did not arrive on top of the hill until 10:00 or 11:00 P.M. this was not as long a wait as it appears. He has said that here at Stavelot, under all these dismal conditions, he had the heavy feeling "the big strike" was going to escape him.*

Well, Peiper was tired. He had had little or no sleep since December 13, nor had his men. He had fought a battle at Honsfeld, one at Büllingen, several skirmishes. As young as he was and as tough as he may have been physically, his body had been absorbing the wear and tear of almost constant motion, in rough vehicles over rough roads, almost without rest from Bliesheim, in front of Cologne. His mind had borne the strain and anxiety of this deep penetration with his flanks unprotected. An erosion of will and judgment occurs with long sleeplessness and extraordinary fatigue even in the strongest man. It seems to have occurred in Peiper here. Thirteen men of 3rd squad, 2nd platoon, Company C, 291st Engineers, with a bazooka and some rifles to make a little noise and do a little damage, plus the mass of vehicles in the town of Stavelot, caused the first long pause in this man's implacable advance and in the end this night's delay cost him his battle.

When Private Bernard Goldstein escaped over the hill, around 7:30 P.M. he came very near running into Peiper's troops gathered at the top of the hill. Hearing them in time, however, he

* Eisenhower, John S. D., *The Bitter Woods* (New York: G. P. Putnam's Sons, 1969), p. 239.

hid, then alternately creeping and hiding, he angled around down the hill on the other side from the road. In the pitch darkness he got lost often, waited a time to try to orient himself, then struggled on. It took him a long time to make his way back to the bridge. It was around 10:30 or 11:00 before he got there. None of his own squad was there, of course. But forty or fifty men, strangers to him, were there, and Pfc. Lorenzo Liparulo was there, in a Company C jeep.

Sometime after midnight Goldstein and Liparulo were ordered, "by some officer," to make a reconnaissance back up the hill. With Liparulo driving, they set out in the Company C jeep, went over the bridge and followed the main road a short distance up the hill. Actually they did not go much farther than the first cluster of houses on the left. Here they stopped, killed the jeep's motor and sat there quietly, alert and watchful. It was about 1:00 A.M.

They sat there for half an hour. For some reason Liparulo took his helmet off — perhaps to hear better. He was holding it on his knees when suddenly, with no warning they had come so quietly, and from both sides of the street, German infantry commenced firing on them. It was as still as death one moment, the next German machine pistols were blazing.

Liparulo was hit in the head and fell over onto Goldstein. Goldstein was hit in the right hip, then rapidly he was hit twice more in the right leg lower down. Believing Liparulo was instantly killed, Goldstein rolled out onto the ground. The firing did not last long, a burst or two and it ceased. The Germans did not approach the jeep to examine it. They retired back up the hill.

Thinking Liparulo had been killed, and himself badly wounded, Goldstein's thought was to get back to the bridge. He could not walk, nor even stand, because of the wound in his hip. Therefore he crawled on his hands and knees every foot of the way back to the bridge. It took him a long, long time. By the

Confrontation on the Amblève

time he reached the bridge the 526th Armored Infantry had come into Stavelot and were guarding it. Fearful they would shoot him, Goldstein called across, identified himself, told them he was wounded and he was coming across. They met him and assisted him and took him to their aid station in the town. He remembers very little more of what happened to him after that.

Sergeant Hensel's squad, leaving Stavelot, had made its slow way in the heavy traffic to Trois Ponts and joined the elements of Company C at the Amblève bridge there.

Colonel Anderson had also taken other steps to defend Trois Ponts. Around 7:00 P.M. he radioed his 51st Engineers at Marche to send him a company from that unit. He asked for a maximum supply of demolitions, mines, bazookas and machine guns. In turn, at 8:00 P.M. the commanding officer of the 51st alerted his Company C, who were at Melreux on the outskirts of Hotton. At 10:00 P.M. the advance elements of Company C, 51st Engineers, consisting of about 75 men, were on their way. They arrived in Trois Ponts at 11:30 and set up a command post in the railway station on the east bank of the Salm. They began immediate preparation of both the Amblève and the Salm bridges for demolition and set up strong roadblocks.

The elements of Company C, 291st Engineers, at the Amblève bridge, were not attached. Instead they were relieved and they now returned to La Gleize, reaching the CP at about 2:00 A.M.

In the meantime, Anderson was worried about the defense of the bridge in Stavelot and apparently he did not know that Sergeant Hensel's squad had left, also. And he was ignorant of First Army's orders for the 526th Armored Infantry to divert one company to Stavelot. He did what he could. He had Company A of the 291st back in the fold now so he radioed Captain Gamble at Werbomont and directed him to send a platoon of his men over "to reinforce the Company C roadblock at the bridge in Stavelot."

This message was received in the schoolhouse command post of Captain Gamble shortly after T/4 Jeff Elliott and Pfc. Red Richardson left with the bazookas for Malmédy. Probably because they were bedded down in the schoolhouse and were handy, Gamble roused up Lieutenant Taylor and told him to get his boys up. "We have to go to Stavelot," he said.

Taylor got his 3rd platoon up and the men sleepily loaded into their trucks. They left Werbomont around 2:30 A.M. with Gamble and Taylor leading and two trucks of 3rd platoon following. It was a slow, cold trip over an icy road in pitch black darkness. Everybody was miserable and tense. In Trois Points they picked up the rumors that were now rife there, that Malmédy had been captured and that Colonel Pergrin and Company B had been lost.

The bottom had suddenly dropped out of the 291st's orderly world. They were split up, nobody knew where anybody else was or what was happening to them, the Germans seemed to be coming from all directions and the whole situation was sheer chaos and confusion. If anything on this black night was making sense to anybody, the men in Lieutenant Taylor's trucks were certainly not aware of it. On Sunday night, December 17, everything was snafu. And the rumors that their own commander and one whole company of their outfit had been lost added considerably to their feeling that they were orphans in the storm.

It was around 4:00 A.M. when Gamble and Taylor led 3rd platoon into Stavelot, and still black dark. Here they found a confusion of 526th Armored Infantry men and 57-mm. antitank guns and a few tank destroyers trying to get set up and deployed. Gamble found an officer who told him the 526th had been sent to defend the town. He did not have much time for Gamble, knew nothing of any 291st roadblock, and had no suggestions to make. He was busy . . . very busy.

Well, Gamble's orders were clear. He was to reinforce the Company C roadblock. He led his little convoy to the bridge

Confrontation on the Amblève

where he found armored infantrymen with machine guns set up, some tank destroyers, and other troops milling about. He saw no sign of any Company C men at the bridge. The infantrymen told him there was no Company C roadblock up on that hill now. They themselves were getting ready to put one up there. But they had assisted the last engineer across the bridge, a wounded man. He had told them German infantry had killed his companion and wounded him.

Gamble and Taylor pondered this news, then decided to push on and see for themselves. They crossed the bridge and proceeded. As they came to the cluster of houses near the bottom of the hill they spotted a jeep bearing the Company C identification parked in front of one of the houses. They investigated and found Pfc. Lorenzo Liparulo lying in the front seat. He was not dead, however. He had been hit three times, in the head, in the chest, and in the left leg, but he was still living.

Gamble detailed somebody to drive the jeep and they brought Liparulo back across the bridge and took him to the 526th's aid station where they turned him over to the medics. They found Private Goldstein there, badly wounded, also. From him they learned something of the details of what had happened. They verified the fact that there was no Company C roadblock, and no more Company C men, on the hill.

With armored infantry, antitank guns and tank destroyers in charge in the town now, with no 291st roadblock to reinforce, Gamble decided to return to Trois Ponts and report the situation to Colonel Anderson. It would have seemed to be well in hand. When they reached Trois Ponts, Colonel Anderson sent them to Haute Bodeux instead of back to Werbomont. Now Company A was split into three parts. Gamble, Taylor and 3rd platoon were in Haute Bodeux. Lieutenant Frank R. Hayes, the administrative officer, the H/S personnel and 2nd platoon were in Werbomont. Lieutenant Walters and his 1st platoon were God knows where — still out of pocket.

As to Liparulo and Goldstein, their war was over. Liparulo

died of his wounds on December 19. Goldstein's hip was operated on that night of December 17–18 and he was evacuated to Paris. He was later flown to England where, strangely enough, he found Captain John T. Conlin, commander of Company B, who was wounded later, in the same hospital.

Goldstein was sent to the States in April of 1945 and he spent one year in a hospital in Massachusetts. Twenty-five years later his hip still troubles him and almost every year he receives treatment for it in the Veterans Hospital in Brooklyn.

In Stavelot, Major Paul Solis, in command of the company of 526th Armored Infantry and its attached platoon of tank de-

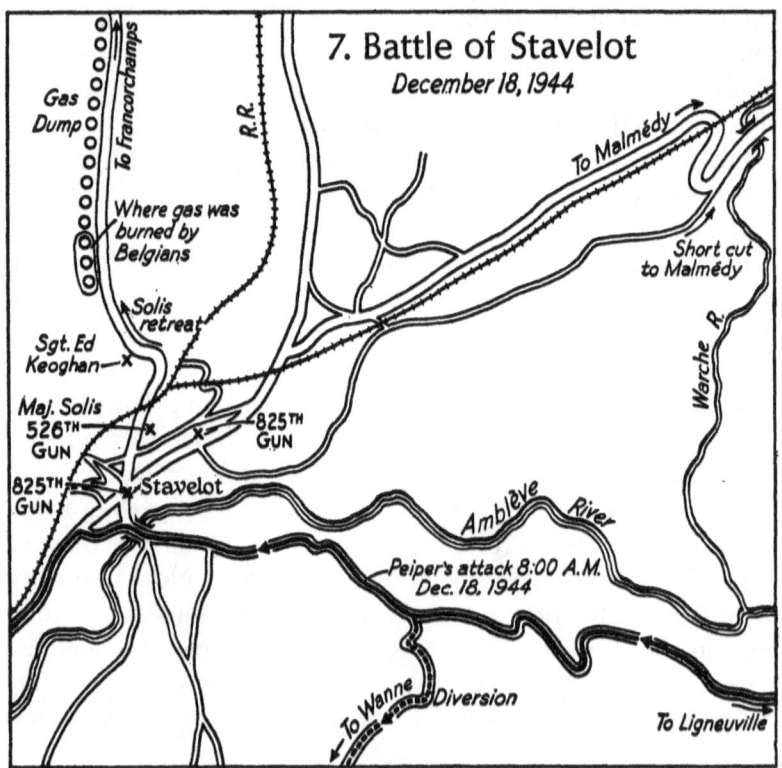

stroyers, worked out his plan of defense. The column had had trouble on the road all night and Solis' units arrived in bits and pieces, not all of them arriving in Stavelot until around 4:00 A.M. Solis decided to defend the bridge with a strong roadblock at the top of the hill across the river, approximately where the 291st roadblock had been. For this he would use two of his 526th rifle squads, with one 57-mm. antitank gun and its crew, and two of the four three-inch tank destroyers belonging to the platoon of the 825th TD outfit.

A branch railroad line, which split off the main line at Trois Ponts, came over to Stavelot, passing around it on the northern edge of the town. The old road to Francorchamps crossed the railroad several blocks north of the town square, near the railroad station. Up this old road, perhaps a mile from Stavelot, an enormous gas dump began, extending between four and five miles, all the way to Francorchamps.

Major Solis, conscious of the need to protect the gas dump, had put two more of his rifle squads and a 57-mm. antitank gun out in front of the railroad crossing on the old road.

The rest of his 526th men and the two remaining three-inch tank destroyers he held in reserve on the main square of Stavelot.

It was between 6:00 and 6:30 A.M. when Major Solis' roadblock detail was finally ready and crossed the old stone bridge and moved out toward the foot of the hill up which they meant to ascend. At that moment Peiper unleashed his predawn artillery barrage preparatory to his attack. The black night sky was suddenly brilliantly lit by the flame of his assault guns, mortars and rocket launchers on the hill and the whole valley of the Amblève thundered with their explosions and blazed with their brilliance.*

* Details of Battle of Stavelot from After Action Reports of 825th Tank Destroyer Battalion, 526th Armored Infantry Battalion, 202nd Combat Engineer Battalion.

Caught by surprise, and in the deadly fire, the roadblock detail was confused. They milled around, then decided to withdraw to the bridge. In trying to turn around, however, both of the tank destroyers and the half-tracks towing them were knocked out. Two members of the gun crews were killed, six men were missing in action, and the rest of the men fled back across the bridge.

Solis quickly ordered one of the 825th's remaining tank destroyers to a position where it could fire across the river. The gun was towed a short distance out the road to Malmédy and put in position beside the home of a citizen of Stavelot, who volunteered to observe for the gun crew. Colonel Pergrin was present when the crew of this gun later reported to Colonel Hansen of the Norwegian Battalion in Malmédy. They told how much help this Stravelot civilian had been to them.

Solis positioned the last tank destroyer gun precisely at the intersection of the main streets in Stavelot — where the Trois Ponts–Malmédy highway crossed the street which led off the bridge and continued on to Francorchamps.

Peiper attacked down the hill at daylight. The artillery barrage continued and between 7:45 and 8:00, just as soon as there was light enough to see, the lead tanks started rolling down the hill. They rolled swiftly until some damage from the gun on the Malmédy road disabled a vehicle or two and caused delay until they could be shoved out of the way.

With the help of the Stavelot civilian, this gun on the Malmédy road was firing away on good targets. Shortly one house on the road that wound down the hill caught fire, then a little later another house was hit and began to burn. Regrettable that the houses were hit, but the shells were also hitting the road.

But the long column appeared invincible and before long it stretched all the way down the hill. The lead tank reached the bottom of the hill and approached the bridge about 8:30. It maneuvered about a little then slowly rumbled out onto the structure. That tank driver's heart must have been in his mouth.

Confrontation on the Amblève

Surely the bridge would blow up under him. But he crossed safely, then the next, and the next and the next. Peiper was across the Amblève.

When the lead tanks debouched onto the street leading from the bridge they came under blasting machine gun fire from the street to their right. This was an antiaircraft artillery battery from 7th Armored Division's Artillery. The tail of the artillery column which had had to depart from their assigned route through Malmédy to St. Vith, they had wandered into the eastern end of Stavelot, from Malmédy, just as the German tanks debouched from the bridge. With their mounted multiple machine guns they did considerable service for the brief time they were engaged. But shortly the commander broke off and moved the battery around the north edge of town and took it up the old road to Francorchamps.

The 202nd Engineers were also taking a hand, blazing away with their machine guns until they saw that the tanks were bypassing the main square and were reaching the Trois Ponts road. They then disengaged and small unit by small unit made their way up the old Francorchamps road.

Straight ahead of Peiper's tanks as they came off the bridge was the last of the 825th's tank destroyers and it was also blazing away. The lead tanks were therefore forced around to the left, onto some crooked, winding streets, to make their way to the Trois Ponts road which was their objective.

As Peiper's tanks began to cross the old stone bridge, Major Solis ordered his troops to withdraw. Those in reserve did so immediately, going, however, out the Malmédy road. Here they alerted the gun crew on this road who joined them, and all continued to Malmédy unmolested.

The crew of the gun at the main intersection in Stavelot was too busy, however, to break off and withdraw immediately. They kept on firing until they saw that the tanks had bypassed them and had reached the Trois Ponts road by other streets.

Then they threw a grenade down the barrel of their gun and they, too, withdrew out the Malmédy road.

Only Major Solis and his two rifle squads, and the crew of his 57-mm. antitank gun positioned out in front of the railroad crossing withdrew up the old Francorchamps road.

It will be remembered that Sergeant Ed Keoghan, platoon sergeant of 3rd platoon, Company C, 291st Engineers, had left Sourbrodt around 2:00 the afternoon before to return to C Company's command post in La Gleize. And that the elements of 3rd platoon had become separated. Sergeant Keoghan had with him two trucks of his men, the other truck having been able to stay with their lieutenant.

Keoghan had been trying all night to get onto a road that would lead him toward Malmédy and La Gleize but had found himself wandering about on a maze of back roads instead. About daylight he finally reached Francorchamps and he thought now he had it made. He would turn south now and go to Stavelot, and from there on to La Gleize.

Shortly before Major Solis withdrew up the old Francorchamps road, Sergeant Keoghan and his men had reached a point on the same road directly overlooking Stavelot. They could hear sounds of the battle from a long way back but Keoghan continued with his men to a position from which he could see down into the town. There he stopped, just in front of a farmhouse which had a cluster of outbuildings around it, and in a field nearby a large haystack.

Keoghan and his men watched the fire fight raging below them and talked about what to do next. Obviously they could go no further on this road to La Gleize. As they were talking together a jeep carrying an American major, and a truck carrying American soldiers came barreling up the hill. It was Major Solis and his men.

Seeing Keoghan and his men, Solis approached him. "Have you got anything to fight tanks with?"

Confrontation on the Amblève

Keoghan shook his head. "I've got one antitank rifle grenade — for a carbine."

"O.K.," the major said. "Position your men in these farm buildings and you take one man with you and get over in that field by that haystack. Guard this road. German tanks are coming."

The major and his men hurried on up the road.

German tanks coming? And they were supposed to guard the road with rifles? But Keoghan did what the major told him. He dismounted his men from the trucks and positioned them in and around the farm buildings as ordered, each with his trusty M-1 rifle. And he obediently took one man with him and positioned himself at the haystack.

It was cold, it was gloomy and they were tired and hungry, and they were scared. The first hour they peered apprehensively down the road expecting enemy tanks any minute. The battle was still raging in the town below the hill.

The second hour they were still apprehensive, still expecting enemy tanks any minute. The battle had died off but they could see the long armored column passing through the town.

The third hour they felt better. Keoghan and his men guarded the road and the haystack for three solid hours. Not a tank ever came anywhere near their road. It was just a long, cold, tedious watch. Around noon Major Solis returned and ordered Keoghan and his men to go back up the road and help the Belgians burn the gas dump. Recall that a detachment from the Belgian Army had the responsibility for guarding the dump. Having given this order the major turned about and went again up the road toward Francorchamps.

Keoghan loaded up his men and started back toward the gas dump. Keoghan was not the only one ordered to help the Belgians burn the gas dump. Sergeant Joe Josephs says that as he and some of his men from Company C, 202nd Engineers, were making their way up the Francorchamps road, they were stopped by Major Solis also and told to lend a hand at the burning. He says they proceeded to the gas dump where some of the five-gallon cans had already been dumped in the ditch and set afire, and using their vehicles they shoved more and more cans into the flames.

Keoghan got nowhere because the road was now not only jammed with various U.S. elements detouring around Stavelot, but 1st Battalion of the 117th Regiment, 30th Infantry Division, was now pouring down the road from Francorchamps to take over the defense of Stavelot.

The advance elements of the 30th had reached Malmédy that morning and the 117th Infantry had just begun to take up its positions there when one battalion of it was ordered to Stavelot to reinforce the 526th Armored Infantry there. They had left Malmédy around 8:30 but had had to circle around by Francorchamps. Lieutenant Colonel Ernest Frankland was their commander. After he got onto the Stavelot road he had met Major Solis who told him Stavelot was now in enemy hands. Frankland's mission was now changed from one of relief to one of assault. He proceeded down the road and detrucked his men. As they marched down the road and passed the burning gasoline, Colonel Frankland ordered the burning to stop. The 117th was on the job now, and they would protect the gas dump.

Sergeant Keoghan inched his way along and finally reached the stacks of gasoline. Clouds of black smoke were still billowing sky-high but the burning had been stopped. At this point Keoghan got fed up. He decided to hell with it. There were enough troops already on this road. So he moved his two trucks on past the burning gasoline and went on to Francorchamps. There he decided to go to Malmédy. He joked with his driver. "Well, the best bars are in Malmédy. If we can't find something to eat there, at least we'll all get a good drink!"

It was now about 2:00 in the afternoon.

*

Confrontation on the Amblève

Colonel Pergrin and Colonel Hansen had learned that Stavelot had been overrun about noon when the bulk of Solis' men arrived in Malmédy. There was shock and consternation and Colonel Pergrin, at least, felt an awful pain that the bridge had not blown the night before. To this day he grieves over that bridge. "If it had only blown that night." But he did all one man could do, with the best he had to do with, and if that one squad of his did not blow the bridge, they had good reason to believe it was no longer their responsibility.

But when Major Solis arrived some time later in the day he brought at least one bit of good news. The 1st battalion of the 117th Infantry Regiment was going back into Stavelot. He also reported that in an attempt to save the gasoline the Belgians guarding the dump had set it afire to stop German tanks from coming up the road and to prevent the whole enormous dump from falling into their hands. Solis was evidently unaware that no tanks had made any effort to go up the road and that the burning of the gasoline had been stopped by Colonel Frankland.

Peiper's attack that morning had two prongs. As he attacked frontally, down the hill toward Stavelot, he sent his two companies of Mark IV tanks along the south bank of the Amblève, by way of Wanne, to attack at Trois Ponts. Believing he might have a hard fight for Stavelot, Peiper sent this column to seize and hold the Trois Ponts bridges for him.* It was a narrow, winding road almost impassable for tanks and this company did not reach the heights above Trois Ponts until after Peiper had reached there by the main highway.

The fact that Peiper got across the Amblève at Stavelot was a bitter blow. It appears to have been caused by a combination of many things. It was a time of great confusion, of lack of communication, lack of clarity in orders, and there was certainly a mis-

* MS. C-004, Kampfgruppe Peiper, p. 10.

take in second-guessing the intention of the German column. Malmédy was so strategic that to everybody it appeared the logical objective. And it was strategic and it was an objective — but for the *12th SS Panzer Division*, not the *1st*. Then, many hands tried to plug the hole at Stavelot, nearly all of them acting in ignorance of other efforts. Units came and went all night in Stavelot, each unit feeling itself relieved as other units appeared. Orders overlapped and were unclear to the point that nobody, until Major Solis and the elements of the 526th Armored Infantry and attached unit arrived, had a clear-cut responsibility. One effort to destroy the bridge was made and failed.

Captain Gamble was ordered to "reinforce the 291st's Company C roadblock," went to Stavelot, found no Company C roadblock to reinforce, found the 526th Armored Infantry there, believed they relieved him of further responsibility, and returned to Trois Ponts to report their presence to Colonel Anderson.

In the event, no engineer unit already stationed in Stavelot, or sent to Stavelot, had the amount of demolitions available to blow the bridge. When 30th Division engineers blew the bridge on the night of December 19, they needed 1000 pounds of TNT to destroy the heavy old structure. But the night of December 17 in Stavelot was as confused and snarled as a ball of raveled yarn. The result was tragedy for many Belgian civilians and a long period of bitter fighting for American units.

13

On this same night, December 17, Lieutenant Bucky Walters and his men of 1st platoon were struggling to reach Trois Ponts. Recall that they had left Grand-Halleux around 4:00 the afternoon before and because of the heavy traffic on the main highways had been compelled to travel on their own logging trails, the firebreaks and narrow forest farm roads.

They had come to grief about 1:00 in the morning. The poor roads had become almost impassable with ice and frozen mud and the blackout conditions of driving made them worse. Attempting to negotiate one of the sharp turns of a narrow road, one of the big bridging trucks traveling with Walters' little convoy skidded on the ice and slid into a ditch. It could not move under its own power. It tells something of the kind of man Bucky Walters was that he did not even think of abandoning the truck. It was a big, heavy piece of expensive equipment. It had to be winched out and saved.

This took hours of hard, cold work. The twilight of false dawn was beginning to streak the sky when it was finally accomplished and the little column could resume its journey. They slipped and slid down a steep hill into the valley of the Salm, and now they were able to get onto the main highway going north. As they approached the lower bridge, the bridge across the Salm some mile and a quarter south of Trois Ponts, it was about

8:00, barely daylight. They were halted by an outpost. Going forward to identify himself, Lieutenant Walters recognized a handful of his own men from his 1st squad, under Sergeant Jean B. Miller. Recall that this squad had been on security detail with Company A and had traveled with Captain Gamble the day before. "What the hell?" Walters said.

"Yes, sir," Miller said. "We got sent down to Trois Ponts to relieve Hinkel and his boys to guard Group. But all hell's busted loose over at Stavelot and nobody is being relieved. Colonel Anderson sent us down here to guard this bridge."

The guns at Stavelot, as Peiper began to roll down the long hill toward the Amblève bridge at this very moment, were a muted thunder and a prescient warning of what might soon be occurring in Trois Ponts. A wispy fog wavered about the men as they talked, rolling and shredding over the river. It was an eerie hour and eerie to hear again the roll of artillery as Peiper's guns bombarded the Amblève valley at Stavelot.

Miller did not know where Captain Gamble was. He and his squad had been sent from Werbomont, he said, but the captain and 3rd platoon had left earlier — to reinforce the roadblock at Stavelot.

Walters said, "O.K. I've got to find somebody and report."

He could not, however, find Colonel Anderson when he reached Trois Ponts, so he decided to go on to Haute Bodeux and report to Battalion. At about this time a Company A jeep came along. In it was a detail sent by Captain Gamble to try to find Walters. When Gamble got back from Stavelot and Walters still had not shown up, his worry boiled over. Where in the devil *was* the man? What had happened to him? So he sent a detail to find out.

Walters followed the jeep to Haute Bodeux and was finally home with Company A's new forward CP. He and his men were exhausted, cold and hungry. It had been a long, long night. They ate some breakfast, of sorts, and then Walters set about trying to find some place for his men to bed down and get a little sleep.

Meanwhile, the sounds of the battle in Stavelot were very clear in Trois Ponts and they lent an urgency to preparations for defense. All of Company C, 51st Engineers, had arrived in Trois Ponts by 8:00 A.M. All, that is, except 21 men left at Melreux as a rear detachment. The bridges across the Amblève River and the Salm in the heart of town were rapidly being wired for demolition and were as strongly guarded as possible.

It is to be remembered that as the 526th Armored Infantry had made its way to Stavelot the night before, slipping and sliding on the road coming from La Gleize to Trois Ponts, the half-track towing one of its 57-mm. antitank guns had slipped a tread and the gun and its crew had had to fall out of the column. This gun and its crew were now attached by the 51st Engineers and positioned in front of the railroad viaduct on the Stavelot road.*

Neither of the railroad viaducts, the one on the Stavelot road or the one on the La Gleize road, was wired for demolition yet. It took an awful lot of TNT to blow a railroad bridge, and a lot of time to prepare it for demolition. The 51st Engineers were working against time, with the sounds of the Stavelot battle in their ears, and they were taking care of first things first.

They had joyfully attached the 57-mm. gun. It was the only artillery in the town. The 51st had brought mines, prima cord, TNT in fairly good supply, but as engineers the only guns they

---

* Details for the Battle of Trois Ponts are in the After Action Reports of the following units: 1111th Engineer Combat Group, 51st Engineer Combat Battalion, 505th Paratrooper Regiment (82nd Airborne Division), and vividly recalled for the author for the four first days by Lieutenant Albert W. Walters who wrote a lengthy account of it, detailed all positions on a map of Trois Ponts, and further confirmed and verified additional details through telephone conversations. S/Sergeant Paul Hinkel also conferred with the author in her home for two days, March 19 and 20, 1965, and gave many details of the battle. Between these two men, who both were present the first four days, a dramatic reconstruction has been possible.

had were their rifles, probably six or eight, .50-caliber machine guns, maybe eight or ten .30-calibers, and eight or ten bazookas at the most. A 57-mm. antitank gun was a real cannon to them.

With the two bridges in Trois Ponts wired and ready to blow if necessary, Colonel Anderson took a look at the other entrances to Trois Ponts. Across the narrow eastern bank of the Salm the road from the heights and the village of Wanne wound down. It crossed the railroad on that side by an overpass which the Germans had destroyed in the fall. Little use was made of that minor road by American forces, so the overpass was only flimsily repaired. Colonel Anderson did not believe this bridge could support tanks, or for that matter that tanks could use the dirt road itself.

But the lower bridge, south of Trois Ponts, on the highway leading to Grand-Halleux and Vielsalm, was really vulnerable. Therefore, around 8:30 A.M. Colonel Anderson ordered the 291st Engineers to send additional strength to the bridge, set up a stronger roadblock and wire the bridge for demolition. Battalion gave the job to Captain Gamble and Gamble gave it to Lieutenant Walters, some of whose 1st squad were already guarding the bridge.

It was about all he could do because Lieutenant Arch Taylor's 3rd platoon, the platoon with Gamble at Haute Bodeux, was already off hunting for paratroopers. The paratrooper scare was very real and, conscious of the possibility of attack from his rear also, Colonel Anderson had ordered out paratrooper details earlier that morning. In addition to those of Lieutenant Taylor's platoon, one squad of 2nd platoon, up at Werbomont, were also out hunting paratroopers. This was Sergeant Tommy Cornes' 2nd squad. There were really no line troops to send to Trois Ponts but Lieutenant Walters'.

Lieutenant Walters was still trying to reorganize his platoon when he received the order to take some men and go back to Trois Ponts. He rounded up some of his 2nd squad, some of his

3rd squad, and he had a few men of his 1st squad he had picked up as he came through Trois Ponts from Grand-Halleux. In all, he took with him the equivalent of two full squads and he also took with him his platoon sergeant, Elio Rosa.

Walters took his men to a hotel on the main street of Trois Ponts and left Sergeant Rosa with them to get set up in the hotel lobby. He proceeded to the bridge site. Here he directed the wiring and the placing of the charges, made sure the bridge was ready to blow and set up the roadblock. The roadblock was positioned across the Salm, beyond the east end of the bridge, with mines laid on the road and machine guns on either side. Security was set up well ahead of the roadblock. Over and over Walters impressed on Sergeant Miller the seriousness of the situation and told him not to fool around but to blow this bridge and blow it good if the enemy approached.

Walters evidently left Miller a truck (Miller's own squad truck and driver, T/4 Merlin Dixon, were back at the hotel) which was low on gas. The men also needed some rations, so when Walters was ready to leave he promised to bring gas and rations as soon as possible. "Later today if I can," he told Miller, "but if things start cracking and I can't get back today, I'll be down first thing in the morning. Now, remember, don't blow the bridge unless the enemy approaches, but if you see Krauts coming, blow her to hell. Keep your men out of sight and don't give your positions away by shooting off at shadows."

Then Walters left Miller in position, with five or six men on the roadblock, and returned to Trois Ponts to report to Colonel Anderson.

While Walters was down at the lower bridge with Miller, the sounds of the fire fight in Stavelot could be plainly heard in Trois Ponts and around 10:45 A.M. Peiper's column was sighted, coming fast from Stavelot. The lead tanks approached the roadblock out in front of the railroad and the 57-mm. antitank gun, manned by its crew of the 526th Armored Infantry and reinforced by six men of the 51st Engineers, promptly opened fire.

The lead tank, a Panther, was hit and it slewed about in such a way that it blocked the road temporarily. The next Panther in line opened fire on the roadblock. Shortly the 57-mm. gun was knocked out and all four members of the gun crew were killed. They were McCollum, Hollenbeck, Buchanan and Higgins. A 51st man, Private Audres Salazar, was slightly wounded by fragments in the leg.

Salazar hurried back across the Amblève bridge and the order to blow the bridge was given. The other five men of the 51st on the roadblock fled through the viaduct and made their escape up the La Gleize road, since they were cut off from Trois Ponts by the destruction of the Amblève bridge. The 51st After Action Report says the bridge was blown at 11:15 A.M.

When the bridge went up, Colonel Anderson issued a series of orders immediately. First, and most important, he had to get word to First Army at Spa, that the German column had arrived at Trois Ponts and that the Amblève bridge had been destroyed. Anderson had begun to dismantle his headquarters, preparatory to moving it, earlier in the morning. He had no radio or telephone communications now. Therefore he sent his Operations Officer, Major Webb, to Spa with this message. Webb's route was roundabout, necessarily, by way of Werbomont and probably La Gleize. His route also went by way of Haute Bodeux to alert the 291st headquarters to begin preparations to move. They were to wait, however, for Colonel Anderson or further orders from him. Where were they moving? He did not know. But probably Modave — First Army's big engineer dump.

The 291st Communications Chief, T/Sergeant John L. Scanlan, remembers his great anxiety about how much time he would have to take down his communications setup. He had to stay with Company A and Company C as long as possible.

Shortly after Major Webb went through, Anderson's Group headquarters moved over to Haute Bodeux. No orders yet.

Confrontation on the Amblève

Colonel Anderson was staying in Trois Ponts a while longer. But they brought word that the German column was turning north toward La Gleize. Now it was C Company's turn to be caught in a squeeze! And a lot more was known about this enemy column now, about its size and strength. Captain Lampp told Scanlan to radio C Company, in the clear, to get out and to get out fast. Now. Move to Modave by most direct route. What about Lieutenant Hayes and 1/Sergeant Smith and 2nd platoon at Werbomont? Alert, but wait for us.

Up at La Gleize, C Company did move fast. Before noon they were on their way, and as the last of their vehicles left the courtyard of their CP in the Château Froidcour, the caretaker was painstakingly removing all signs of the U.S. Army star in its garden. Discretion was the better part of valor now. When the Germans had been pushed back Company C returned to La Gleize and the château to look for some abandoned equipment. Corporal Edmond Byrne said the walls of the château were pitted and smoke-blackened from the battle in La Gleize, and that La Gleize civilians told him about the caretaker removing the U.S. star from the garden.

When the Amblève bridge went up with a thundering explosion and every color of the rainbow, Peiper heard it and saw it and observed the debris flying in all directions. It angered him, for he correctly judged that there was little strength in Trois Ponts — only a handful of men, but they had blocked him and despair ate at his heart. He had needed this bridge badly, and nobody knew it better than he. Under interrogation by U.S. authorities after the war, he said if he could have captured the bridge at Trois Ponts intact, and had had fuel enough, it would have been a simple matter to drive through to the Meuse early that day.

But his nemesis was catching up with him. The overnight delay at Stavelot had given the 51st Engineers (Company C) time to reach Trois Ponts and wire the bridges, while the 291st fronted on roadblocks. And one 291st roadblock at Stavelot had tilted the scale which caused the delay. Engineers — they were to wreck all his plans, until time ran out and the big guns and armor and infantry could move in.

He studied his map and saw that the only thing left for him to do now was swing north toward La Gleize. There was a bridge across the Amblève near there, in the little hamlet of Cheneux. Maybe that bridge would be intact. Maybe he could beat the engineers to it. He radioed his tank commander of the column which had proceeded to Trois Ponts on the south bank of the Amblève and ordered the tanks to return to Stavelot and follow him.*

Across the river from Peiper's column, on a height of land which gave him a good view, Colonel Anderson watched the Germans intently through his field glasses. He saw them swarm down into the area between the viaduct and the blown Amblève bridge, and he saw one German soldier kill, without any provocation whatever, an old Belgian man and woman who by the bundles they were carrying, were only trying to evacuate their home. Colonel Anderson may not have known the old couple, but they lived next door to the 291st motor pool and the men of the 291st had come to know them well.

Unseen by Colonel Anderson, Peiper's men also swarmed into another house near the motor pool and killed ten people, among them a young lad and a pregnant woman. These Belgians were also known to the men of the 291st, and later after the Germans were pushed back south of the Amblève on December 24, T/4 Jeff Elliott drove Sergeant Paul Hinkel and a colonel from the 78th Infantry Division back into the town. They went into the cellar of this home where the bodies of the murdered civilians still lay. The pregnant woman had been stabbed innumerable times in the stomach. Many men of the 291st saw these bodies before they were finally buried.

* MS. C-004, Kampfgruppe Peiper, 15-26 December, 1944, p. 7.

Confrontation on the Amblève 245

As Peiper's column turned northward to La Gleize, Colonel Anderson had to send another messenger to Spa with this news, for this movement menaced First Army headquarters itself. The messenger chosen was Captain Lundberg, the 1111th Group's Motor Officer. A route by way of Werbomont was laid out for him and Lundberg left, by jeep, immediately, driven by Private James N. Snow.

In addition to their defensive positions all along the west bank of the Salm River, the 51st Engineers had also set up a roadblock across the Salm that morning, on the heights — on the road that approached from Wanne. At about noon the roadblock saw three German tanks coming up this road. The men of the 51st opened fire with an AT rocket launcher (bazooka) in an effort to stop the tanks but they were not successful. The tanks came on. They were, of course, the lead tanks of the company of Mark IVs that Peiper had sent by the secondary road south of the Amblève, which led through Wanne.

All three leading tanks opened fire on the men of the 51st and they had to get out in a hurry, under the blazing fire of the tanks' big 75-mm. guns and their machine guns. The men on the roadblock recrossed the Salm to safety without losing any men.

It was about now, shortly after 12:00 noon that Lieutenant Walters returned to Trois Ponts from the lower Salm bridge. He had found Colonel Anderson and the two men stood talking together outside the hotel which had housed Anderson's headquarters until a short while before. Across the street from them, Sergeant Paul Hinkel, whose security detail was still guarding Anderson's small CP detachment, watched the two men. Suddenly a burst of machine gun fire from the heights across the river sprayed the wall of the hotel, just above their heads. Hinkel recalls that the two men looked up, observed the pattern of machine gun bullets, went on talking a moment or two longer, then separated. Colonel Anderson was at that moment attaching

Lieutenant Walters and his men to the 51st Engineers and directing him to report to their commanding officer.

At the conclusion of their conversation, Anderson went into his headquarters to finish closing it down. Walters went to look for Captain Shober, commander of the detachment of 51st Engineers. When the Amblève bridge was blown, Shober had moved his command post from the railroad station on the east bank to the post office on the west bank of the Salm. Walters found him, and Shober told him to hold his men in reserve in case more demolitions were needed. Walters then went to the hotel where his own men were set up and made sure his equipment was all under cover and ready.

From where Sergeant Hinkel was standing he could see the German tank column on the height of land across the river. It was bumper-to-bumper. About that time Walters' platoon sergeant, Elio Rosa, approached Hinkel and he also saw the long tank column. He said, "Sarge, what are we going to do?"

Hinkel said, "Well, we're here. We better get set up over by the lumberyard and make the best stand we can."

The column of tanks, however, did not come on down the hill into the east section of Trois Ponts. The road was a dirt track and from the amount of bazooka and machine gun fire loosed on them, they knew there was at least some strength in this town. One tank, prowling down the hill, was disabled by a bazooka rocket.

The appearance of this column on the heights created a critical situation, however, and Colonel Anderson now felt that he must destroy the bridge across the Salm, lest greater strength assemble up on the heights and attack in force. The bridge was already wired and ready to go. Accordingly the order was given to blow it.

At 1:00 P.M. the bridge was blown. At some time the night before, during the passage of 7th Armored's Artillery through Trois Ponts, a big 105-mm. howitzer tank destroyer had skidded and slid off the road crashing into one of the pillars of the bridge and partially destroying it. The big vehicle rested in the edge of the water. The crew had worked all the rest of the night trying to get it out without success. Because of the heavy flow of civilians fleeing ahead of Peiper's column, from Malmédy and all the villages south of it, from Stavelot and its environs, the road could not be blocked. Finally the crew decided to wire it for demolition and destroy it after dark when it was hoped the flow of traffic might ease and a safe period would ensue.*

In spite of the damage done to the pier at the east end of the bridge, the blow on the bridge was not perfect. The floor went, but the piers and girders were only wrenched and damaged. Vehicles could not use the bridge but infantry could swarm across it easily and a determined attack could pose a threat. Shortly after the bridge was blown, therefore, Captain Shober ordered Lieutenant Walters to position his men so as to guard the blown bridge from foot soldiers. The west part of Trois Ponts was built around and flowed up onto the shoulders of a hill. Walters positioned his men up on the shoulder so as to overlook the bridge and bring it under fire from their machine guns. Shober spread his 51st men all along the west bank of the Salm overlooking the confluence with the Amblève. Sergeant Paul Hinkel and his security detail were now attached by the 51st and meshed into the defenses along the west bank. Their gun emplacement was precisely at the west end of the blown bridge.

When the Salm bridge was blown at 1:00 P.M. Colonel Anderson shut down his advance command post and went to Haute Bodeux. Preparations had been under way most of the morning for Battalion's move, but the radio setup had not yet been taken down. Now with the German column turning north at Trois Ponts it was necessary for Colonel Anderson to take further action against blocking its access to the main Huy road. He ordered Captain Lampp to send a detail of men to guard the Habie-

* Sergeant Paul Hinkel to author, personal conference, March 19 and 21, 1965.

mont bridge and wire it for demolition. This bridge across the Lienne Creek between Trois Ponts and Werbomont had now become crucial.

Since Werbomont was nearer the bridge than Haute Bodeux, and since Company A's 2nd platoon was in Werbomont, it was decided to give this job to them. Lieutenant Alvin Edelstein, 2nd platoon's leader, was in Haute Bodeux at the time. So Werbomont was radioed and Sergeant Edwin Pigg, the platoon sergeant, was ordered to take a strong detail to the bridge and begin work on it. The radio message advised that Lieutenant Edelstein would meet the detail at the bridge.

Preparations for the displacement of Group and Battalion were now stepped up and since obviously the movement to Modave would occur shortly and the convoy would travel by way of Werbomont and would cross the Habiemont bridge, it was decided that Lieutenant Edelstein should travel that far with the convoy.

South of Trois Ponts at the lower Salm bridge, Sergeant Miller and his men had also seen the enemy tanks on top of the hill. He and his men watched them as they maneuvered around. But they knew they had nothing to fear from the tanks at the moment. There was no road down off the hill in their direction. In order to reach the bridge the tanks would have to turn around, go south, come down off the hill and approach the bridge from the south. But there was nothing to prevent the foot soldiers from pouring down the hill, and shortly they did precisely that.

Miller and his men watched them come down the hill. Miller's men were well dug in and hidden from view. He cautioned them not to open fire and give away their positions. Miller let the infantrymen reach the bottom of the hill. He let them approach the bridge, cautiously, watchfully. Tautly his men waited and watched Miller's hand on the exploder. It must have seemed an eternity to them as Miller waited and waited.

He let the German foot soldiers come up onto the road. Let

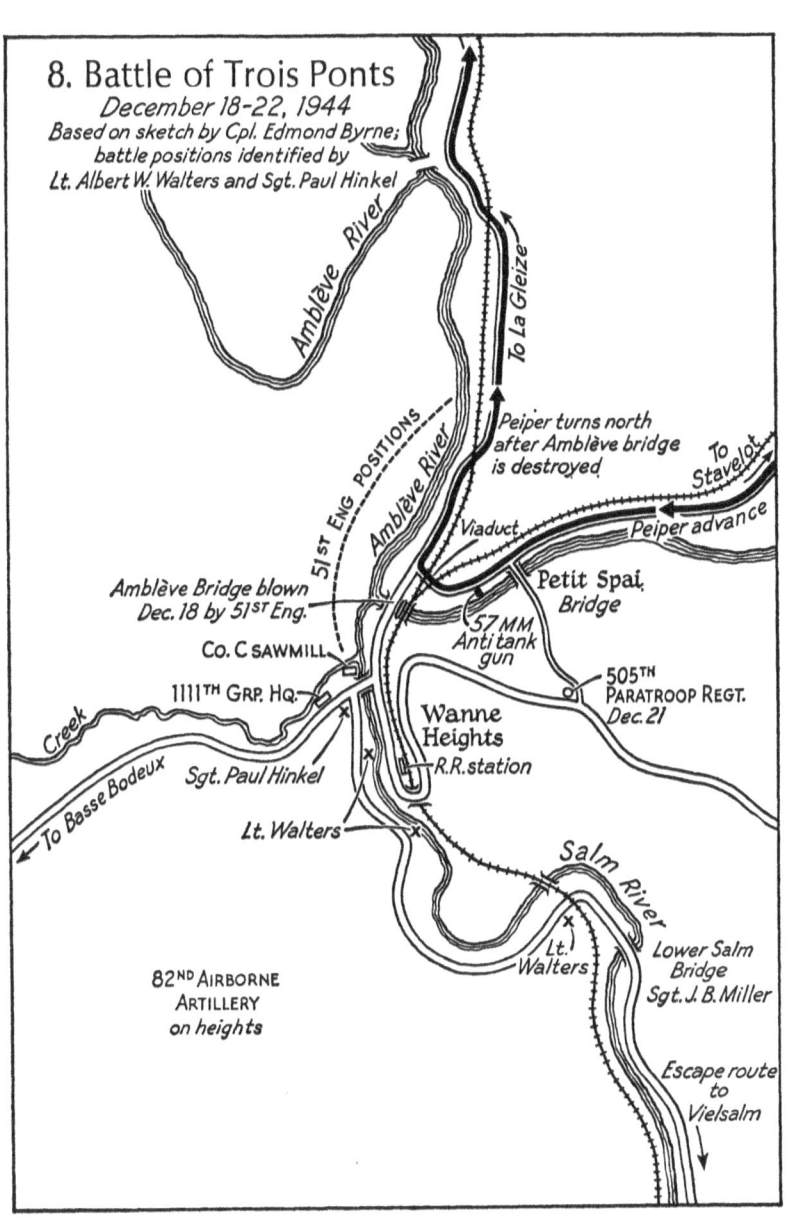

them remove the mines. He let several of them actually get onto the bridge and begin to examine it for demolitions, while others clustered about the bridge approach. Not until then did he pull the exploder. Up went the bridge, taking several Germans with it, injuring many others.

It was a good blow and in the fog of dust and debris Miller and his men loaded into their truck and headed rapidly down the road to Grand-Halleux and made it by the skin of their teeth. It was a week before he and his men worked their way around by back roads to rejoin Walters and Company A at Modave.

Around 2:00 P.M. a new commander for the engineer forces in Trois Ponts arrived. Lieutenant Colonel Harvey Frazer, commander of the 51st Engineers, had been advised that Trois Ponts was the hinge of an important defense line being prepared and that it was a "hold at all costs" position. He therefore decided to send the Battalion's Executive Officer, Major Robert B. Yates, to take over the defense. The forces in Trois Ponts now included various straggler units as well as Lieutenant Walters and his men and Company C of the 51st Engineers. It was a happy decision Colonel Frazer made, for Major Yates proved to be staunch, aggressive and imaginative.

The night before, December 17, the situation all along his First Army front had looked so desperate to General Hodges that he had telephoned General Bradley and asked for SHAEF's only reserve units, the 82nd and 101st Airborne Divisions. After a consultation with General Eisenhower, Bradley telephoned Hodges that they were being released and asked where he wanted them. At that time Bastogne seemed to be the hottest spot in the First Army sector and Hodges asked that the divisions be sent there.

The units had just recently returned from participating in the British action around Arnhem and Nijmegen in Holland and

Confrontation on the Amblève

were resting near Mourmelon and Reims. Hastily they were rounded up, loaded up and started north.

A new corps, the XVIIIth Airborne, had just been formed to direct the airborne divisions. Major General Matthew Ridgway was given command of it and was in his London headquarters at this time. Major General James M. Gavin, commander of the 82nd Airborne Division, was its acting commander on the Continent, however. He decided to go to Spa for a personal conference with General Hodges. By the time he arrived in Spa, the morning of December 18, the situation had changed and the greatest threat to First Army was now Peiper's column. Hodges had just learned that Peiper had gotten across the Amblève at Stavelot. Now First Army headquarters, all the big supply installations, everything north of the Amblève was threatened. Hodges therefore ordered Gavin to shift his own 82nd Airborne Division to Werbomont instead of Bastogne. Hodges had to have some strength on his right flank.

Gavin radioed the change in destination to the 82nd and left to make a personal reconnaissance of the Werbomont area and set up an assembly point. He had just left when General Leland S. Hobbs, commander of 30th Infantry Division, arrived.

Hobbs' division had reached its assembly point, Eupen, during the night. At midmorning on the 18th, Hodges telephoned Hobbs at Eupen and asked him to come to Spa for a conference. Anticipating action, Hobbs brought his 119th Regiment with him as far as Theux, five miles north of Spa, where he told them to wait. He would meet them again after his conference with Hodges and he expected then to have further orders for them.

While Hodges and Hobbs were conferring together, Colonel Anderson's messengers arrived, first Major Webb with the news that Peiper was now at Trois Ponts and the Amblève bridge had been destroyed, and then Captain Lundberg with the more alarming news that Peiper had turned north at Trois Ponts. Shortly afterward, about 1:00 P.M., General Pete Quesada, commander of the 9th Tactical Air Command, sent word that the long snaking German column had been spotted by reconnaissance planes and that its head was now in the vicinity of La Gleize.

This was disastrous news. Without knowing the intention of the enemy, Hodges had to try to second-guess him. Peiper could proceed on down the Amblève and cut First Army's rear installations, or he could turn westward at La Gleize and go to Werbomont. There he would most certainly prevent the 82nd Airborne from assembling and he could also probably reach the Meuse. Hodges therefore ordered Hobbs to move his 119th Regiment rapidly and to split it, sending part of it to La Gleize and Stoumont to meet Peiper should he continue straight north, sending at least one battalion over to Werbomont and down the Trois Ponts road to screen the 82nd's assembly.

Hobbs left immediately to carry out these orders. It necessarily took time. But he managed to get the 119th Regiment over to Remouchamps that afternoon. The battalion detached and sent to Werbomont was Major Hal McCown's 2nd Battalion, reinforced with one tank destroyer company.

General Quesada's message concerning the finding of the long German column grew out of his own activity that same morning. Flying weather was bad but not impossible and there was at least no ground fog. Small planes had been sent up as soon as word reached First Army headquarters that the Germans were across the Amblève. Flying a long oval over the hills and valleys they not only located the head of Peiper's column as it neared La Gleize, they also spotted the entire, long, coiling length of it, winding like a serpent as far as twelve or fifteen miles back, just south of Malmédy. Quesada threw everything he could into the air, Thunderbolts, Mustangs and the fast British-made plane, the Typhoon.

The earliest planes in the air were those of the 365th Fighter

Group, reinforced by the 300th and 506th fighter squadrons who, about 1:00 P.M., swept down on the German column as it passed through Stavelot and stretched out onto the plains behind it.

In Malmédy, perched up on his hill overlooking the Gdoumont road, Private Bernie Koenig watched these planes making their endless, relentless circles over the column, diving, bombing and strafing. He said it was like watching a movie from a front row seat. The Thunderbolts came in in formations of four, peeling off and diving, bombing and strafing, then swooping up to make their long, long circle to come back in again. Whatever their target was, Koenig thought, it was really taking a plastering. It was, and an infinite amount of damage was done to both the vehicles and men of the column.

Colonel Ernest Frankland took a hand in doing some damage in Stavelot, also. Attached to his infantry battalion was a platoon of tank destroyer guns from the 843rd TD Battalion. He positioned them on the hill above the town and they ranged in on the enemy column passing through the town below and added their firepower to the bombing.

When fog rising from the river blotted out the target around 4:00 P.M. and the planes had to go home, Frankland sent two companies of his infantrymen into a frontal attack on the central part of the town. Here they were astonished and temporarily confused because they ran smack into what seemed to be U.S. units, in U.S. vehicles and uniforms. They were Skorzeny men, of course. But Frankland's men quickly discovered the disguise because these units were certainly shooting at them. Angered by this deception they fought back hard and before dusk succeeded in taking the center of the town.

By full dark the two infantry companies held about half the town, but better still, the 118th Field Artillery Battalion, 30th Infantry Division, was moving in behind them and taking up positions on the hills northeast of the town. When these guns were in place and found the range, targeting in on the river crossing, they put a stop to any more vehicular crossing of the Amblève in Stavelot. Bitter fighting would occur for two more days as General Mohnke tried desperately to get more troops across to strengthen Peiper's spearhead, but nothing could avail against the American artillery.

On the night of December 19, a detachment of 30th Division engineers succeeded in destroying the old stone bridge. The structure was so massive that it required in the neighborhood of 1000 pounds of TNT to blow it.*

Another witness to a segment of the bombing attacks by friendly planes that afternoon were the men in Trois Ponts. From their position overlooking the Salm bridge Lieutenant Walters and his men also watched the long, sweeping elongated circle of planes bombing and strafing along the Trois Ponts road and north of it. The big Thunderbolts and Typhoons looked wonderful to them as they made their long fast sweeps for almost two hours.

Also among those on the ground who saw friendly planes were some of the men of the detail sent from Werbomont to wire and guard the Habiemont bridge. Lying on the ground near the platoon truck, having no duty except to guard it and drive it away when it was necessary, T/4 Louis Kovacs watched the sweeping planes. They were bombing something not far north of the bridge and while that meant the 9th TAC was on the job, it also meant the enemy was far too near this blasted bridge for comfort. Fearful that the enemy might be approaching on their own side of this creek, Kovacs concentrated on keeping an intent eye on the byroad which came down from Forges through the woods.

When the radio message from Haute Bodeux ordering a detail to wire and guard the Habiemont bridge was received at the schoolhouse in Werbomont, its urgency was clear. Sergeant Ed-

* Major General Ernest Frankland (USAR) in letter to author, June 18, 1969.

win Pigg hurriedly rounded up as strong a detail as was available — mostly 3rd squad of 2nd platoon, whose squad leader was Sergeant R. C. Billington, beefed up with a few men from the 2nd squad who had not gone on the paratrooper hunt. These were the only line troops in Werbomont now, the others being in Trois Ponts, fanned out in paratrooper hunts from Haute Bodeux, and with Colonel Pergrin in Malmédy.

Sergeant Pigg also had a transportation problem. The only truck big enough to hold the men and all their equipment was the platoon truck, but it had burned-out valves from making the trip back from Amblève without sufficient oil. Its top speed was about ten miles per hour and it was notional about going at all. If Hooks Kovacs ever killed the engine, it would not start again without a strong push from the men. Nevertheless, it would have to do.

The men hurriedly loaded up the crippled truck with mines, prima cord and TNT, and set out from the schoolhouse at about 1:30 P.M. How many men were on this detail is not precisely known, but among them were:

>S/Sgt. Edwin Pigg, 2nd platoon sergeant
>Sgt. R. C. Billington, 3rd squad leader
>Cpl. Fred R. Chapin, assistant 3rd squad leader
>Cpl. Harry Bossert, assistant 2nd squad leader
>Pfc. Abraham Miller, 3rd squad
>Pfc. Shorty Nickell, 3rd squad
>Pfc. Harry Sansbury, 3rd squad
>Pfc. Thorne, 3rd squad
>T/4 Edward Lufsey, 2nd squad
>T/4 Louis Kovacs, platoon truck driver
>Pvt. Johnny Rondenell, 2nd squad

They went eastward on N-23. It was a winding and serpentine road up and down hills, with curves doubling back on curves. The men met many civilians fleeing from Trois Ponts, Basse Bodeux and the nearer villages. They were on foot, on bicycles, some pushing handcarts with their belongings. When the men occasionally stopped briefly to talk to them, they all reported that German tanks were in Trois Ponts. Progress toward the bridge was slow, partly because of the many refugees on the road but also because of the snail-like speed of the crippled truck.

Around 3:00 P.M. the truck finally arrived at the bridge. On the near side, the west end of the bridge, was a single building, a small café. Sergeant Pigg instructed Kovacs, the truck driver, to turn the truck around, headed for home, to keep the motor running and to stay near it. "If we have to blow the bridge," he said, "walk, not run, to the truck, then start out slow, in low gear, and give the boys a chance to catch up. Then take off."

He told the men, "If we have to blow the booger, it'll be every man for himself. Make the truck if you can, but if you can't, head out on foot."

Two men, Pfc. Harry Sansbury and T/4 Edward Lufsey, were sent across the bridge to a point position as security. Sergeant Billington and the assistant squad leader, Corporal Fred Chapin, went under the bridge with the men and set to work on the wiring. Sergeant Pigg stayed on top.

Chapin was the demolitions expert of the squad. Now he and Billington gauged the type of blow that was needed, the amount of TNT, the kind of wiring to be done. Dynamite charges were wired to all the piers, connected with prima cord, then wires were run from both sides of the bridge to be hooked to the detonator. It was not an easy job nor one that could be hurried, although the men worked rapidly.

Around 4:00 P.M. the convoy of Battalion and Group, displacing from Haute Bodeux to Modave, arrived at the bridge site. A messenger from First Army Engineer, had arrived at Haute Bodeux between 2:30 and 3:00 P.M. with verbal orders to move. They were to go to Modave and the 291st was to be assigned to the 84th Infantry Division. What 291st? Battalion and a handful of men from A and C Companies? Well, O.K.

Group and Battalion were ready and left almost immediately. The convoy crossed the Habiemont bridge without stopping,

Confrontation on the Amblève 257

and the men under the bridge were aware only that a convoy of some kind had crossed. With them, however, were Lieutenant Edelstein and two or three more Company A men, who dropped out of the convoy at the bridge and joined the detail.

Shortly after the arrival of Lieutenant Edelstein, General James M. Gavin showed up at the bridge and talked with him about a flimsy bridge farther down the creek near the hamlet of Forges. Edelstein told him he had demolitions enough only to do a good job on the Habiemont bridge. He also told him that the bridge at Forges was so light that 291st trucks had been forbidden to use it. Only jeeps were allowed to cross it. It would not carry tanks, Edelstein said.

When Gavin left First Army headquarters after his conference with General Hodges, it will be recalled that he went to Werbomont to make a personal reconnaissance of the area his 82nd Division would be responsible for. Precisely what time General Gavin arrived at the schoolhouse headquarters of Company A in Werbomont is not known, but presumably it was after the bridge detail left. The Administrative Officer, Lieutenant Frank R. Hayes, was the only officer at the CP when General Gavin arrived. He recalls giving Gavin information regarding houses available for headquarters, also that a detail had been sent to the Habiemont bridge.

At thirty-seven, General Gavin was one of the youngest general officers in the Army. He had made quite a name for himself. He had fought in North Africa, Sicily and Italy. He had jumped with his men on June 5 into Normandy, and he had jumped with them in Holland only a short time before. He did not linger long at the Company A headquarters, but left to make his reconnaissance of the area, and by 4:00 P.M. or shortly afterward he stopped by the Habiemont bridge to talk briefly with Lieutenant Edelstein.

Meanwhile, when Peiper turned north at Trois Ponts he had a tortuously winding road down the canyons of the Amblève River to La Gleize. Arriving there finally around 1:00 P.M. he made all haste to the village of Cheneux to see if his luck was in with the bridge across the river there. It was. The bridge at Cheneux was intact.

Company C, quartered in La Gleize until noon that day, had received no orders at all concerning this bridge. Shortly after Peiper decided to turn north, Company C was ordered to move to Modave. The only officers in La Gleize were lieutenants, platoon leader rank, and lieutenants do not go around blowing fine big bridges on their own initiative. It is an excellent way to get a court-martial in case error is made.

Just beyond Cheneux the road makes a very deep horseshoe bend. The German column was traversing this bend when Quesada's planes homed in on it and began their deadly mission. Much damage was done in the bombing, but perhaps the worst damage was in the time lost. Peiper had to scatter his vehicles and men into the woods and sweat out not only the bombing period, which lasted until the fog rose and hid them, around 3:30 or 4:00 P.M., but he had also to shove disabled vehicles off the road and get going again. Then he proceeded as rapidly as possible toward the main highway which led to Huy, the destination on which his eyes had been fixed for so long. Once he hit the highway, his map showed one more bridge, and a critical one, across a small creek named Lienne. If he found that bridge intact, he had it made. It must have been as anxious a time as he lived through on his entire long thrust.

Peiper's column now had some of the Tiger Royal tanks of the 501st Tank Battalion mixed in. This unit had come up as Peiper delayed at Stavelot with quite a few of the big, lumbering monsters with the 88-mm. gun which since the days of Rommel in the North African desert had wreaked such damage on Allied aircraft, tanks and troops. A long-barreled gun, its range was enormous and it was of such high velocity that its shells, when piercing armor, burned the edges of the hole and curled them outward. This gun and the smaller self-propelled assault guns

Confrontation on the Amblève

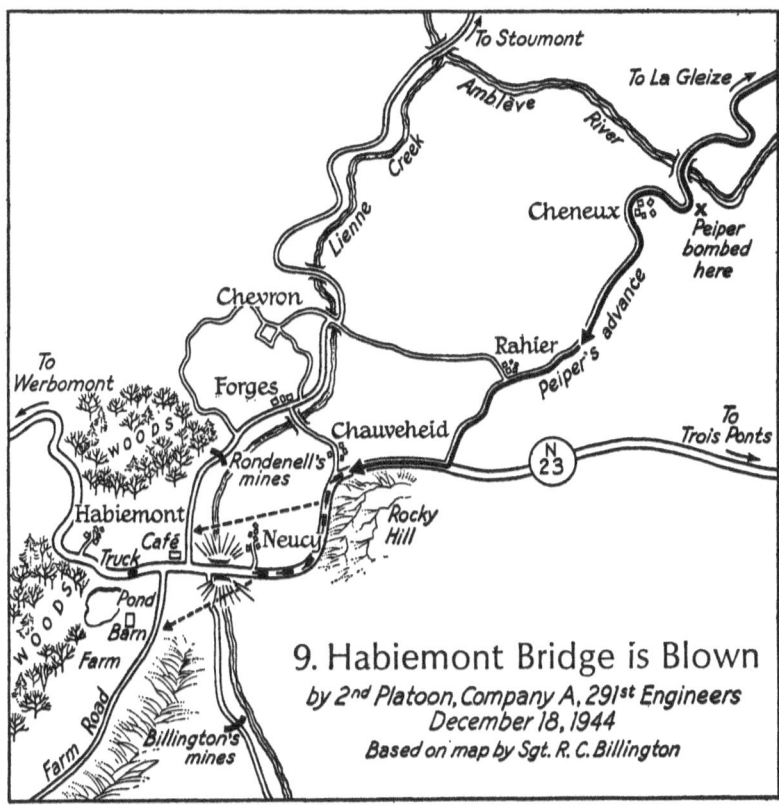

9. Habiemont Bridge is Blown
by 2nd Platoon, Company A, 291st Engineers
December 18, 1944
Based on map by Sgt. R. C. Billington

which the German infantry leaned on so consistently were the envy of all American commanders.

Peiper's route on the east side of the Lienne brought him out onto Highway N-23 just below the village of Froidville. He reached it about 4:30 P.M.

At almost exactly this same time the men of 2nd platoon finished wiring the Habiemont bridge. A friendly argument broke out between Sergeant Pigg and Sergeant Billington as to where to put the detonator. Pigg said, "Hell, Bob, put the damned thing out where you can see!"

Billington, who figured he was going to have to turn the key, did not think it was very important whether he could see German tanks or not. He could hear them, and it was far more important that they should *not* see him. The detonator was therefore put in an old German sentry box about 100 feet back from the bridge. The wiring to it was run along the road in a ditch.

This was only part of the job, however. The bridge ready to blow, Lieutenant Edelstein told the men to link up some mines. Two roads intersected here at the bridge, on the west bank of the creek, and he thought they should be protected. One road led north to Forges, the other road went south to Lierneux. Billington was told to take a detail to the right, the south, and Corporal Harry Bossert drew the road going north, to the left. Billington took three or four men with him, among them Pfc. Abraham Miller and Pfc. Thorne. Bossert took three or four, among them Private Johnny Rondenell. Corporal Fred Chapin was given charge of the detonator at the bridge, with Pfc. Shorty Nickell.

The men linked up their daisy chains and both details set out. Recall that the sun had set at 4:35, and that the twilight would last only thirty-eight minutes. By the time the men left on their mine-laying details the light was growing pretty dim.

As Corporal Chapin kept his watch in the old German sentry box, what he could see beyond the wired bridge was a short stretch of straight road, then a sharp bend left, where for a considerable distance the road ran parallel to the creek before bending right again around a rocky, cliffy hill which it climbed. Along the parallel stretch of road there was occasionally a thin line of trees, but in between were open clear spaces.

As daylight swiftly faded, now, around 4:45 P.M., Chapin suddenly spied the German armored column rolling along that parallel stretch of road. The light was so dim, now, that he peered to make certain he was not imagining things. But he was not. As ghostly as they looked in the light, they were real — a

Confrontation on the Amblève

long column of German tanks, plain in the open spaces, shadowy behind the trees.

Just as he made certain, a Tiger Royal tank, probably Peiper's own, fired its 88-mm. gun. Obviously the tankers had seen the engineers at the bridge. The shell was simply a warning. It did no damage, hitting off to the left. But Chapin flinched, ducked and looked wildly around for the lieutenant, and saw him motioning frenziedly, blow! Blow!

Chapin turned the key and saw the streak of blue lights, the heaving blast of dust and debris and knew he had a good blow. He quickly unhooked the detonator from his dead wire and hooked it to the other. Again he turned the key, but the explosive used had been so excellently gauged, the blow was so good and so powerful that it had wrecked the wiring on the other side. Actually the one blow had done a beautiful job, had got an almost perfect destruction of the bridge.

Only a few vehicles behind the lead tanks, Peiper heard and saw the bridge go. Up she went in rainbows and thunder, an expert, beautiful demolition job. Peiper could only sit with a leaden heart and face the fact that time and his luck had entirely run out on him. Though he would battle desperately for five more days to escape the box he was now caught in, it was here he faced the inevitable end. And he could only sit helplessly, pound his knee and swear, "The damned engineers! The damned engineers!"

In the meantime, Corporal Chapin had unhooked the detonator and salvaged it, then he turned to catch up with Shorty Nickell, who was already running back up the road toward the truck. And now the tanks were approaching just beyond the bridge. They opened up with their machine guns. For a time the dust and debris of the blast hid Nickell and Chapin but as the fog of dust cleared they were in plain sight of the tanks. They were running desperately, weaving up the road, to make the truck, which was pulling out. Suddenly a machine gun bullet cut the canteen from Chapin's cartridge belt and sliced into the belt itself so that it fell down around his knees and tripped him. He rolled into the ditch and hoisted the belt up, then crawled on his hands and knees until the road bent around a corner. Nickell, ahead of him, was running as fast as his short legs would carry him, and Chapin now took out after him. As they caught up with the truck eager hands reached out to pull them in. Out of breath, hearts pounding, they sank onto the floor of the truck, a good job well done, and a miss as good as a mile.

When the bridge blew the two men on point, Lufsey and Sansbury, were cut off. They fled into the woods in the opposite direction and made their way to Trois Ponts where they linked up with the Company A men there. They were listed as missing in action, however, for quite a while.

When the bridge blew Kovacs, the truck driver, followed his orders. He walked, not ran, to the truck, put it in low gear and started off slow. Sergeant Pigg suddenly threw himself up onto the seat beside him and Kovacs heard several men scrambling into the back of the truck. Slowly Kovacs tried to accelerate to ascend the hill. It was a joke, he thought, telling him to go slow. There was no other way the truck would go. A good, fleet-footed runner could catch him at his top speed! Which was precisely what Chapin and Nickell had just done behind him.

All in the truck now who were going to make it, what they most wanted to do was get out fast, or as fast as Kovacs could nurse the old vehicle along. Each time they came into an open space without any sheltering trees the tanks across the creek poured machine gun fire on them. The men in the back stayed pretty low until the truck finally reached the top of the hill and could open up to its maximum speed of ten miles per hour.

Not far down this ridge road they met an officer and a detachment of tank destroyers who stopped them and asked questions concerning the enemy. The 2nd platoon had plenty to tell them concerning the enemy and one of the men had a little more than plenty. He asked why the hell they weren't down at

Confrontation on the Amblève

that bridge with their tank destroyers instead of sitting on their rumps up here on this hill! Sergeant Pigg told him to shut up and he gave the officer information about the tanks and told him the bridge had been destroyed. Then Kovacs nudged the truck onward to Werbomont. It was now around 5:30 P.M. or perhaps a little later.

The officer and the tank destroyers were a platoon of the 823rd Tank Destroyer Battalion which had been assigned to Major Hal McCown's 2nd Battalion, 119th Regiment, 30th Infantry Division, which, it will be remembered, had been ordered earlier in the afternoon to go to Werbomont to screen the assembly of the 82nd Airborne Division.

When the 2nd platoon truck reached the schoolhouse they found the command post gone. Vamoosed. Vanished. There were only some 82nd Airborne troops who had taken over the schoolhouse. They knew nothing about the 291st Engineers and Company A. What to do now? "Well," Sergeant Pigg said, "let's just keep going to the rear. We'll find 'em some place."

That suited the boys just fine — the more rearly they got the better they would like it. They were worried about the lieutenant, however, and they kept trying to raise him on the walkie-talkie radio in the truck. Nothing but silence. Finally Kovacs said, in disgust, "Hell, Sarge, throw the damned thing away. Let's go to Paris for a few days and come back and look for the outfit when this is all over."

Pigg shook his head. "We'll just keep moving around. We'll find 'em."

Sometime during the night as they moved on up the road toward Huy they found the vehicles of the 629th Engineer Light Equipment Company, the 1111th Group unit which had displaced from Malmédy the night before. This outfit welcomed them, gave them some food and they turned in for some sleep.

When the bridge blew, the mine detail which went up the road northward to Forges scattered into the woods, and in its cover most of the men made a dash to catch the truck and most of them did. Corporal Harry Bossert missed it. Private Johnny Rondenell, separated from the others, didn't even try to catch it. He just burrowed deeper into the woods and decided to wait until dark.

On the road which went south, Sergeant Billington had led his mine detail on a shortcut across the hill and through a farmyard. They came out above the road they were to mine, on a steep bank down which they would have to slide. Just as they reached this steep bank they heard tank engines and looking up they saw the five tanks Peiper had sent to the main bridge. At about the same time the tankers saw them and opened up with their machine guns. Under fire, Billington and his men slid down the bank, pulled their daisy chain across the road and scrambled back up the bank. They heard the bridge go, with a thundering explosion, saw blue lights and flame and a big cloud of black smoke and Billington said, "Thar she blows!"

As he and his men fled back down the farm road the machine guns continued to fire at them and they hit the ditch alongside and inched forward. They could look up and see the bullets hitting the crown of the road but they were safe in the ditch. They crawled in the ditch until they reached a barn where they made a fast-diving approach behind its shelter and stood there shaking and puffing. And now the men wanted to try to make the truck. Billington said, "Go ahead. Me, I'm gonna walk." Billington was twenty-seven years old and he figured that was too old to be dodging machine gun bullets. The other men took off but he stayed put behind the barn until the firing died down a little, then he made use of the bank of a small pond to creep around to the road.

The truck was long gone by now. Nobody at all was on the road. And Billington now felt very lonely and thought perhaps

Confrontation on the Amblève

this war was going to end for him right shortly. He trudged on up the long winding hill.

Sometime after he reached the top of the hill he bumped into Pfc. Thorne and Pfc. Abraham Miller of his own detail, who had missed the truck, and Corporal Harry Bossert. They plodded on up the road together. Within a few minutes they were overtaken by a jeep, which pulled up beside them. Their eyes bugged when they saw it carried two stars. A general, yet! They gave the officer their best salutes and answered his questions. Yes, sir, the bridge was blown. How many Kraut tanks? Three or four, perhaps five. The men, of course, had no idea these were simply the lead tanks of Peiper's powerful armored column.

The officer was General Gavin who told them to pile on and he would give them a lift into Werbomont. He also gave them some advice. He told them to attach themselves to some outfit pretty quickly or else they would be picked up and sent to a collecting center.

Arrived in Werbomont, the men went to their quarters and found their house totally deserted and all their personal gear and equipment gone. They judged, correctly, that it had all been gathered up by Lieutenant Hayes and 1/Sergeant Smith and taken with them when the command post moved out.

The men went to the schoolhouse and ate some K rations and bedded down for the night. During the night their quarters became very crowded as more and more of the 82nd Airborne men kept moving in.

The next morning an officer of an antiaircraft outfit attached to the 82nd came in and asked for volunteers to accompany him on a special mission. He had lost some of his men and he wanted to look for them.

The 82nd's orders had been so urgent and they had left Mourmelon, near Reims, in such a hurry that more than one small unit had been left behind. Moreover, their orders had been changed after they got under way, and their destination had been shifted from Bastogne to Werbomont. Inevitably some units had lost their way. Billington and his men, remembering General Gavin's advice, volunteered and were promptly attached. The officer looked for his men as far south as Metz, in France, and thinking they might have gone into Bastogne he even managed to get there looking for them. Billington and his men had several days of a hair-raising ride dodging Germans, and when the officer headed back north again and they spotted some 291st men on a roadblock near Huy, they decided to bid the antiaircraft officer goodbye. Here, they said, is where we get off. They joined the roadblock crew and were home again.

Back in Werbomont the evening of the 18th, Major Hal McCown and his 2nd Battalion of 119th Regiment, who were to screen the assembly of the 82nd Airborne at Werbomont, arrived shortly after 5:00 P.M. Security was set up and a reconnaissance force was sent out. This team confirmed the destruction of the Habiemont bridge, then went a short way up the road which went north on the west side of the Lienne. Here they were fired on by Peiper's tanks across the creek. It was full dark and the terrain was strange to McCown, so he dispersed his tank destroyers along the ridge near the road in the vicinity of Habiemont.

Over on his side of the creek Peiper was probing for a bridge on which he could cross a light reconnaissance force. There were several light, flimsy bridges between Cheneux and the Habiemont bridge. On one of these he sent across a detachment of half-tracks, and they prowled southward along the road which led through Forges.

Now, Private Johnny Rondenell was still hidden in the woods between the Habiemont bridge and the hamlet of Forges, and he still had his daisy chain of mines with him. He heard the clanking of half-tracks. He did not know how they could have crossed the creek but they were definitely on his side of the creek and had no business being there. He decided this was the time to

Tiger Royal tank near Petit Spai, undamaged except for engine trouble. Note white flag of surrender. Capt. James H. Gamble, commander Company A; Lt. Arch L. Taylor, 3rd platoon leader, Company A

T/5 Vincent Consiglio, who was trapped in a house surrounded by German tanks for 12 hours, December 21, 1944, at Malmédy

First Lieutenant Albert W. Walters, 1st platoon, Company A, 291st Engineers

Warche River bridge after being blown

Company B emplacement near big viaduct. Radio Operator Frederick Bryans holding binoculars; Sgt. Munoz using radio phone

Big railroad viaduct blown on December 22, 1944, under direction of Lt. Frank W. Rhea; 1000 tons of TNT were used

Bomb damage in Malmédy, December 24, 1944; all that was left of Col. Pergrin's command car. *Below:* 291st Engineers fighting fires the same day

Wreckage caused by bombing at Malmédy; 291st rescue crews at work

Christmas Eve in the command post at Malmédy. A toast to peace. *L to r.*, Capt. Sheetz, Capt. Kamen, Lt. Colbeck, Lt. Rhea, Lt. Joehnck (hidden), Col. Pergrin, Lt. Kirkpatrick, Lt. Stack, Capt. Moyer, Lt. Davis

January 23, 1945: Men of Company C beginning to sweep snow from bodies of victims of the Malmédy massacre. Ruins of Madame Adele Bodarwé's café in background and undamaged home of Henri Lejoly

Bodies of victims uncovered and tagged with numbered markers. Here over a dozen lie in one small heap
U.S. Army Photograph

Last bridge in Belgium, double-triple Bailey over the Our River near Lanzerath. Built for 82nd Airborne, February 3–5, 1945, in 40 hours by Company A and Company C in a blizzard and under artillery fire

Battalion Staff near Rheinbach, Germany, in March, 1945, just after award of Presidential Unit Citation. Note that officers promoted have not yet changed the rank insignia on their helmets!
Front row, l. to r.: Col. David E. Pergrin, Maj. Lawrence R. Moyer, Capt. William L. McKinsey, Maj. Edward L. Lampp, Lt. Donald Gerrity
Back row: Capt. James H. Gamble, Capt. Frank W. Rhea, Capt. Warren R. Rombaugh, unidentified man, Lt. Thurston K. Lowrie, Capt. Paul Kamen

make use of his daisy chain. Because he waited to make certain they were enemy vehicles, he hauled his necklace of mines across the road as the lead half-track was practically on top of him. Then, in the phrase that was used at least a million times during the Battle of the Bulge, "all hell busted loose." The half-track went up with the mine explosion and the vehicles following cut loose with their machine guns. Rondenell ran for cover deep into the woods.

After a brief period in which the Germans removed the remainder of the mines, he heard the half-tracks clanking on southward. They went on to the Habiemont bridge, crossed the highway there, and continued southward for some three or four miles before turning around and returning to the highway. Here they probed toward Werbomont and ran into McCown's tank destroyer guns, a brief skirmish occurred and several more half-tracks were destroyed. The reconnaissance column turned around then and fled, recrossing the Lienne to join the main Peiper column.

Here, perhaps more than at any other place in his advance, Peiper must have regretted having no heavy bridging equipment with him. During the remainder of the night he could easily have reinforced any of the light bridges across the Lienne to support his tanks. Instead he was helpless, and there was nothing to do but lead his entire column back up to La Gleize. Passing through Cheneux on the way he left a strong detachment to guard that bridge and prevent the Americans from seizing it. It might at least offer him an escape hatch later.

Private Johnny Rondenell spent the night in the woods and the next morning began his long trek to find the rest of 2nd platoon, or anybody from Company A or the 291st. He kept moving along to the rear until he found the 291st at Modave, some four or five days later.

*

Recall that Colonel Anderson had moved Group and the 291st from Haute Bodeux between 2:30 and 3:00 P.M. on the receipt of verbal orders from First Army Engineer, and that they had crossed the Habiemont bridge around 4:00 P.M. Colonel Anderson had felt considerable concern about the two officers he had sent, about half an hour apart, with messages to First Army headquarters at Spa — Major Webb and Captain Lundberg. He had no way of knowing whether they had reached Spa safely or not. He was not to learn until the next day, when Major Webb arrived in Modave, that they had both reached Spa safely and that preparing to return they had joined forces, traveling together but in separate jeeps. According to Major Webb, Captain Lundberg's jeep was in the lead and they had followed a route over secondary roads from Spa which led down the east side of the Lienne Creek, through Chessions and Forges, debouching onto the highway through the hamlet of Habiemont. Obviously they must have crossed the Habiemont bridge shortly before it was blown, because they ran straight into Peiper's lead tanks and Captain Lundberg and his driver were killed. Major Webb, behind him, and his driver had time to jump from their jeep and escape into the woods. Knowing that Captain Lundberg was carrying written orders from First Army Engineer to back up the verbal orders already sent for Anderson to move to Modave, Major Webb and his driver made their way to Modave. The missed connection at the bridge was very close. Had Captain Lundberg and Major Webb been half an hour earlier, they would have met Group and the 291st Battalion in convoy at the bridge.

Group and the 291st missed running into the head of Peiper's column themselves only by this same period of time. The tail of their convoy cleared the bridge not much over thirty minutes before Peiper's tanks debouched onto the highway.

The 291st's Communications Chief, John Scanlan, remembers the anxiety with which this entire segment of the road was trav-

Confrontation on the Amblève

ersed. Captain Edward Lampp led the 291st segment in a jeep. The trucks followed with the best riflemen of H/S Company positioned in the rear, to be ready to take whatever action rifles could take if this German armored column suddenly appeared. Scanlan and one of his radiomen, Corporal Thurston, rode in the last vehicle in the convoy, in Captain Lampp's command car.

In the vicinity of the bridge, or perhaps nearer Werbomont, in one of the innumerable halts that had to be made on the refugee-laden road, there was suddenly a frantic pecking on the isinglass window of the command car. The road had been crowded with Belgian refugees from the time they had left Haute Bodeux. Here were two, an old man and his wife. Scanlan opened the door to speak with them. "Take us with you, Monsieur, please," the old man pleaded. "We are Jewish. We lived through the Nazi occupation before but we cannot stand any more."

Scanlan and Thurston were in the back. A command car carries three easily in the back seat. Both Scanlan and Thurston were on the lean side. They looked at each other, then without a word moved over and made room. The old man and his wife got in, so relieved that they burst into tears. They rode all the way to Modave, and safety, in Captain Lampp's command car.

At another lengthy halt somewhere along the way Captain Lampp came back to the rear of the column and asked Scanlan if he could possibly raise the 84th Division on the radio. He was anxious to let them know the 291st was on its way! Scanlan shook his head. The only operable radio was a walkie-talkie, with a distance of three to five miles. Captain Lampp must have known this — but he was trying.

Colonel Anderson and his headquarters arrived in Modave around 8:00 P.M. and set up in the beautiful and historic old Château de Modave. Battalion did not arrive until much later, between 11:00 and midnight. Captain Lampp had only fragments of the 291st with him. Colonel Pergrin and the men in Malmédy were believed lost. Two platoons of Company A were scattered. Only a handful of Company C men were present. But the core of Battalion was still operative, functioning directly under Colonel Anderson and Group now.

They found shelter within the ancient stone walls of the château, in the enormous chambers with the great fireplaces. They knew nothing of its long history. They thought it was a castle that belonged to "some rich guy," and they built fires in the huge fireplaces and tried to get warm, ate K rations and bedded down.

Men trickled in for days. Lieutenant Edelstein found the headquarters the second day and promptly went looking for his men. He found Sergeant Pigg and the platoon truck with the 629th Light Equipment Company, manning roadblocks, tucked them under his wing and brought them home. Billington and his men came stumbling in several days later, then Rondenell, until finally 2nd platoon of Company A was almost back together again. Lieutenant Walters and 1st platoon were still at Trois Ponts.

Peiper, in the meantime, had taken over La Gleize. Arriving back there around midnight of the 18th, he set up his command post in a farmhouse near the château which until that morning had been occupied by Company C, the 291st. Probes made shortly by the 119th Infantry indicated they were in Stoumont by now, and Peiper had to take Stoumont in order to reach the next bridge across the Amblève which was at Targnon. He therefore laid his plans to attack Stoumont at dawn.

14

T̲HE 82ND AIRBORNE DIVISION had been detrucking in the vicinity of Werbomont all night of the 18th and morning of the 19th. By noon General Gavin had one regiment, the 504th, in Rahier pushing toward Cheneux, which Peiper still held. His 505th Regiment had built a temporary bridge across the Lienne Creek and was pushing toward Basse Bodeux.

General Matthew Ridgway, commander of the XVIII Airborne Corps, who had been in England when the German offensive opened, arrived in Werbomont the morning of the 19th, also. Ridgway had been telephoned the night of December 16, but most of his headquarters was maintained in London and he required 55 of the big C-47s to transport his staff and all their equipment to Belgium. He went first to see General Middleton at Bastogne and spent the night of the 18th there. He drove on to Werbomont by automobile the next morning, arriving about noon.

When General Ridgway arrived in Werbomont he had just been given command of the front from Stavelot to Werbomont, which meant he took over the responsibility for Trois Ponts and for Stoumont and La Gleize as well. Shortly his command would be enlarged until he commanded nine divisions and his front would extend for 65 miles.

*

Meanwhile down at Trois Ponts, the day of the 18th once Peiper turned north had passed fairly quietly, with the elements of the 51st Engineers spread out along the west bank of the Salm River, and with Lieutenant Bucky Walters and his men dug in overlooking the destroyed bridge. All units exchanged frequent rifle and machine gun fire with the Germans across the river, but no attempt was made by the enemy to put any men across.

The night of the 18th, however, was spectacular. Recall that a big 105-mm. howitzer tank had skidded into the river twenty-four hours earlier, that it could not be retrieved and that its crew had finally wired it for demolition. About dark they blew it up. Fine. It could not be used by the Germans now.

About an hour after the tank was blown up, a shell suddenly exploded from the east end of the destroyed bridge and zoomed out over the town. A few moments later another shell fired off and zoomed out into space. Everybody in Trois Ponts ducked for cover. The Krauts were finally shelling the town with their artillery, it was thought.

Shells began thundering more and more frequently, but they seemed to have no target. In their gun emplacements Lieutenant Walters and his men watched them. The shells exploded with much thunder and then went zooming off in erratic and totally senseless courses. German artillery never fired that erratically. If there was one thing German gunners were, it was precise and their aim was always good. But these shells were going straight up, wildly left, wildly right, any direction at all, like fireworks, and as if some idiot were doing the observing. The west bank of Trois Ponts was too good a target for that kind of aimless shooting.

More and more men became enthralled with the spectacular display and risked being decapitated by sticking their heads up to watch. Major Robert Yates, Executive Officer of the 51st Engineers, had arrived in Trois Ponts around 2:00 that afternoon to take command of the 51st unit there. Sergeant Paul Hinkel and

Confrontation on the Amblève

his guard detail had been meshed into the 51st defenses on the west bank. Sergeant Hinkel recalls that Major Yates approached his gun emplacement shortly after the thundering blazing spectacle began and said, "What the hell *is* that stuff? Where's it coming from? What are they trying to do over there?"

It was probably Major Yates who sent a detail to find out what was happening and learned it was a freak. The shells were coming from the destroyed M–7 tank. They were entirely harmless. The heat from the burning tank had started the 105-mm. shells to simmering. When they got hot enough they started to detonate and shoot off in whatever direction they happened to fly. But they were not exploding. They were just sizzling out into space. But they made a lot of noise, they put on a marvelous show and the whole thing caught the fancy of all the men and they watched them with the glee of kids watching fireworks. They hoped the enemy was being properly impressed. They hoped the Germans would believe the town was much more strongly defended than it actually was.

It is also said that Major Yates got another idea from all this false show of strength. He took about eight trucks and ran them up and down a hill all night, up the hill in the dark, down the hill with full lights on, in the hope the enemy would believe reinforcements were arriving all night. With the entire strength in the town consisting of one company of the 51st Engineers (minus 27 men), two squads of the 291st Engineers and a few scratch details of men, such as Sergeant Paul Hinkel's, a few Company C men left at the sawmills to guard equipment, and stragglers who kept trickling in, if the enemy could be fooled into thinking there were more it would be helpful.

At daylight on the 19th, Lieutenant Walters went to his CP at the hotel and collected some rations for Sergeant Miller and his men, and some gasoline for Miller's truck. He set out then for the lower Salm bridge. The railroad coming up from the south crossed the highway with an overpass about 400 yards this side of Miller's bridge. Walters drove under the overpass and stopped. He could see the bridge had been blown. Miller's orders had been to blow the bridge only at the approach of the enemy, so Walters knew that obviously the enemy had tried to get across this bridge, too.

Becoming cautious now, he left his jeep and crawled along a ditch to the bridge site. He saw enemy infantry prowling about up on the hill north of the bridge site, but he found no signs of Sergeant Miller and the five or six men on the roadblock. The truck was also gone, so Walters decided Miller and his men had escaped toward Grand-Halleux. He returned to Trois Ponts and reported to Major Yates that the lower bridge, south of Trois Ponts, had been destroyed.

In the light of this information, Yates decided to redeploy Walters' men. He ordered one squad to guard the site of the destroyed lower bridge. And he spread the remainder of Walters' men into two positions on the west bank of the river, below the upper Salm bridge. Yates was already using Sergeant Paul Hinkel and his guard detail, with some 51st men, precisely at the upper Salm bridge site, remember. Walters put his first detail just below that point and positioned the others as ordered.

Trois Ponts was entirely cut off, now. Major Yates had no communications of any kind with anybody, anywhere. The 1111th Group had displaced to Modave. Yates' own 51st-Battalion commander had his plate full with the rest of the battalion around Hotton. Yates had around 200 men to defend Trois Ponts, but they were behind their blown bridges and they had good positions guarding the river bank. They were in good spirits and they had no doubt they could hold on until reinforced, and Major Yates intended for somebody to know they needed reinforcing. Although he was without communications, he kept patrols constantly probing. If an outfit with any strength came along, Yates meant to know about it.

At about 9:00 that night a patrol sent out by Major Yates

Confrontation on the Amblève 275

met a patrol from the 82nd Airborne's 85th Reconnaissance Squadron. This was a unit of Colonel William Ekman's 505th Parachute Regiment. Ekman's men had now pushed into Basse Bodeux, Haute Bodeux and into the hills behind Trois Ponts. But they thought Trois Ponts was in enemy hands. They had expected to have to make a fight of it to recapture the town. Instead, when the patrols met, it was learned that the 51st Engineers and their attached units, among them Lieutenant Walters and his 1st platoon of the 291st Engineers, were very much in command of the whole west bank.

Well, great! Things were looking up for engineers and paratroopers both.

After the seesaw battle in Stavelot on December 18, General Leland Hobbs, commander of the 30th Infantry Division, poured reinforcements into the town, sending over the other two battalions of the 117th Regiment from Malmédy, the 743rd Tank Battalion and a platoon of the 823rd Tank Destroyer Battalion. Recall that the tank destroyers were positioned the night of the 18th so as to cover the bridge crossing and from the time they took up their positions no more German vehicles could cross.

Across the river, however, the entire pocket bounded by Highway N-32, the Amblève and the Salm, was now in the hands of General Mohnke's troops from *1st SS Panzer Division*. The rear march groups were coming up and the Stavelot crossing was an imperative for them if the *Liebstandarte Adolf Hitler Division* was to fulfill its glorious mission, spearheaded so ably by Kampfgruppe Peiper.

Therefore, directly across from Stavelot considerable strength was massing and they were to try fanatically, under Mohnke's desperate orders, to get across by any means and recapture the town.

Not only did the 117th have to repel these fanatic assaults to cross the river, they had an enemy on their flank to contend with. All day of the 18th the enemy had poured across the stone bridge, including not only Peiper's task force, but the reconnaissance section of the southern march group which had been ordered to join Peiper.

The southern task force, which had usurped the *Fifth Panzer Army*'s road in front of St. Vith and made traffic chaos of it and been long delayed, had finally arrived in assault positions in front of Poteau around 2:00 A.M. December 18. Here they ran into the solid resistance of CCR, 7th Armored Division, and were entirely stalled. Mohnke had then ordered the strong reconnaissance section north to mesh into Peiper's column now crossing at Stavelot.

Radioed the night of the 18th at La Gleize that Stavelot had been retaken by the Americans, Peiper had sent elements of this reconnaissance section to recapture the town for the Germans. It was the troops of this section which infested the tiny hamlets of Ster, Parfondry and Renarmont, outlying Stavelot, and committed so many massacres of helpless Belgian civilians in them and along the road between Stavelot and Trois Ponts.

They also made a considerable nuisance of themselves on the fringes of Stavelot as the 117th hung on in the town by tooth and toenail.

At noon on December 18, General Hermann Priess had moved his *I SS Panzer Corps* headquarters to Holzheim. He had been out of touch all day of the 17th with General Mohnke and his *1st SS Panzer Division* because Mohnke was traveling right behind Peiper's advance. The night of the 18th, however, Mohnke was in radio contact again.

Mohnke, in turn, had been out of touch with Peiper, who had much difficulty with his radio. On December 19 Mohnke reported to Priess that radio contact with Peiper had been restored and he gave Priess Peiper's situation. Peiper had captured

Confrontation on the Amblève

Cheneux, La Gleize and Stoumont, but he was almost out of fuel, he was low on ammunition, and he could go no further unless he was reinforced.

Priess by now had assessed his *I SS Panzer Corps* situation. The *12th SS Panzer Division* had bogged down in its attempts to take it three routes in the north and any further advances in that area were doubtful. Priess's only hope to move forward, then, lay with Peiper.

The *2nd SS Panzer Grenadier Regiment* was closing on the Amblève across from Stavelot. It was making fanatic attempts to cross the river. Knittel's reconnaissance battalion was already across and, under Peiper's orders, was trying to recapture Stavelot. Mohnke's *1st SS Panzer Grenadier Regiment* was hung up by CCR, 7th Armored Division, at Poteau. Priess therefore ordered Mohnke to close up his division, bring his *1st Grenadiers* up to the Amblève near Trois Ponts and attack strongly to get everything he could across the river and keep Peiper's thrust moving.

Priess had nothing with which to reinforce Mohnke, except some artillery. Mohnke would have to make his assault with what he had, but it must be a do-or-die effort. Peiper had to be kept alive if possible.

When the bridge at Stavelot was blown, Mohnke began to mass his forces on the heights across from Trois Ponts. Recall that there was a light bridge across the Amblève some short distance beyond the railroad viaduct on the Stavelot road. This was the Petit Spai bridge. And it would have to do when Mohnke launched his drive to reach Peiper in La Gleize. These assembled units of Mohnke's dominated the heights across the Salm from Trois Ponts and constant small-arms fire was exchanged with them by the engineers holding along the west bank of the river, and the engineers at listening posts reported considerable movement going on each night.

If any attempt by Mohnke's engineers was made to reinforce

the flimsy Petit Spai bridge so tanks could cross on it, it was not good enough, as later events will show.

Up north of Trois Ponts Peiper attacked Stoumont at dawn on the 19th and by 10:00 A.M. he had pushed the 3rd Battalion of the 119th Regiment, 30th Infantry Division, out of the town. Actually he had pushed them a short distance behind Targnon, but at this strategic moment, just as Peiper was driving beyond Targnon, the 119th's forces were reinforced by tanks from the 740th Tank Battalion and a fierce battle ensued. By the end of the day Peiper decided to break off the battle for Targnon and concentrate his forces at Stoumont. He has said he did not have enough fuel left to continue westward if he took the Targnon bridge. He expected an air drop of fuel, and some was dropped but it was so widely scattered it was of little use to him.

Morning on December 20 laid a dense fog over the entire Amblève valley and a light mist fell in some areas. In this ghostly shroud, one battalion of the *2nd SS Panzer Grenadier Regiment* crossed over the Petit Spai bridge near Trois Ponts and moved on to La Gleize to join Peiper.*

These men were to add considerably to the cost the 504th Parachute Infantry, attacking at Cheneux that night, would have to pay for that position. Peiper already held the bridgehead, his opening to the south, and he strongly reinforced it when this battalion arrived with elements of their infantry, his mortars, machine guns and assault artillery. Two companies of the 504th's 1st Battalion were cut to pieces as they tried to take the bridgehead the night of the 20th. On the morning of December 21, General Gavin ordered the entire regiment into the battle and by late afternoon of that day the fight was over. But it cost the regiment 225 dead and wounded, mostly from the two assault companies. When the 504th took Cheneux, however,

---

* Cole, Hugh M., *The Ardennes: The Battle of the Bulge* (Washington: Department of the Army, 1965), p. 352.

Confrontation on the Amblève

Peiper's opening to the south was gone. The net was drawing tighter about him.

Between 9:00 and 11:00 A.M. of the 20th, the German artillery on the heights across the Salm shelled Trois Ponts. Remember that Lieutenant Bucky Walters had three gun positions now — at the lower Salm bridge, south of Trois Ponts, and two below the upper Salm bridge on the west bank. The 51st Engineers were spread all along the west bank above him, with the enemy across on the heights on the east bank.

The 505th Parachute Infantry, of the 82nd Airborne Division, was now deployed on the heights behind Trois Ponts, and at 1:00 P.M. on the 20th, Colonel William Ekman, the regimental commander, arrived in Trois Ponts. He went immediately to Major Yates' command post to confer with this man who had been stoutly hanging on to the town. When he walked into the CP of the 51st Engineers the two men shook hands and Yates said, laconically, "I'll bet you guys are glad we're here."

They were. Delighted. The engineers at Trois Ponts saved the paratroopers a fight to retake the town.

The paratroopers were noted for their offensive stance and Colonel Ekman immediately began preparations to throw his men across the river to drive the enemy back. The immediate job was to repair the upper Salm bridge to get them across and the 505th's engineers went to work on it.

They finished the job that same afternoon, and Colonel Ekman, commander of the 505th Parachute Infantry, began to put his bridgehead across the Salm. Lieutenant Colonel Benjamin H. Vandervoort, commander of the 505th's 2nd Battalion, sent his Company E across the repaired bridge to a position on the heights of Wanne hill.

The morning of December 21, General Mohnke started to move his heavy equipment, tanks and tank destroyers toward the Petit Spai bridge to cross. The first vehicle to attempt the crossing on the flimsy bridge was a tank destroyer. As it rumbled out onto the light structure its weight was too much and the bridge collapsed. The big tank destroyer settled into the water up to its turret. Infantry could still cross on the wreckage, but not another vehicle could get onto the north bank until and unless the bridge could be repaired or a new bridge built.

In Trois Ponts the engineers on listening post duty had again heard German troop movements all night. On this morning of the 21st, therefore, Major Yates led a patrol across the Salm on a reconnaissance. He and his men observed the German engineers struggling in the deep, strong current as they tried to build a new structure just above the collapsed bridge. As they returned to Trois Ponts, Yates' patrol was seen and fired on by the enemy and Major Yates was wounded in the arm. He escaped the enemy fire by plunging into the Salm and swimming across under water. From his post at the west end of the Salm bridge, Sergeant Paul Hinkel and his men watched the narrow escape of Major Yates and covered him with small-arms fire.

Reporting what he had seen to Colonel Ekman, Yates had his wound dressed and continued on duty. The 82nd's artillery was deployed on the heights behind and above Trois Ponts and Ekman called for an intense fire to be laid on the Petit Spai bridge site. This effectively stopped the efforts of the German engineers to work on the new bridge. It was a suicide mission from there on and they never did get a new bridge built.

But Mohnke was shifting tanks, artillery and infantry around on the Wanne hill this same morning and now Company E of the 505th's 2nd Battalion, occupying a bridgehead on Wanne hill, found themselves in trouble. Around 11:00 that morning a company of German infantry, led by self-propelled guns, was seen on a road which ran past the position occupied by the paratroopers. A section of bazookas was able to knock out the assault guns, but the eight men of the section were overrun and either killed or captured in the skirmish.

Company E radioed that they could now see German tanks

maneuvering around them and more infantry infiltrating up the draws and forest trails. They were in danger of being entirely encircled and cut off, they said.

Their commander, Colonel Vandervoort, asked for help from the 456th Parachute Field Artillery Battalion, which was positioned on the heights west of Trois Ponts. The artillery laid down an intensive artillery barrage for about an hour and a half. During this period Colonel Vandervoort was trying to reach Colonel Ekman by radio for orders concerning the bridgehead. Unable to reach him, at 1:30 P.M. Vandervoort sent his Company F to the support of Company E. Stringers had been laid across the Salm bridge so that light vehicles could cross, and a jeep towed a single 57-mm. antitank gun over with Company F. This gun was manned by a crew under Lieutenant Jake Wurtich who kept the gun in action against the German tanks until it was knocked out and he himself was killed.

The enemy tanks were unable to maneuver successfully because of the muddy slush and the battle on the hill across the Salm from Trois Ponts became a series of bitter hand-to-hand fights, and the 82nd infantrymen suffered heavy losses. Vandervoort threw one more platoon across, but by then Colonel Ekman had returned to Trois Ponts and Ekman ordered an immediate withdrawal of the troops in the bridgehead. In the daylight this was almost as dangerous as continuing the fight.

The engineers of the 51st and the 291st, in their positions lining the west bank of the Salm, received orders to cover the retreat of the paratroopers. Lieutenant Walters and his men in their positions were alerted. It could be assumed that the enemy would attack on the heels of the retreating infantry. Each of Lieutenant Walters' emplacements had one or two .30-caliber machine guns and the men had their rifles.

Walters and his men waited. Suddenly on the cliffy hill directly across the river from them the infantry-paratroopers came pouring over, running and stumbling and falling, to escape the enemy closely pursuing them. Walters and his men were ready, but they gazed, astounded, as Vandervoort's paratroopers came unbelievably right on down over the cliffs, jumping from rock to rock, many of them trying to jump into the river, some being killed by their leaps, some being able to reach the bottom in one way or another and swim the river to safety. Others came down paths and fled over the repaired Salm bridge. It was a desperate, hard-pressed retreat.

The Germans, following closely on the heels of the retreating paratroopers, swarmed down the cliff and attempted to force a crossing over the bridge. Two platoons drove hard onto the bridge itself, and now Lieutenant Walters and his men cut loose with their machine guns and rifles, the 51st Engineers did the same, and exactly at the bridge Sergeant Hinkel and his men, meshed into the 51st positions, were violently engaged in hand-to-hand combat as the enemy infantry surged onto the bridge. But such a barrage of machine gun and rifle fire met the attacking Germans that not one of them lived through the assault. The engineers held steady all along the west bank under the attack and after a short hot fight the danger was over.

At 3:00 P.M. in the middle of the hot fighting around the Salm bridge, Major Yates received a message from Colonel Anderson ordering him to withdraw from Trois Ponts. Now that the 82nd Airborne was there, Anderson wanted and needed his engineers elsewhere. Disengagement at the moment was entirely impossible. Not only did Yates have his hands full at the Salm bridge, but also the Germans were trying to put infantry across the railroad bridge, now destroyed, down at the lower bridge. Here Lieutenant Walters' men on their outpost position helped repel that brief attempt. Everywhere the enemy was thrown back.

At 4:30 P.M. when the situation had been stabilized again, Major Yates sent for Lieutenant Walters and told him he was relieving the 291st elements and that he himself was under orders to withdraw. "And thanks, Walters," he said, "for a job well done."

Walters collected his men and their gear, loaded them into the trucks and, just at dusk, wearily led them toward Haute Bodeux where as far as he knew the command post was still located. The battle of Trois Ponts was over for him.

About the time he left Trois Ponts the 82nd Engineers blew the Salm bridge — for the second time.* At 7:30 P.M. Major Yates began to withdraw his men of the 51st, completing this by 8:00 and at 11:30 that night Yates and the 51st's Company C reported to their battalion headquarters in Marche.

Driving the short distance to Haute Bodeux, Walters thought how wonderful it was going to be to get a good wash-up, a hot meal and a good night's sleep. That was what he thought. He arrived in Haute Bodeux to find the 291st gone, of course. Nobody home at all. "Well," he told his men, "everything is snafu, as usual. We're out on the hook again."

They talked it over and Sergeant Elio Rosa, the platoon sergeant, recalled that there was a gas dump up north some place, and if they headed in that direction they might find some of the outfit's vehicles there. Or they might find somebody who knew something about the outfit.

So, in the pitch dark, again sliding about on an icy road, hungry, tired, sleepless for several nights, they started off. They went by N-23, toward Werbomont. The 82nd Airborne had built a temporary bridge across the Lienne Creek so their 505th Regiment could advance to Trois Ponts. Here Walters and his men ran into an 82nd roadblock and were halted. The guards told them to dismount, all of them, and approach with their hands up. The little unit obeyed. And then to Walters' consternation he could not find his ID card. Somehow, sometime, some place in the confusion at Trois Ponts he had lost it. He could not prove who he was at all, and with General Ridgeway's headquarters in Werbomont the men of this 82nd roadblock were not having any of his efforts to tell who he was, where he had been and what he had been doing. At gunpoint he and his

---

* 505th Parachute Infantry AAR.

men were marched off to the stockade and held prisoner, under arms!

They waited for an hour, furious at being treated like this by men of the very same outfit they had so recently covered with their machine guns and rifles as they retreated pell-mell down the cliff at Trois Ponts, for whom they had stuck their own necks out. Neither anger nor persuasion worked. "Wait for the interrogator," they were told, and all they could do was wait. The paratrooper-jeep team scare was working overtime and the 82nd was taking no chances.

Finally an officer to interrogate them arrived. A few judicious questions proved to him that Walters had indeed been at Trois Ponts fighting, that the men with him were indeed 291st Engineers, and that neither he nor they were saboteurs or Operation Greif commandos. They were released and Walters was told where the 291st was now located. "Straight up the Huy road," he was told, "the engineer dump at Modave."

It was midnight now, and it was snowing, the first snow in this section of the Ardennes since the offensive began. Walters and his men plowed along up the road, dark, cold and homeless.

It was nearing daybreak when they figured they should be somewhere near Huy, perhaps within four or five miles of it. Another roadblock loomed up ahead of them. Again they were ordered to halt, and again told to dismount and advance, hands up, to be recognized. Again they obeyed. Quickly. Men on these roadblocks all over the Ardennes did not want any fooling around.

Walters led his little detachment forward and then dropped his hands and laughed. The sergeant in charge of the detail dropped his jaw and said, "My Gawd, Lieutenant, we thought you'd been killed!"

He was Walters' own Sergeant Williams, his 2nd squad leader. "What are you doing here, Williams?" Walters asked.

"We been on some damned roadblock ever since we left

Haute Bodeux," Williams said, "just one after another. Kraut paratroopers are all over the place, they say. We're supposed to keep a lookout for 'em."

Walters inquired about the rest of the outfit and learned where they were. He was home, finally. All he had to do was, somehow, get to that castle Williams told him about, report and then just lie down, any place, any corner, and stay there for as long as the war would let him.

Six hours later he was directing his men as they laid new minefields in the fresh-fallen snow.

15

In Malmédy, meanwhile, these had been days of continued tension and preparation, and further strengthening of the town.

In the dark, predawn hours of December 18 the units of the Norwegians, and those of the 526th Armored Infantry and its attached platoons of tank destroyers, streamed into the town and were hurried into their positions.

For the men on the 291st outposts in Malmédy it had been a long, cold, extremely tense night. As has been said, the morning of December 18 was dark and overcast, but with no ground fog. When the officers made their rounds of the outposts, the men reported much movement of vehicles, engines starting and approaching the outposts, then receding, but nothing had ventured very near the roadblocks. The enemy attack expected at daylight did not come. Some of the tension felt all night died down. On some roadblocks shifts were rotated and the cold, sleepy men on duty all night were taken into town and fed and allowed a few hours of rest. On others there was no relief.

Private Bernie Koenig came down from his perch up on the hill overlooking the Gdoumont road and had a cold breakfast of K rations, then he climbed right back up to his post again.

Out beyond the B Company roadblock, on N-32, along the hill overlooking Five Points, Sergeant Sheldon Smith's squad remained strung out in their posts until noon. Shortly after full daylight, about 8:30, they heard a motorcycle coming up the road. It zoomed into view, carrying two German soldiers, one driving, the other riding in the sidecar attached. Smith's men had orders not to fire at anything and give away their positions, unless they were attacked. They let the motorcycle pass.

About ten minutes later they heard machine gun fire up at the B Company roadblock and judged the boys there had knocked out the motorcycle.

The men on the roadblock had also heard the motorcycle coming and they had watched it approach. They, too, were under orders not to fire unless something actually tried to pass the roadblock. They saw the motorcycle stop at a farmhouse. Tensely they watched as the driver got off and approached the house. A woman came out in the yard and pointed in their direction. They concluded she had given away their positions. When the driver remounted the motorcycle, therefore, and the woman had gone back in the house, they opened fire on it with their machine guns. The driver was hit and killed and the motorcycle plunged out of control into the ditch.

Sometime later, when the bodies of the dead Germans were examined their identification showed they were from one of the units of the *3rd Parachute Division*. Elements of this division were coming into place along the shoulder marked by Highway N-32, from Morschheck, near Büllingen, to south of Malmédy.

The incident was promptly reported to Colonel Pergrin and shared with Colonel Hansen. It was believed to be a reconnaissance probe and it reinforced the opinion that when the enemy was in sufficient strength Malmédy would be attacked.

It will be remembered that around dark the evening before, Lieutenant Tom Stack had been sent to Spa to take the first survivors of the massacre to First Army headquarters. He had had no difficulty going to Spa, but getting back to Malmédy was another matter altogether. He ran into the Norwegians moving down the road, now, and he could not get onto it. So at Francorchamps he detoured over to Verviers and headed down the road to the Mon Rigi crossroads.

This took a lot of time with the roads as crowded as all of them were with heavy traffic. It was around 5:30 A.M. when he neared the crossroads. He was stopped at a roadblock manned by some 30th Infantry Division troops. "Where you going, sir?"

"To Malmédy."

The guards laughed. "You'd better try something else, sir. Malmédy was captured by the Germans yesterday. We've been sent down here to retake it."

Stack was Irish and his Irish immediately got right up on its high horse. "Now, you listen to me! The 291st Engineers are in Malmédy and it has not been captured! I know. I have been there. I was sent by my battalion commander to Spa last night with some of those boys that got shot up at that crossroads. Malmédy wasn't captured then, and it isn't captured now. I got out last night and I can get back in today . . . if I can get past you!"

The guards talked it over and perhaps it was Stack's word that he had carried wounded survivors to First Army's headquarters which made them take him to their commanding officer. It turned out that this was an outpost of the 30th Reconnaissance Troop. The officer to whom Stack talked realized he had somebody here who had some information of vital importance. He therefore got in touch with 30th Division headquarters which, at that time, was in Eupen.

Recall that the 30th Infantry Division had been ordered to move from the north down to the V Corps sector, to come under command of General Gerow, had begun their movement at 4:30 the afternoon before and had been moving all night. General Gerow had ordered General Leland Hobbs to assemble at

Eupen, where he meant to use the division to back up the 2nd and 99th Infantry Divisions on the Elsenborn shoulder. The news of the German armored column at Malmédy, however, made Gerow change his mind and issue orders to Hobbs to divert his lead regiment to Malmédy. Gerow understood that Malmédy was in the hands of enemy paratroopers by now, and his orders to Hobbs were to retake Malmédy.

Lieutenant Tom Stack was finally escorted clear to the top, into the presence of General Hobbs himself, to whom he told his story of the 291st again. "My colonel is there, sir," he said, "and we have roadblocks on every road and there is no enemy inside Malmédy!"

He answered General Hobbs' questions. "Yes, sir, an armored column passed the crossroads southeast of Malmédy yesterday afternoon, but they pivoted south. Except for a probe or two, the enemy has not attacked at Malmédy."

Hobbs chuckled at Stack's Irish vehemence. "Well," he said, "that's the clearest information concerning the situation I've had yet. The 30th has been ordered to Malmédy. You lead the way, Lieutenant, and my Reconnaissance Troop will follow you."

The I & R platoon and other elements of the 30th Reconnaissance Troop were alerted and the little convoy proceeded down the road from Eupen. At 8:30 A.M. Lieutenant Thomas Stack led the first elements of 30th Infanty Division into Malmédy. The Reconnaissance Troop reported to Pergrin and Hansen that the 30th's lead regiment was also on its way. It was wonderful news. They were going to get some artillery and more infantry into Malmédy. Malmédy was going to be backed up.

The 3rd Battalion of the 117th Regiment moved into Malmédy almost on the heels of the Reconnaissance elements and took up position in the hills north and east of the town, and the 2nd Battalion moved into position between Malmédy and Stavelot. But the 1st Battalion, commanded by Lieutenant Colonel Ernest Frankland, was shortly ordered to move to Stavelot to reinforce the 526th Armored Infantry there. They displaced and moved toward Stavelot by way of Francorchamps. The direct route was under Peiper's artillery fire, as he got his attack at Stavelot under way about the time Colonel Frankland left Malmédy.

Shells fell all day during the 18th in Malmédy, but there was no other action, and elements of the 117th Regiment continued to arrive and take up positions all morning.

Around noon all the 291st roadblocks on the southern perimeter along the railroad were relieved by men of the 526th Armored Infantry. They were Company C roadblocks.

Other roadblocks manned by the 291st were no longer needed because of the stronger perimeter defense now possible. These were inner defense roadblocks, inside the town. Late that afternoon Private Bernie Koenig came down from his perch on the hill to find that his squad on the Gdoumont road was no longer needed because men of the 117th Infantry were positioned all around it.

He had been up on that hill, entirely alone, for almost twenty-eight hours, cold, hungry, thoroughly and miserably uncomfortable. He had seen absolutely no sign of the enemy and even his position made no sense to him. But that is not the point. The point is that he stayed there. He did not say to hell with it and go wandering off in search of warmth or food or sleep. With as much sense of duty as Pergrin, who did not say to hell with Malmédy, Bernie Koenig and dozens of others like him stuck at their cold, miserable posts until those posts were either absorbed or relieved.

All the other 291st roadblocks were kept in position and continued to be maintained by 291st men.

One unit of 291st men manned a roadblock late that afternoon that had not been ordered by Colonel Pergrin and about which he knew nothing.

Confrontation on the Amblève

Recall that Sergeant Ed Keoghan had set out with the rest of 3rd platoon, Company C, from Sourbrodt around 2:00 the afternoon before, under orders to return to La Gleize. That he had got lost from the platoon leader, but with two trucks of men had kept trying all night to get onto some road that would take him home. Recall that he had wandered by accident into the edge of the Stavelot fight, been commandeered by Major Solis to guard the old road to Francorchamps, was finally relieved around noon, headed back up to Francorchamps, then decided at that point to go to Malmédy.

He did just fine until he approached the S-bend of the road in the outskirts of Malmédy. It was now about 3:00 P.M. and here he was stopped by an officer of 2nd Battalion, 117th Infantry Regiment. A roadblock was being set up and the officer ordered Keoghan and his men to take it over. Once more Keoghan obeyed orders, detrucked his men and they took over the roadblock. They had had nothing to eat since breakfast the day before and they had been riding around so continuously and were so cold that Keoghan was worried about them. But when an officer gives an order, unless your own commanding officer is present you obey.

Soon, however, there were plenty of infantrymen in the vicinity, so that when about 4:30 a big bridging truck approached the roadblock and Keoghan noticed it bore 1111th Group identification, he was delighted. He talked with the driver and learned the truck was under orders to proceed to Modave and join Group there. Keoghan determined to go with him. He had to get his men fed and into some kind of shelter soon or he was going to have some casualties.

He sought the officer who had put him on the roadblock and explained the situation. He ran into an understanding officer who told him to go ahead. He had more men coming in all the time and they could spare him. Keoghan therefore attached himself to the big bridging truck and hung on to it like a leech.

They had to go all the way around by Liège and down the Meuse to Huy and it was after 4:00 A.M. when they finally drove into the courtyard of the Château de Modave. But they were finally home.

Keoghan spoke directly to Colonel Anderson and pled for immediate hot food and shelter for his men. "They've been in open trucks, Colonel," he said, "since day before yesterday. Some of them are in pretty bad shape."

Colonel Anderson went into high gear. To anybody within hearing distance he shouted, "Get those boys out of those trucks immediately! Get them inside! And get plenty of hot food down them at once!"

Keoghan himself was so exhausted he staggered when he walked. But he had his men home, now, and he could find something to eat and go to sleep for a while himself.

There was a flurry of intense excitement at the N-32 roadblock about 4:45 that afternoon. The men, still Lieutenant Colbeck's Company B men, reinforced by some infantrymen from the Norwegian Battalion, saw an American jeep approaching up the road. It was a lowery time of the day, and hard to see plainly, but as it came nearer they could tell there were four soldiers in the jeep itself and two riding the front deck. All of them wore the American uniform, but by now the news had spread through all units in the First Army sector that Germans were masquerading as Americans, so any strange vehicle or soldier was held in suspicion.

All the men on the roadblock, therefore, tensely studied the jeep trying to read its identification on the bumper. When the jeep came close enough they could finally make out the figures 106 on it, which identified it as belonging to the 106th Infantry Division. Somebody said, "That outfit isn't anywhere near us. That jeep's a phony!"

At about the same time one of the men on the front deck of

Confrontation on the Amblève

the jeep jumped off and ran toward the roadblock, yelling, "They're Krauts! The men in that jeep are Krauts!"

The occupants of the jeep fired at the soldier as he ran toward the roadblock, but missed him, and the other soldier riding the hood now jumped off and escaped. Desperately the driver of the jeep tried to turn around, but the vehicle was caught in the machine gun fire from the roadblock. One of the occupants jumped and fled and was killed as he tried to reach the woods. The other three surrendered.

They were, of course, one of Skorzeny's jeep teams, but the 106th marking on the vehicle identified it as recently captured somewhere in the vicinity of St. Vith. The men riding the hood were genuine Americans who had been captured. The German prisoners were embarrassed and crestfallen. They had approached confidently, believing Malmédy was in German hands.

They were not alone in this belief. The BBC radio was reporting that Malmédy had fallen to the Germans, and the Germans themselves had spread the information so widely that only those units actually in Malmédy knew the city had not fallen.

Around 11:00 P.M. that night of December 18, Colonel Pergrin was ordered by First Army Engineer to go to Spa and begin to work out the withdrawal of the 291st from the Malmédy defenses. Colonel W. H. Carter, First Army Engineer, now believed there were enough troops in Malmédy without them, and he badly needed all his engineers in the new barrier line being erected in front of the Meuse.

Pergrin took Captain Sheetz, Captain Conlin and Captain Moyer with him, along with those elements of B and C Companies already relieved from roadblock duty. These included Bernie Koenig's squad of B Company and Corporal Edmond Byrne's squad of Company C, as well as others.

They reached Spa about 1:00 A.M. and went directly to the Hôtel Britannique, the old headquarters of General Hodges.

The hotel was practically deserted. First Army had evacuated Spa at 4:00 P.M., only small ragtag units being left to move the last elements and equipment. The officers found rooms and the enlisted men bedded down on the balcony of the grand ballroom. They all anticipated a good long sleep.

It was short-lived. Behind Pergrin at Malmédy such vigorous protests about the 291st's withdrawal had gone to First Army that Colonel Carter had to weigh them. The 291st was too integrated into the defenses, it was said. They were manning all the important roadblocks. They had wired the bridges and railroad overpasses, and they had laid minefields. They were badly needed if more minefields had to be laid and if the bridges had to be destroyed.

In the end 30th Infantry Division won and a runner was sent to Pergrin ordering him back to Malmédy. He had slept two hours.

He roused up his men and they struck out for Malmédy at about 5:00 A.M. The fog was extremely heavy the morning of December 19, very thick even for the Amblève valley which experienced almost constant, pea-soup morning fogs all winter. And it was a widespread fog, reaching up and enveloping the 30th Infantry's 119th Regiment getting ready to do battle with Peiper at Stoumont, and blanketing Stavelot and Trois Ponts as well.

Just as Pergrin and his men reached the S-bend, where the road from Spa joined the Stavelot-Malmédy road, in this heavy fog, the enemy forces south of the Amblève laid on an intense predawn artillery barrage. Pergrin's driver, T/4 Curtis Ledet, did the best he could to speed through it, but shell fragments peppered the vehicle and scarred the windshield. It was an immense relief to reach Sergeant McCarty's outpost at the big railroad viaduct and be identified and let through.

The 120th Regiment of 30th Infantry Division had now taken over the defense of Malmédy. After the hard battle Colonel

Frankland's men had had in Stavelot the day before, the other battalions of the 117th Regiment were shifted over there. Colonel Pergrin now reported to the commanding officer of the 120th and a new approach to the perimeter defenses was worked out. The 120th's 1st Battalion was taking positions on the left flank in the hills east of Malmédy and was tied into 1st Infantry Division's units west of Waimes. Lieutenant Colbeck's unit on the Gdoumont road in that vicinity was therefore relieved. The 120th's 3rd Battalion was given the responsibility of protecting the town on the south and southwest, which included a large portion of the highway leading to Stavelot. But Sergeant McCarty's two roadblocks, one at the wooden bridge over the Warche River near the paper mill on the Stavelot road, the other at the big railroad viaduct, were kept. The 120th's 2nd Battalion was held in reserve near the regimental command post in Beverck, north of Malmédy.

Colonel Hansen's Norwegians were also attached to 30th Infantry, as were the 526th Armored Infantry and the tank destroyer company. With the exception of one company, the Norwegians were positioned near Beverck. Their Company B was spread along the high railroad embankment which lay south of Malmédy. The 526th and tank destroyer positions remained the same as first set up, their big guns practically poking through the railroad overpasses to cover the small roads coming up from the south.

The 291st was now ordered to set up machine gun emplacements all along the railroad embankment. They were also ordered to lay deeper minefields and to wire more railroad bridges for demolition.

Fortunately, Pergrin's old CP had not been usurped. He could return to it and begin his new assignments at once. He turned over to Lieutenant Frank Rhea and Lieutenant Donald Davis the job of putting the guns along the embankment and spreading the 291st men available.

Some of Lieutenant Rhea's squads had gone with Colonel Pergrin to Spa and on their return they waited for orders in a building in downtown Malmédy. Artillery fire was very heavy and as the shells crumped all around them they wished they could get moving some place else.

When Rhea came for them finally, about daylight, they moved on foot out to the south edge of town, went on beyond their old sawmill and out the Route de Falize. Along the road somewhere, before they reached the railroad, they stopped at a house which had been evacuated by its owners and Rhea took it over for his command post. Rhea set his security and the men put a .30-caliber machine gun at a second-story window which faced south.

Then Rhea set up his schedule of shift rotations for his men at the gun emplacements behind the railroad embankment. Bernie Koenig's squad, Rhea's 1st squad, with Sergeant Munoz in charge, drew an emplacement near the big railroad viaduct. Between Rhea and Davis machine guns were dug in and men posted all along the embankment and by 8:30 or 9:00 A.M. the first shifts of B and C Company men were in position.

The defense of Malmédy south of town now made a large U. One arm lay on the highway N–32 and extended eastward with 120th Infantry into the hills and touched 1st Infantry Division near Waimes.

The railroad embankment due south of Malmédy was the broad base of the U. Here Company B of the Norwegians and the 291st Engineers were in strong defense, backed up by the tank destroyers and antitank guns.

The west arm of the U reached down the road toward Stavelot, past the big railroad viaduct, past the paper mill and the wooden bridge over the Warche River, to the S-bend, and beyond it linked up, rather loosely, with the 117th Regiment which extended out into the hills from Stavelot.

Confrontation on the Amblève

All inside the large U was open space with excellent fields of fire. It was rimmed by trees but it extended for 500 yards directly in front before the wooded hills rose beyond it.

Although the units in Malmédy did not know it, massing in front of them now, in the hills south of this open space, was most of Skorzeny's *150th Panzer Brigade*. These were his own regular troops, the Wehrmacht and Luftwaffe battalions he had demanded and got, not the jeep team commando units which had fanned out on intelligence and reconnaissance details.

On the night of December 17, Sepp Dietrich had called a staff conference at his *Sixth Panzer Army* headquarters in Manderfeld. Skorzeny arrived about midnight and he had pressed for a new assignment for his combat troops. It was not possible, now, he insisted, for his men to achieve their mission of seizing the Meuse bridgeheads. The advance had been too slow. His men should be used, he now insisted, as regular ground troops with the *1st SS Panzer Division*.

After arguing Dietrich agreed and the commander of *I SS Panzer Corps*, SS General Hermann Priess, told Skorzeny to move his troops into the vicinity of Malmédy and report to General Mohnke at his headquarters in the Hôtel du Moulin in Ligneuville. Skorzeny set up, as we have already noted, in the chalet of Peter Rupp and his wife, not far from the hotel.

On December 19, the same day the 291st was attached to the 120th Regiment and was spreading itself along the railroad embankment, Skorzeny's men were assembling only a few miles south of them. And to the east, all along the northern shoulder, *I SS Panzer Corps* was massing during the 18th and 19th for a big general assault. On the 18th, SS General Hermann Priess moved the *12th SS Panzer Division*, which had been held up in front of the twin villages Krinkelt-Rocherath, and had slipped it southward and around to Büllingen. It was swelled there by other units which had finally taken Losheimergraben.

On the 19th, German General Staff officers paid a visit to the battle zone to learn what had kept the *Sixth Panzer Army* from exploiting the breakthrough made by the Peiper task force. Irritably they insisted that this entire northern shoulder, from Elsenborn through Malmédy, must be reduced and the right wing of *Sixth Panzer Army* must be brought abreast of Peiper's kampfgruppe which was now twenty miles west at Stoumont.

This conclusion had probably been arrived at in the higher echelons of command before the General Staff arrived to consult with Dietrich. They made their suggestions but failed to tell him how he might achieve this breakthrough, through 2nd Infantry Division and 99th Infantry Division, holding farthest east on the Elsenborn shoulder, or 1st Infantry Division at Dom Butgenbach and stretching to Waimes, and although the Germans did not know it yet, 30th Infantry Division holding from Waimes through Malmédy. They told Dietrich that obviously he had to have more room to maneuver, therefore he must break through somewhere along this northern shoulder. Then they left it to Dietrich to figure it out and try to do it. He kept hammering away and began to plan an all-out effort for December 21.

By the afternoon of December 20, the 120th Regiment was occupying all of its positions and late that afternoon, about 4:30, Sergeant McCarty was told he could pull his Company A men off the wooden bridge near the paper mill on the Stavelot road. Company K of the 3rd Battalion, 120th Regiment, were now in good positions on the bend of the road at this point and were well dug in out in front of the wooden bridge. The bridge was wired for demolition, minefields had been laid and the situation appeared to be well in hand. The engineers could be relieved. Thankfully the Company A men went into Malmédy for a good night's sleep. Sergeant McCarty himself turned in at the B Company command post for the first whole night of sleep since December 17.

Confrontation on the Amblève

Colonel Pergrin's radio operators in Malmédy were totally exhausted by now. Since the morning of December 17 the three men had done their best, round the clock, to stay on top of all the communications, but Corporal Andy Moore, Pfc. Daniel Haran and Sergeant Bill Crickenberger were just about used up.

Furthermore, as the various new dispositions had been made when 120th Regiment came into Malmédy and Pergrin knew his men were going to remain integrated into the defenses indefinitely, he wanted better communications with them. He wanted some walkie-talkies out on those roadblocks and at the gun emplacements, so he could keep in touch.

Therefore, late in the afternoon of December 20, he sent Sergeant Corcoran of H/S Company to find Battalion and bring in the Communications Chief, T/Sergeant John L. Scanlan. Through First Army Engineer, Pergrin now knew where Battalion was, although he remained out of communication with them. Pergrin also decided to have Warrant Officer John K. Brenna, Assistant S–1, come to Malmédy. Records were getting in a big mess. Nobody in Malmédy, least of all Pergrin, had had time to keep the records.

Corcoran left late in the afternoon. His route went by Verviers to Liège and down the Meuse to Huy and Modave. All around Robin Hood's barn, but all other routes were now closed.

The night of the 20th there occurred what so many men had been fearing. Two American infantrymen were killed by a patrol made jittery and nervous over the paratrooper and jeep team scare. It took a brave man to go from one outpost to another during this time. The men were inclined to shoot first and ask questions later. Lieutenant Colbeck has said that he approached even his own outposts when making a tour of inspection with great care and caution. That night there was a sadness in the lines as the word of the two men killed was passed along. "For God's sake," the men were told, "be careful."

The afternoon of the 20th, also, Lieutenant W. L. Colbeck, leader of Company B's 1st platoon, had a little time to think about himself. He badly needed to clean up and shave. But his personal gear was in the trailer in which he had been living in Stavelot. He decided, now, to make a trip to Stavelot and recover his effects.

He went by the back road, up to Francorchamps and down the old road by the gas dump which had now been evacuated. By the time he arrived in Stavelot, the 117th Regiment had control of the town.

Colbeck made his way out the Trois Ponts road to the sawmill. He was appalled. What he found there was a shambles. Peiper's men had smashed every piece of equipment and burned the mill. Colbeck's trailer was also a wreck. They had rampaged through it and taken all of his personal gear, then they had totally wrecked it. The kitchen setup was also vandalized. Nothing that could possibly be of any use had been left.

But worst of all was the news the civilians gave Colbeck concerning the massacres. Remember that right next door to the sawmill stood the Legaye home. It had been the scene of one of the most brutal of the massacres.

Because it was a large, imposing home, with full basements underneath, many neighbors had gathered there when Peiper attacked on the 18th. All day of the 18th and the 19th they had remained in safety, undetected by the German troops.

On the 19th some American troops occupied the upper floors and sniped at the enemy occasionally. The men warned the Belgian civilians to be quiet and they would be safe. But by dark the Americans had left.

About 7:00 in the evening the German troops arrived at the house and searched through it, finding the civilians in the basement.

The SS troops rounded up the civilians in the cellars and prodded them into the garden where they lined them up against the hedge. There were twenty-three of the civilians. They were

Confrontation on the Amblève

mostly women, a few old men, and there were four children, four, seven, eight and nine years old. The SS troops then shot them down in cold blood, using pistols and rifles.

One woman, a Madame Regine Gregoire, was spared. She was a refuge from Manderfeld, in the combat zone, and she spoke German. Believing her to be German, therefore, the troops shoved her out of the way, with her children. But she was a witness to the whole horror and testified concerning it before the War Crimes Commission later.*

These were not all the civilians murdered in Stavelot, but they were the largest group killed at one time.

At the time Lieutenant Colbeck heard and believed that the owner of the sawmill and his young daughter had been killed in this group. The entire family who operated the hotel where Colbeck had stayed when he first went to Stavelot had been among the group, and their children were two of the four shot down and killed.

The massacre stories seem to be endless. Wherever the soldiers of *1st SS Panzer Division* went, Lodomez, Wanne, Petit Spai, Trois Ponts, Stavelot, Ster, Renarmont, Parfondry, they killed the civilians, senselessly and uselessly. Entire families were wiped out, even to one baby only nine months old.

Hitler's directive to his armies had been that their behavior should be guided by the behavior of the local populace. Stavelot and Trois Ponts were centers of the Belgian Resistance movement and many of the people in both towns engaged in active Resistance activities. Apparently German sympathizers betrayed this knowledge, or German spies reported it. Innocent Stavelot and Trois Ponts civilians paid the price, with their lives, for the loyal Belgian patriots engaged in the Resistance activities.

Lieutenant Colbeck returned to Malmédy feeling sick over what he had seen and heard.

* Eisenhower, John S. D., *The Bitter Woods* (New York: G. P. Putnam's Sons, 1969), p. 263.

16

THAT AFTERNOON, the 20th, one of Skorzeny's men was captured in the outskirts of Malmédy and he was interrogated that night at the 120th's headquarters. Among other things, he said that a strong attack against Malmédy would be launched around 3:30 the following morning.

This word was immediately sent to all commanders and to most of the men in the defense lines. Colonel Pergrin received his message sometime after midnight. Everything now tightened up, waiting to see.

The Skorzeny attack was part of the big general assault Dietrich was planning for the entire northern shoulder, of course, and if Malmédy could be captured it would be a real wedge and opening. The important road net northward would be wide open and it might provide Peiper, who was now known to be in trouble, an escape route. But more important it would furnish Dietrich an opening through which to pour his men, push around behind the Americans and perhaps even yet get across the Meuse north of Liège. Also, the gas depots known to have been in Malmédy would furnish badly needed fuel.

It should not be forgotten that, based on the report of the merchant marine captain, Skorzeny's man, it was believed there was no great strength in Malmédy. On the basis of this imprecise report, Skorzeny had laid out his attack plan. He would attack in two prongs. He would send one group straight north on the highway N–32 and hope to open that road. He would send another group west and attack up the highway N–23. He had no heavy artillery, so there would be no heavy artillery bombardment in preparation. Instead, he would achieve tactical surprise. He did not expect much resistance and assumed he could roll right into the town within an hour or so. He expected to be in the heart of Malmédy by daylight.

From midnight, all Dietrich's troops along the northern shoulder were ready. On the dot at 3:30 A.M., from Butgenbach to Malmédy the great attack began. Immediately all the U.S. units along the line knew they had a battle on their hands, for the enemy fought with a fierce and unremitting fanaticism. The Americans settled down to hang on and repulse, and they did. There was no break anywhere on the shoulder line. But at the end of the day they knew they had seen some of the fiercest fighting in the war.

Sometime after midnight, Captain John Conlin, B Company's commander, and Colonel Pergrin awakened Sergeant McCarty. Both of them knew an attack against Malmédy was expected, but Sergeant McCarty was not told. He was simply roused up and told to find his men and take them back out to the wooden bridge.

McCarty could not find the Company A men who had been on that roadblock. When they were relieved that afternoon they had scattered into the various quarters being used by the 291st for some well-earned rest. McCarty sensed an urgency in the order to take some men back out to the wooden bridge and he did not waste too much time looking for the original roadblock men. He simply reached into the quarters of a mixed group of men, mostly mechanics and specialists, sleeping near the Company B command post, and pulled out T/5 Vincent Consiglio, Private William Mitchell and Private Joseph Spires.

Consiglio was a B Company motor mechanic. Mitchell was an old-line Army man, also with H/S platoon, Company B. Spires was one of the Company A men who had come into Malmédy with the machine guns the night of December 17. McCarty shook them out and said, "Come on, boys, wake up. You've got to go out and guard a bridge."

McCarty drove them out in a jeep. It was about 3:00 A.M. when they left the CP. As they drove out N-23 they passed under the big railroad viaduct where one of the men on the roadblock pulled a necklace of mines aside to let them pass. The night was very cold and very clear. On the drive out both McCarty and Consiglio noticed how bright the stars were, after so many pitch-dark nights of murk. And at this hour there was not the slightest wisp of fog.

McCarty pulled up at the big brick paper mill on the right side of the road, just before the wooden bridge over the Warche was reached. "The bridge is already wired," he told the men, "but the detonator isn't hooked up. Now, the infantry is dug in about fifty yards beyond the bridge, and some TD boys have a machine gun at the far end of the bridge. All you have to do is hook up the detonator and if anything gets through the infantry, turn the key and blow the bridge."

"Where's the detonator?" Spires asked.

"The boys said they put it on the windowsill of that paper mill," McCarty said.

"O.K."

The men were armed only with their rifles. They did not constitute another roadblock. Their job was simply to blow the bridge if Germans broke through the infantry.

McCarty turned the jeep around and started back to town.

The men never even had time to find the detonator. Suddenly the entire area was brilliantly illuminated and in the bright light of hundreds of flares the infantry and tanks of the enemy were seen approaching, *not* up the road toward the bridge, but across an open field to the left, all guns beginning to fire as the scene was suddenly lit up.

Confrontation on the Amblève

What had happened was that the U.S. infantry had strung trip wires all across this open field to the left of the road, and as the enemy silently approached across the field to get into position for their attack they circuited the trip wires and set off all the flares. Vincent Consiglio has said the light was so bright a newspaper could have been read without any difficulty.

The three men were confused by the direction of the enemy's approach. Instead of coming up the road to cross the Warche River on the bridge, as the men had been warned they might do, here they were coming from the left. The river curved away south just below the bridge and the Germans were therefore under no necessity to capture the bridge. They were already above the river.

The men were sitting ducks in the bright light. They fled across the street to a house directly opposite the paper mill. They burst into the house and startled the occupants out of a sound sleep. The house, it turned out, was the command post of a platoon of the 823rd Tank Destroyer Battalion, attached to the infantry, who had several three-inch towed guns positioned behind it, and several .50-caliber machine guns also dug in behind the house.

A captain was in charge and his quarters were in the kitchen, at the back of the house. The TD men got on the ball at once, under the captain's orders, and gun crews were in position and firing across the field behind the house shortly.

The situation inside the house was confused for a little while as men sought window positions from which to fire, and a handful of infantrymen from Company K poured in, also seeking shelter. In all, there would eventually be 33 men in the house. Finally they got themselves sorted out after a fashion with men in positions at all the windows. The house had two stories and a basement. The TD medics had an aid station already set up in the basement.

Consiglio took up a position at a kitchen window and the TD

captain asked him to observe for him as he gave the range to his gun crews back of the house. By this time enemy infantry and tanks were beginning to swarm up into the back area. Consiglio remembers calling the distances to the captain, "300 feet!" — "250 feet!" as the enemy approached. Then a TD man appeared and took over working with the officer.

Consiglio ran down into the basement. He found a window over a coal bin which looked onto a driveway beside the house. He clambered up on the coal to fire out the window. Sometime later the enemy infantry were swarming all over the yard and started tossing hand grenades into the basement. The infantry was thrown back and then a tank rumbled up the driveway and lumbered past Consiglio's window so close he could have reached out and touched it. It stopped and just sat there. Like practically every other American soldier in the Battle of the Bulge, Consiglio thought it was a Tiger Royal. It was actually a Panther disguised as a U.S. Sherman. Skorzeny had no Tigers and all his Panthers had been plated over with the slanted sides of the Sherman and the American star painted on them.

But when Consiglio peered out the window and saw the big tank, its gun muzzle turning, searching, like the trunk of some great prehistoric monster sniffing its prey, he was too low to see the star. He concluded, however, he was in a decidedly unhealthy position, so he fled upstairs. He ran clear up to the second floor into a bedroom. There he found Spires firing out a window which looked down toward the wooden bridge. Consiglio took a position beside him and both men continued firing their rifles.

Two tanks then approached up the road and crossed the bridge and came on, guns blazing, toward the house. They joined the others which had come into the area across the field, and all the tanks started maneuvering about the house.

Then the big tank clanked out of the driveway and went down the road, crossed the bridge to the far side, maneuvered

Confrontation on the Amblève

around a bit and finally turned around and took up a position where it could fire at the paper mill and the house. Almost immediately it began to shell the house with its big 75-mm. gun. The men called them 88s. One of the shells hit the kitchen of the house. Consiglio ran down to see if he could find Mitchell. Neither he nor Spires had seen him since the battle began.

When Consiglio ran into the kitchen all the men in there had been killed, including the TD captain. He ran into the front room on the first floor and bumped into Mitchell, who had found a bazooka. "Help me get into this gear," he told Consiglio, "I'm gonna get that bastard."

Consiglio helped Mitchell on with the vest bazookamen wore when firing and Mitchell went to the front door to go outside. He opened the front door, then apparently changed his mind and closed it and went to the front window and started to crawl out. Just then a machine gun sprayed the whole front of the house with a long burst and Mitchell fell headfirst through the window, killed instantly. Consiglio says that to this day he can close his eyes and see him, going headfirst out the window, but killed.

Consiglio went a little crazy then. He ran out the back door to a machine gun dugout. The gunner was dead. He pushed the body aside and swiveled the gun toward the field and just held the trigger down and sprayed and sprayed the enemy in the field. He did not know how long he fired. Then a tank nosed around the corner of the house and he had to abandon the machine gun. A one-room, one-story wing was built on one side of the house. Consiglio ran in there. There were only dead men in the room. A TD man who had been firing from the window was lying fallen beside his rifle. He had been shot precisely between the eyes.

Consiglio then ran back up to the bedroom and joined Spires at the south window. They continued firing and all count of time was lost. The battle simply went on and on, surging toward

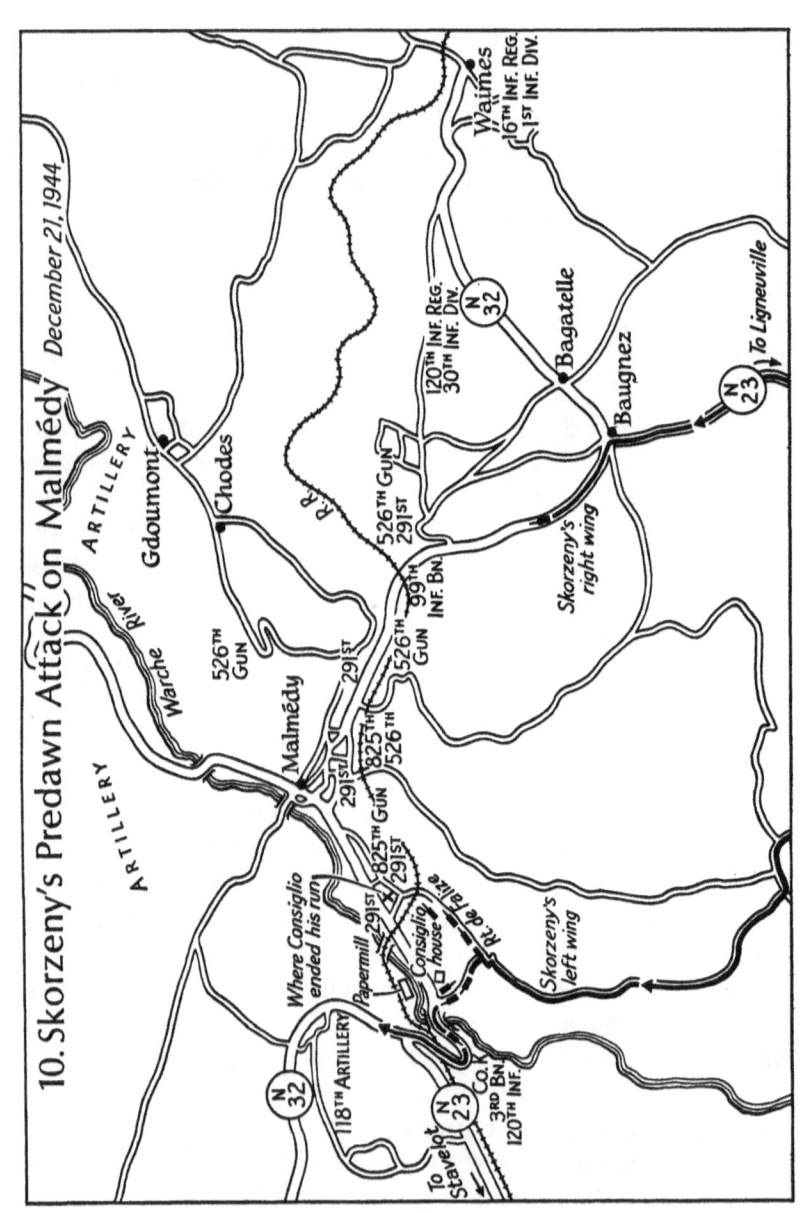

Confrontation on the Amblève

the house, then receding, then surging back again. Consiglio does not remember when daylight came. All reports of the battle say that there was a very heavy fog along about daylight. Consiglio remembers no fog at all. To the contrary, his recollection is that they had excellent vision.

At some time during the morning Spires suddenly cried out that he was hit. Consiglio pulled him back from the window and laid him on the floor. Spires was holding his right arm. When Consiglio examined it, he saw that a bullet had entered the right wrist, on the back side, and traveled up the arm to emerge at the elbow. The bones in the wrist and elbow were crushed. He then remembered the medics and the aid station in the basement. He picked Spires up in his arms and carried him to the basement which was already crowded with wounded men. He laid Spires down and tried to find a medic to treat his wound.

About that time the gunners on the three-inch guns outside came running into the basement. "We can't hold them," they shouted, "they're all over the place. We can't stop them!"

But somebody, an officer or an NCO, rallied them and they went out to try again. They were all killed.

Consiglio found a medic and turned Spires over to him. Then he went back up to the second-story window. A thick fog had settled over the valley at daylight, but now, around 10:00 A.M., it was lifting and the infantry all along the railroad embankment south of Malmédy saw the action around the house and the paper mill and opened fire. The artillery in the hills north of Malmédy found the range and started plastering the area. The house in which the men were trapped was now getting fire not only from the enemy, but from the railroad embankment and from the artillery also. It was rapidly becoming a deathtrap.

The big tank down at the wooden bridge got hit just then and all five men of its crew came boiling out of the turret. They ran across the bridge up the road toward the house, then they swerved, seeking shelter. Some huddled in a ditch along the road, and two found shelter in an unfinished structure. All were flushed out and picked off, one by one. Finally the last of the crew came running right up the middle of the road. Consiglio had an excellent shot. He drew a bead on the man, squeezed the trigger and saw him drop in mid-step.

The battle seemed endless. It went on and on, surging and swirling all about the house, the paper mill, the bridge and into the field.

When the attack opened after McCarty had let the three men out at the wooden bridge, he raced for the roadblock position at the railroad viaduct. Here he had several men dug in right beside the viaduct, almost under it, with a machine gun, a bazooka team and a daisy chain of mines across the road. One of the men in this position was Pfc. Wiley N. Holbrook of Company A. They were well dug in and as McCarty reached them, enemy shells, mortars and rockets were hitting all around them. They hit their foxholes and got as low as possible, hoping nothing would land on top of them.

The right wing of Skorzeny's attack had been launched, with tanks and infantry, straight up N–32 toward the crossroads. Here his men ran into the 120th's men of the 1st Battalion and the elements of the 291st Engineers in the roadblock on N–32.

The lead vehicle, a half-track, hit the mines and exploded, sending its equipment and its occupants high into the trees on both sides of the road. The men were wearing American uniforms. One of them, only wounded, lay helplessly beside the road, screaming in the anguish of his burns.

The artillery behind 1st Battalion opened up early and laid a heavy rolling barrage on the road. Many of Skorzeny's men quit under the heavy fire and surrendered. One prisoner had been a ballet manager before the war and had taken his troupe to the

United States. In excellent English he told his captors, "You can never win the war. We have so many new secret weapons."

They had none to use that morning in this right wing attack. It lasted about an hour, then Skorzeny's men had had enough and fell back.

There was one more incident. The night before, three Germans had driven a captured M–8 Scout car up toward the Five Points crossroads. It had hit a mine and one wheel of the car had been sent spiraling. The Germans had taken shelter in a house near the crossroads.

Now, as the battle along this road died off, these Germans in the house spied a jeep left by some tank destroyer men near the house. They mad a dash for it and then tried to rescue the man wounded when the half-track blew up. They rode boldly up in front of the roadblock, the jeep was challenged and in heavy, accented English one of the Germans yelled, "You are crazy!" He dragged the wounded man into the vehicle.

The men on the roadblock opened up with rifle grenades, bazooka and their machine gun and blasted the jeep sky-high. Two of the occupants were killed and the other two were captured.

This was the end of Skorzeny's right wing attack.

Skorzeny's left wing attack, which consisted of his strongest unit, had moved in column up the Route de Falize from the vicinity of Bellevaux. Abreast of the wooden bridge, one section of the column had taken a farm road that crossed the field over to the paper mill. The rest of the column had continued up the Route de Falize. The column following the farm road had tripped the flares which opened the battle prematurely for Skorzeny on that flank.

The tanks on the Route de Falize continued up that road, guns now blazing, and Company B of the Norwegians, in position on top of the railroad embankment, opened up with everything they had. Through the portholes of the railroad overpasses, the antitank guns of the 526th Armored Infantry and the three-inch guns of the 825th Tank Destroyer Battalion added all their firepower.

About that time the lead tank struck the minefield out ahead of the Route de Falize overpass and was set afire. The other tanks maneuvered around it and the infantry poured past it and charged the whole railroad embankment from the big railroad viaduct on the west to the railroad station on the east. Again and again they charged, screaming, "Surrender or die!" Their fanatic charges reached clear to the foot of the embankment. Again and again they tried desperately to set up their machine guns, and paid a dreadful price for their efforts.

For the first time in the war, the new proximity fuse shells were used at Malmédy. The new shells, which exploded in the air in the proximity of the target, caused some panic among the Germans, who were accustomed to shells that exploded when they hit. Some flung down their arms and raced for the embankment to surrender. In the main, however, Skorzeny's men were too tough to panic long and more than one hundred died in the futile effort made against the railroad embankment.

Private Bernard Koenig had just left the 3rd platoon command post to take his turn at the gun emplacement manned by 3rd platoon when the attack began. He was still some distance from the position. He hit the dirt and lay there for thirty minutes, sheltered to some extent on the lee side of the embankment. When the intensity of the artillery fire died down a little, he ran for the foxholes at the gun position. From there he watched the German tank burning in the predawn darkness like a Roman candle, a torch of light sending off sparks.

At the roadblock defended by Sergeant McCarty's men at the big railroad viaduct the men reacted promptly as the tanks and infantry rolled nearer. It was impossible to know the strength of the enemy, but occasionally, in the flare of artillery fire, or in the light from the burning tank, the infantry could be seen charging.

Confrontation on the Ambléve 313

The men fired everything they had, rifles, machine guns and bazookas.

At another position, Corporal Isaac O. McDonald suddenly remembered that the safety catches on the daisy chain of mines across the road had not been thrown. He dashed out to throw them, and earned himself a Bronze Star.

At still another gun emplacement, near one of the 526th's antitank guns, a mortar shell landed and killed an infantryman and knocked down T/5 John T. Noland, a bulldozer operator now serving as infantryman. He bounced back up, and fearful that the tanks would reach the overpass, ran out to drag a daisy chain across the road. This earned a Silver Star for him.

In the middle of the fight at the railroad embankment, and just as dawn was coming, another mortar shell hit in some trees near McCarty's men. A tree splintered and sent its fragments in all directions. Pfc. Wiley Holbrook was hit by the fragments of this tree-burst and was instantly killed. The back of his head was literally sheared off. A big, good-humored man, Holbrook had been at this roadblock since the night of December 17.

The entire attack up the Route de Falize against the railroad embankment lasted about two hours, but it was a fierce, hot fight during that time, with the enemy often at the very foot of the embankment. Then the artillery and the fierceness of the Norwegians in repelling the attack began to tell and Skorzeny's men slowly fell back, leaving their dead and dying, their burning tanks and disabled vehicles to litter the field.

The detachment which had gone toward the paper mill and the main Stavelot road pushed their infantry to the fore and poured around the house in which Consiglio, Mitchell and Spires had taken refuge — the TD command post — and spilled over the wooden bridge into the Company K positions beyond. The men of Company K made a fight of it but eventually had to retire to the paper mill.

At the paper mill, Pfc. Francis Currey, a BAR man of Company K, fired his own weapon with vigor. Then he found a bazooka, but it had no rockets. A TD half-track at the house across the street was said to have some rockets in it. Currey dashed across the road to find the rockets. He dashed back with them and loaded for another man who blasted the turret of a tank and knocked it out. This may have been the tank Consiglio thought was hit by artillery fire.

Seven or eight tanks were maneuvering around a house below the bridge, and the infantrymen at the paper mill decided this house was being used as a base of operations. Currey went out with a bazooka alone and fired into the tanks around the house. Then he dashed across the street again and found some rifle grenades in the TD half-track. From a flank position he fired all the grenades at the house.

His grenades gone, Currey ran to the half-track and started firing its .50-caliber machine gun, but he could not get a good range of fire from there. He abandoned it and seeing a .30-caliber machine gun nearby ran for it and opened a burst of fire on the Germans below the bridge. The fight around the paper mill and the bridge went on and on, very hot and fierce, as it also swirled around the house in which the TD men, a handful of Company K infantrymen and Consiglio and Spires were trapped.

At about 2:00 that afternoon the men trapped in the house were all grouped in the basement. They took a count. Out of thirty-three, only twelve were left alive. Consiglio said, "Somebody has got to get out of here and go for help or we'll all be wiped out."

One man said, "Who'd be fool enough to try? You're a dead duck the minute you stick your nose out of this house."

Consiglio said, stubbornly, "If somebody will go with me, I'll try."

There was a silence and then one of the infantrymen, a corporal from Company K, said, "I'll go. Maybe one of us will get through."

Consiglio said, "O.K. Let's go."

The other men thought they did not have a chance but the two men were now determined. They went up to the first floor and mapped out a plan. "We'll cut across the road," Consiglio said, "through that mill yard, then down the hill to the river, cross the river and make for the railroad tracks. If we make it to the tracks, we can head on up toward Malmédy. And don't stick with me," Consiglio warned the corporal, "stay on your own. We'll have a better chance of making it."

They put a full clip in their rifles then took off their cartridge belts. "Ready?" Consiglio asked.

"Ready," the corporal answered.

Consiglio went first, flinging open the front door of the house. He hit the dirt running. "I never ran as hard or as fast in my life," he said. "I really had wings on my feet. They started firing at us as soon as we broke out of the house. You never know how fast you can run until you've got bullets nipping at your heels!"

Each man running on his own, zigzagging, they both made it across the road, through the gates of the mill yard, down between the buildings, down the hill to the river. "I think I just walked on the water," Consiglio said, "I don't remember even making a splash!"

On the far side of the river he noticed that the corporal had made it, too, and separated by some twenty or thirty feet each man pulled himself up the railroad embankment with the help of shrubs and little bushes. It was a very steep embankment. Consiglio remembers it as being at least a sixty-degree grade. Together, now, they fled down the tracks. Shortly the tracks bent east and they had to cross the little river again, this time on the railroad trestle. Negotiating the trestle, they then slid down the embankment on the sheltered side onto a dirt road. They eased up into a trot now, feeling fairly safe. Both men were shaking all over, wet to their necks, both almost totally out of breath and Consiglio had a bad stitch in his side.

Suddenly they trotted right into a .50-caliber machine gun positioned on the road with two men on guard. "Halt!" the guards shouted.

Consiglio and the corporal halted, their hands flying up over their heads. Out of breath, almost ready to drop, Consiglio could not for the life of him think of the password. He blurted out the first thing that came into his mind, and to his horror it was the German word for surrender. "Kamerad!" he cried, on a long exhaled breath.

One second later, thinking they had themselves two Germans disguised in American uniforms, the two machine gunners were on top of Consiglio and the corporal. They grabbed them by their collars at the back of their necks and shook them as if they had been puppy dogs. Still shaking them they dragged them across the road to the yard of a house where they flung them face down in the mud and slush. One of them stood guard over them while the other went in the house. He emerged a moment or two later with a captain. Gruffly the captain told the guards to bring the two men inside the house, and the guards poked, prodded and shoved them into the building.

It was the command post of Company K. Inside, the captain gave them a little time to get a breath or two. "Who are you?" he said then, "and where did you come from?"

The two men, haltingly and still breathing very hard, identified themselves satisfactorily, and then Consiglio told about the long fight around the house. "They're all being killed," he said, "there are only twelve left now. The Krauts are all over the place out there!"

"I know the Krauts are there," the captain said, "but it's impossible you've come from that house. I've got telephone to my men out there and they say the Krauts captured that house early this morning and are using it for a CP."

With some understandable heat Consiglio said, "They didn't capture it! We're still there. Or at least what's left of us. You've got to believe me, sir, and you've got to send somebody out there and get those men out."

Confrontation on the Amblève

The captain did believe him finally and ordered two half-tracks, with multiple machine guns mounted on them, to be sent to the relief of the men in the house. The corporal was home now and could relax, but the captain took Consiglio to the 3rd Battalion command post in Malmédy.

Consiglio says this was a "real high-class" command post, with a big map room and a lot of brass. Here he repeated his story and got the feeling that the officers in this CP were learning some details for the first time of what had actually occurred out near the wooden bridge. They seemed to Consiglio to be confused about the events of the entire day. They were bewildered enough to believe the enemy had broken through and their tanks were roving around behind the lines.

When he had told his story again, Consiglio was allowed to go back to his own CP. It was now around 4:00 in the afternoon. And now he told his story once more, this time to Colonel Pergrin. By now reaction had set in and he was shaking all over. He was also wet and filthy and hungry and totally exhausted. Pergrin said he looked like a water-drowned rat, slime and mud all over him and his eyes like dark holes in his head. He was sent to his quarters where he could finally collect himself and get warm and dry, get some food and some sleep. It had been a long, long day and T/5 Vincent Consiglio had had himself very much of a battle.

The battle around the paper mill and wooden bridge slowly subsided toward the middle of the afternoon. Artillery had really turned the tide. They had plastered the fields south of Malmédy with over 3000 rounds of fire. Skorzeny threw in the sponge, after a long and desperate try, disengaged his men and slowly pulled them back along a six-mile ridge line.

He had received the word early that his right wing attack had not worked and he had accepted it philosophically. He had not counted too much on it, anyhow. But when a couple of hours went by and he had no news from his left wing attack, he became perturbed. At daylight he walked to the crest of a hill from which he had a good view of the widespread field and the S-bend on the Stavelot road. Looking through his field glasses he could see the battle swirling hotly along the bend and around the paper mill. He noticed that six of his Panthers, camouflaged as Shermans, were hopelessly embattled with the Americans and he was dismayed. These were the tanks which had been intended to cover the left flank of the main attack up the road.

He also saw that Foelkersam, who was commanding the main attack, was in trouble around the paper mill and wooden bridge. This left wing assault was not going well at all, either.

Along toward the middle of the morning the first of his troops arrived at Skorzeny's position on the hill. They told him they had run into solid and strongly defended positions and they could not be taken without heavy artillery support. Skorzeny had no heavy artillery. General Mohnke was pouring fire on the town, but Skorzeny had to depend on his tank guns and his assault guns.

Combat cars started bringing the wounded back. But Foelkersam held grimly on around the S-bend and the paper mill, the tanks continuing to maneuver and cover the infantry as they slowly disengaged. Skorzeny now felt extreme anxiety for Foelkersam, who was a close personal friend. He now felt this whole affair was stupid, and he wanted Foelkersam to break it off. Obviously Malmédy was not lightly defended at all!

Finally he saw Foelkersam approaching on foot, limping badly, leaning on the arm of a medical officer. As he approached Skorzeny he grinned weakly then lowered himself gingerly to the ground. He confessed that he had been wounded in the rump. It was painful as the devil and Skorzeny could laugh if he liked but sitting was not at all comfortable!

Skorzeny set up a ring of rocket launchers to protect their position against counterattack (which was not attempted) and held a staff conference. About then the tank commander limped in. He had reached the artillery positions, he said, and had over-

Confrontation on the Amblève

run one battery, but he had then been thrown back. Skorzeny says he lost every tank he had.*

The artillery positions were those of the 117th Infantry Regiment, which linked in the S-bend with the 120th positions. They had fought a grim battle along the line, not knowing precisely where their own sector ended.

Skorzeny then gave orders, about the middle of the afternoon, for all his men to fall back and he formed them in a very thin line along the crest of the hill for about six miles. The American artillery was now firing very heavily. It systematically pulverized the small village of Ligneuville.

He remained in position in the hills south of Malmédy, however, until December 28, when he was pulled out, relieved by an infantry unit and sent to a sector east of St. Vith.

The battle at Malmédy had far-reaching repercussions. Reports were that the town had been overrun and that the enemy tanks had penetrated as far north as Burnenville. Two battalions of antiaircraft artillery with 90-mm. guns were rushed to take up positions to build a defense in depth as far back as the division command post at Beverc̆é.

An air of malaise had hung over Malmédy from that fateful Sunday, December 17 — a mystery and a fear. Part of it was psychological. The city was known to be strongly pro-German. It was also full of refugees from the German border towns who were German in all their habits and thinking and loyalties. The 526th Armored Infantry had reported they were fired on by a sniper as they entered the town the night of December 17.

The 3rd Battalion, 120th Regiment, reported that in the darkness of the early morning preceding the Skorzeny attack on December 21, a woman guided German troops up the dirt road toward their positions, firing a burp gun as a directional guide.

* Details of German side of battle in Skorzeny, Otto, *Skorzeny's Special Missions* (London: Robert Hale Limited, 1957).

The men on the 291st roadblock on N-32 believed that a woman had given away their positions to the two paratroopers on the motorcycle the morning of December 18. And it was believed an agent had observed for the big 310-mm. guns on the morning of December 16.

Worst of all was the mournful knowledge that bodies of an unknown number of American soldiers lay dead at the crossroads, frozen as they had fallen when massacred. There were some dark thoughts that perhaps pro-German civilians had had something to do with that, too.

It was an unhappy town, perhaps a fated town, and a pall hung over it. The Norwegians and the men of the 120th Regiment disliked it intensely, feeling the citizens were not on their side at all, feeling their flanks were wide open because of so much pro-German sentiment in the town. Even the 291st, who knew the Malmédy people better than the Norwegians or the infantrymen, felt it to some extent.

And the rumors would not die that the Germans had control of it. Each time the rumors were laid, they were only partially laid, by only those elements who gained firsthand knowledge. And now, on the night after the battle, the rumors gained fresh fuel for their fires. Nobody in command knew quite what had happened in Malmédy that day and everyone feared the worst.

17

For several days Manteuffel's *Fifth Panzer Army* had been posing a very dangerous threat farther west. He had isolated St. Vith and Bastogne and his forces were now streaming westward past both towns.

Within forty-eight hours of the launching of the German offensive the Allied command had diagnosed the intention as the crossing of the Meuse in the vicinity of Liège and steps had been taken quickly to harden the shoulders and keep the offensive crowded into one narrow corridor of advance. But Eisenhower had also been determined that this advance must be halted east of the river. It must not be allowed to cross the Meuse.

On December 18, therefore, late in the afternoon SHAEF made its first move to bolster a barrier line on the Meuse. The 17th Airborne and the 11th Armored Divisions, both in England, were ordered to the continent. Neither unit, however, could be expected to arrive in position for some days.

Montgomery had also recognized the threat to his rear and the trap in which his entire 21 Army Group might be caught. On his own initiative he had started moving some troops south. At 5:30 on December 19, Montgomery ordered General Horrocks to move his XXX Corps from Holland to the area behind the Meuse between Liège and Brussels and gave him the Guards Armoured Division and the 43rd, 51st and 53rd Infantry Divisions, as well as three armored brigades.

In the meantime, however, scattered units of engineers were spread in front of the river to guard crossroads, wire bridges, lay minefields, set up machine gun and bazooka emplacements and, in general, delay or check the enemy in any way possible. And the enemy included paratroopers and jeep teams wearing U.S. uniforms. Every unit committed to the Meuse barrier line was jittery about these German infiltrations and was extremely conscious of security against them.

On December 19, Colonel Anderson, at Modave just in front of Huy, was ordered to put all the engineers of his 1111th Group he could muster into this Meuse barrier line. He could not muster many. He did not have the slightest idea where his 296th Battalion was. Swallowed up, somewhere north of the Elsenborn shoulder. He had also lost all contact with the 202nd Battalion temporarily assigned to him on December 11.

Two companies of his 51st Battalion were deeply involved in a long line of defense near Hotton, and its third company was at Trois Ponts. Almost half of his 291st Battalion was either in Malmédy or killed or captured, so far as he knew. At Modave he had one platoon of Company A intact, Lieutenant Arch Taylor's 3rd platoon. He had a handful of Lieutenant Walters' 1st platoon of Company A, but most of it was in Trois Ponts. He had a handful of Lieutenant Edelstein's 2nd platoon of Company A, but the rest of it was scattered, following the destruction of the Habiemont bridge.

He had the 291st H/S Company, and he had the specialists, the mechanics, radio operators, cooks, clerks, of two H/S platoons, Company A and Company C. He had handfuls of Company C men with not a single platoon intact.

Of line troops, therefore, he had only the equivalent of slightly more than one company. The assignments were nevertheless made. The Company A units were sent to fixed positions. Lieutenant Taylor's 3rd platoon was sent to Hamois, on the main Dinant-Huy highway, where they were ordered to

Confrontation on the Amblève

wire the bridge over the Bocq River and set up a roadblock in front of it and guard it. They were also to lay minefields around it.

One squad of Lieutenant Walters' 1st platoon was at Modave, so it, with Sergeant Abe Caplan in charge, was sent to Emptinne to guard the crossroads there.

Other elements of Company A, a scattered mix of 1st and 2nd platoons, were sent to guard the Barvous Condroz crossroads, and Company A's command post was moved there.

Corporal John King, Company A clerk, remembers that security at the CP was stretched so thin by all the jobs the men were doing, including the mechanics, cooks and radio operators, that there came a day when a Bing Crosby movie was shown at the CP and there were so few men present that only one man at a time could see the movie.

It was on one of these days, too, that there was a paratrooper scare at the command post. The kitchen setup was in an outbuilding several hundred feet from the headquarters. Corporal King was working alone that morning in the orderly room. Suddenly Mess Sergeant McCarl burst into the room and grabbed a rifle. "Some damned snipers just fired at me," he shouted, "and I think I saw 'em. They're a couple of paratroopers and they're out behind some bushes near the barn!"

King grabbed a rifle, too, and he and McCarl made a strategic advance, from one sheltered position to another. Finally they charged the bushes, sure they had cornered the enemy. Fortunately they did not fire. A Belgian farmer would have lost his cow if they had! But credit them with heart. A mess sergeant and a company clerk were not going to let any German paratroopers escape if they could help it.

Company C was sent hopping, skipping and jumping all over the place to lay minefields — at Nettine, at Hogne, at Sinsin, Rabosse and Heure. Not until December 24 was any unit of Company C assigned a fixed position. They laid so many minefields they lost count of them, and most of the time they did not have the slightest idea where they were. Captain Bill McKinsey, at Battalion, however, kept an accurate record of them. But the men were sent out, with an officer or NCO, to a bridge, a culvert, a railroad crossing, and told to lay a field so deep, so wide, right here. With frozen fingers they dug their mines into the frozen ground, and moved on, frequently under enemy artillery fire.

Corporal Al Schommer, radioman in Company A, remembers a time when Captain Gamble took him along as he visited positions. At a particular position, under a slight hill, the captain got out of his command car to talk to the men in the foxholes. His driver, John Coupe, also got out to walk around and try to get some feeling in his feet. About that time Schommer's radio came to life and he was busy taking down the message. With a head-set on he heard nothing else. Finished with the message he looked up to see Coupe frantically signaling him. Then he noticed the snow was black with exploded shells. An artillery barrage had been laid on the position from over the hill. Nobody was hurt.

Reinforcements for the Meuse barrier line were rapidly being ordered in, meanwhile. On December 18, General Hodges had called Major General J. Lawton Collins to his headquarters in Spa and directed him to pull his VII Corps out of the line near Düren, in the north, and move it onto the Marche plateau.

The conference took place around noon on the 18th. Word arrived during the conference that the German armored column had turned north at Trois Ponts and was approaching dangerously near Spa, and Hodges' staff was recommending that the headquarters move back to their rear installations at Chaudfontaine. Hodges coolly continued his conference with Collins while his staff began preparations to move.

Collins' VII Corps was already depleted. His 1st Infantry Division was with V Corps, in the line near Butgenbach and

Confrontation on the Amblève   325

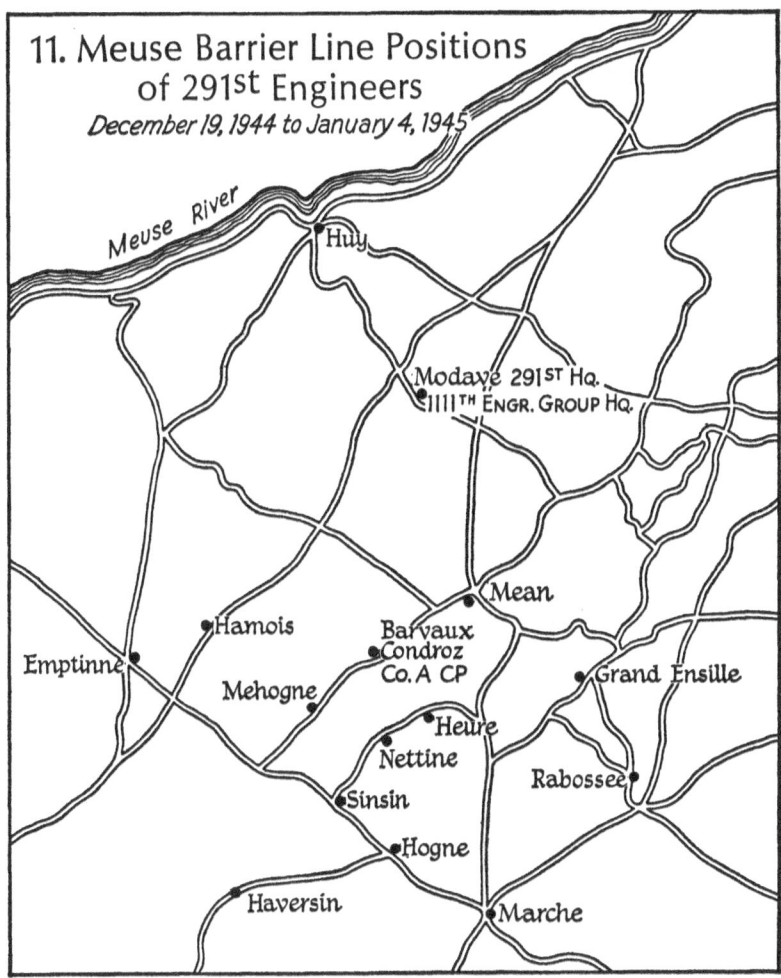

Waimes. His 4th Infantry Division was fighting desperately with VIII Corps near Echternach in Luxembourg. Hodges told Collins he could have the 84th Infantry Division, fighting in the north at Geilenkirchen, but already ordered to displace south and take up a position around Marche, to the west of Ridgway's XVIII Airborne Corps. And Collins could have a new division, the 75th Infantry, just arriving in France. He would also have the 2nd and 3rd Armored Divisions.

Collins would therefore move south and west as rapidly as possible and make his headquarters astride the Huy road at Mean. Understood, and Collins left to head north and begin moving.

On December 20, however, General Eisenhower made a momentous decision. He looked at the map long and thoughtfully. General Omar Bradley, commanding the 12th Army Group, was headquartered in Luxembourg City. First Army headquarters, which had displaced from Spa on the 18th to Chaudfontaine, and later to Tongres, west of the Meuse, was a long way from Bradley. Communications were extremely poor already and might be cut entirely at any time. For political reasons it was not a good idea to move Bradley's headquarters. But how could he command First Army, now so beleaguered, from where he was?

Eisenhower decided it was impossible. He therefore drew a line from Givet, on the Meuse, to Prum, which divided the battlefield in half and determined to hand over command of the top half to Field Marshal Montgomery, leaving Bradley to command the lower, or southern half. In effect, this meant leaving Bradley with little but General Patton's Third Army, because VIII Corps of First Army had been hit so hard that it was practically inoperable by now.

Eisenhower knew this would create some problems and probably cause some misunderstandings. It did plenty of both, but it had much more far-reaching effects than problems and misunderstandings. Any British commander leading American troops would have had his problems. American commanders were firm believers in keeping an offensive stance. Since the days of General Ulysses S. Grant, who held and acted on the theory that the best defense was usually offense, this had been an unshakable tenet of commanders in the United States Army. With

Confrontation on the Amblève

them, you simply did not wait around getting ready to fight. You did not wait until your lines were tidy and just sit and hold a position. You kept putting on pressure, where you could, with what you had.

Montgomery, of all British commanders, had a totally different concept. It has been said that he was a master of the set battle. Perhaps. Certainly he was obsessed with the notion he must have his lines tidy and masses of men and matériel behind him before going on the offensive. In fact, he did not easily take the offensive at any time. He was extremely cautious. He had been unforgivably slow attacking after the Normandy landings. And he had allowed the enemy to escape from the Falaise pocket by being as slow as molasses in January in closing the gap on the entrapped Germans there. The Allied officers whom the best Wehrmacht officers in the German army most admired, respected and feared were Lieutenant General George S. Patton, Major General Matthew Ridgway and Major General J. Lawton Collins. They were all aggressive, dangerous men. The Allied commander they had the least respect for was Montgomery. They considered him an old maid and they always knew precisely what he was going to do.*

Furthermore, Montgomery's success at El Alamein had gone to his head. He was the darling of the British press and he had become such a hero that he began to believe his own publicity. Nobody knew quite as much about commanding as Montgomery. He was arrogant, tactless and he was an egotist to the marrow of his bones. For months he had been trying to maneuver

---

* As early as El Alamein and Rommel's dreadful defeat there and his long desperate 800-mile retreat into Tunisia, it began to be known to German commanders that Montgomery was cautious. Rommel expected Montgomery to close and finish him off as with low fuel supplies and ammunition and transportation he daily improvised and moved farther back. It never happened. And at the end, escaped, Rommel said: "The British commander had shown himself to be overcautious. He risked nothing in any way doubtful and bold solutions were completely foreign to him." Rommel Papers, B. H. Liddell Hart, ed. (New York: Harcourt, Brace and Company, 1953), p. 360.

Eisenhower into giving him command of all the Allied ground forces, and for months he had also been trying to get Eisenhower to commit himself to one thin thrust at Berlin — Montgomery of course to lead it, Eisenhower to give him all the American troops and supplies he needed to make the thrust, and halt everything else.

Now, Eisenhower turned over command of all the American troops north of the line Givet-Prüm to Montgomery. It was to be a very, very expensive decision. Montgomery took over the V Corps, the XVIII Airborne Corps and Collins' VII Corps. And he immediately began to talk of tidying the lines, withdrawing from St. Vith, creating a firm defense on the Meuse and holding in position until the "German runs his course."

The American commanders were appalled. Hodges, Collins, Ridgway and Gavin all protested vehemently. But Montgomery was giving the orders now and he was adamant. Tidy up the lines. Fall back. Specifically, he ordered Collins, who was beginning to move to the farthest west position, on the right flank of the XVIII Airborne Corps, not to get committed anywhere on his front. Montgomery was planning to begin his counterattack, on the far west of all places, with Collins' Corps. The Americans wanted to jump off from the northern shoulder. Montgomery insisted that Collins could not support his corps in a counterattack on the single road from Malmédy to St. Vith. Collins, who could always be blunt, said not too discreetly, "Maybe you can't sir, but we can." He added, "If you're not careful, Field Marshal, the result will be the same as at Falaise. Rather than cut off the Germans, we will simply push them out of the bag." *

But the Germans had something to say about all this, too. On December 19, Manteuffel, prodded by his own High Command to get farther west as rapidly as possible, ordered three armored divisions to shake loose and get moving. They were, nearest the

* Eisenhower, John S. D., *The Bitter Woods* (New York: G. P. Putnam's Sons, 1969), p. 352.

Salm, the *116th Panzer Division*; along the Ourthe River, the *2nd Panzer Division*; and farthest west, the *Panzer Lehr Division*. Recall that Manteuffel's Army was Wehrmacht, not SS.

The *2nd Panzer Division* was able to break loose from the assault on Bastogne and begin a drive for the Meuse in the direction of Dinant. The division commander was Colonel Meinrad von Lauchert. The unit had broken through on December 16 across the Our River in Luxembourg, had then taken Clerf, then moved into the attack on Bastogne. It was a crack division which had given an excellent account of itself in Normandy and during the retreat across France. Lauchert was a steady, able commander. All three German armored divisions constituted a serious threat in the west, but in particular the *2nd Panzer* streaked out and by December 21 was nearing Ciney and Celles only a few miles from Dinant.

The 84th Infantry Division, in the line along the Roer up north, disengaged and began moving south on December 20. Advance elements set up headquarters on December 21 in Marche.

By this time General Maurice Rose's 3rd Armored Division was split into two combat commands. One was backing up 30th Infantry Division's 119th Regiment in the effort to pocket Peiper at La Gleize and Stoumont, and the other was engaged in the fighting around Hotton. Third Armored was still fighting under attachment to XVIII Airborne Corps, though it would come under Collins' VII Corps when he was in place.

The 84th position was to the right of 3rd Armored, and the remnants of the 291st Engineers were attached to the 84th Division.

Collins' 2nd Armored Division was on the road moving south and west during the 21st and 22nd, and closed in position west of the 84th on the night of the 22nd.

Now the entire Allied line was in place. It began on the far left, at Monschau, and curved around Elsenborn, Butgenbach and Malmédy, then bent west along the Amblève River. Then it made a radical turn north at Trois Ponts to La Gleize, as well as another turn south along the Salm River to Salmchâteau, where it bulged out around St. Vith, then it stretched thinly westward to Givet on the Meuse.

In order it was defended by V Corps, farthest left to and through Stavelot, where XVIII Airborne picked up and extended to Vaux Chavanne, near Manhay, where VII Corps took over. It was a very untidy line indeed and one Montgomery's neat mind could not tolerate. He therefore ordered 7th Armored to withdraw from St. Vith and fall back to the 82nd Airborne's lines, which he also ordered to be redrawn, by a withdrawal, to a neater line, Trois Ponts–Manhay.

When the 84th Infantry Division closed in the Marche area, an anomalous situation with regard to the 291st Engineers arose. The commanding officer was fighting in Malmédy and came under the 30th Infantry Division, which was attached to V Corps. But the 291st officially was now attached to VII Corps and specifically was assigned in support of the 84th Infantry. All of the positions the 291st, officially, was guarding fell within that sector.

It could not have mattered less to the men of Company A and Company C. The weather had turned brutally cold and whoever they were supporting they were out in foxholes in it, under artillery fire as the front moved west, feeling a little as if the whole world had fallen in on top of them. None of them ever expected to see Colonel Pergrin and the men in Malmédy again. And furthermore, nothing made much sense to them now. They were operating in chaos. They simply went where they were told to go, did what they were told to do, froze in the cold, went hungry and without sleep, and hung on, hour by desperate hour. Guard duty, when ten minutes turned a man into one raw, suffering, continuous paroxysm of shuddering, and an hour could freeze his clothing so stiff he could no longer shudder. His shift in a foxhole when he grew gradually so cold that even his mind went numb. Days and nights that ran together in an endless snowy, bitter, miserable world, when a man could not think any farther ahead than this job, right now, this minute and dumbly hope he could last through it.

18

The night of December 21 in Malmédy was a time of exhaustion, tension and apprehension. Skorzeny's men had fought fanatically and they had come much too close to the railroad embankment to suit the men in command at Malmédy. Additional measures must be taken, they felt, and they conferred together to decide what they should be.

That night, also, Sergeant Corcoran brought T/Sergeant John L. Scanlan, the 291st's Communications Chief, and three more radiomen into Malmédy, with five walkie-talkie radio sets. The other radiomen were Bryans and Murphy from Company C and Nick Theodoseau from Company A. Scanlan also brought identification panels, wiring and other communications equipment. Warrent Officer John K. Brenna came, also, to take over administration and records.

When Corcoran had arrived at Modave early in the morning of the 21st, he brought the first word Battalion had had from the colonel since communications had been lost the night of December 17. A cloud was lifted, Corcoran got a joyous welcome and everything the colonel needed, fast. He and the men he brought back with him were in Malmédy by 8:00 P.M.

When Scanlan walked into the CP the first person he saw was Sergeant Ralph McCarty. McCarty looked like something dragged up from the gutter. He was filthy dirty, he badly

Confrontation on the Amblève 333

needed a shave, and he was so exhausted his eyes were sunk holes in his face. He was drinking a cup of coffee. He looked and saw Scanlan. "Hi, Scan," he said, "what are you doing here?"

"The colonel sent for me," Scanlan said. "What are *you* doing here?"

McCarty told him, and told him about the battle that day. "I lost two good men," he said. "And I thought for a while my own time had come. And you know, Scan, what my greatest regret was? That I would never get to see my boy. I hated that worse than anything."

McCarty had been married about one month before leaving the United States. On D-day, June 6, a son had been born. McCarty's wife had kept him posted on the boy's progress in daily letters. "When it was hottest out there," McCarty said, "I thought, I'll never see my boy."

Scanlan shook his head and went on to his own work. The colonel wanted walkie-talkies in the major outpost positions. Scanlan took his men and equipment and set out, with a guide. Just as he set out, at 8:00 P.M. a heavy artillery bombardment began. Ducking the artillery fire Scanlan positioned his men. He put a radio near the big railroad viaduct, at the gun emplacement manned by Sergeant Munoz and his 1st squad of Rhea's platoon. He put Corporal Frederick Bryans on it.

Then he drove around to the N–32 roadblock and put one there, placing Pfc. Nick Theodoseau on it.

He put a third radio out on a hill near the S-bend on the Stavelot road. The 120th's 3rd Battalion were stationed out there, with only a handful of the 291st C Company men mixed in. Pfc. Dennis Murphy was put there.

When he returned to the command post and reported, Colonel Pergrin felt greatly relieved. The experience that morning, without communications with his men in their outposts, had been galling for him. He did not want a repetition of it.

※

On this same day, December 21, Baron Friedrich August von der Heydte, commander of the paratroopers dropped the early morning of December 17, reached a decision.

After von der Heydte had landed, around 3:00 that morning, a handful of men had gathered around him and they had proceeded to the crossroads of Mon Rigi where they found another handful of men assembled.

In all, 125 men made their way to the rendezvous point north of Malmédy. They had with them only the arms and ammunition with which they had jumped, and no food. Supplies were to have been dropped earlier at various depot points. As best they could, by the light of the flares, they searched for these depots of supplies and found only four or five of them. They found no food and very little in the way of arms and ammunition. They did find their radio, but as von der Heydte had feared it had been damaged beyond use in the drop.

By noon of the 18th he had gathered his men into a base camp in the middle of the forest. There, one of his patrols brought another officer, a Lieutenant Kayser, and 150 men he had gathered up. Lieutenant Kayser was feeling full of the mission. He wanted to find the enemy and attack immediately. Von der Heydte was more realistic. "With 300 men?" he said, "and no heavy weapons?"

The most he could do was harass. He sent out far-ranging patrols, behind Stavelot, as far as Werbomont, around Liège. He ambushed small units, captured a few prisoners, frightened civilians. He made it seem as if several thousand paratroopers were active behind the lines. He believed his mission was a failure and as far as its primary objective, to keep reinforcements from reaching the vital northern shoulder, was concerned, it was. Not one thing he did helped Dietrich at all. But beyond all hope of success the operation succeeded in creating fear, suspicion and confusion, and in wasting the time of hundreds of units sent out searching for his men.

Not until after the war did von der Heydte learn why so few

of his paratroopers rendezvoused at Mon Rigi with him. Partly because of the high winds, but mostly because of the heavy antiaircraft fire, the flight of planes had been badly scattered and his men had been dropped helter-skelter. One group had been dropped well behind the German lines, near Bonn. One group had been dropped behind the U.S. lines in Holland. Most of these had been rounded up and captured, but their capture added to the belief that an enormous drop had been made, over a very wide and general area.

It all added up to the picture — paratroopers in Holland, the dummies dropped all over, the squadron of planes scattered everywhere and the billowing parachutes actually seen north of Malmédy — all together formed the seedbed for chaos and panic. Nobody knew *how* many paratroopers had been dropped, or where. Not even the most optimistic German commander could have hoped for the mass panic induced by the news of the paratroop drop. And because the entire *3rd Parachute Division* was being used as ground troops and infantry, very much like the U.S. 82nd and 101st Airborne Divisions, every time one of their men was captured it was assumed he had been dropped in. And this covered some very wide territory indeed.

There was never, in the entire Battle of the Bulge, but the one parachute drop. Hitler had entirely lost faith in paratroopers and had to be talked into the only one made. However, the 300 men who rendezvoused with von der Heydte accomplished as much psychologically as 3000 would have.

But now, on December 21, von der Heydte's men were without food and ammunition. In four days only one JU–88 had flown over with a drop which contained a few more arms, a container of water and some cigarettes. He had had no messages whatever from his superior officers and it was plain to him that the offensive was not going as expected. Dietrich had certainly never showed up, as promised, north of Malmédy. Von der Heydte could see for himself that the American strength was pouring down from the north to reinforce the Elsenborn shoulder. He therefore decided he was doing no good where he was and he determined to lead his men eastward and back to the German lines.

They ran into a strong American patrol as they crossed the Helle River, behind Monschau. There was a hot brief battle in which one more of his men was seriously wounded. Von der Heydte could see only enemy strength, all of it armored, all around him. He therefore broke up his men into groups of three and sent them to make their own way back to the German lines as best they could.

With only his executive officer and orderly he continued toward Monschau, which he believed to be in German hands. In the outskirts of the town he came upon a farmhouse into which he stumbled. He was in very bad condition. His broken arm was troubling him, he had had no food for several days and he believed his feet to be frozen.

At the farmhouse he learned that the Americans held Monschau. Very well. He could go no farther. He would surrender. He sent a note to the American commanding general, thinking him to be General Maxwell Taylor, commander of the 101st Airborne Division. They had been opposite each other in Normandy. Von der Heydte appealed to Taylor's chivalry and said he wanted to surrender. Instead of General Taylor, the Monschau area was held by the 99th Division's 395th Infantry, Lieutenant Colonel McClernand Butler commanding, and the 38th Cavalry Reconnaissance Squadron under Lieutenant Colonel Robert E. O'Brien. It was the 99th Division, therefore, who accepted von der Heydte's surrender.

He was brought into Monschau, fed and given medical attention, treated as chivalrously as he could have expected. Believing he had failed utterly, it was not until the war was over that he learned how badly he had scared the entire U. S. Army.*

* B–823, Oberstleutnant Friedrich August Baron von der Heydte, "Kampfgruppe von der Heydte."

Confrontation on the Amblève

In Malmédy, on the 22nd of December, in the aftermath of the battle the day before the 120th Regiment was understandably nervous about the defenses. The officers felt that the battle had been much too close a thing and they were also certain the attack would be renewed.

The Company K lines out by the paper mill had been stabilized at the river, and the wooden bridge had now been blown, but the infantry wanted more reassurance than that. They asked Colonel Pergrin to destroy the big railroad viaduct and the Route de Falize overpass on the road next to it. To destroy highway bridges was one thing. A highway bridge was easily rebuilt. But a railroad bridge, especially one as huge as the old, stone-arched viaduct, was very difficult both to destroy and to rebuild. To rebuild it required special equipment, and for as long as it was out of commission an entire railway system was disrupted. Engineers had been working all over France and Belgium to rebuild the railway systems. Pergrin hated like sin to blow that big stone buster.

But the infantry officers insisted and finally a direct order came from the 120th's commander. Pergrin had no alternative except to blow the two railroad bridges.

The job of blowing the big viaduct was turned over to Lieutenant Frank Rhea. He assigned his own 1st squad, Sergeant Munoz in charge, to haul blocks of TNT to the top of the bridge, which was some 60 feet above the highway. But first the body of Pfc. Wiley Holbrook had to be removed so it would not be buried in the debris of the demolition. It lay, still, where he had fallen, almost under the viaduct. Koenig was one of the four men detailed to carry the body away. He had grown accustomed to seeing dead men, he thought, but the sight of this man, a 291st man, affected him so that he felt sick at his stomach the rest of the day.

In all, 1800 pounds of TNT were put on one of the stone piers, and 500 pounds were put on the crown. At 2:00 P.M. the order was given and up she went. It was a perfect blow. All the stone understructure fell on the road and blocked it almost to the top of the embankment. It also was the biggest boom the men had ever heard! But one thing was dead sure. Nobody could approach Malmédy up the Stavelot road again.

The Route de Falize overpass was blown a little later that afternoon. Now, two roadblocks no longer had to be maintained.

The infantry, still nervous, however, wanted the highway bridge over the railroad out in the S-bend beyond the paper mill, wired. It was not thought necessary to destroy it, but they wanted it ready to go. Sergeant McCarty, with no roadblock to oversee now, took a detail of men and did that job.

Squad Sergeant Sheldon Smith, 1st squad, 3rd platoon, Company C, and one of his men, Pfc. Zaleski, were sent out to guard the wired bridge in the S-bend. An infantry captain was well dug in on the back side of the hill nearby. Smith and Zaleski dug their own foxhole immediately beside him. The captain was guarded at all times by a huge sergeant who carried a BAR. Smith and Zaleski figured the safest place for them was near the captain and his big bodyguard. They kept the detonator in the dugout with them.

That night, December 22, Lieutenant Frank Rhea's 3rd platoon drew a cold, rough job. With two railroad bridges blown and a third one wired for destruction on the south, the infantry wanted a lot more mines in that field south of the railroad embankment, too. They did not want the enemy getting to the foot of that embankment again. A request went to Colonel Pergrin to take care of it, please.

Rhea's 3rd platoon were living nearest the field. They got the job. About midnight, feeling very jittery about the whole thing, they drove out through the overpass on the Route de St. Vith and went on out the road for perhaps half a mile. Then they unloaded and set to work. It seemed to the men they made a hell of a lot of noise. The enemy was not very far away, and the wreck of the burned-out German tank was there to remind them of it. But it was a job that could not be done quietly. The ground was frozen so hard it was like iron. The night was clear, star-shiny and as cold as Siberia. The men chipped away with picks and shovels that rang clatteringly with every stroke on the iron-hard ground, trying to hurry, tense with anxiety and fear, until they had at least partially buried the mines.

It took a couple of hours, but they saw no enemy, heard none and with great relief drove back to their quarters without a shot being fired. Shaking with cold they griped that surely the infantry would feel safe now.

The following day, December 23, Sergeant McCarty took out two details. One was to look for German tanks which were thought to have broken through the seam between the 120th and the 117th on the day of the battle and got to the rear of the lines. He and his men searched until midafternoon, up as far as Francorchamps, but saw nothing of any enemy.

Late that afternoon he was ordered to take a detail out N-32, beyond the roadblock, and wire the trees along the highway for demolition. He and his men had almost completed the job, they were on the last two or three trees when McCarty stepped under a tree and happened to look up. Fifteen feet up in the tree, hanging in the crotch, was the body of a dead German, in American uniform except for his boots which were regular German issue. McCarty started looking around and some twenty feet away he found the tire of a jeep high in another tree.

How the dead German and the jeep tire got blown up into the trees was a mystery to McCarty, but the men on the roadblock could have told him. It was the jeep carrying U.S.-dressed Germans they had blown up the evening of December 20.

Between these two details which kept him out of Malmédy all day, McCarty missed a tragic event.

A little after 2:00 P.M. that afternoon, on the first clear, cold day on which the Air Force could fly extensively, the first U.S. planes had appeared over Malmédy. The sight of them raised a cheer and lifted the hearts of every man who saw them. Everybody went out to watch them.

Suddenly a heavy and intense antiaircraft fire opened on the planes from the German guns south of Malmédy, and all the planes flew away.

Around 4:00 P.M. a small flight of six medium bombers with fighter escorts appeared over Malmédy, and again all eyes were lifted. A heartfelt wish went with them, wherever they were going, that they would have good hunting.

But unbelievably, before the astonished eyes of everybody watching, they dropped their bombs on the heart of Malmédy! It was not possible! Their own planes! Bombing their own men in Malmédy!

But it was. A carpet of bombs was rained down on the town and several homes were totally destroyed. The streets were completely blocked with debris.

The wounded, the killed, were everywhere. People were buried under the rubble and muffled cries came from beneath the masses of debris. The spectacle was horrible. The men of the 120th pitched in to help dig people out, and a cry went up for the engineers to clear the streets, and soon the 291st's bulldozers were plowing the wreckage out of the way. Then buildings started to burn. The men of the 291st worked like demons to help get the fire under control, although without city water it had to be done with a bucket brigade. All men not on the defense line were called out to help, and they turned out, helping dig people out, assisting the wounded to aid stations, laying out the dead.

The 291st suffered no losses. Most of the men were quartered in the southern edge of town and the homes in that area did not receive any bombs. Most of the men were on duty along the railroad embankment and at the roadblocks, and they were not

Confrontation on the Amblève

bombed. It was the heart of the town that received the bombs.

The 291st worked frantically putting the bright orange identification panels on the roofs of the tallest buildings and out on the hills. And the commanders of various units telephoned or radioed their headquarters. Malmédy is *not* in German hands! Colonel Ward of the 120th Regiment sent a messenger to General Hobbs, and General Hobbs blasted First Army headquarters. Aghast, First Army assured him it would not happen again. It was horrible, terrible, an inexplicable mistake had been made, somehow, some way. But it would *not* happen again.

19

By December 23, Colonel Jochen Peiper up at La Gleize was almost out of supplies. Nothing his commander, General Mohnke, had devised had worked. Airdrops had been unsuccessful and the desperate attempt to float supplies down the Amblève to him had also failed.

And nothing Mohnke had tried to do to reinforce Peiper with more troops had worked. When the *1st SS Panzer Grenadier Regiment* moved up from Poteau into the Wanne sector, Mohnke had been able to get it across the Amblève on the Petit Spai bridge. But the collapse of the bridge under the weight of the first piece of heavy equipment kept him from being able to support this infantry regiment with artillery or tanks.

The 3rd Armored Division, one of whose combat command teams was supporting the 30th Division in their drive on La Gleize and Stoumont, sent a task force down into the Amblève pocket near Trois Ponts. This task force was reinforced with elements of the 117th Infantry in Stavelot and finally with 30th Division's reserve battalion from Malmédy. These units effectively prevented any of Mohnke's troops from reaching Peiper.

Late that afternoon of December 23, Peiper was in radio contact with Mohnke. His situation had become hopeless and he wanted an order permitting him to break out. He did not get it.

Confrontation on the Amblève

He was told he could break out only if he brought his vehicles and his wounded with him.

Peiper knew he could not do that. There was a ring tightly closed around him. He had to walk out. He could never take wounded men and his vehicles out with him. There was not enough fuel left in his tanks even if he could fight his way through.

He decided to do it his own way. He had an important prisoner, Major Hal McCown, commander of 2nd Battalion, 119th Regiment, 30th Infantry Division. When the 82nd Airborne took over at Werbomont, McCown had brought his unit back to fight at Stoumont. He had been captured when he was on a reconnaissance. Now Peiper sent for McCown and wanted to make a deal with him. He said he would release all the American prisoners he had taken, except McCown who would be held as hostage, if McCown would sign an agreement that when the German wounded were sufficiently recovered they also would be released. Then when Peiper's men were returned to him, he would release McCown.

McCown told him he had no authority to sign such an agreement and if he did it probably would not be honored by American commanders. Nevertheless Peiper insisted. McCown said he would sign a document saying he had heard Peiper make this offer. Peiper produced another American officer and both he and McCown signed the agreement Peiper drew up.

At 1:00 the following morning, December 24, Peiper led what was left of his great kampfgruppe, which had so arrogantly and so proudly ridden roughshod over so many, southward, on foot, through the woods fringing La Gleize. There were 800 of them. He left a rear guard to demolish the tanks, trucks and guns. He left a medic to stay with his wounded until they were taken into custody by the Americans. And he left, according to his agreement, some 170 prisoners he had taken. He took Major McCown with him.

McCown has said that the column moved so quietly in the new-fallen snow that an outpost only 200 yards away could not have heard them.

They made their way southward toward Trois Ponts. When daylight came the sun rose clear and bright. The column moved slowly on, staying hidden in the forests. A little after dark they crossed the main highway between Basse Bodeux and Trois Ponts and continued south, skirting around Trois Ponts. Shortly after midnight that night, only about three miles south of Trois Ponts, they brushed into an 82nd Airborne outpost near Bergeval, and there was a noisy, if brief, skirmish. During this skirmish Major McCown saw his chance to escape and took it. He fled toward the Americans, was not missed, and approached the outpost in safety by whistling a popular American song.

Peiper's column crossed the Salm about two miles below the bridge Sergeant J. B. Miller had blown, but they had to swim its dark waters. They were fired on as they crossed the river and Peiper was slightly wounded. Clambering out they moved on to Wanne where they found the *1st SS Panzer Division* command post.

Behind at La Gleize on the morning of December 24, the American task force scheduled to attack went into La Gleize on schedule. They expected a sharp fight and got one, a fierce small battle, with the fifty men of the rear guard Peiper had left behind. Almost to a man they died rather than surrender. Knowing what their own outfit had done to prisoners, they must have preferred death to capture.

Not an American was killed and the 119th Regiment liberated the 170 American prisoners, took over 300 wounded German soldiers, put out the fires begun when the rear guard had tried to demolish the vehicles, and counted their booty. Between Stoumont and Trois Ponts it amounted to 28 tanks, 70 half-tracks and 25 artillery pieces.

The only Germans left north of the Amblève now were tiny

Confrontation on the Amblève

pockets in the hills between La Gleize and Stavelot and Trois Ponts. It would take time to hunt them all down and eliminate them, but the great threat of Peiper's spearhead had been ended. And the northern shoulder had proved it was safe. Nothing was going to break through along that line. First Army could finally turn all of its attention to the line along the Meuse and the threat which three Panzer divisions driving westward posed there.

Like a long, broad snake Manteuffel's *Fifth Panzer Army* was stretched with its body coiled about Bastogne and its head flicking a three-pronged tongue at Namur, Dinant and Givet.

Recall that this western area was roughly divided into three sectors by the natural river systems. Three rivers flowed northward to make the dividing lines, the Salm, the Ourthe and the Lesse. Probing up the Salm sector toward Namur was the *116th Panzer Division*. Up the Ourthe sector toward Dinant was the *2nd Panzer Division*. And farthest west, toward Givet, was the *Panzer Lehr Division*.

Montgomery was guarding the river crossings on the Meuse with elements of his XXX British Corps. But out in front of the river was the network of engineers, in a barrier line of roadblocks, minefields, machine gun emplacements and bazooka teams. Three or four men here, three or four there, they held almost every crossroads in the barrier line, every bridge, culvert and railroad crossing.

The 51st Engineers were occupying such positions in a bending arc from Hotton to Champlon, a distance of around twenty-two miles. They could help blunt the movement of the *116th Panzer Division*.

The fragments of the 291st Engineers now occupied fifteen scattered positions, in a network of defenses around Ciney and on the Marche plain. They were in the path of the *2nd Panzer Division*.

The British, however, sent probes from the Meuse as far as

Marche. Sergeant Abe Caplan's squad of 1st platoon, Company A, were holding their crossroads position at Emptinne, north of Marche. They had a minefield laid, a daisy chain for the road, a bazooka and a machine gun. Day and night they rotated guarding the crossroads.

On December 22, they saw a column of tanks approaching from the north. Enemy? From that direction? Immediately alert, they held their fire until they could make certain. Something about the tanks did not look German, but neither were they American Shermans.

As the lead tank got within hailing distance the turret flew open and a head emerged and a shout was heard, "Don't shoot! Don't shoot! We're English!"

They were told to dismount and come forward to be identified. Caplan's men were taking no chances on a German ruse. The commander of the small column was taken to the CP for questioning. He was good-natured about it. "We have come all the way from Holland," he said, "to help you beat the Nazis, and this is the welcome we receive."

He identified himself, beyond question, as an officer of the 2nd Household Cavalry Regiment, XXX British Corps. They were on a reconnaissance, he said, to Marche. "We are along the Meuse. Backing you up."

Well, it was great news to learn somebody was backing them up. The men of 3rd squad, 1st platoon, let the small column pass, happier than they had been for days. If the British were up that way, northwest, they did not have to worry about Germans from that direction. They even thought they might be relieved in a day or so.

It did not happen until January 4.

It will be remembered that when Field Marshal Montgomery was given command of the entire northern half of the battle area his first thought had been to tidy up the long, looping lines held by XVIII Airborne Corps. Especially was the great bulge in the "fortified goose-egg" at St. Vith intolerable to him. He had ordered the 7th Armored and its attached units to withdraw from the St. Vith area. This took place on December 23, and the enemy promptly took advantage of the withdrawal to shift Dietrich's armored divisions over to support Manteuffel's drive. The emphasis, and the concern, had left the northern shoulder since Dietrich's failure on December 21. It was all placed on Manteuffel's thrust now.

The American generals were all vehement in their protests of this tidying up of the lines, and of Montgomery's plan for launching the counteroffensive so far west. In particular, Ridgway and Collins were vehement and Montgomery finally visited both commanders to explain his plans personally to them. Neither commander liked the plans but there was nothing to do but obey. To Collins, Montgomery emphatically stated that he did not want his corps to get involved in battle. He was merely to get into position. He was to get into position, and hopefully he would lead the counterattack on December 25.

Manteuffel's *2nd Panzer Division* changed those plans. By the night of December 23, the forward elements of this division were south of Ciney, only four miles from Dinant.

December 24 was a day of bright, clear sun and arctic air, a perfect flying day. The Air Commands jubilantly put up their planes in strength. All day everything that could fly, Mustangs, Typhoons and Thunderbolts, flew one sortie after another, strafing, bombing, clobbering all the German divisions caught below without cover. It was a terrible day for the enemy.

Sergeant Ed Keoghan and his men of 3rd platoon, Company C, 291st, were at Sinsin that day, with a roadblock on the main Marche-Namur highway, just north of Marche. They watched the planes flying over, very low, to strafe and bomb the German *2nd Panzer Division* near Ciney.

Keoghan was sitting at the machine gun position on a snowbank beside the road, achingly cold, and he looked up once as a Thunderbolt flew by at treetop level. The pilot saw him, grinned happily, gave him a thumbs up, and then waggled his wings as if to say, "We're taking care of them for you, now," and flew on. Nothing so lifted the hearts of the ground troops as the sight of these friendly planes, so many and so mighty, flying again.

All that day reports of the German armored column at Conneux, near Celles and Ciney, kept reaching the headquarters of Major General Ernest N. Harmon, commander of the U.S. 2nd Armored Division of Collins' VII Corps. The 2nd Armored had closed into its assembly area, about twelve miles north of Marche, the night of the 22nd. The next morning Harmon had sent patrols out and at Leignon, near Ciney, one of these patrols had been shot up by the enemy.

Now the Air Command was reporting this enemy, in strength, coiled up in a natural pocket at Conneux. Harmon wanted to get at them. It was a great opportunity. But he had been ordered by Collins, who had been ordered by Montgomery, not to get involved.

When he heard that one of his patrols had been shot up in Leignon, however, he did not ask anybody's permission to do something about it. He dispatched his Combat Command A promptly, under the command of Brigadier General John Collier, in the direction of Ciney.

Collier found no enemy in Ciney itself. Instead he found elements of the British 29th Royal Tank Brigade. This brigade had been apprised of a strong enemy force approaching from the south, the *Panzer Lehr Division.*

Harmon now felt there was no further use hiding the presence of his division. He therefore ordered Collier to proceed southward to Haid. Then he got a report that the British had been forced back to Dinant, and American planes were getting heavy flak from Celles. Harmon then ordered his Combat Command B

Confrontation on the Amblève

to move west and back up CCA by occupying Ciney. At the same time he sent two battalions of self-propelled artillery into firing positions.

Then, having practically committed his division, Harmon proceeded to try to get official permission to attack. It took him a long time and there was a little stretching of truth but he finally got it. He happily roared, "The bastards are in the bag!" And that same night, Christmas Eve, Colonel Meinrad von Lauchert's *2nd Panzer Division*'s fate was sealed.

20

IT DID HAPPEN AGAIN.

On December 24, Christmas Eve, they were still digging out from the bombing the day before in Malmédy. Colonel Pergrin and Captain Moyer were directing a work detail from Company C who were trying to extricate some men of the 120th Infantry trapped in a cellar under what had been their company kitchen. It was in the heart of town. The men had just finished making an opening through the rubble into the cellar and Pergrin and Moyer had squeezed through inside. Captain Conlin stood outside in the street to keep an eye on a very dangerous wall which was still standing.

It was 2:30 P.M. And now a flight of eighteen B-24 (Liberator) heavy bombers flew over and what the medium bombers did the day before was nothing compared to what the eighteen B-24s did on this day, December 24. They leveled the main square and the whole central part of the town. Various company and platoon CPs of the 120th Regiment took direct hits and many of their men were buried in the debris. Fire immediately broke out and went raging through the devastated buildings and whole blocks lay in heaps of rubble. Civilian casualties were enormous and Army aid men worked desperately caring for the Belgian wounded on every hand. The dead were laid row on row on the school playground and covered with whatever could be found in the midst of the destruction.

Confrontation on the Amblève

As the bombs rained down on the principal square, the dangerous wall Captain Conlin was watching collapsed and Colonel Pergrin and Captain Moyer were buried in the cellar that had just been opened. Pergrin was injured with numerous cuts and bruises, especially on his back which took the brunt of a falling timber. Moyer escaped injury beyond cuts and sprains and bruises.

It took them an hour to dig their way out, and when they did they found Captain Conlin lying in the street, one leg severely damaged. When Pergrin saw it he thought privately, "He may lose that leg."

Conlin was carried to the aid station and from there he was evacuated to a field hospital and later evacuated to England. There he and Private Bernard Goldstein, wounded at Stavelot, ran into each other and exchanged news. But it was the last the 291st ever saw of the "wild, fighting Irishman." The war did not stop for one wounded man. And the city was burning and the 291st were told to see if they could save it.

Captain Moyer was given charge of the fire-fighting details and he organized the men efficiently. As night came on and the cold grew intense it was very difficult. The city's fire-fighting equipment was almost totally useless. The city was without water and the pumps were frozen. Every man of the 291st not actually on a defense position was turned out to help. They worked all night. Moyer brought the water booster from the 291st's water detail unit and found he could make it work with the city's equipment. All night the fires were fought. Entire streets were burning. There were hours when it looked as if the whole town would go up in flames. But the men stuck with it and kept fighting, first in one building, then another.

In some cases buildings were dynamited to make a firebreak. Sergeant Walter J. Smith, 2nd platoon, Company B, had charge of one such demolition job. He wired the building precisely as he would have a bridge, then stood outside and turned the key to bring it down. The destroyed building kept the fire from spreading.

In another building, Lieutenant Tom Stack and Lieutenant Leroy Joehnck were in a basement trying to put out a fire in a burning coal bin with buckets of water. The smoke grew so intense they had to escape. When they opened a window to clamber out the steam from the fire gushed over them and Lieutenant Joehnck was parboiled about his neck and ears.

It was a holocaust and a tragic, tragic Christmas Eve.

At some time during that evening, Pergrin and his officers gathered in the shabby basement room which was his command post. Some of the B Company men had gone out earlier and cut a small fir for a Christmas tree. A few businesses were still trying to stay open and they had been able to buy a handful of ornaments and some tinsel. The tree was brave and beautiful that night of Christmas Eve. In lieu of gifts the men put pictures of their loved ones around the base of the tree.

A bottle of champagne had been found in the supplies abandoned by the 44th Field Hospital. Colonel Pergrin had been saving it for Christmas. Now he opened it and with his officers gathered around him he poured it into tin cups, enamel cups, paper cups, water glasses, whatever could be found to hold it, and they drank a toast together — to Captain Conlin, because he was much on their mind. And to the new commander of Company B, Captain Frank Rhea. And to peace — to an early peace.

Somebody took a picture of them, cups and glasses lifted, and they look like men resurrected from the dead. They are so tired, so disheveled, so sleepless. Their eyes are so rimmed with weariness and their clothing is so bedraggled. And most of them could not muster a smile, even for the photographer. Strain, pressure, anxiety shows on the faces of all. And grief. Conlin was gone, and they had just learned they had lost another man. Private Edward Barker, Company B, had been on a work detail in the middle of town when the bombs rained down. He had been

Confrontation on the Amblève 353

killed. Pfc. John J. McVay had been hurt, and Sergeant Martinez, of Rhea's platoon, had suffered concussion. But then there was hardly a man of the 291st in Malmédy who was not cut or bruised or burned by now. Such injuries largely went unnoticed.

The officers only had a moment, to eat and drink their toast. Then it was back to fight the fires, dig out people, clear the streets, blow up buildings, pull down dangerous walls, help the wounded, lay out the dead. Selflessly, without sleep or food, the men of the 291st details worked all through another night.

Out along the Meuse on Christmas Day, Harmon's 2nd Armored Division moved to the attack in two task forces. As the two task forces moved out of Ciney, support for them moved down the main road N-36 *toward* Ciney. At Hamois, on this road, Lieutenant Arch Taylor and his 3rd platoon, Company A, had been guarding a bridge since December 20.

Now, December 25, they had just received an order to blow the bridge, the enemy was approaching. Taylor and his men got ready to destroy the bridge. Just before they turned the key, however, a detachment of MPs arrived in hot haste and told them to forget it. The bridge would not be blown after all. It was needed for *American* armor moving south. Well, glory hallelujah! Maybe the tide was turning out here!

Taylor pulled his men off the bridge and they went to the top of the hill and watched the elements of Harmon's division roll their tanks across the bridge and on to the battle. It was a sight for sore eyes. They had been retreating long enough, and it was high time Americans took the offensive.

Captain Gamble had promised all his men a hot Christmas dinner on this day. He meant well, but it did not work that way. When Mess Sergeant McCarl and Lieutenant Frank Hayes left the CP with the kitchen truck, fully intending to drive to every Company A position with a good hot Christmas dinner for the men, the truck ran into enemy fire as it came into the area and had to turn back. The men had cold K rations that day the same as all the days before. Taylor's men consoled themselves with the thought that with things looking up they might be relieved pretty soon. They had nine more days to go yet!

On security at Modave that day, Sergeant Billington and his men ate flapjacks somebody cooked over an open fire in the fireplace of the great hall of the château. As they ate their flapjacks they read the latest issue of *Stars & Stripes*. It said, "All the troops of Uncle Sam's armies will have a turkey dinner on Christmas Day."

The men whooped and Billington laid the newspaper on the fire and watched it burn. So much for the veracity of *Stars & Stripes*!

But at Malmédy the men of Company B and Company C did have a turkey dinner. Most of them. It was taken to the gun emplacement and roadblock positions. It missed Sergeant Sheldon T. Smith and Pfc. Zaleski in their dugout on the hill in the S-bend of the Stavelot road, however. The railroad embankment was the safe perimeter and that was as far as the hot dinners went.

Smith and Zaleski were not entirely forgotten however. The chaplain of the 120th Regiment paid a visit to the captain in the dugout next door and when he had finished his visit with the captain he came over to see Smith and Zaleski. He gave them each a Christmas present — a clean, new, dry pair of socks! Zaleski went down to a house where the infantry kept a fire going and warmed his feet and put his dry socks on. Then Sergeant Smith went. It was the finest Christmas present they could have had — warm, dry feet for a while.

Malmédy was still burning that morning. The biggest fires were under control, but smoldering fires were scattered all over the central part of the town. Men of the 291st ate their Christmas dinners then went right back to work fighting the fires. Since the afternoon of the 23rd they had been doing this. Most of them were at the point of exhaustion but they continued working.

Around 4:30 P.M. a flight of bombers again flew over Malmédy and once again the city was bombed. This time, however, they evidently saw the identification panels which had now been plastered all over the town. This time, when the planes were sighted, everybody took cover, and bitterly said, "Here comes the American Luftwaffe again."

The leading squadron dropped their bombs, but the next flight turned aside without dropping theirs. Painfully and doggedly the men of the 291st went to work to help put out the new fires that were started. They wondered if this place was doomed to be bombed daily until the end of the war, and what was haywire with the 9th Tactical Air Command? What had they done in Malmédy that the 9th should try so hard to annihilate them?

Christmas Day, and another gift of bombs.

But it was to be the last. For weeks 9th Tactical Air Command would stubbornly refuse to concede that an error had been made. Perhaps the heavy flak on December 23 had reinforced the belief that Malmédy was in German hands. There had been nothing but confusion about the town from the beginning. It was as if the place were fated, rent by its own divided loyalties, known to be a seedbed of pro-Nazi sentiments, gloomed over by its own malaise. Even the Germans had been confused about it. The American units sent to defend it were defending a position, not a place, for they had no love of the place. Except perhaps Company B of the 291st, who had fonder and happier memories of it. After December 17 it was the town of infamy, the sick town of the massacre. It is believable that General Quesada's men took a peculiar pleasure in bombing it. To destroy it would be one way of evening the score a little.

But finally General Hobbs convinced them — Malmédy was not in German hands. And the air strikes were called off. Christmas Day was the last day the town was bombed.

The bombings ceased but the daily artillery fire continued.

Since the night of December 17 when Peiper's artillery first began shelling the town, Malmédy had suffered daily. The shelling was not incessant or continuous but it was daily. There would be periods of two or three hours when no shells fell. Then suddenly an intense barrage lasting for half an hour perhaps would be loosed on the town. Neither the soldiers nor the people knew when to expect these bombardments.

On the afternoon of December 26, in a quiet spell, Private Bernie Koenig met a girl. He was off duty and was visiting around in the vicinity of the old sawmill where he and the men of Company B knew many of the people. When one is twenty, war is not all misery, and a pretty girl is still a pretty girl. She took Koenig home with her to meet her family, and the family welcomed him and the girl played "Lili Marlene" for him on the piano. Suddenly a heavy artillery barrage began. Koenig was caught between his own natural feelings of panic, his intense desire to find shelter and the need to appear a brave U.S. soldier before these Belgian people. He conquered his fear and sweated it out, a shaking, brave, twenty-year-old U.S. soldier.

December 26 was a routine day for the other men of the 291st — that is, they rotated shifts at the gun emplacements on the railroad embankments, they worked all day fighting the still smoldering fires, they dug people out of the ruins, they bulldozed the streets and they came in for the evening meal exhausted and hungry.

The kitchen setup for Company B was directly across the street from the command post. The wash-up area, where the men washed and scalded their mess kits, was outside. The men had already eaten that night and most of them had finished washing their kits. A cook, T/4 Burnie Hebert, came outside into the wash-up area. Suddenly an 88-mm. shell whistled in and sheared off half of Hebert's right leg. It then plowed into some sand about twenty feet away, without exploding.

Hebert's leg was ruined and it was amputated that night in a field hospital. But lives of many Company B men were saved when the shell failed to explode. In so compact an area a bursting shell would inevitably have killed most of the men present.

This was to be the last blow Malmédy gave to the 291st. During that day, December 26, First Army Engineer, Colonel W. H. Carter, finally got his 291st Engineers back. He was able to order 30th Infantry Division to release them. Late that evening Colonel Pergrin received word to report to General Hobbs' headquarters. He spruced up as best he could for the interview, but he had no change of uniform so the burned, torn, dirty uniform which had not been off his back since the battle of Malmédy began nine days earlier had to do. Nor could he do anything about his cuts and scratches and bruises. He could only shave and brush his hair, put on a tie and tuck it in properly and hope he did not smell too high.

At 30th Division headquarters he was met by General Hobbs himself. "Colonel," the general said, "I would like to have you and your fighting engineers permanently attached to my division. You have rendered invaluable service in Malmédy. But you have earned and you well deserve a rest now. You are hereby relieved of your assignment to this division."

The interview was concluded when he handed Pergrin a copy of the commendation he was that day forwarding to First Army. It read:

> 1. Upon the arrival at the town of Malmédy, Belgium, of the 30th Infantry Division, among other elements located there was the 291st Engineer Combat Battalion (Minus), commanded by Lt. Col. David E. Pergrin. Since occupancy by this division, the town has been completely organized for all around defense, and defended by the 120th Infantry of the 30th Infantry Division, with attachments. During the period of occupancy and active defense, Col. Pergrin and the officers and men of his unit based in the town of Malmédy, rendered outstanding service in assisting in such all around defense. They laid extensive minefields, prepared demolitions, established roadblocks and defended and strengthened that

defense both locally and in depth every day during its occupancy. They also rendered heroic and gallant service in fighting fires covering large areas of the town, these fires having been caused by bombs from our own American bombing planes. As a result of this bombing many buildings were demolished, streets were littered with debris and many fires were started. In overcoming all of these difficulties the 291st Engineer Combat Battalion gave every possible assistance. They have also been integrated into the scheme of local defense, and at the date of writing of this letter it is still possible that this town may be attacked by a force of sufficient size to necessitate their utilization in a combat role.

2. This commendation is fully justified and I am certain that during the period the battalion was located in the town of Malmédy, Belgium, they performed as efficient and necessary service as could have been possible in any locality. While serving in an attached capacity to the 30th Infantry Division, this engineer combat battalion exhibited fine energy, initiative and capacity for soldierly effort.

Be it noticed that the commendation was still protesting the withdrawal of the 291st and justifying its continuing attachment, even though General Hobbs was obeying orders and releasing them.

Well, fine. This was the military reward for duty well done. It was the official recognition that Pergrin's decision not to run away had been recorded and approved. What Pergrin felt was less than elation. He was glad the 291st had been recognized and honored. But what he mostly felt was weariness and continued anxiety about the rest of the battalion. He knew battalion headquarters was at Modave, but beyond that he did not know but what his entire command now consisted of only the men he had with him in Malmédy. He had had no news of the others since Scanlan and Brenna had come in the night of December 21, five days earlier. For all he knew they had been overrun, killed, captured or scattered to the four winds. What he wanted most, now, was to get his men out of Malmédy, get to Modave, give

Confrontation on the Amblève

them a well-earned rest, let them sleep round the clock, pull the entire unit together again, if there was a unit.

He spent most of that night working out the withdrawal with his officers, then he left the next morning for Modave.

Company C of the 291st were scheduled to withdraw first and they left Malmédy on the 27th, but Company B was scheduled to withdraw last. The men of the 291st were not all withdrawn from Malmédy until December 31. Those on the gun emplacements on the railroad embankment were the last to be withdrawn. Company B's 3rd platoon was one of the last elements to leave. If they looked back as they drove away they saw a city that looked like all bomb-cratered, wrecked towns, a shattered skeleton, fire-gutted and dead, a shambles. Rats and stray cats and dogs prowled in the ruins of the homes.

Malmédy had indeed been a city of doom.

Colonel Pergrin reached Modave on the 27th. When Captain Lampp saw him he barely recognized him. He said, "My God, Colonel, you look like you'd been through hell."

"I have," Pergrin said grimly, "ten days of it."

He ate, slept, bathed and felt like a human being again, then he set about pulling the battalion together for regrouping. He found it pretty difficult to do.

By the morning of December 26 the enemy drive to the west had been stopped, but the situation remained so fluid it took time for Pergrin to pull his men back from their positions on the Marche plains. Colonel Anderson had scattered the men of Company A and Company C so widely they could not immediately be withdrawn. Anderson ordered the 51st Engineers to take over many of their positions. Recall that except for the unit at Trois Ponts the 51st had been in the Marche area the entire time. But the 291st's new assignment was in their own old area — Trois Ponts, Malmédy and Spa. They had somehow to be pulled out and put together again for this new assignment.

On December 27, therefore, the 51st took over a few of the Company A and C positions — the bridge in Barvaux Condroz, the minefield at Nettinne, the roadblock and minefield at Hogne, the bridge at Heure and the culvert position that Sergeant Ed Keoghan and his men had guarded at Sinsin. All of the Company C men were thus relieved on December 27, and they returned to Modave.

Company A's relief was not yet in sight. In fact, they were even given further assignments. On December 27 they laid a mine necklace at Sinsin. They wired a bridge and laid mines at Grand Ensille. They laid crater charges at Somal. They wired a bridge and laid mines at Moressee. On December 28 they went out again and laid a minefield at Mehogne, and on December 29 they reinforced the minefields at Somal and Mehogne. On December 31 they wired a bridge at Haversin, west of Marche, and laid a minefield.

Next day, January 1, most of these positions set up by Company A on the 27th, 28th, 29th and 31st of December were taken over by the 300th Engineers and the 308th Engineers.

But the crossroads guarded by Sergeant Abe Caplan's unit at Emptinne, and the highway bridge and minefield guarded by Lieutenant Arch Taylor's 3rd platoon, were not relieved until January 4. In fact, they were not relieved at all. By January 4 the situation had stabilized to the extent that the necessity for them no longer existed. The enemy had been pushed back far enough so that they could simply be withdrawn. On this day, Company A's command post, Captain Gamble and these men were ordered back to Modave. They got there just in time to load up and move with Battalion to Spa on the following day, January 5, to begin their new assignment.

The men who had been in Malmédy had had a few days in which to rest and be refitted. Nearly every man of Company B and Company C who was in Malmédy had to draw a completely new outfit of clothing. Living in their uniforms, fighting fires in them, digging out civilians from cellars, tearing down walls, huddling in foxholes at the outposts and along the railroad embankment, hitting the mud when the shells rained in, or the bombs, they arrived in Modave looking like waifs, torn, burned, singed, cut, bruised, scratched, and to a man filthy dirty. Clothing that had been through all that could not be cleaned and repaired. It could only be discarded. It was done and now the men, rested and clean, were ready for the next job.

Among the tattered remnants who had been working under Colonel Anderson to help blunt Manteuffel's sharp drive, Company C had also had a few days' rest to sleep and recuperate. But Company A came in last, straight from their foxholes and bridges and minefields, and went right on into the new assignment.

Company B wore Malmédy like a bright feather in their cap, and were entitled to. They had stuck when everything else had left and when they had every reason to expect an assault by an immensely strong armored column and when they did not know when, or if, they could be reinforced. For their valor they deserved every honor and every credit. There was no shirking in the ten days they helped defend the town. They stayed when they were totally alone and they did not leave until they were relieved. Colonel Pergrin's reports to First Army gave General Hodges the first and most important information he got of Peiper's column, and in time for Hodges to begin his own moves. It was of inestimable value to have him in Malmédy at that time.

Without taking any credit from the men in Malmédy, it must be said, however, that two squads not in Malmédy at all did more than anybody else to bring about Peiper's downfall and to end the threat in the Amblève sector. First, the 3rd squad of 2nd platoon, Company C, of the 291st, made an incalculable contribution with their roadblock near the top of the hill at Stavelot. By being there, by making a little noise, by slightly disabling one Panther tank, they created a psychological condition which convinced Peiper the U.S. were present in strength. He decided to wait until morning to attack and historians agree that he lost his battle right there and then. His overnight delay gave the 51st Engineers time to reach Trois Ponts and prepare the bridges there for demolition, to blow them in his face the next morning. This delay also gave Company A, 291st, time to get back to Werbomont from Amblève, and this was of great strategic importance.

For it was Sergeant Billington's 3rd squad of 2nd platoon, Company A, under Lieutenant Alvin Edelstein's capable direction, who put the cork in the bottle which effectively sealed Peiper in, when they blew the bridge near Habiemont. Peiper had nowhere to go except back to La Gleize and time was given the 119th Regiment of the 30th Infantry Division to give battle to him there. Time was given to Major McCown to move his battalion to Werbomont and screen the 82nd Airborne's assembly. If Peiper had gotten across the Lienne Creek the afternoon of December 18, not a thing would have stood in his way. McCown's battalion had not yet reached Werbomont, and the 82nd was yet a long way from arriving. Peiper would easily have made his Meuse crossing.

But Sergeant Billington's squad, and a few men of 2nd squad, perhaps fifteen men, stopped him cold. Nobody knew how important their action that day was, however, and the men have remained mostly unsung until this day. Only one of them, Private Johnny Rondenell, received a citation. The man who so efficiently gauged the wiring and demolitions for the bridge and who himself turned the key on a beautiful blow has never really been known. This mention of Corporal Fred Chapin must be his only medal.

Unaware of the importance of what they had done, these men joined with the rest of the battalion in wholehearted admiration for the men of Malmédy and never once begrudged them their medals.

21

On January 3, the Allied counteroffensive jumped off, as planned by Montgomery, along the northwest front. General Collins badly wanted to move his VII Corps behind Malmédy and advance southward to St. Vith. Montgomery would not hear to it, but he did grant Collins one concession. He allowed him to sideslip his corps east of the original line to advance down the Liège-Houffalize road, rather than require him to advance as far west as the Huy-Houffalize line.

The VII Corps and the XVIII Airborne Corps led the attack which moved southward. Patton's Third Army advanced northward, to meet Collins at Houffalize. General Leonard Gerow's entire V Corps was kept inactive along the whole northern shoulder from Monschau to Malmédy.

The counterattack was a painful, slow, miserable, plodding, desperate affair. The weather was abominable. Since December 27 snow and more snow and more snow had fallen, until men often moved in the white wastes of the Ardennes plateaus almost waist deep in the stuff. Sleet fell on top of the snow and turned the roads into skating rinks, on which tanks and all other vehicles skidded about. And the cold was brutal. The mercury in the thermometer fell right out the bottom. To be outside in it for an hour was to be punished achingly. To stand guard at a roadblock, on a crossroads or bridge for several hours caused so much suffering that even the commanders winced at having to rouse men to go out. Good commanders did all they could to relieve the suffering of their men, finding blankets, extra clothing for them, trying to see to it they got hot food. But during this period of agonizingly slow advance perhaps the worst enemy was the cold. Men simply could not keep a strong will, a fierce determination to fight. Increasingly they huddled in houses in whatever town they took and often had to be brutally driven out of them.

The attack proceeded exactly with the effect of one of the 291st's big bulldozers. It simply shoveled the enemy slowly back, down in front of the northern shoulder. It did not, as Eisenhower wanted, destroy their effectiveness.

On the German side, the High Command had waited tensely for the blow of the counterattack. They fully expected the Americans to take advantage of their possession of Malmédy and thrust through the now very weak *Sixth Panzer Army* positions there, toward St. Vith. This would have entrapped all their divisions in the west, precisely as Gerow, Collins, Hodges, Ridgway could see for themselves, and so badly wanted to do. It was what the Germans most feared and could do the least about. Hitler was insisting that Manteuffel continue his drive west. As long as Hitler would not allow Manteuffel to settle for anything less than a Meuse crossing, his armored spearheads had to be supported. Almost all of the *Sixth Panzer Army*'s amored divisions had been sent to support Manteuffel. All Field Marshal Model could do, as he anxiously watched Malmédy, was to scramble together two ordnance companies to create one single operational tank company from the armored debris the *1st SS Panzer Division* had saved from the Amblève debacle.

Late in December, however, it became apparent to them that the counterattack was going to be made from the northwest and that Patton's Army would come up from the south. They could meet this attack well enough. Almost all of their strength was in

Confrontation on the Amblève

position to face such an attack. When the counteroffensive opened, therefore, on January 3, the Germans recognized that at best it could only snip off the nose of their salient. It could not even begin to entrap their divisions. The Obercommando West War Diary records Rundstedt's comment: "They have settled for the small solution."

Montgomery was the one who settled for it. And it may be that in making what he thought was a sensible, practical decision and giving command of First Army over to Montgomery, Eisenhower actually made one of his worst command decisions. Montgomery's cautious decision to launch the counteroffensive from the west certainly prolonged the battle, and it did not destroy the enemy's divisions beyond further effectiveness. The Germans fought toughly for every foot of ground, gave ground reluctantly, requiring immense sacrifice of American lives, and finally were back on their own jump-off line of December 16. They were weakened, of course. But not beyond still fighting and it took another three months to reach the Rhine. Had the trap envisioned by the American generals been sprung and the German divisions bitten off and rendered entirely ineffective, the war might have been shortened by several months.

The 291st's new role lay with the XVIII Airborne Corps. They were now relieved of their long attachment to the 1111th Group and assigned to the 1186th Engineer Group. The 1111th remained attached to VII Corps.

Specifically, the 291st was to support both the 30th Infantry Division and the 82nd Airborne as they held in position along their fronts, Trois Ponts–Malmédy, inclusive, both preparing to jump off when Montgomery gave the word.

On January 5 the 291st moved to their new quarters in the vicinity of Spa. Here they stayed five days and Colonel Pergrin made some administrative changes. It will be recalled that he was without an Executive Officer all during the period of the heaviest fighting. He now offered the post to Captain Edward Lampp, who received a promotion to major. Major Lampp asked permission to stick with his own job, Operations Officer. Pergrin then offered the job to Captain Moyer, who took it and was promoted to major.

Since this left Company C without a commander, Lieutenant Warren Rombaugh was given the company and a captaincy. Which left 2nd platoon without a leader. Lieutenant Tom Stack was given the platoon.

Lieutenant Frank Rhea had taken over Company B on December 24 when Captain Conlin was wounded in Malmédy, and made a captain. But his 3rd platoon was left without a commander. The best possible man was right at hand, in Pergrin's opinion. He therefore gave M/Sergeant Ralph W. McCarty a field commission as second lieutenant and gave him B Company's 3rd platoon.

Third platoon had mixed emotions about this. To a man they had been devoted to Lieutenant Rhea. They were proud of him and glad he had got the company but he had occupied such a solid position in their hearts they hated to give him up and they strongly believed nobody could fill his shoes.

McCarty did not try to fill Rhea's shoes. His own fitted him well enough. The morning after he received his battlefield commission he stepped outside his own quarters and slushed through the snow over to the company area. The first man he met proceeded to try one on for size. He pulled up shortly and gave the new platoon leader a smart salute. The only trouble with it was, it was a left-handed salute. McCarty gravely returned the salute. With his left hand. The men cherished him for his own sake forever after.

On January 10 the outfit moved near Francorchamps and started back over the same old ground doing the same old things. They went down to Trois Ponts and built two Bailey bridges there for the 82nd Airborne. Under machine gun and artillery

Confrontation on the Amblève

fire from those same old heights of Wanne, Company A built a Bailey across the Amblève to replace the one blown by the 51st Engineers in Peiper's face on December 18, and Company C built one across the Salm where Sergeant J. B. Miller blew up some of Peiper's infantry that same day.

On January 13 the order finally came for the 30th Infantry Division, in Malmédy, to go on the offensive. For ten irreparably lost days following the opening of the counteroffensive this division had been kept sitting there, idle. By the time the 30th was allowed to take the offensive, the Germans had been shoveled down in front of them.

It was a long, hard road back, now. The 30th moved from one hill to another, from one patch of forest to the next, from one small village to another. The enemy had had time to mine much of the area, so on January 18 the 291st was brought into Malmédy and its units went out to clear the roads ahead of the 30th as they painfully and slowly moved toward St. Vith again.

In Malmédy Company B built a Bailey across the Warche where the old wooden bridge, fought around so bitterly on December 21, had been destroyed. Actually, Company B built three bridges at this site. First, in November of 1944 they had built the wooden bridge. Then they put in the Bailey, which later they took out when they had built a timber trestle under it. Company B had good reason never to forget the tiny Warche River.

During the last weeks of January, some of the men of Company C drew the painful assignment of helping to find the bodies of the men massacred at Five Points. The massacred men still lay where they had fallen, frozen now in their grotesque positions, and covered with heavy snow. It was a grim task, finding them, gently sweeping the snow from them, revealing all the horror, then placing numbered markers on each body. The entire field had to be swept to make certain none were missed.

The bodies were then taken to be viewed and inspected minutely by the Inspector General and his court. His findings would be the foundation of the evidence presented by the U.S. in the trial at Dachau of Dietrich and Priess and Peiper and the men of the *1st SS Panzer Division* who took part in the killings.

Shortly thereafter the 291st said goodbye to the sad little town of Malmédy and moved southward with 30th Infantry. They built a 60-foot double-single Bailey at Plance for the 119th Regiment and a 40-foot double-single at Pont.

At Poteau, where Company A had run into the immense logjam of traffic on December 17 and where Captain Gamble had taken to the woods and led his men home by way of logging trails and firebreaks, the 291st built a 110-foot triple-single Bailey.

They cleared snow from the roads for the 119th, cleared mines ahead of them, kept the air strips swept so the liaison planes could land and take off, and they built two landing strips at Montenau, Lieutenant Arch Taylor's old home. In the flesh he could reassure the people he had not been killed on December 17.

On January 23, exactly one month from the day the 7th Armored had withdrawn from the St. Vith area, they retook it. Brigadier General Bruce Clarke got the honor of marching his Combat Command B first into the shattered little town.

The following week the 291st reached Deidenberg and stayed for a few days in the farmhouses nearby and in the cellars of the village. In the yard of one farmhouse was the fresh grave of a German soldier, marked by his helmet.

On January 31 the 291st was reattached to the 1111th Group and ordered to Lanzerath, the town of twenty-three houses and one church, where Peiper had jumped off for his long, swift advance westward. On the German border nearby they built a bridge for the 82nd Airborne across the Our River, one end of it in Belgium, the other in Germany.

It was here that Lieutenant Ralph McCarty had his encounter with a major. The men of the 291st avoided majors when possible. A strange captain did not usually have enough weight to swing it around much, and a colonel had too much sense, but majors fell between two stools, always bucking for that silver bird on the shoulder. McCarty was directed to take a bulldozer to the bridge site and report to an Airborne major. McCarty lumbered up on a big dozer, dismounted and reported. The officer returned his salute, then waved one nonchalant hand at the 100-foot chasm of the Our River and said, "Fill it up."

McCarty said, "Yes, sir," crawled on the dozer and rumbled away. He did not return.

The bridge was a double-triple Bailey. It was snowing and sleeting and there was artillery fire. Company A and Company C built the bridge, completing it in forty hours, all hands working in a blizzard round the clock.

Before the bridge was finished, as soon as men could clamber over the framing, Sergeant Frank Dolcha, 3rd platoon, Company A, took a handful of men across and swept the road for mines and removed them. Then the 291st bulldozers lumbered across and plowed the snow off the road for the 82nd's vehicles.

The last bolts were hammered in, the last joints welded. The bridge was finished. The frozen, bone-weary men of Company A and Company C stepped back to let the 82nd Airborne Division begin their crossing. They leaned on their tools, their eyes red-rimmed from sleeplessness and streaming from the cold wind. Their hands were skinned and metal-burned and bloody. Their knees were sagging and their backs ached from the God-awful weight of the iron panels. But in forty hours, in a blowing blizzard, under artillery fire, they had put this monster up, and it was a damned good job. And the 82nd was crossing the Our with dry feet.

A truck loaded with paratroopers rumbled up. As its tires started singing on the metal floor of the bridge, a paratrooper leaned out the back and yelled at the exhausted engineers: "Why the hell don't you rear echelon bastards ever come up front and fight?"

Epilogue

Hitler's gamble had failed. Although Allied harmony heaved and strained and cracked a little under the pressure of his offensive, it did not give way. He did not get his new war.

He came closer than he knew, perhaps. For between the days of December 27 and 31 there was such a crisis in Command that it would have made him dance with joy.

In an effort to get Field Marshal Montgomery moving with a counterattack Eisenhower went to his headquarters to see him on December 27. Returning to Versailles he penned a memorandum to Montgomery. In summary it contained the basic plans for destroying the enemy forces west of the Rhine and the preparations for crossing the Rhine in force with the main effort in the north with Montgomery's 21 Army Group.

Eisenhower thought he had made it very clear that in the offensive toward the Rhine crossing Bradley would move his headquarters north into close proximity with Montgomery's headquarters, and for the drive across the Rhine all decisions concerning detailed or emergency coordination between Bradley's 12th U.S. Army Group and Montgomery's 21 Army Group would be vested in Montgomery, but Bradley would still have full operational control of his 12th Army Group.

Montgomery chose to interpret it differently and on December 30 Eisenhower received a letter from him which sent the famous Eisenhower temper right out the roof. One paragraph of the letter in particular incensed Eisenhower for it read to him like an ultimatum. Montgomery even suggested the wording of a directive to be issued to Bradley. Montgomery, of course, was still plugging hard for full control of the Rhine offensives. In fact, he only wanted one — his, and he wanted Eisenhower to give him everything, men and material, for it and to halt everything else until he had achieved it.

Eisenhower cooled down but he decided the time had come when Montgomery had to be dealt with, finally and conclusively. In short, he was going to face the Combined Chiefs of Staff with an ultimatum. Either he or Montgomery must go. They could no longer work together. He composed a telegram, short and to the point, asking that either he or Montgomery be relieved.*

It had not yet been sent, however, when Montgomery's chief of staff got wind of the high feelings at SHAEF and took things into his own hands. It was obvious to him that faced with such an ultimatum Montgomery would be the one to go. The Combined Chiefs of Staff would not consider relieving Eisenhower. Eisenhower, too, knew this and he had suggested that he could work happily with Sir Harold Alexander.

Montgomery's chief of staff, Major General Francis de Guingand, flew to SHAEF and did some very fast talking. In the end Eisenhower agreed to hold his telegram twenty-four hours. But he laid the law down to de Guingand. He said that Montgomery *and* the British press which idolized Montgomery, had put Bradley in an impossible situation. The British press had given the impression, ever since Montgomery was given command of the northern sector of the Ardennes battle, that he had been forced to come to the rescue of the Americans because Bradley had failed. Furthermore, Eisenhower said that Montgomery was

---

*Eisenhower, John S. D. *The Bitter Woods* (New York, G. P. Putnam's Sons, 1969), pp. 382–383.

Confrontation on the Amblève

using what he *knew* to be a temporary expedient to push his demands to be given the job as overall commander. And the whole mess had simply become intolerable to the Americans.

General de Guingand arrived back at Montgomery's headquarters at 4:30 P.M. on December 31. Within a few minutes he was explaining to Britain's most glamorous soldier that he was within inches of being relieved of his command.

Montgomery was baffled. The man was actually so insulated in self-confidence that he did not know what he had done. To him it simply made sense. He was the best commander in the field. He was really better than Eisenhower. Everybody should recognize that. Therefore, in wanting a totally free hand, and everything the Americans could give him to back him up, he was only wanting what was sensible. But when de Guingand reminded him the Americans were furnishing most of the men and practically all of the materials of war, as well as the Supreme Commander, and that if that Supreme Commander faced the Combined Chiefs of Staff with a choice between himself and Montgomery, not even Churchill could save him, Montgomery began to realize what a mess he was in.

But if Montgomery was supremely tactless in his blind egotism, he was also capable of doing the handsome thing. He wrote a full apology to both Eisenhower and Bradley, promising his loyal cooperation in all decisions. Although he continued to irritate the Americans over and over, the situation never came so close to coming unglued again as during these critical days.

On March 8 the 291st Engineers were once again in a most strategic position for an important assignment. They happened to be very near the little town of Remagen on the Rhine when the famous Ludendorff Bridge was taken by the 9th Armored Division.

They heard the news before turning in that night and figured they would cross with the 78th Infantry, whom they were supporting, in a day or two. But they were rolled out at midnight and ordered to Remagen to build a floating treadway to expedite the build-up of the bridgehead across the river.

Captain Bill McKinsey of Pergrin's staff was plotting the bridge site by daylight the next morning and the advance elements, Company A to be precise, arrived shortly afterward. The remainder of the 291st continued arriving throughout the day and, working round the clock, they had the long floating treadway ready to use thirty-two hours after beginning.

It might have been done faster if the artillery fire had not been so heavy that one entire pontoon section of the bridge was blown out of the water and had to be rebuilt. But at 5:00 on the afternoon of March 11 the first trucks of the 78th Infantry Division rolled across. It was the longest tactical bridge built in Europe during the entire war, and the 291st had another feather in their cap. To Malmédy and the Amblève Line they now added the first bridge built across the Rhine and the battle star of Remagen.

They guarded the bridge until March 17. Saw their first V–2 rockets and the battalion headquarters narrowly escaped being buried by one. Saw their first jet-propelled planes sweeping lightning-fast down the river. They witnessed the collapse of the Ludendorff Bridge and rescued many of the survivors, men caught on the bridge when it fell, as they floated down the stream to their treadway. They pulled them out of the river and carried them to their aid station and once again 291st medics gave aid to survivors of an unforeseeable incident.

They lost one man killed at Remagen, Private Merion Priester, and had eighteen men wounded, all by artillery fire.

Then they were assigned to the 99th Infantry Division for the reduction of the Ruhr. When that had been done, the 99th, and the 291st with it, were assigned to Patton's Third Army and they all went speeding down into Bavaria. The primary objective was to liberate as many prisoner-of-war camps as possible and to prevent any movement of German High Command to the redoubts in the southern mountains.

They lost three men during this movement. Captain Paul Kamen, who had brought the medical supplies to Malmédy through Peiper's artillery fire the night of December 17, was killed on the autobahn near Kissengen. The 291st convoy was strafed by a couple of Luftwaffe jet-propelled planes. Staff Sergeant Douglas Swift, also of the medical section, was killed at the same time.

Then, just four days before the war's end, they suffered their last casualty. On the Danube Company A was waiting in an apple orchard for their bridge assignment. Mortar fire from a little village across the river suddenly screamed in. Private Arnold Hall was sleeping in a truck. A shell hit a tree, the fragments flew in all directions and one went through the side of the truck and pierced Hall's head, killing him instantly as he slept.

The war ended finally as they were bivouacked on the Isar River just north of Munich. They went on into Munich and took over the job of working German prisoners who were cleaning up the debris of the city.

And now the point system started to break up the outfit. Some high-point men, with 85 points or more, left Munich as early as August and were home by the end of September. Others did not reach home until December.

The core of the battalion embarked on the *St. Albans Victory* on October 11, 1945, and arrived at Hampton Roads on October 20. The 291st Engineer Combat Battalion was officially inactivated that same day. Lacking three days they had been an outfit two years and nine months.

In the 11 months from June 1944 to the war's end, May 1945, they traveled almost 3000 miles on the continent of Europe, making 48 different stands. They built 44 Bailey bridges, 30 of them in France, Luxembourg and Belgium, 14 in Germany, and 20 timber trestle bridges. They built a floating treadway across the Rhine, the longest tactical bridge on the continent, and they built another floating treadway across the Danube.

They had eight men killed and 93 wounded. They won five battle stars: Normandy, Northern France, Ardennes, Rhineland, Central Europe. They were awarded the Presidential Unit Citation and the French Unit Croix de Guerre. They brought home a written commendation from the Third Army Engineer in which he called them the "crack engineer outfit in Europe."

These damned engineers had a short life but they gave a damned good account of themselves.

APPENDIXES

BIBLIOGRAPHICAL NOTES
AND ACKNOWLEDGMENTS

BIBLIOGRAPHY

APPENDIX A

Decision No. 246

Translation
On proposal of the Minister of National Defense,
THE PRESIDENT OF THE PROVISIONAL GOVERNMENT OF THE REPUBLIC,
CITES TO THE ORDER OF THE DIVISION

291st Engineer Combat Battalion

"Elite Unit which distinguished itself in remarkable manner, in the course of the German offensive in Belgium.

Having been ordered to prevent the enemy from using the roads to the south and east of Malmédy and to insure the defense of the city itself, gave proof of the most absolute scorn of danger in accomplishing its mission under particularly violent and accurate fire.

In spite of repeated attacks, by forces superior in number, resisted all attempts at infiltration and proved its real qualities of courage and daring."

This citation includes the awarding of the Croix de Guerre with Silver Star.

Paris, 15 July 1946

By Order: General of the Army JUIN
Chief of the General Staff
for National Defense

Signed: A. Juin

A TRUE COPY:
Paul M. Jewell, Captain, CE

APPENDIX B

Presidential Unit Citation

The following is quoted from General Order No. 30, Hq. First US Army, dated 18 Feb 45:
"*I BATTLE HONORS (291st ENGINEER COMBAT BATTALION)* — As authorized by Executive Order No. 9396 (Sec I, Bull. 22, WD, 1943), superseding Executive Order No. 9075 (Sec III, Bull. WD, 1942), and under the provisions of Section IV, Circular No. 333, War Department, 1943, the following unit is cited for extraordinary heroism and outstanding performance of duty in action:

The *291st Engineer Combat Battalion*, United States Army, is cited for outstanding performance of duty in action against the enemy from 17 to 26 December 1944, in Belgium. On 17 December 1944, at the beginning of the German Ardennes break-through, the *291st Engineer Combat Battalion* was assigned the mission of establishing and manning roadblocks south and east of Malmédy, and with the defense of the town itself. The battalion set up essential roadblocks and prepared hasty defenses. Shortly thereafter, numerically superior enemy infantry and armored columns moving the direction of Malmédy were engaged. Though greatly outnumbered and constantly subjected to heavy enemy artillery, mortar and small arms fire, the officers and men of the *291st Engineer Combat Battalion* stubbornly resisted all enemy attempts to drive through their positions. Repeated attacks were made by enemy armor and infantry on roadblocks and defensive positions and, in each instance, were thrown back with heavy losses by the resolute and determined resistance. The determination, devotion to duty and unyielding fighting spirit displayed by the personnel of the

291st Engineer Combat Battalion in delaying and containing a powerful enemy force along a route of vital importance to the Allied effort is worthy of high praise.

It is with my utmost satisfaction and esteem that as your Battalion Commander I have the pleasure of forwarding to you the above citation — one of the highest honors that can be bestowed on a unit as a whole. You are hereby awarded The Distinguished Unit Badge and are authorized to wear it as a permanent part of your uniform.

The glory with which you may wear this Badge is characteristic of the extremely high merit for which this citation is presented.

DAVID E. PERGRIN
Lieutenant Colonel, CE
Commanding

BIBLIOGRAPHICAL NOTES
AND ACKNOWLEDGMENTS

EXCEPT FOR THE BROAD PICTURE of the entire Ardennes offensive, this book has been written from primary sources. For the 291st Engineer Combat Battalion it is to a considerable extent oral history. The skeleton of their story is contained in their Unit History, and in the After Action Reports and Service Journals, but it is only a skeleton and had to be given flesh, muscle, nerves and tissue by personal conferences, endless correspondence, telephone calls and many written accounts. The men of the 291st have told their story themselves, and they have told it magnificently.

Proceeding on the theory that "one witness is no witness," in almost every case there are at least two, sometimes three or four witnesses to each event. There are a few exceptions, as in the case of T/5 Vincent Consiglio's running battle all day in the house by the paper mill in Malmédy. No other 291st men were present to witness most of it. As also with Private Bernard Goldstein's escape over the hill at Stavelot and the tragic reconnaissance later. Nobody but Private Goldstein was involved, or survived.

No conversation or dialogue has been manufactured, nor were any thoughts put into the minds of the men. Such conversations and thoughts as are used were told to me or written to me.

Colonel Pergrin, who commanded the 291st Engineers, has been devotedly faithful. In March 1965, he and three other officers of the 291st, and four men of the 291st, representing the action at Malmédy, Trois Ponts and Werbomont, spent a memorable weekend in my home. The entire period of March 19 to 21 was one long conference with these men and one eight-hour session was taped.

In addition, Colonel Pergrin furnished me with his entire file of personal records and private papers, which included his roster of officers with their vital statistics, his valuable scrapbook and all the official battalion photographs, his log of headquarters movements from Camp Swift, Texas, to Munich and war's end. They included his records of all men wounded, and where and on what date, and his records of all citations and awards, both individual and for the unit. A number of maps he used were also included. These records were infinitely helpful.

For the specific battles along the Amblève in which the 291st played an important role, the primary sources were the After Action Reports, Service Journals and Unit Histories of the U.S. Army units involved at Malmédy, Stavelot, Trois Ponts, La Gleize and Werbomont. All military records of World War II are now lodged in the files of the General Services Administration, National Archives, Washington, D.C. A list of those reproduced for me and used by me to any extent is included in the Bibliography.

For the enemy side of the picture I have also relied on primary sources. An invaluable collection of manuscripts prepared by German military commanders in 1945 after the war ended, under the direction of the U.S. Military History Section, is also available in the National Archives. For the Sixth Panzer Army, I have made use of the paper prepared by its chief of staff, Brigadeführer der Waffen-SS Fritz Kraemer, "Operations of the Sixth Panzer Army During the Ardennes Offensive." For the 1 SS Panzer Corps, I have made use of the paper of its commander, General der Waffen-SS H. Priess, "Commitment of the 1 SS Panzer Corps During the Ardennes Offensive." And for the composition, strength, route of advance and detailed accounts of battles for Kampfgruppe Peiper there are three manuscripts, C-004, Ethint #10 and Ethint #11. Baron von der Heydte's paper on the operations of his paratrooper brigade was used, as was the Ethint manuscript of an interview with Otto Skorzeny concerning Operation Greif and the 150th Panzer Brigade.

Secondary sources, in the form of books already published about the Battle of the Bulge, were used only for the general picture. First and constantly I relied on the official military history of the Battle of the Bulge, *The Ardennes: The Battle of the Bulge*. Commissioned by the Department of the Army and written by Dr. Hugh M. Cole as a part of the long record of the U.S. Army in World War II being compiled, it hardly falls into the category of secondary sources. It is truly a textbook of the Battle.

Other books which have been of value are: Forrest C. Pogue, *The Supreme Command*, also a part of the Department of the Army's history of World War II; Dwight D. Eisenhower, *Crusade in Europe*; John S. D. Eisenhower, *The Bitter Woods*; Robert E. Merriam, *Dark December*; Otto Skorzeny, *Skorzeny's Special Missions*; Omar N. Bradley, *A Soldier's Story*; John Toland, *Battle: The Story of the Bulge*; Field Marshal Montgomery, *Memoirs*.

Colonel H. W. Anderson, USA (Ret), commander of the 1111th Engineer Combat Group, of which the 291st was a part, gave valuable assistance in details concerning the activities of Group, particularly at

Bibliographical Notes

Trois Ponts on December 18, 1944. He patiently replied to several letters requiring many details. It was good to have his interest and assistance.

Major General Ernest Frankland, USA (Ret), commander of 1st Battalion, 117th Regiment, 30th Infantry Division, was helpful concerning the burning of the gasoline dump near Stavelot, and with details of the destruction of the old stone bridge at the same place. I am grateful for his courteous attention.

All photographs were provided by men of the 291st Engineers and Colonel Pergrin, unless otherwise indicated. My brother-in-law, Kenneth E. Giles, gave me invaluable assistance by reproducing for print all the 291st photographs. What he was able to do with old, sometimes badly faded, usually very small photographs was amazing and I am deeply indebted to him.

For unvarying courtesy in many demands made on them, I am obligated to Mr. Edwin R. Flatequal, Archivist of the National Archives, to Mr. Robert Wolfe, Specialist in German Records of the National Archives, and to the U.S. Army Photographic Section in the Pentagon.

The editors at Houghton Mifflin Company, particularly my own editor, Anne N. Barrett, have been dedicated and tireless in their interest and efforts, always sustaining and encouraging, and I am profoundly grateful.

My husband, who was on the cadre which formed the 291st and was with it to war's end, has been a walking encyclopedia on 291st habits and ways, their lore and tradition. He knows full well the debt I owe to him.

Spout Springs
Knifley, Kentucky
June 26, 1969

Janice Holt Giles

BIBLIOGRAPHY

Books

Ayer, Fred, Jr., *Before the Colors Fade*. Boston: Houghton Mifflin Company, 1964.
Baldwin, Hanson W., *Battles Lost and Won*. New York: Harper & Row, 1966.
Blumenson, Martin, *The Duel for France, 1944*. Boston: Houghton Mifflin Company, 1963.
Bradley, Omar N., *A Soldier's Story*. New York: Henry Holt & Company, 1951.
Bryant, Arthur, *Triumph in the West*. New York: Doubleday & Company, 1959.
Butcher, Captain Harry C., *My Three Years with Eisenhower*. New York: Simon and Schuster, 1946.
Churchill, Winston S., *Triumph and Tragedy*. Boston: Houghton Mifflin Company, 1953.
Cole, Hugh M., *The Ardennes: The Battle of the Bulge*. Washington: Office of the Chief of Military History, Department of the Army, 1965.
Draper, Lieutenant Theodore, *The 84th Infantry Division in the Battle of Germany, November 1944–May 1945*. New York: Viking Press, 1947.
Eisenhower, Dwight D., *Crusade in Europe*, New York: Doubleday & Company, 1948.
Eisenhower, John S. D., *The Bitter Woods*. New York: G. P. Putnam's Sons, 1969.
Farago, Ladislas, *Patton: Ordeal and Triumph*. New York: Ivan Obolensky, Inc., 1963.
Foley, Charles, *Commando Extraordinary* (Otto Skorzeny). New York: G. P. Putnam's Sons, 1955.

Bibliography

Gallagher, Richard, *The Malmédy Massacre*. New York: Paperback Library, 1964.
Gilbert, Felix, ed., *Hitler Directs His War*. New York: The Oxford University Press, 1950.
Greenfield, Kent R., ed., *Command Decisions*. New York: Harcourt, Brace and Company, 1959.
Guderian, General Heinz, *Panzer Leader*. New York: E. P. Dutton & Company, 1952.
Guingand, Major General Sir Francis de, *Generals at War*. London: Hodder and Stoughton, 1964.
Hart, B. H. Liddell, *The German Generals Talk*. New York: William Morrow & Company, 1948.
Ingersoll, Ralph, *Top Secret*. New York: Harcourt, Brace and Company, 1946.
Manchester, William, *The Arms of Krupp*. Boston: Little, Brown and Company, 1968.
Marshall, Colonel S. L. A., *Battle of the Bulge* (Selection in *History of World War II*). Reader's Digest Company, 1969.
Martin, Ralph G., *The G.I. War, 1941-45*. Boston: Little, Brown and Company, 1967.
Martin, Ralph G. and Harrity, Richard, *World War II*. Greenwich, Conn.: Fawcett Publications, 1962.
Merriam, Robert E., *Dark December*. Chicago: Ziff-Davis Publishing Company, 1947.
Montgomery, Field Marshall, Viscount of Alamein, *Memoirs*. Cleveland: World Publishing Company, 1958.
Patton, George S., Jr., *War as I Knew It*. Boston: Houghton Mifflin Company, 1947.
Pogue, Forrest C., *The Supreme Command*. Washington: Office of the Chief of Military History, Department of the Army, 1954.
Ridgway, Matthew B., *Soldier: The Memoirs of Matthew B. Ridgeway* (As told to Harold H. Martin). New York: Harper and Brothers, 1956.
Shirer, William L., *The Rise and Fall of the Third Reich*. New York: Simon and Schuster, 1960.
Skorzeny, Otto, *Skorzeny's Special Missions*. London: Robert Hale Limited, 1957.
Smith, General Walter Bedell (with Stewart Beach), *Eisenhower's Six Great Decisions*. New York: Longmans Green, 1956.
Toland, John, *Battle: The Story of the Bulge*. New York: Random House, 1959.
Toland, John, *The Last 100 Days*. New York: Random House, 1966.
Trevor-Roper, H. R., *The Last Days of Hitler*. London: Macmillan & Co., 1947.

Warlimont, Walter, *Inside Hitler's Headquarters, 1939-45.* New York: Frederick A. Praeger, 1964.
Wilmot, Chester, *The Struggle for Europe.* London: Collins, 1957.

MAGAZINES

American Legion Magazine: "The Battle of the Bulge."
  Part I, "Hitler Plans the Impossible" (January, 1966)
  Part II, "Disaster and Reaction in the Ardennes" (February, 1966)
  Part III, "The Bulge is Erased" (March, 1966)
American Heritage, "A Few Men in Soldier Suits," Helena Huntington Smith, August, 1957.
Field Artillery Journal, "The Massacre at Malmédy," Virgil T. Lary, February, 1946.

NEWSPAPERS

All issues of *Stars & Stripes*, and *Yank*, for December 1944 through January 1945.

PERSONAL ACCOUNTS

Manuscripts written for author by men of the 291st Engineer Battalion:
  Billington, Sgt. R. C., Company A
  Byrne, Cpl. Edmond, Company C
  Caplan, Sgt. Abraham, Company A
  Chapin, Cpl. Fred R., Company A
  Colbeck, Lt. Wade L., Company B
  Courvillion, Pvt. George J., Company A
  Dymond, Pfc. Louis T., Company A
  Dixon, T/4 Merlin E., Company A
  Elliott, T/4 Jeff, Company A
  Gamble, Capt. James H., Company A
  Getz, Pfc. William, Company C
  Hayes, Lt. Frank R., Company A
  King, Cpl. John A., Company A
  Koenig, Pvt. Bernard L., Company B
  Kovacs, T/4 Louis, Company A
  McCarty, Lt. Ralph W., Company B
  Melton, Sgt. Albert D., Company C
  Morris, Cpl. Eugene, Company C

Bibliography

    Pergrin, Col. David E., Battalion Commander
    Rhea, Lt. Frank W., Company B
    Scanlan, T/Sgt. John L., H/S Company
    Schommer, Cpl. A. C., Company A
    Sheetz, Capt. Lloyd B., Battalion Staff
    Smith, S/Sgt. Walter J., Company B
    Stack, Lt. Thomas F., Company C
    Taylor, Lt. Archibald L., Jr., Company A
    Walters, Lt. Albert W., Company A

    Typescript of eight-hour taped conference with Col. David E. **Pergrin,** Capt. James H. Gamble, Lt. Arch L. Taylor, Lt. Ralph McCarty, Sgt. Paul Hinkel.

    Typescripts of personal interviews and/or telephone conversations with:
    Billington, Sgt. R. C., Company A
    Caplan, Sgt. Abraham, Company A
    Colbeck, Lt. Wade L., Company B
    Connors, Pfc. Joseph, Company B
    Consiglio, T/5 Vincent J., Company B
    Dymond, Pfc. Louis T., Company A
    Elliott, T/4 Jeff, Company A
    Gamble, Capt. James H., Company A
    Goldstein, Pvt. Bernard, Company C
    Hayes, Lt. Frank R., Company A
    Hensel, Sgt. Charles, Company C
    Hinkel, Sgt. Paul J., Company A
    Keoghan, Sgt. Ed, Company C
    Leary, Pfc. John L., Company C
    McCarty, Lt. Ralph W., Company B
    Melton, Sgt. Albert D., Company C
    Morris, Cpl. Eugene, Company C
    Pergrin, Lt. Col. David E., Battalion Commander
    Rhea, Lt. Frank W., Company B
    Russo, Pfc. Carl, Company C
    Scanlan, T/Sgt. John L., H/S Company
    Smith, Sgt. Sheldon T., Company C
    Smith, S/Sgt. Walter J., Company B
    Stack, Lt. Thomas F., Company C
    Taylor, Lt. Archibald L., Company A
    Walters, Lt. Albert W., Company A

Official U.S. Government Sources

After Action Reports, Unit Journals, Unit Histories for December 1944 through January 1945:
First U.S. Army
30th Infantry Division
 117th Regiment
 119th Regiment
 120th Regiment
82nd Airborne Division
 505th Paratroop Regiment
84th Infantry Division
99th Infantry Division
 394th Infantry Regiment
99th Infantry Battalion (Separate)
526th Armored Infantry Battalion
825th Tank Destroyer Battalion
14th Cavalry Group
49th AAA Brigade
1111th Engineer Combat Group
291st Engineer Combat Battalion
51st Engineer Combat Battalion
202nd Engineer Combat Battalion

Manuscripts, *National Archives*

A Series:
A-877, General der Waffen-SS H. Priess, "Commitment of the 1 SS Panzer Corps During the Ardennes Offensive" (Dec. 16, 1944–Jan. 25, 1945)
A-924, Brigadeführer de Waffen-SS Fritz Kraemer, "Operations of the Sixth Panzer Army" (1944–45)

B Series:
B-823, Oberstleutnant Friedrich August Baron von der Heydte, "Kampfgruppe von der Heydte."

C Series:
C-004, Oberst (W-SS) Jochen Peiper, "Kampfgruppe Peiper" (Dec. 15–26, 1944)

Ethint Series:
Ethint 10, Oberst (W-SS) Jochen Peiper, 1 SS PZ Regt. (Dec. 11-24, 1944)
Ethint 11, Peiper, "1 SS PZ Regt." (Dec. 16-19, 1944)
Ethint 12, Oberst (W-SS) Otto Skorzeny, "Ardennes Offensive, an Interview with Obst. Skorzeny" (Aug. 12, 1945)

INDEX

AAA Brigade, 49th. *See* Antiaircraft Artillery Brigade, 49th
Aachen, 14, 31, 60, 64, 72, 99, 100, 187
Afst, 143
Ahrens, Sgt. Kenneth, 166, 167, 169, 171
Airborne Corps, XVIIIth, 251, 271, 325, 328, 329, 330, 346-47; and Allied counteroffensive, 363, 365
Airborne Division, 17th, 321
Airborne Division, 82nd, 250-51, 252, 257, 263, 265-66, 271, 343, 362; in battle of Trois Ponts, 279, 280-82; roadblock near Lienne Creek bridge, 283-84; ordered to redraw line, 330; skirmish with Peiper's men, 344; and Allied counteroffensive, 368-69
Airborne Division, 101st, 250
Albert Canal, 110
Allied counteroffensive, 363-69
Allied Front. *See* Western Front
Alzette River, 101-2
Amay, 106
Amblève, 114; Company A in, 52-57, 73-78; on Peiper's march route, 118, 134-35; German tanks seen headed for, 75, 138; Peiper's diversion through, 138-40, 146, 196, 212
Amblève River, 15-16, 43-44, 46, 59, 106, 118; Peiper crosses at Stavelot, 230-31, 235-36, 251, 252; crossing by Germans stopped, 253-54; Peiper crosses at Chenoux, 258; on Meuse barrier line, 330

American retreat of Dec. 17, 74, 76, 78, 190-201
Anderson, Col. H. W., 8, 11-12, 23, 24, 58, 186, 197, 236; orders of Dec. 17, 70-71, 219, 225; and Pergrin's messages from Malmédy, 86, 91, 189-90; at Trois Ponts Dec. 18, 238, 240, 241, 242-43, 244-46; move from Trois Ponts, 247-48, 268; at Modave, 269-270, 292; orders engineers to leave Trois Ponts, 282; ordered to put engineers on Meuse barrier line, 322; and reassembling of 291st Engineers, 359, 361
Anderson, Roy, 161
Andler, 118, 119, 139, 142-43, 144, 146
Antiaircraft Artillery Brigade, 49th, 52, 134-35, 206; in Ligneuville, 208-209; evacuation to Lambermont, 210, 212-13
Antwerp: British enter, 99; objective of German offensive, 100-101, 108, 109
Ardennes battle. *See* German offensive; Allied counteroffensive
Ardennes forest, 39, 45
Ardennes front (Monschau to Echternach), 14-15, 21-23, 100, 101
Armored Division, 2nd, 325, 329, 348, 353
Armored Division, 3rd, 326, 329, 342
Armored Division, 7th: move to St. Vith, 60, 71-72, 78, 83, 92, 139, 147, 150; Combat Command R of, 156, 209, 276, 277; roadblock on N-33,

Armored Division *(cont'd)*
  196–97; skirmishes at Kaiserbaracke and Recht Dec. 18, 212; AAA battery at Stavelot, 231; withdrawal from and re-entry into St. Vith, 330, 347, 368
Armored Division, 9th, 144–45, 373; Combat Command B of, 22, 23–24, 55, 56, 107, 111; service train in Ligneuville, 209–11
Armored Division, 10th, 71
Armored Division, 11th, 321
Armored Field Artillery Battalion, 440th, 92, 163, 175–76
Armored Infantry Battalion, 526th, 188, 199–200, 205, 206; lost half-track and antitank gun, 200, 239–40, 241–242; and battle of Stavelot, 224–32, 236, 289–90; in Malmédy, 286, 295, 311–12, 313, 319
Army, First, 4, 11, 12, 14, 15–16, 19, 105; assignment to capture Urft-Roer dams, 20–21; communications, 28–30; comb-out of Germanic Belgian towns, 32–33; importance of Malmédy to, 47; security alert issued by, 58; movements of Dec. 17, 63–64; armored divisions loaned to, 71–72; Hitler's plans against, 105, 110; warned of assembling of German tanks, 113; Pergrin's reports to, 181, 187, 361; Peiper's movements and blowing of Trois Ponts bridge reported to, 242, 245; evacuation of Spa headquarters, 293–94, 324, 326; and U.S. bombing of Malmédy, 341; and Meuse barrier line, 345, 365
Army, Third, 6, 14, 19, 23, 110, 219, 326, 363, 374. *See also* Patton, Lt. Gen. George S., Jr.
Army, Seventh, 14, 99–100
Army, Ninth, 14, 19, 20, 71, 107, 187
Army Group, 6th, 14
Army Group, 12th, 14, 19, 98, 188, 326, 371
Army Group B (German), 99, 102
Arnhem, 250
Arnhold, Pvt., 165
Auw, 81
Aywaille, 45, 118

Bagatelle, 151, 161
Bailey, Sir Donald, 3
Bailey bridge, 3–4
Baraque Michel, 106, 132
Barker, Pvt. Edward, 352–53
Barse, 118
Barvaux Condroz crossroads, 323, 360
Basse Bodeaux, 43, 255–56, 275
Bastogne, 71–72, 101, 102, 144, 187, 250, 251, 265–66, 271, 329; isolated by *Fifth Panzer Army*, 321, 345
Bauers, Pfc. Charles, 207, 215–17
Baugnez. *See* Five Points; Five Points massacre
Bavaria, 374–75
Belgium: Germanic area of, 30–34; Gauleiter assigned for, 111
Bellevaux, 311
Bereldange, 102
Bergen Op Zoom, 105
Bergeval, 344
Berterath, 81, 141
Bevercé, 118, 295, 319
Bevis, Cpl., 55–56
Billington, Sgt. Robert C., 26, 30, 196, 197, 354; and blowing of Habiemont bridge, 255–56, 259–60, 264–66, 270, 362
Bjornstad, Major, 188, 198
Blankenheim, 124
Blankenheimerdorf, 121
Bliesheim, 120
Bocq River, 322–23
Bodarwé, Mme Adèle, 155–56, 157, 158, 172. *See also* Madame Bodarwé's café
Bodarwé, Louis, 155–56
Bolero construction program, 7–8
Bomal, 210
Bonn, 335
Born, 13, 35, 80; Company A's move to, 24, 27–30, 34, 38–52, 55, 111, 140; Germanic character of area, 30–34; Dec. 17 in, 78, 81; on German march route, 118, 139; Peiper's diversion southward through, 140, 146–47, 211; 14th Cavalry Group's retreat from, 140–49
Bossert, Cpl. Harry, 255, 260, 264, 265
Bouck, Lt. Lyle C., 131

Index

Bradley, Lt. Gen. Omar N., 14, 19, 20, 22–23, 71, 250, 326; and crisis in Allied command, 371–73
Brandenberger, Gen. Erich, 110
Brenna, W.O. John K., 299, 332, 358
Bressoux, 118
British military units: Army, Second, 14; 21 Army Group, 14, 19, 321, 371; Armoured Division, 11th, 99; Corps, XXX, 321, 345, 346; Guards Armoured Division, 321; Household Cavalry Regiment, 2nd, 346; infantry divisions, 321; Royal Tank Brigade, 29th, 348
Brussels, 321
Bryans, Cpl. Frederick, 332, 333
Buchanan, of 526th Armored Infantry, 242
Buchholz, 131, 132–33
Buffone, Pfc. Francis, 9
Büllingen, 13, 31, 32; German attack of Dec. 17, 70–72, 137, 174, 209; on German march route, 118, 134–35; gas dump at, 123; Americans taken prisoner at, 137, 138, 161; *12th SS Panzer Division* moved to, 297
Burnenville, 319
Butgenbach, 13, 21, 75, 137, 174, 298, 303, 324–25; Germanic character of, 31, 32; road intersection west of, on Dec. 17, 68–69, 135; German breakthrough, 70–72, 73, 91, 93, 209; on German march route, 119; 99th Infantry Division headquarters moved from, 136; on Meuse barrier line, 329–30
Butler, Lt. Col. McClernand, 336
"Buzz bomb alley," 134–35, 206, 209, 210
Byrne, Cpl. Edmond, 84 n, 192, 243, 293–94

Camp Swift, 5, 16
Canadian Army, First, 14
Caplan, Sgt. Abraham, 82–83, 323, 346, 360
Carentan, 9
Carter, Col. W. H., 23, 185–86, 293–94, 357
Carville, Maj. Richard, 70

Cavalry Group, 14th, 108, 117; 18th Reconnaissance Squadron, 21, 81; Company A, 820th Tank Destroyer Battalion, 22, 130; Troop A, 32nd Reconnaissance Squadron, overrun at Honsfeld, 133; positions in Losheim Gap, 140–41; retreat from Born and Wallerode, 140–49
Cavalry Reconnaissance Squadron, 18th. *See* Cavalry Group, 14th
Cavalry Reconnaissance Squadron, 32nd. *See* Cavalry Group, 14th
Cavalry Reconnaissance Squadron, 38th, 336
Celles, 329, 348
Chambois, 98
Champion, Sgt. Malvin, 76, 79, 80
Champlon, 345
Chapin, Cpl. Fred R., 255–56, 260–62, 362
Château Froidcour, 66, 243
Chaudfontaine, 12, 324–26
Cheneux, 43, 244, 257–58, 266, 267, 271, 276–77; attacked by 504th Parachute Infantry, 278–79
Cherbourg Peninsula, 9
Chinlund, Lt. Joe, 219
Chodes, 64, 85, 88, 183
Christmas Eve and Christmas Day, 1944, 350–55
Ciney, 329, 345, 347, 348–49, 353
Clarke, Brig. Gen. Bruce, 147–48, 368
Clerf, 329
Clotten, Sgt., 165
Colbeck, Lt. Wade L., 45, 65, 69, 72, 84 n, 174–75, 178, 295, 299; and Malmédy defense plans, 87–90; roadblock near Five Points, 155, 292–93; trip to Stavelot for gear, 300–301
Cole, Pfc., 207
Collier, Brig. Gen. John, 348
Collins, Maj. Gen. J. Lawton, 14, 98, 324–26, 327, 329, 348; and Montgomery, 328, 347; and Allied counteroffensive, 363, 364
Cologne, 112
Communications: at "seam" near Lanzerath, 22; loss of, during German offensive, 29–30, 78, 114, 115; of Company A on move to Born and

Communications (cont'd)
Amblève, 38-39, 53, 55; break on telephone line from Haute Bodeux to Trois Ponts, 56-58, 59; jamming by Germans, 57; from Group to Malmédy closed down, 86; Haute Bodeux to Malmédy Dec. 17, 189; lost in Trois Ponts, 242, 274; reinforced in Malmédy, 332

Company A, 101-2, 366-67, 375; in Werbomont, 12, 24-27, 34, 35, 53; ordered to Born, 24, 27-30, 34, 111; en route to Born and Amblève, 38-52, 114, 117; at Amblève, 52-54, 55, 56, 57; security detail at Trois Ponts, 61; on Dec. 17, 72-83, 139-40; 3rd platoon truck fired on, 79-80, 151; machine gunners sent to Malmédy, 195, 197, 202; return to Haute Bodeux and Werbomont, 195-98, 202-3, 362; bazookas taken to Malmédy, 201, 202-6; unit ordered to Stavelot, 225-27; and blowing of Habiemont bridge, 248, 254-57, 259-65, 362; on evening of Dec. 18, 269-70; elements in Malmédy with 120th Infantry Regiment, 298, 303, 332; elements on Meuse barrier line, 322-23, 330-31, 346, 353-54; reassembling of, 359-60, 361; and bridge across Our, 368-69; and bridge across Rhine, 374

Company B, 12, 13, 24, 29, 33-34, 36-37, 361, 366, 367; bridges built by, 44, 46, 102; sawmill in Stavelot, 45, 48, 65; and shelling of Malmédy Dec. 16, 48-50; on Dec. 17, 65-69, 70, 174-86; defense of Malmédy set up, 84-94; roadblock on Highway N-32, 88, 155, 178-79, 184-85, 292-93, 320; German armored column seen moving from Thirimont, 93-94, 151; elements sent from Malmédy to Spa and back, 293-94; elements in Malmédy with 120th Infantry Regiment, 295-96, 303-20, 350-53, 356-57; withdrawal from Malmédy and reassembling of, 359, 360-61

Company C, 12-13, 29, 36, 43, 101-2, 366, 367; sawmills run by, 24, 44; on Dec. 17, 61, 62-65, 188-94, 291; ordered to Malmédy, 177; roadblock above bridge at Stavelot, 177, 190, 191, 192, 207-8, 213-17, 220-21, 225-227, 229-30, 236, 238, 243-44, 361-362; detachment at Trois Ponts, 218, 225; ordered to Modave, 243, 258, 270; roadblocks at Malmédy relieved, 290; elements sent from Malmédy to Spa and back, 293-94; elements in Malmédy with 120th Infantry Regiment, 296, 332, 333, 338, 354; elements on Meuse barrier line, 322, 323-24, 330-31, 347-48, 350; reassembling of, 359-61; recovery of bodies at Five Points, 367-68; and bridge across Our River, 368-69

Conlin, Capt. John T., 13, 48, 49, 50-51, 54, 55, 228; in Malmédy Dec. 17, 67, 176, 180; and Malmédy defense plans, 69, 72, 84, 86-87; trip from Malmédy to Spa and back, 293-94; in battle at Malmédy, 303; and bombing of Malmédy by U.S. B-24 planes, 350-51, 352

Conneux, 348

Consiglio, T/5 Vincent, 68, 84 n, 88, 303-10, 313-17

Corcoran, Sgt., 299, 332

Cornes, Sgt. Tommy, 240

Corps, V, 12, 14, 15, 60, 108; assignment to take Urft-Roer dams, 21, 22-24; seam at joining with VIII Corps, 22, 117, 130; on Meuse barrier line, 324-25, 328, 330; and Allied counteroffensive, 363

Corps, VII, 14, 21, 99, 324-26, 328, 329, 330, 363

Corps, VIII, 14, 15, 21, 22, 23, 60, 108, 113, 187; seam at joining with V Corps, 22, 117, 130; and Meuse barrier line, 325, 326

Coupe, John, 324

Courvillion, Pfc. George, 53-54

Crickenberger, Sgt. Bill, 189, 299; on reconnaissance with Pergrin, 177-80, 182-83

Currey, Pfc. Francis, 313-14

Dachau trial, 368
Dalhem, 105, 120, 125

Index

Damon, Lt. Col., 148–49
Danube River, 375, 376
Daub, Carl R., 168
Davis, Lt. Donald T., 190–93, 295, 296
Death's Head units, 120, 161
Deidenberg, 52, 78, 80–81, 140, 368
Dennington, Cpl., 38–39, 202–3
Devers, Lt. Gen. Jacob L., 14
Devine, Col. Mark, 140–49
Diaz, Pfc., 197
Diefenthal, Maj. Josef, 122, 137, 139, 159, 210
Dietrich, Gen. Sepp, 105–6, 109, 117, 125, 132, 297, 347; attack on northern shoulder, 298, 302, 303, 368; and 3rd Parachute Battalion, 334, 335
Dinant, 110, 329, 345, 347, 348
Dishaw, Sgt. Charles, 88, 173, 179, 184–185
Dixon, T/4 Merlin, 241
Dobyns, Samuel, 161, 166, 167
Dolcha, Sgt. Frank, 369
Duggan, Lt. Col. Augustine, 148
Dymond, Pfc. Louis T., 53, 57

Echternach, 110, 325
Edelstein, Lt. Alvin, 30, 196, 270, 322; and blowing of Habiemont bridge, 248, 257, 260, 261, 362
Eifel, 122, 134. *See also* Schnee Eifel
Eisenhower, Gen. Dwight D., 15, 19, 22–23, 71, 112, 250; German plot to kidnap, 104, 127–28; creates Meuse barrier line and gives command of top half to Montgomery, 321, 326–328, 364, 365; crisis with Montgomery, 371–73
Ekman, Col. William, 275, 279–80, 281
Elliott, T/4 Jeff, 10, 76, 77–78, 139–40, 226, 244; delivers bazookas to Malmédy, 203–6
Elsenborn, 13, 60, 70, 75, 107, 329
Elsenborn shoulder, 289, 298, 322, 335–336
Emptinne, 323, 346, 360
Engel, Gen. Gerhard, 124, 125
Engineer Combat Battalion, 51st, 8, 11–12, 322; Company C of, and battle of Trois Ponts, 225, 239–47, 250, 272–73, 274–75, 279, 281–83, 362; on

Meuse barrier line, 322, 345, 359–60
Engineer Combat Battalion, 168th, 76
Engineer Combat Battalion, 202nd, 219; Company C of, 219–20, 231, 233–34
Engineer Combat Battalion, 254th, 136
Engineer Combat Battalion, 291st: activation, 5; NCO cadre, 5, 6, 9; training, 5–7; designation, March, 1943, 6; assigned to 1111th Engineer Combat Group, 8; in England, 8; in France, 9–11, 33; in southern Belgium and Luxembourg, 10, 11, 101–2; at Hockai, 11, 102; positions Oct.–Nov., 1944, 11, 12–13, 32; assigned as security battalion of Group in Trois Ponts area, 12; headquarters at Haute Bodeux, 12; character of men, 16–18; communications, 28–29; motor pool, 44–45, 244; on night of Dec. 17–18, 226, 286; headquarters moved to Modave, 242, 248, 256–57, 268–70; elements in Malmédy with 120th Infantry Regiment, 295–96, 297, 298–299, 350–59; elements on Meuse barrier line, 322–23, 329, 330–31, 345–46, 347–48; released by 30th Infantry Division and commended by Hobbs, 357–58; in Allied counteroffensive, 365–69; at Remagen, 373–74; in Germany and Austria, 374–75; end of duty, 375–76
Engineer Combat Battalion, 296th, 8, 12, 322
Engineer Combat Battalion, 300th, 360
Engineer Combat Battalion, 308th, 360
Engineer Combat Group, 1111th, 8, 11, 14, 23, 365, 368; headquarters at Trois Ponts, 12, 28, 44; communications, 28–30; security alert received by, 58; headquarters moved to Modave, 248, 256–57, 268–70. *See also* Anderson, Col. H. W.
Engineer Combat Group, 1115th, 6
Engineer Combat Group, 1186th, 365
Engineer Combat Regiment, 82nd, 5, 6
Engineer Light Equipment Company, 629th, 70, 91, 136, 185–86, 263, 270
Engineer Maintenance Company, 962nd, 70, 185–86

Engis, 118
Ettelbruck, 101-2
Eupen, 13, 24, 31-33, 72; Skorzeny unit captured near, 127; 30th Infantry Division moved to, 187-88, 251, 288-89
Eupen District, 31-34
Eupen road, 85, 90
Eupen-St. Vith highway, 48

Falaise, 98, 327, 328
Faymonville, 23-24, 144-45, 209-10
Field Artillery Battalion, 118th, 253-54
Field Artillery Observation Battalion, 285th, Battery B serials, 91-94, 151-152; arrival at Five Points, 155-57; shelling and surrender of, 157-64; execution of prisoners, 165-70; survivors of massacre, 170-72, 179-81, 183, 184-85, 195, 201-2; recovery of bodies, 367-68
Field Evacuation Hospital, 44th, 47, 174
Fifth Column, 32-33
Fighter Group, 366th, 138
Five Points (Baugnez), 51-52, 311; roadblock on Highway N-32 near, 84, 88, 199, 286-87, 292-93, 311, 319; Battery B of 285th Field Observation Battalion heads for, 92, 94; German tanks at, 139; on German march route, 149-50, 151. *See also* Five Points massacre
Five Points massacre, 155-70, 320; survivors of, 170-72, 179-81, 183, 184-185, 195, 201-2; heard by Company B, 173-74, 178-79; reported to First Army headquarters, 181; publicized as Malmédy Massacre, 172 n, 181-182; recovery of bodies, 367-68
Fleps, Pvt. George, 165, 166-67
Foelkersam, German officer, 318
Ford, Pfc. Homer, 155, 157-59, 160-61, 167, 171, 179, 181
Forges, 254, 257, 260, 264, 266
Fort Belvoir, 7, 8, 26
Francorchamps, 46, 118, 187, 291, 339, 366; gas dump south of, 46, 123, 229, 300; withdrawal of Americans from Stavelot toward, 232; burning of gas dump, 233-34, 235

Frankland, Lt. Col. Ernest, 234, 253, 289-90, 294-95
Frazer, Lt. Col. Harvey, 250
Frederick the Great, 98
French Army, 14
French II Corps, 99-100
Fresina, Cpl. Vincent, 53-54
Friedmann, Pfc., 207
Froidville, 43, 259
Führer. *See* Hitler, Adolf

Gadziola, Pfc., 207, 214, 216
Gamble, Capt. James H., 24-30, 34, 35, 203, 238, 240, 368; leads Company A to Amblève, 42-53, 56; move from Amblève Dec. 17, 75-78, 81-82, 138, 140, 196-98; ordered to Stavelot, 225-27, 236; on Meuse barrier line, 324, 353, 360
Gavin, Maj. Gen. James M., 251, 257, 265-66, 271, 278, 328
Gdoumont road, 64, 183; roadblocks on, 85, 88, 290, 295
Geilenkirchen, 235
German-Belgian border towns, 30-34
German breakthrough: rumors of, 53-54, 56, 63; security alert regarding, 58; on 99th Infantry Division front, 65, 69, 70-72; at Butgenbach, 70-72, 73, 91, 93, 209; at St. Vith, 76, 77, 82-83; at Losheim Gap, 81, 117
German infantry, 115
German offensive: Hitler's concept, 97-101; plan for attack, 101; buildup, 102-7; opening day postponed, 104; Hitler's instructions to generals, 107-111; northern shoulder, 108, 132, 146, 363, 364; secrecy of, 111-13; opening of, 114-17; march routes, 118-19; assault on northern shoulder, 297-98, 302, 303, 334, 345; assault on northern shoulder at Malmédy, 302-20; and Meuse barrier line, 321; Peiper's spearhead ended, 345; drive to west stopped, 359, 360; and crisis in Allied command, 371-73
Gerow, Maj. Gen. Leonard T., 21, 22, 23, 60, 117, 288-89, 363, 364
Givet, 326, 328, 330, 345
Goebbels, Joseph Paul, 99

Index

Goldstein, Pvt. Bernard, 207, 213 n, 214–17, 223–25, 227–28, 351
Grand Ensille, 360
Grand-Halleux, 13, 32; Company A's 1st platoon at, 24, 35, 36, 54; move from, 56, 75, 82–83, 237
Grant, Gen. Ulysses S., 326
Green, Capt. Seymour, 209–11
Gregoire, Mme Regine, 301
Grohe, Gauleiter, 111
Guingand, Maj. Gen. Francis de, 372–373

Habiemont, 42
Habiemont bridge, 43, 102; wired and blown, 247–48, 254–57, 259–63, 362
Hahne, Pfc., 207
Haid, 348
Hall, Pvt. Arnold, 375
Hallschlag, 125
Hamois, 322–23, 353
Hansen, Lt. Col. H. D., 188, 198–201, 206, 287, 289, 295
Hanssen, Col., 121
Haran, Pfc. Daniel, 299
Harmon, Maj. Gen. Ernest N., 348–49, 353
Haute Bodeux, 43, 69, 275, 283; battalion headquarters in, 12, 24, 55, 56; telephone line to Trois Ponts cut, 56–58, 59; Dec. 17 in, 61–62, 189–90; Lampp sent to CP at, 86; radio contact with Malmédy lost, 201; Walters reaches, 238–39; battalion headquarters leaves, 242, 268; Group headquarters moves to, 242–43, 247, 256
Haversin, 360
Hayes, Lt. Frank R., 30, 42, 53, 76, 77–78, 203, 243, 257, 265, 353–54
Hayes, Lt. Col. John R., 7
Hebert, T/4 Burnie, 356–57
Hechler, Maj. Kenneth W.: Peiper's account of Stavelot told to, 221–22
Heeresbach, 144
Heerlen, 71, 92
Helle River, 336
Hensel, Sgt. Charles: and roadblock above Stavelot bridge, 207–8, 213–18, 221–22; at Trois Ponts, 218, 224

Heppenbach, 118, 134, 138, 139
Hernandez, Pfc. Louis, 197
Heure, 323, 360
Heydte, Baron Friedrich A. von der, 104–6, 109, 132, 334–36
Higgins, of 526th Armored Infantry, 242
Highway N-15, 42
Highway N-23, 42, 43, 45, 51, 52, 255–256; viaduct on, 45, 85; on German march route, 118, 159, 259; at Five Points, 157; Skorzeny's attack along, 303
Highway N-26, 119
Highway N-32, 47, 48, 51, 52, 85; on Dec. 17, 64, 66–67, 68–69, 93, 94, 178; roadblock near Five Points, 84, 88, 199, 286–87, 292–93, 311, 319; on German march route, 119, 146, 151; American defense positions on, 193–194, 296, 320; Skorzeny's attack along, 302–3, 310–11; wiring of trees on, 339
Highway N-33, 45: on 7th Armored Division route, 72, 83, 196–97
Highway N-36, 353
Himmler, Heinrich, 129
Hinkel, S/Sgt. Paul, 61, 238, 239 n, 244, 245; in battle of Trois Ponts, 247, 272–73, 274, 280, 282
Hitler, Adolf, 123, 129, 182, 188, 335, 364, 371; political distinction between sections of Belgium, 32; concept of Ardennes offensive, 97–101; and *Sixth Panzer Army*, 98–99, 100, 108–109, 112, 117; "unalterable" plan, 102; instructions to Skorzeny, 102–3; opening day of offensive postponed, 104; headquarters moved to Ziegenberg, 107; meeting with division commanders and speech to, 107–11, 123–24; and Wehrmacht, 108–9; success in maintaining secrecy, 111–13; directive to armies regarding civilians, 301
Hitzfeld LXVII Corps, 115
Hobbs, Maj. Gen. Leland S., 188, 251–252, 275, 288–89, 341, 355; releases and commends 291st Engineers, 357–58
Hockai, 11, 102

Hodges, Maj. Gen. Courtney H., 12, 14, 21, 23, 60, 250, 251–52, 324–26, 328, 364; reports of Pergrin to, 187, 361
Höfen, 115
Hoge, Brig. Gen. William M., 23–24, 144–45, 210
Hogne, 323, 360
Holbrook, Pfc. Wiley, 197, 310, 313, 337
Holland, 14, 105, 111, 335
Hollenbeck, of 526th Armored Infantry, 242
Hollerath, 117, 118
Holzheim, 139, 276; 14th Cavalry units in, 143–44, 146
Honsfeld, 32, 75, 118, 131; Peiper in, 133–35, 146; American planes over, Dec. 17, 68, 74–75, 135
Horrocks, Maj. Gen. Percy B., 321
Hotton, 274, 322, 329, 345
Houffalize, 42, 363
Hungary: Skorzeny in, 102
Hürtgen Forest, 14, 19–20, 22, 100
Huy, 42, 110, 118, 124, 212, 258, 263; blocking access to, 247; 291st roadblock near, 266, 284

Infantry Battalion (Separate), 99th. See Norwegian Battalion
Infantry Division, 1st, 187, 295, 296, 296, 298, 324–25
Infantry Division, 2nd, 21, 22, 141–42, 187; attack toward Urft-Roer dams, 22, 23–24, 60, 115–17, 209–10; German offensive considered counterattack against, 54, 56, 70; on Elsenborn shoulder, 288–89, 298
Infantry Division, 4th, 20, 22, 325
Infantry Division, 8th, 21
Infantry Division, 28th, 20, 22, 113
Infantry Division, 30th, 187–88, 251, 294, 298, 330, 342; engineers blow Stavelot bridge, 236, 254; 30th Reconnaissance Troop, 288–89; drive on La Gleize and Stoumont, 342, 343; 291st Engineers released by, 357–358; and Allied counteroffensive, 367, 369
Infantry Division, 75th, 325–26
Infantry Division, 78th, 21, 373–74
Infantry Division, 84th, 256, 269, 325, 329, 330
Infantry Division, 90th, 98
Infantry Division, 99th, 21–22, 23, 60, 81, 108, 112, 187, 374; break through line of, 65, 69, 70–72, 209; resistance to Germans, 115–17; Intelligence and Reconnaissance platoon, 22, 130–31, 141; forces at Buchholz overwhelmed, 131, 132–33; headquarters moved from Butgenbach, 136; loss of contact with 14th Cavalry, 142, 144; on Elsenborn shoulder, 288–89, 298; accepts von der Heydte's surrender, 336
Infantry Division, 106th, 22, 35–36, 52, 53, 112, 140, 141; 7th Armored Division ordered to help, 60, 71–72; regiments in Schnee Eifel, 110, 143, 144, 145; loss of contact, 142
Infantry Regiment, 16th: en route from Aachen to Waimes, 63–64, 127
Infantry Regiment, 26th, 60, 137; ambulance of, 92–93, 157, 161, 183
Infantry Regiment, 117th, 234, 235, 275–76, 289–90, 291, 294–95, 296, 300, 319, 342
Infantry Regiment, 119th, 251, 252, 263, 266, 278, 294, 329, 368; enters La Gleize, 344
Infantry Regiment, 120th: in command at Malmédy, 294–97, 298–99, 302–20, 333, 337–41; Company K of 3rd Battalion, 298, 305–10, 313–17, 337; and bombing of Malmédy by U.S. B-24 planes, 350–56
Infantry Regiment, 394th, 133–34
Infantry Regiment, 395th, 336
Infantry Regiment, 423rd: 2nd Battalion, 52, 57
Intelligence, Allied: overconfidence of, 111–13
Irox, 118
Isar River, 375

Jodl, Col. Gen. Alfred, 97, 101
Joehnck, Lt. Leroy H., 71, 352

Index

Jones, Maj. Gen. Alan W., 52, 57, 150; and Col. Mark Devine, 141–48
Jones, Lt. Alan W., Jr., 145
Josephs, Sgt. Joe, 219–20, 233–34

Kaiserbaracke crossroads, 140; Devine-Peiper skirmish at, 147–48; Peiper at, 149–50, 211; skirmishes of Dec. 18, 212
Kamen, Capt. Paul, 195, 201, 375
Kampfgruppe Peiper, 121–23, 124, 275; advance elements in Büllingen, 134, 136, 137; section sent north of Ligneuville, 139, 164; northern route of, 139, 151; at Five Points, 158–72; at Ligneuville, 208–12; at Stoumont, 298; leaves La Gleize, 343–45. *See also* Peiper, Lt. Col. Jochen
Kampfgruppe von der Heydte, 106, 334–36; supplies dropped for, 36, 54; parachute drop postponed, 107, 132; drop of Dec. 17, 59–60, 132, 334–35
Kaplita, Capt. Walter, 195
Kayser, Lt., 334
Kean, Maj. Gen. William B., 181
Keitel, Field Marshal Wilhelm, 97
Kelakos, Major, 210
Keoghan, Sgt. Ed, 62–65, 232–34, 291–292, 347–48, 360
King, Cpl. John, 323
Kingston, Kenneth, 168
Kirkpatrick, Lt. John C., 65–66, 190–191, 217–19
Knittel, Maj. Gustave, 121, 123, 277
Kobscheid, 21, 81, 140–41, 142
Koenig, Pvt. Bernard, 34 n, 50, 67, 84 n, 85 n, 356; at roadblock on Gdoumont road, 90–91, 183, 184, 194, 253, 286, 290; trip from Malmédy to Spa and back, 293–94; in battle of Malmédy and aftermath, 296, 312, 337
Koewitz, Cpl., 165
Kovacs, T/4 Louis, 254, 255–56, 262–63
Kraemer, Gen. Fritz, 105–6, 109–10, 121–22
Krenser, Lt., 149
Krewinkel, 81, 140–41, 142, 143
Krinkelt, 32, 119, 297
Kronenberg, 125

La Gleize, 32, 43, 66, 118; Company C at, 12–13, 24, 36; Dec. 17 in, 61, 62, 188–92; Company C's 3rd platoon ordered to, 65, 291; unit of 51st Engineers at, 225; Company C's headquarters moved from, 243, 258; Peiper's swing toward 243–45, 251–52; Peiper at, 257–58, 267, 270, 276–77, 278, 329; comes under Ridgway's command, 271; on Meuse barrier line, 330; Peiper leaves and Americans enter, 342–45; German pocket near, 344–45
Lambermont, 210
Lampp, Capt. Edward R., 8, 69–70, 86, 189–90, 243, 247–48, 359; en route to Modave, 269–70; promotion to major, 366
Lanzerath, 21–22, 81, 118, 140–41, 142, 368; Peiper's drive to, 126, 128, 129–132; 14th Cavalry's effort to retake, 143
La Reid, 200
Lary, Lt. Virgil T., 92, 152, 156, 162–164, 166, 167; escape of, 169–72, 185, 201–2
Lassen, Lt. Phillip, 87, 88, 157
Lauchert, Col. Meinrad von, 329, 349
Leary, Pfc. John, 207, 214, 216
Ledet, T/4 Curtis, 294
Legaye residence, 45, 300–301
Leignon, 348
Lejoly, Henri, 155, 157, 158, 160, 167
Lesse River, 345
Liebstandarte. See *Panzer Division, 1st SS*
Liège, 11, 13, 15, 42, 44, 187–88, 208, 321; and Hitler's plan of attack, 101, 106, 108, 109–10, 117; unassigned men in Malmédy ordered to, 176; paratroopers near, 334
Liège Province, 12
Lienne Creek, 42–43, 271, 283, 362; Peiper's route along, 258–59, 266–67
Lienne valley, 42–43
Lierneux, 43, 118, 260
Ligneuville, 32, 67, 79, 114, 151, 164, 319; on 7th Armored Division route, 72, 92, 175; on Peiper's march route, 118, 134–35, 149; Peiper's plan to

Ligneuville (cont'd)
envelop, 135, 139; Germans enter, 208-12
Liparulo, Pfc. Lorenzo, 217-18, 223-24, 227-28
Lippspringe, 107, 132
Lodomez, 301
Longuyon, 11, 102
Losheim, 32, 118, 124, 125, 126, 128
Losheimergraben, 12, 105, 115, 118, 135, 297
Losheim Gap, 14, 21, 22, 108; German breakthrough at, 81, 117; 14th Cavalry units in, 21, 140-41
Lufsey, T/4 Edward, 255, 256, 262
Lundberg, Capt., 245, 251, 268
Luxembourg, 20, 31, 44, 110, 111, 113; 291st Engineers in, 10, 11, 101-2
Lynch, Pfc. Francis, 207, 214, 216, 217

McCarl, Mess Sgt., 323, 353-54
McCarty, M/Sgt. Ralph W., 84 n, 177-178, 180, 183, 298, 368-69; and roadblocks on Stavelot road, 182, 194, 202, 294, 295; in battle of Malmédy and aftermath, 303-4, 310, 312, 313, 332-33, 338, 339; promotion to lieutenant, 366
McClements, Pfc. John, 207
McCollum, of 526th Armored Infantry, 242
McCown, Maj. Hal, 252, 263, 266, 267, 343-44, 362
McDonald, Cpl. Isaac O., 197, 202, 313
McKinsey, Capt. Bill, 324, 374
McVay, Pfc. John J., 353
Madame Bodarwé's café, 157, 158, 160, 171-72, 178, 182. See also Bodarwé, Mme Adèle
Magliocco, Sgt., 193
Malmédy, 15, 35, 36, 102, 118; Company B in, 12, 13, 24, 29, 33-34, 36-37, 48; Germanic character of, 31, 32-34, 319-20; touched by Company A en route to Born, 42, 46-47, 50, 114, 117; importance of, 47, 187-88, 236; shelling of Dec. 16, 48-50, 54-55, 114, 209, 320; Dec. 17 in, 65, 67, 69, 174-86; Pergrin moves to, 70-71,

72; on 7th Armored Division route, 72, 150; defense organized, 84-94; opening guns of "Malmédy Massacre" heard at, 94, 151; Skorzeny unit in and report to Skorzeny, 127, 157, 302; and Kaiserbaracke crossroads, 149-50; reinforcement of, 187-206, 286-90; shelling of Dec. 18, 201, 290, 296; believed in German hands, 204, 269, 288-89, 293, 319, 320, 355; retreat from Stavelot to, 231-32, 235; civilian refugees from, 247; 291st roadblocks relieved, 290, 295; attack of Dec. 19, 294; defense under 120th Infantry Regiment, 294-97, 298-99; Skorzeny's attack on, 297, 302-20, 332; on Meuse barrier line, 330; railroad bridges blown and more mines laid, 337-39; bombed by U.S. B-24 planes, 340-41, 350-56; Christmas in, 354-55; withdrawal of 291st Engineers from and reassignment to, 358-360; and Allied counteroffensive, 363, 364, 367
Malmédy District, 31-34
Malmédy Massacre. See Five Points massacre
Malmédy-St. Vith highway, 147, 148, 149, 151, 328
Malmédy-Spa back road, 85; abatis defense on, 90, 193, 198
Manderfeld, 32, 118, 139, 141, 297
Manhay, 330
Manteuffel, Baron Hasso von, 110, 142, 321, 328-29; drive toward Namur, Dinant and Givet, 345, 347, 361, 364
Manx, Marthe, 201
Marche, 11-12, 324, 325, 329, 330, 348, 359; British probe toward, 345-46, 347
Marmegen, 121
Martin, "Mother," 193
Martinez, Sgt., 353
Massara, Pvt. James P., 166, 167-68, 169-71, 184
Matthews, Col. Church M. U., 150
Mayes, Maj. J. L., 143
Mean, 326
Mehogne, 360
Melreux, 225, 239

Index

Melton, S/Sgt. Albert D., 84 n, 190, 193
Menil, 117, 118
Merlscheid, 81, 141
Metz, 19, 265
Meuse barrier line, 293, 321–31, 345–349; on Christmas Day, 353–54
Meuse River, 19; and Hitler's plan of attack, 101, 103, 106, 108, 109–10, 111, 123, 124, 297; German march routes crossing, 117, 118; threatened by Peiper, 243, 252
Meyrode, 77, 144, 146
Middleton, Maj. Gen. Troy, 14, 21, 22, 60, 144–45, 271
Military Police, 518th, 47, 156
Miller, Pfc. Abraham, 255, 260, 265
Miller, Sgt. Jean B., 238, 241, 248–50, 273–74, 344, 367
Mitchell, Pvt. William, 303–4, 307, 313
Modave, 118, 332; assembling of 1111th Engineer Combat Group units at, 242, 243, 248, 250, 256, 258, 267–70, 284–85, 291; 291st units at, Dec. 19, 321–22; Christmas in, 354; reassembling of 291st Engineers at, 358–61
Model, Field Marshal Walther, 99, 102, 105, 364
Moderscheid, 139, 150
Mohnke, SS Gen. Wilhelm, 117, 121–124, 211, 212, 342; and attempt to retake Stavelot, 254, 275–76; at Petit Spai bridge, 277–78, 279–80; and battle at Malmédy, 297, 318; failure to help Peiper, 342–43
Mon Rigi crossroads, 60, 93, 288; traffic jam of Dec. 17, 63–64; road signs changed by saboteurs, 63–64, 127; German paratroopers' rendezvous at, 334–35
Monschau, 21, 23, 24, 108, 115, 329, 336, 363
Monschau-Echternach line. *See* Ardennes front
Montenau, 13, 24, 28, 31, 32, 34, 35, 52, 368; move of Company A's 3rd platoon from, Dec. 17, 75–76, 78–81
Montgomery, Field Marshal Sir Bernard L., 14, 23, 98, 112; and Meuse barrier line, 321, 326–28, 330, 345, 346–47, 348; and Allied counteroffensive, 363, 365; crisis with Eisenhower, 371–73
Moore, Cpl. Andy, 299
Morello, Pfc. Angelo, 197
Moressée, 360
Morris, Cpl. Eugene, 207, 213, 214, 216
Morschheck, 137, 287
Mortain, 10
Mourmelon, 251, 265
Moyer, Capt. Lawrence R., 177, 189–193, 217, 293–94, 350–51, 366
Munich, 375
Munoz, Sgt. 90, 184, 296, 333, 337
Murphy, Pfc. Dennis, 332
Mussolini, Benito, 102

Namur, 101, 110, 345, 347
Nessonvaux, 118
Nettine, 323, 360
Nickell, Pfc. Shorty, 255, 260, 261–62
Nijmegen, 250
Noland, T/5 John T., 313
Norwegian Battalion, 188, 198, 199–200, 206, 286, 287, 292, 296, 320; attached to 30th Infantry Division, 295; Company B of, 295, 311–12
November, 1944, Allied offensive, 19–21, 100

O'Brien, Lt. Col. Robert E., 336
Oliver, Cpl. Rufus, 56
Omaha Beach, 9
Ombret Rausa, 118, 124, 212
Ondenval, 139, 151
Operation Greif, 103–4, 127
Ormont, 125
Our River, 329, 368–69; bridge at Andler, 142–43, 144, 146
Ourthe River, 329, 345

Paderborn, 58, 106, 107, 132
Palmer, Pfc., 197
Paluch, T/5 Theodore, 168, 171–72, 183
Panzer Army, Fifth, 110, 117, 142, 276, 321, 345
Panzer Army, Sixth, 98, 100, 105–6, 108–10, 112, 120, 146; attack of Dec.

Panzer Army, Sixth (cont'd)
17, 115–17, 125, 142; conference at Manderfeld, 297; ordered to reduce northern shoulder, 298; and Allied counteroffensive, 364
Panzer Battalion, 506th, 146
Panzer Brigade, 150th, 103–4, 126, 297
Panzer Corps, I SS, 117–24, 276–77, 297
Panzer Division, 1st SS (Liebstandarte Adolf Hitler), 119–21, 126, 142, 161, 211, 275, 297, 364, 368; march routes, 117, 118; southern march group, 118–119, 123, 139, 142, 146, 276; Peiper given command of kampfgruppe, 121–23; begins to move, 125; and attempt to retake Stavelot, 275–76; murder of civilians by, 276, 300–301; remnants of Kampfgruppe Peiper reach command post, 344
Panzer Division, 2nd, 329, 345, 349
Panzer Division, 12th SS (Hitler Jugend), 106–7, 117–18, 119, 134, 212, 236, 276; postponement of parachute drop, 107, 126, 132; at Büllingen, 297
Panzer Division, 116th, 328–29, 345
Panzer Grenadier Regiment, 1st SS, 120, 121, 123, 139, 142, 143, 277, 342
Panzer Grenadier Regiment, 2nd SS, 120, 121, 122, 139, 212, 277, 278
Panzer Lehr Division, 329, 345, 348
Panzer Regiment, 1st SS, 120, 122, 139
Parachute Division, 3rd (German), 119, 139–40, 335; penetration of Losheim Gap, 117; advance of, 126, 142, 143, 146, 287
Parachute Field Artillery Battalion, 456th, 281
Parachute Infantry Regiment, 504th, 271, 278–79
Parachute Infantry Regiment, 505th, 271, 274–75, 279, 280–82, 283
Parachute Regiment, 9th (German), 126, 130, 136
Paratroopers, German: rumors of, 58–59, 66, 174; security alert regarding, 58, 85; drop of Dec. 17, 59–60, 132, 334–35; in woods near Sourbrodt, 63; hunt for, 240, 285; killed near Malmédy, 286–87, 320; fear of, and death of two Americans, 299; infiltration of Meuse barrier line, 322; surrender of, 355–36
Parfondry, 276, 301
Paris, 10
Patch, Lt. Gen. Alexander M., 14, 99–100
Patton, Lt. Gen. George S., Jr., 19, 71, 99–100, 327, 364. *See also* Army, Third
Peggy's tavern, 26, 30
Peiper, Lt. Col. Jochen, 121–26, 128–129, 368; drive to Lanzerath, 126, 128, 129–32; in Honsfeld, 133–35, 144, 146; in Büllingen, 135, 137; diversion southward through Amblève, Deidenberg and Born, 138–40, 146–47, 196, 211; at Kaiserbaracke, 147, 149–150; arrival at Stavelot, 196, 208, 212–213; at Ligneuville, 211–12; delay at Stavelot, 221–23, 243–44, 258, 361–62; diversion of Mark IV tanks around Wanne, 222, 235, 245, 248, 264; attack on Stavelot Dec. 18, 229–31, 235, 238, 276, 290; crosses Amblève at Stavelot, 230–31, 235–36, 251; approaches Trois Ponts, 241–42; at Amblève River bridge in Trois Ponts and swing toward La Gleize, 243–45, 251–52, 272; at La Gleize, 257–58, 267, 270, 329; in Cheneux area, 258, 271; route along Lienne Creek, 258–59, 266–67; at Habiemont bridge, 260–61, 265; reconnaissance group and probe toward Werbomont, 266–67; at Stoumont, 270, 278, 294, 298, 329; and German attempt to retake Stavelot, 276; situation Dec. 19, 276–77; loses Cheneux, 278–279; and attack on northern shoulder, 298, 302; leaves La Gleize, 342–45
Pepinster, 118
Pergrin, Col. David E., 7–9, 12, 18, 29, 63, 84 n, 174–75, 299; assignment to support CCB of 9th Armored, 23, 107; orders Company A to Born, 24–28, 111; and Capt. Conlin, 50–51; shelling of Malmédy reported to, 54–55; check on Company A at Born and Amblève, 55–56; security alert received by, 58, 59; breakthrough re-

Index

port of Conlin to, 69–70; move to Malmédy Dec. 17, 70–71, 72, 127; orders Company A to return to Werbomont, 72–73, 76; defense of Malmédy set up, 84–94; hears "little FOB outfit" fired on, 94, 152; Five Points massacre reported to, 170; and survivors of Five Points massacre, 172 n, 179–81, 183; and 440th Armored Field Artillery Battalion, 175–176; and reinforcement of Malmédy, 176–77, 183, 187–206, 289; determination to stay in Malmédy, 176–77, 198–99; orders Company C to Malmédy, 177, 188–89; reconnaissance toward Five Points, 177–80, 182–83; reports to First Army, 181, 187, 361; ordered to send units away from Malmédy, 185–86; interview with Lt. Virgil T. Lary, 201–2; and failure of Stavelot bridge to blow, 219, 220–21, 235; believed lost, 269, 330; and Dec. 18 in Malmédy, 287; ordered to Spa and back to Malmédy, 293–94; attached to 120th Infantry Regiment, 295; Skorzeny's attack and aftermath, 302, 303, 317, 333, 337, 338; and bombing of Malmédy by U.S. B-24 planes, 350–52; receives release and commendation from Hobbs, 357–58; removal to Modave and reorganization of battalion, 358–61; administrative changes made by, 365–66

Perkins, Lt. John J., 62–63, 64–65
Petit Spai, 301
Petit Spai bridge, 45, 277–78, 279–80, 342
Pigg, Sgt. Edwin: and blowing of Habiemont bridge, 248, 254–56, 259–260, 262–63, 270
Pioneer Company, 3rd SS, 166, 168–70
Pioneers, 122
Plance, 368
Poetschke, Major, 139, 159–60, 164, 166, 212, 222–23
Polish Mounted Rifle Regiment, 10th, 98
Pont, 150, 368
Poteau, 80, 81, 140, 276, 277, 342, 368; traffic jam at, Dec. 17, 78; on German march route, 118, 119; 14th Cavalry units in, 147, 148
Priess, SS Gen. Hermann, 117, 119, 126, 276–77, 297, 368
Priester, Pvt. Merion, 374
Prisoners of war, German: Hitler's demand for "wave of terror," 111; Peiper sets pattern of killing at Honsfeld, 135; at Büllingen, 138; at Ligneuville, 210–11. *See also* Five Points massacre
Profanchik, survivor of Five Points massacre, 168, 171
Proximity fuse shells, 312
Prum, 326, 328

Quesada, Maj. Gen. Elwood R. ("Pete"), 181, 251–53, 258, 355

Rabosse, 323
Rahier, 43, 271
Railroads: from Luxembourg to Liège, 44; from Stavelot to Malmédy, 47, 85; Malmédy defense positions along, 192–93; from Trois Ponts to Stavelot, 229
Recht, 72, 78, 80, 81, 92; on 7th Armored Division route, 92, 139, 150, 175; on German march route, 118, 139, 140; 14th Cavalry units in, 146–147; skirmishes of Dec. 18, 212
Recht River, 146
Reem, William, 167, 171, 180
Reims, 251
Remagen, 373–74
Remouchamps, 118, 200, 252
Renarmont, 276, 301
Renson, Red Ball, 88, 156–57
Reppa, Lt. Bob, 133, 144
Rhea, Lt. Frank W., 66, 67–69, 72, 84 n, 174–75; American planes sighted by, 68, 135; and Malmédy defense plans, 86–87, 90, 184, 194; in Malmédy with 120th Infantry Regiment, 295–96, 333, 337–39; promotion to captain, 352, 366
Rhine River: Allied offensives against, 19–21, 100, 112, 365, 371; bridges across, 102, 373–74, 375–76
Richardson, Pfc. Red, 203–6, 226

Ridgway, Maj. Gen. Matthew, 251, 271, 283, 364; and Montgomery, 328, 347
Robertson, Maj. Gen. Walter M., 23, 141. *See also* Infantry Division, 2nd
Robertville, 118
Rocherath, 32, 119, 297
Roer River, 19–20, 329
Roer River dams, 20–21, 112, 115–17. *See also* Urft-Roer dams, attack toward
Rolfes, Bob, 194
Rombaugh, Lt. Warren, 190–92, 207, 217, 218, 366
Rommel, Field Marshal Erwin: quoted on Montgomery, 327 n
Rondenell, Pvt. Johnny, 255, 260, 264, 266–67, 270, 362
Rosa, Sgt. Elio, 241, 246, 283
Rose, Maj. Gen. Maurice, 329
Roth, 81, 140–41, 142
Route de Falize, 85, 193, 296, 311–13; overpass blown, 337–38
Route de St. Vith, 85, 193, 338–39
Rumors: of German breakthrough, 53–54, 56, 63; of German parachute drops, 58–59, 66, 174
Runstedt, Field Marshal Gerd von, 99, 102, 112, 113, 365
Rupp, Peter, 210–11, 297

Saar sector, 71
Saboteurs, German. *See* Spies and saboteurs
St. Albans Victory, 375
St. Lô, 10
St. Vith, 31, 35, 52, 57, 211, 363; move of 7th Armored Division to, 60, 71–72, 78, 175; German attack on, 76, 77, 82–83, 187; on German march route, 110, 119, 181, 276; Col. Mark Devine's reports to headquarters at, 141, 144–45, 147–48; and Kaiserbaracke crossroads, 149–50; isolated by *Fifth Panzer Army*, 321; Allied withdrawal from, 328, 347; on Meuse barrier line, 330; retaken by Americans, 367, 368
St. Vith-Vielsalm-Menil highway, 117
Salazar, Pvt. Audres, 242

Salmchâteau, 11, 102, 330
Salm River, 43–44, 328–29, 344, 345; parachute drops reported west of, 36, 54; on German march route, 118; on Meuse barrier line, 330
Salm River bridges. *See under* Trois Ponts
Sandig, Col., 121
Sansbury, Pfc. Harry, 255, 256, 262
Santa Elena, 8
Sart, 118
Scanlon, T/Sgt. John L., 28, 34 n, 38–39, 55–56, 62, 150 n, 189, 242–43; en route to Modave, 268–70; brought to Malmédy, 299, 332–33, 358
Schaeffer, Cpl. Gerhard, 165
Scheid, 125
Schmidt, T/5 Warren, 164, 185
Schmidtheim, 121, 125
Schnee Eifel, 14, 21; 106th Infantry Division regiments in, 110, 143, 144, 145
Schommer, Cpl. A. C., 55, 57, 74–75, 135, 138, 202–3, 324
Schönberg, 146
Schoppen, 139, 149–50, 151, 161, 212
Schutzstaffel (SS), 119–20
Schwammenauel Dam, 20
Self, W.O. Coye R., 194
Self-propelled assault guns, 258–59
Seraing, 118
Seventh Army (German), 110
Seyss-Inquart, Artur von, 111
SHAEF, 250, 321, 372
Sheetz, Capt. Lloyd B., 8, 64, 69–70, 84 n, 181, 293–94
Shober, Capt. 246, 247
Siegfried Line. *See* West Wall
Simon, Gauleiter, 111
Simpson, Lt. Gen. William, 71
Sinsin, 323, 347, 360
Siptrott, M/Sgt. Hans, 165, 166
Skorzeny, Lt. Col. Otto, 102–4, 106, 121, 126–28, 211; attack on Malmédy, 297, 302–20, 332
Skorzeny units, 103–4, 122, 124–25, 126–27, 157, 302; on Stavelot road, 204–5; in Stavelot, 220, 253; blown up near N-32 roadblock, 292–93, 339; jeep-team scare and death of two Ameri-

Index

cans, 299; infiltration of Meuse barrier line, 322
Smith, Sgt. Sheldon T., 84 n, 190–91, 193–94, 286–87, 338, 354
Smith, S/Sgt. Walter J., 48, 65, 84 n, 251–52
Smith, 1/Sgt. William H., 27, 30, 54, 57, 76, 77, 197, 203, 243, 265; reconnaissance of Dec. 17, 74–75, 135, 138
Smith, survivor of Five Points massacre, 168, 171
Snow, Pvt. James N., 245
Solis, Maj. Paul, 200; and battle of Stavelot, 228–36, 291
Somal, 360
Sombernon, 100
Sosa, Pfc., 207
Sourbrodt, 12, 13, 24, 31, 32, 36, 60, 118; Dec. 17 in, 62, 65, 191, 291
Spa, 13, 15–16, 107, 110, 118, 187; First Army headquarters in, 12, 29, 30, 32; gas dumps around, 123; Anderson's messengers sent to, 242, 245; conferences of Dec. 18, 251–52; evacuation of First Army headquarters from, 293–94, 324, 326; elements of 291st Engineers in, Dec. 19, 293–94; 291st Engineers reassigned to, 359, 360, 365
Spies and saboteurs, German, 59, 63–64; *See also* Skorzeny units
Spires, Pvt. Joseph, 197, 303–4, 306, 307, 313, 314
Sprenger, Pvt. Gustav, 168–69
SS. *See* Schutzstaffel
Stack, Lt. Thomas F., 71, 84 n, 176–77, 180, 181, 182, 366; return to Malmédy, 287–88, 352
Stars & Stripes, 354
Stavelot, 13, 15, 24, 32, 107, 118, 294; touched by Company A moving toward Born, 42, 45–46, 114; Company B sawmill in, 45, 48, 65, 300; Amblève River bridge, 46, 86; Dec. 17 in, 65, 67, 82; on 7th Armored Division route, 72, 176; roadblock above bridge, 177, 190, 191, 192, 207–8, 213–217, 220–21, 225–27, 229–30, 236, 238, 243–44, 361–62; Peiper at, 196, 208, 212–13, 221–23, 300–301; units of

526th Armored Infantry diverted to, 199, 200; evacuation of 49th AAA Brigade through, 210, 212–13; wiring of bridge and failure to blow, 218–20, 230–31, 235, 236; battle of, 229–36; bridge destroyed, 236, 254, 277; civilian refugees from, 247; retaken by Americans, 253–54; comes under command of Ridgway, 271; German attempt to retake, 275–77; 1st Battalion, 117th Infantry, ordered to, 289–90, 300; murder of civilians in, 300–301; on Meuse barrier line, 330; German paratroopers near, 334; German pocket near, 344–45
Stavelot road, 204, 239; Company B roadblocks on, 182, 194, 202, 294, 295; on night of Dec. 17–18, 195, 204–5, 208, 212–13; and defense of Malmédy, 296, 298; blocked off, 338
Steinfort, 101
Ster, 276, 301
Stoumont, 43, 252, 271, 294; Peiper at, 270, 276–77, 278, 294, 298, 329; 30th Infantry Division's drive on, 342, 343
Swift, S/Sgt. Douglas, 375

Tactical Air Command, 9th, 251–53, 254, 258, 355
Tank Battalion, 740th, 278
Tank Battalion, 743rd, 275
Tank Destroyer Battalion, 612th, 136
Tank Destroyer Battalion, 820th. *See* Cavalry Group, 14th
Tank Destroyer Battalion, 823rd, 263, 275; command post of, in battle at Malmédy, 305–10, 317
Tank Destroyer Battalion, 825th, Company A of, 188, 199–200, 206; at Malmédy, 188, 199–200, 206, 312; in battle of Stavelot, 229, 230, 231–32
Tank Destroyer Battalion, 843rd, 253
Targnon, 43, 270, 278
Taylor, Lt. Archibald L., 34–35, 52, 240, 368; move from Montenau Dec. 17, 75–76, 78–81, 140, 146, 151; ordered to Stavelot, 226–27; on Meuse barrier line, 322–23, 353–54, 360
Taylor, Maj. Gen. Maxwell, 336

Theodoseau, Pfc. Nick, 202–3, 332, 333
Theux, 118, 251
Thirimont, 79, 93–94; on Kampfgruppe Peiper's march route, 139, 151, 212
Thorne, Pfc., 255, 260, 265
Thurston, Cpl., 55, 61–62, 268–69
Tiger Royal tanks, 258–59
Tilff, 188
Timberlake, Brig. Gen. E. J., 52; and move of 49th AAA Brigade from Ligneuville, 208–10, 212–13
Tintari, Lt. Martin, 190
Tondorf, 121
Tongres, 326
Treaty of Versailles, 31
Trois Ponts, 13, 15, 32, 54, 294, 322; 1111th Engineer Combat Group headquarters in, 12, 28; touched by Company A moving toward Born, 42, 43–45, 114; bridges of, 43–44, 102; telephone line to Haute Bodeux cut, 56–58, 59; Dec. 17 in, 61, 71, 190; on 7th Armored Division route, 72, 83, 176, 246–47; on German march route, 118, 212; roadblock at Amblève River bridge, 190, 191, 192, 218, 225; roadblock on Stavelot road, 204; Peiper sends tanks toward, 222, 235; preparation of defense, 225, 237–41; Amblève River bridge wired and blown, 239, 242, 243, 251; Salm River bridge wired, blown, repaired and blown again, 239, 246–47, 279, 283; lower Salm River bridge wired and blown, 240–41, 248–50; battle of, 241–250, 272–75, 279–83; civilian refugees from, 255–56; comes under command of Ridgway, 271; German reinforcements ordered to, 277; civilians murdered at, 301; on Meuse barrier line, 330; German pocket near, 342, 344–45; 291st Engineers reassigned to, 359, 366–67
Tucker Bridge, 9

Udenbreth, 118, 119
Urft-Roer dams, attack toward, 22, 23–24, 60, 107, 141, 209–10; German offensive considered counterattack to, 54, 71. *See also* Roer River dams

Vandervoort, Lt. Col. Benjamin, 279, 281–82
Vaux Chavanne, 330
Verviers, 13, 72, 92, 118, 187
Vianden, 110
Vielsalm, 13, 24, 35, 45, 110; on 7th Armored Division route, 72, 78, 82; on German march route, 117, 118; 14th Cavalry units in, 141, 142; 440th Armored Field Artillery Battalion en route to, 175–76
Vogt, Pvt., 165
Volksgrenadiers, 12th, 119, 124; attack on Losheim, 125, 145
Volksgrenadiers, 18th, 142, 145
Volksgrenadiers, 277th, 119

Waimes, 32, 190–91, 295, 296, 298; 16th Infantry Regiment en route to, 63–64, 127, 324–25
Wallerode, 118, 139, 140, 146
Walters, Lt. Albert W., 35–36, 54, 56, 212, 322, 323; move from Grand-Halleux Dec. 17, 75, 82–83, 195, 197–198, 237–39; in Trois Ponts, 240–41, 245–46, 247, 250, 254, 270, 272, 273–74, 275, 279, 281–82; en route to Haute Bodeux and Modave, 283–85
Wandre, 118
Wanne, 44, 45, 83, 301, 342; on German march route, 118, 211–12; diversion of Mark IV companies around, 222, 235, 245, 248, 264; Kampfgruppe Peiper remnants reach, 344
Wanne hill: and battle of Trois Ponts, 245, 279, 280
Warche River, 47; bridge near Malmédy, 46, 194, 202, 295, 298, 303–5, 337, 367
"Watch on the Rhine," 102, 104, 112. *See also* German offensive
Ward, Col., 341
Webb, Maj., 242, 251, 268
Weckerath, 140–41, 143
Wehrmacht: Hitler and, 108–9
Weiss, Pvt. Jacob, 168–69
Werbomont, 13, 15, 32, 42, 110; Company A in, 12, 24–27, 34, 35, 53; Company A's departure from, 38–42, 114; return of Company A to, 73,

Index

75, 76, 197, 202–3, 362; assembly of 82nd Airborne in, 251, 252, 257, 263, 265–66, 271, 343, 362; Habiemont bridge units return to, 263, 265; Germans probe toward, 267; Ridgway in, 271, 283; paratroopers near, 334
Wereth, 144, 146
Western Front, Dec., 1944, 14–15, 25; Monschau-Echternach sector, 14–15, 21–23, 100, 101, 108
West Wall, German, 20, 99
Wetengel, Cpl., 165
Wettling, Pfc., 207

Williams, Sgt., 82, 212, 284–85
Wilson, Lt. Robert, 206
Winterspelt, 210
Wischeid, 143
Wolfe, Capt. Peter, 219
Wurtich, Lt. Jake, 281

Yates, Maj. Robert B., 250, 272–73, 274–75, 279, 280–81, 282–83

Zaleski, Pfc., 338, 354
Zeigenberg, 107